D0392475

Gentleman of the Senate

Gentleman of the Senate

Orrin Hatch
A Portrait of Character

Lee Roderick

PROBITAS PRESS

Gentleman of the Senate

Probitas Press, LLC, 2115 National Press Building
Washington, D.C. 20045
1-800-383-1212 ext. 1010

Library of Congress Catalog Card Number 00-132901

Includes bibliographical references and index.
ISBN 09673432-1

First Printing 2000

Printed in the United States of America

For Angela, Eric, Justin, Kimberly, Matt, and C.C., with their father's hope that they too will become portraits of character.

Contents

Acknowledgements . . . . *ix*
Introduction . . . . *xi*

Part I

1. *A Gentleman Up Close* *1*
2. *The Early Years* *13*
3. *Molding the Man* *20*
4. *Into the Arena* *29*
5. *Labor Law 'Reform'* *42*
6. *Growing Into a Giant* *55*
7. *The Club* *63*

Part II

8. *Suffer The Children* *77*
9. *Women and Families* *91*
10. *Health and Longevity* *104*
11. *The AIDS Crisis* *114*
12. *Education* *124*
13. *Toward a Colorblind Society* *134*
14. *And Justice For All* *143*

15. *Patriotism and Foreign Policy* 154
16. *Religious Freedom* 170

Part III

17. *Clinton and Gore* 183
18. *Bill and Monica* 199
19. *The Impeachment* 213
20. *Utah and the West* 230
21. *Orrin at Ease* 246
22. *Friends* 256
23. *Music Man* 267
Epilogue 281
Sources 301
Index 321

Acknowledgments

I ESPECIALLY THANK MY FRIEND and fellow author Bob Henrie for his steadfast support, which helped sustain the research and writing of this book over many months. Thanks also to Chuck Canfield and Mac Christensen for their encouragement.

Other colleagues or friends who were important along the way include Jay Bernhisel, Scott Bradley, Donna Falkenborg, Bob Gilliland, Bob Mouritsen, and Barbara Richardson.

Scott Springer, my ace research assistant, helped lighten the load. Marie Woolf, a talent nonpareil, designed the jacket. Kathy Allred, my creative, accommodating typesetter, kept the project on track even when it meant working weekends. Paul Rawlins and Lyle Mumford shared useful advice on various aspects of production.

Senator Hatch's staff was consistently helpful in locating various documents, allowing me to comb through files, and answering numerous questions about the Senator's activities and views. Thanks especially to Patricia Knight and Kris Iverson in Washington, D.C., and Melanie Bowen and Heather Barney in Utah.

Orrin Hatch and his wife Elaine were unfailingly open and cooperative, never trying to curb an avenue of inquiry even if it brought to the surface memories with some pain attached.

My mother, Karla Mouritsen Roderick, who gave me the writing gene, kept me well supplied with treats during endless hours at the computer.

Most importantly, my gifted wife and best friend Yvonne Maddox

Roderick cheerfully and masterfully shouldered all the burdens of home and family to allow her husband to write another book. She also read the manuscript and offered many helpful suggestions.

To each of you, my heartfelt thanks.

Introduction

AS I COMPLETED MY FIRST BOOK ON Senator Hatch in 1993, *Leading the Charge: Orrin Hatch and 20 Years of America*, William F. Buckley, in a critique, wrote that "I found myself at the end of the book hoping Lee Roderick would ten years from now give us another volume on Senator Hatch, into the 21st century."

Not likely, I thought. My long-suffering wife and children largely had gone without their husband and father for a year, I was exhausted, and besides, in almost 500 pages I had written nearly everything I thought worth writing about Hatch.

William Jefferson Clinton changed my mind. In 1993–his first year in the White House–Clinton was generally considered of dubious character. By the start of 1999 when I began the present volume, he had become uniquely infamous–the first U.S. president to be justifiably impeached. (One other president, Andrew Johnson, also was impeached, but largely for political reasons arising from the Civil War.)

"Bill Clinton may not be the worst president America has had," George F. Will noted, "but surely he is the worst person to be president." Fifty-eight American historians agree. Responding to a survey by C-Span, released on Presidents Day 2000, they put Clinton at the very bottom of forty-two chief executives in "moral authority"–one rung below Richard Nixon, who resigned in disgrace.

Intriguingly, it was Orrin Hatch–the president's polar opposite in integrity–who could have saved Clinton that harsh judgment of history. As Clinton increasingly became tangled in the web of lies he spun to hide his affair with Monica Lewinsky, Hatch, publicly as well as privately, clearly told the president how he could extricate himself before it was too late. Their personal conversations are detailed for the first time in these pages.

Hatch's example of character, courage, competence, and compassion is a badly needed antidote to the dark legacy of the Clinton-Gore years. Their administration has induced a cynicism that has infected our country like a disease, lowering our opinion of public officials and institutions, and turning us more inward and less likely to involve ourselves in civic affairs.

My hope is that readers of *Gentleman of the Senate* will take heart and resolve to become involved, knowing that, even in a tawdry time, we still have public servants like Senator Hatch who serve tirelessly and honorably, for the right reasons.

In the late evening of June 18, 1999, Senator Hatch flew into Salt Lake City from Washington and met downtown with about a hundred associates. "I'm going to run for president of the United States," he told us. "I'm not running for ego or self-aggrandizement. I'm running for my country."

Too much was wrong with America's current leadership, he added, and "I can't sit back any longer and see these things go on." Hatch publicly threw his hat into the ring two weeks later. Almost nobody gave him a prayer of winning the GOP nomination. And six months and $2 million later, a prayer was about as close as he came. While some Hatch supporters wanted to point the finger of blame elsewhere, the Senator took full responsibility.

"I knew that by getting in late, by raising money from small donors, and by refusing public funds, I was defying conventional wisdom and the odds were extremely long. I knew that I would be criticized. I also knew it would be far more comfortable not to run. But the goal of public life is service. In a democracy, each of us has an obligation to step forward if we believe we can make a difference for the better."

More recently, in May 2000, Senator Hatch–along with Utah Governor Mike Leavitt–was booed by some boorish extremists at the Utah Republican Convention. This ugliness, despite the fact that Leavitt is one of the best governors in the state's history, and Hatch is the most accomplished legislator in the past half-century to represent Utah in Washington. Without him there, says former Wyoming GOP Senator Alan Simpson, the Clinton-Gore administration would have "picked Utah like a chicken."

Several hours after the booing, I was standing next to Senator Hatch in a box overlooking the convention floor as vote totals were announced. Nominees had to get 60 percent to avoid a primary contest; Hatch got 61.5. The Senator winced, then gathered his family and staff around him.

Obviously shaken by the close call, yet without a trace of bitterness, he said, "When we leave this room, I don't want any of us complaining about the outcome here. Let's be grateful we don't have a primary, and let's go out with our heads held high and run a tough, good race right through to November."

Noted Supreme Court Justice Joseph Story, writing a century and a half ago, said the structure of America "has been erected by architects of consummate skill and fidelity; its foundations are solid...and its defences [sic] are impregnable from without. It has been reared for immortality...."

Nonetheless, he warned, "It may perish in an hour by the folly, or corruption, or negligence of its only keepers, the people. Republics are created by the virtue, public spirit, and intelligence of the citizens. They fall when the wise are banished from the public councils, because they dare to be honest, and the profligate are rewarded because they flatter the people in order to betray them."

I thought of Story's warning as I watched two honorable, highly effective civil servants treated in a most uncivil way. In Hatch's case, there has always been a solid, highly vocal minority of voters who would banish him from the public councils in a flash if they could. While critics come from both ends of the political spectrum, they are noisiest from the far right.

That is ironic, since Hatch is a solid conservative in most respects–not out of convenience but out of deeply held belief. He once defined conservatism as "the commitment to conserve the freedom that is unique to America...We seek to preserve these values not because they are old, but because history has proven that they are best."

But because Hatch refuses to move in lock step with self-anointed leaders of the far right, he is often a target of their ire. Early in 1997, after a critical article on Hatch appeared in newspapers around the country, former president George Bush wrote him from Houston to say "Barbara and I read the attached article in our local paper at 6 a.m. today. It didn't ruin our entire day, but it came close.

"...Here you are with a 100% conservative voting record having to put up with a load of crud from these people who should be supporting you all the way. Most of them have groups with few members, a mailing list they dun to support themselves, and an open mouth on every subject. They get more pleasure attacking Republicans than they do attacking Democrats. They did it to me plenty, but I thought they would spare you, for you truly don't deserve [it]."

Hatch long ago chose to march to the beat of an inner drummer, whatever others say. He belies many stereotypes of prominent public figures. He lives modestly, would rather stay at home and read than socialize, prefers the company of friends to that of VIPs, and genuinely considers his wife Elaine, their six children, and nineteen grandchildren his "greatest blessing."

The Senator is a prodigious worker, sponsoring legislation that routinely leads to national headlines, as well as numerous measures that pass unnoticed by the general public. Probably no current Republican in Congress has put his imprint on more U.S. laws. Some are sweeping and historic–such as reducing the capital gains tax from 28 to 20 percent to keep America's economy soaring; sharply reducing the cost of many medicines by fathering the modern generic drug industry; or creating child care and child health insurance programs for poor families.

Senator Hatch strongly believes in less government, more local control, and more individual responsibility, and tries to solve problems without creating new bureaucracies. He was the leading congressional sponsor of a constitutional amendment to balance the federal budget, and helped exert the pressure that led to current budget surpluses. He routinely seeks to have federal funds flow to states as block grants, giving states greater flexibility in spending them.

At the same time, the Senator has great empathy for those who have been dealt a particularly bad hand in life. He believes an important and legitimate role of government is to help those unable to help themselves, but who would if they could. He has worked hard for children, women and others facing discrimination, abused citizens, the elderly, and the mentally or physically impaired.

Long before presidential candidate George W. Bush in 1999 labeled himself a "compassionate conservative," Hatch described his own approach that way. A *Washington Post* reporter did some digging and concluded that "The very first mention of a compassionate conservative that I found came...in 1981" in a *New York Times* story on how Senator Hatch saved the Job Corps from budget cutters.

Hatch is surprisingly versed and experienced in foreign affairs as well. He played a key role in helping to end the Cold War, as explained in the chapter on foreign policy. The Senator is widely credited with having one of the best minds in Washington–a reason he is on the short list of the TV networks, ready on a moment's notice to discuss breaking news in the U.S. or abroad.

There is one more dimension to Hatch that is essential to any understanding of him. He was reared in a strongly religious home, served as a full-time missionary during his formative years, and remains a faithful, Sunday school-teaching Christian. His innate kindness and concern for others is a reflection of what Christ taught, and what Hatch learned in his home from two loving parents.

In 1994 his mother Helen, who would die within a year at age eighty-nine, took pen in hand and, in clear cursive, sent her son a one-page letter that summarizes him well.

Aug. 17, 1994

Beloved Orrin,

...I wish to thank you for your thoughtfulness and caring, and your letters which help to educate me.

Every time I think of you, I think of Kipling's "If."

lst verse

If you can keep your head when all about you
    are losing theirs and blaming it on you;
If you can trust yourself when all men doubt you,
    But make allowance for their doubting too;
If you can wait and not be tired of waiting,
    Or, being lied about, don't deal in lies;
Or being hated, don't give way to hating,
    And yet don't look too good, nor talk too wise.

4th verse

If you can talk with crowds and keep your virtue,
    Or walk with kings, nor lose the common touch,
If neither foes nor loving friends can hurt you,
    If all men count with you, but none too much:
If you can fill the unforgiving minute
    With sixty seconds' worth of distance run,
Yours is the earth and everything that's in it,
    And–which is more–you'll be a man, my son!

This poem I believe was written for the Spartans, but in my heart, I have

> always believed it was written for you...I want you to know I'm more than proud of you, and love you too much I think.
>
> Your Mother, Helen

Helen Hatch once told me that she kept my first book on Orrin by her bedside, and that, next to the scriptures, it was her favorite book. I'd like to think she would have enjoyed this one too.

Lee Roderick
June 2000

Part I

1

A Gentleman Up Close

Senator Hatch is a fine Christian gentleman . . . someone of unquestioned high reputation.

–Garrison Keillor

GENNADY AND NATASHA KASSIN were a young couple in the former Soviet Union who came to the attention of Orrin Hatch early in the 1980s. They were Jewish dissidents who heroically helped other dissidents seek basic freedoms, including the right to emigrate. The Kassins were under constant surveillance by the KGB and faced the threat of imminent imprisonment in Russia's dread gulag system for political troublemakers.

Touched by their plight, described to them by other dissident leaders, Orrin and his wife Elaine announced they were "adopting" the Kassins, in an attempt to throw a thin security blanket over them from afar. The Senator warned Soviet leaders of his special interest in the Kassins, and put pressure on successive regimes, from Leonid Brezhnev to Mikhail Gorbachev, to treat them humanely. His intervention almost certainly was what kept the Kassins out of prison.

Assisting Hatch was Anatoly Sharansky, a celebrated world symbol of freedom who was imprisoned for nearly a decade in the gulag for promoting the cause of Soviet Jewry. Sharansky kept in close touch with the Senator by wire and telephone to request help for the Kassins. Finally, Sharansky and the Kassins were allowed to emigrate to Israel, where Sharansky became a powerful cabinet minister and where the Hatches hosted the Kassins to a celebration dinner at the King David Hotel a decade after adopting them.

Senator Hatch is famous for lending a helping hand to those who need it. Pundits and political cartoonists sometimes characterize him as stiff, distant, and puritanical. Those who know him well know better. Hatch believes passionately that the levers of government should be used to help those who cannot help themselves, and he goes far out of his way to do so.

"Compassion is what most defines Orrin," says Ruth Montoya, the Senator's personal assistant since the mid-1980s. "He'll do whatever it takes to help those in need. His heart really bleeds for people." When Democrats temporarily regained a Senate majority in the 1986 elections, Hatch, as outgoing chairman of the Labor and Human Resources Committee, was forced to cut the GOP staff from one hundred to about thirty. "He agonized over it," says Montoya. "It just about killed him."

A litmus test of a public figure's civility is how he treats his own family and employees. In the Senator's case, current and former staffers alike–on and off the record–are remarkably consistent in saying he is the kindest man they have ever worked for. They relate both large and small things, including his insistence that everyone simply call him "Orrin." Long after they leave his staff, his proteges–collectively called "Hatchlings" around Washington, where they fill numerous jobs he has helped them land–call the Senator for advice on everything from career moves to personal relationships.

Their loyalty has been earned by a thousand acts of kindness. One time a young male staff member was assigned to shepherd through the Senate a bill by Hatch that provided for a seven-day pass to national parks in Utah. When the staffer reported that everyone involved had signed off on his bill, Hatch went to the Senate floor and brought up the parks amendment, which easily passed on a voice vote.

Unfortunately, however, the aide had assumed too much. Senator Dale Bumpers, D-Arkansas, chairman of the national parks subcommittee, had not been consulted about the bill and was livid at its passage. His staff having seriously breached senatorial courtesy, Hatch was forced to withdraw the amendment and apologize both publicly and privately to Bumpers. Then he had to contact the Utah media and retract a statement praising the bill's passage.

"What is remarkable about this incident," recalls Kris Iverson, the Senator's legislative director, "is the way Orrin dealt with the young staffer. Most senators would have royally reamed him out for such a mistake. Instead, Orrin calmly took him aside, pointed out the errors, and issued immediate forgiveness."

Another staffer, Becky Shipp, had a different problem. Her sister Julie was getting married and needed the wedding dress transported from Utah to Washington. The Senator himself made the delivery–taking the dress beside him in its own airline seat.

Close observers, even Hatch himself, point to his generous nature as also his weak spot. Occasionally he has been embarrassed because of misplaced trust. "Probably my worst fault and my best fault is that I am loyal and fight for people, even if they don't always deserve my efforts," says Hatch. "People have tried to change me, and it doesn't work."

When Ruth Montoya had a baby in July 1994, she took maternity leave for six weeks and worried what to do next. "Orrin looked at me and said, 'I know what you're going to do–bring Leo to work with you.'"

"Oh, sure!" Montoya laughed.

"No, I'm serious," he insisted. He was and she did. Montoya worked part time for the next four months, taking little Leo with her to the Russell Senate Building, right outside the Senator's private office. The baby spent most of the time on Montoya's desk or in a stroller behind it. Charles Sherrill, Washington correspondent for KSL Television in Salt Lake City, got wind of the unusual arrangement and dropped by to do a story on Ruth and Leo. But the story didn't air because, he said, it looked too good to be true.

Larry Block, a staff member on the Senate Judiciary Committee, chaired by Hatch, recalls when he had emergency heart surgery. "I was nervous about the operation and how it would affect my job," says Block. "But Orrin called every day to assure me I'd have a job when I returned. His concern and support were a very important part of my astonishing recovery."

In 1997 press secretary Heather Barney had surgery in Utah without telling her boss. "I didn't want to bother Orrin, but when he found out about it after the fact, he called immediately and said 'I really wish you had told me you were going to have an operation. I would have prayed for you.'" More recently Barney had another operation. No sooner had she been wheeled out of the recovery room than the Senator was on the line, offering encouragement. During convalescence, she received four mor encouraging calls from Orrin or Elaine.

"Periodically I will bring to Orrin's attention stories from the newspaper of people going through hard times," says Barney, a dark-haired, bright-eyed surrogate for Hatch in political forays around the state. "There have been a number of times that Orrin has gone to hospitals to visit people, or has written personal letters of encouragement. Many times these are people he has never met before."

The Senator does such things quietly, with no apparent ulterior motive. He seems to have a sixth sense about others' needs. Among thousands of Mormon missionaries serving throughout the world in 1998, one young man from Cache Valley, Utah was struggling mightily to cope with the rigors of his two-year assignment in Michigan. On the brink of bagging his mission and going home, he reluctantly agreed to give it a final try. Months later, after much fret and sweat by his mission president, parents, and a professional counselor, the young elder had overcome his problems and was totally engaged and soaring in his volunteer service.

Only after he was over the hurdle did the missionary casually mention in a letter to his parents that, out of the blue during his time of crisis, two letters of encouragement had arrived from Senator Hatch. His parents had never mentioned their son's difficulty to Hatch, and were stunned that the Senator somehow was moved to write him, helping to save his mission.

Backed by what one Utah publication called the state's "most responsive congressional staff," Senator Hatch goes far out of his way to help constituents. Federal agencies respond, knowing he will not back down. "Your name is magic!" wrote a Mr. Jensen, one of many who have sought help with the Internal Revenue Service. "IRS told us that there was no appeal to their decision. When my wife said, 'I'm going to write Senator Hatch about this injustice,' there was a 180 degree turn around on IRS's part....We appreciate your reputation and you!"

George Thomas Scott just wanted to be an American–and thanks in part to Hatch he was, for a single day, before he died. An emigrant from Scotland at age sixty-one, Scott wed a Utah pen pal, Jessie, and had ten years of idyllic marriage, their own home, a new car, and money to travel–dreams fulfilled in America that would have been impossible back in Scotland. Scott's goal was to become a U.S. citizen, but he was diagnosed with cancer and told he had four months to live. With the clock ticking, Hatch got immigration agents to expedite the paperwork.

In November 1988, Scott, seventy-one and weighing just eighty pounds, sat bright-eyed in his wheelchair in a judge's chambers, answering questions about his adoptive country and responsibilities of citizenship. Too weak to raise his arm, Jessie held it up for him as Scott repeated the oath of allegiance. "Congratulations," said the judge to Scott, who was grinning broadly, "you are now a U.S. citizen." Less than twenty-four hours later, Scott died in his wife's arms.

When Hatch's name comes up in casual conversation, it is surprising how often people volunteer their own examples of his unsolicited compassion.

Pulitzer prize-winning Washington columnist Jack Anderson, for example, suffers from Parkinson's disease, which often causes his hands to shake profoundly, making it extremely difficult to type. Anderson was at his home in Bethesda, Maryland one day when he got a phone call from a doctor at nearby National Institutes of Health. The doctor explained that NIH was experimenting with new therapies for Parkinson's, and invited Anderson over to see what could be done to help him.

"I had no idea why they called me," said Anderson in an interview. "But I learned from a doctor that Senator Hatch had seen me on a TV news show with my hands shaking. He took it upon himself to call NIH to request that I be included in their treatment program for Parkinson's." Doctors prescribed a medication which gave Anderson some relief, allowing him freedom from tremors for two hours at a time.

The Senator has put himself on the line numerous times for citizens in no position to do anything for him–often at political cost. Early in his Senate career, for instance, he backed a bill to protect the constitutional rights of the mentally ill, prisoners, and other institutionalized citizens. Although other conservatives protested, the Utahn explained that such citizens are "unique in their inability" assert their own rights and are "people whom society has basically ignored."

The bill passed the Senate by a single vote–Hatch providing the margin of victory–with its sponsor, Senator Birch Bayh, D-Indiana, writing to thank him for "the spirit of compromise and fairness which marked your treatment" of the measure. "Without your help this important piece of legislation might not have been reported [by the Judiciary Committee]."

Hatch is also noted for easing the burdens of prominent Americans in their times of personal trial, often taking heat for doing so. It is a selfless trait that has endeared him to colleagues on both sides of the political aisle, and has helped make him an effective legislator.

In May 1981, Senator Harrison (Pete) Williams, a New Jersey Democrat, was convicted of bribery and conspiracy in an FBI sting operation known as Abscam. The liberal Democrat, organized labor's leading Senate supporter, had frequently sparred with Hatch on the Labor Committee. Early in 1984, having exhausted legal appeals, Williams was about to be sent to a federal penitentiary in Danbury, Connecticut. That night he telephoned for help–not to his fellow Democrats and liberals, but to Hatch. Williams asked Hatch to ask the Justice Department to send him to a prison closer to home so that his family could visit more easily. Hatch agreed, and two weeks later, Williams reported to prison in neighboring Allentown, Pennsylvania.

During the 1988 campaign, the Utahn defended another Democratic senator. Dennis DeConcini, running for reelection in Arizona, was under fire after his brother had invested in land along the Central Arizona (water reclamation) Project, then sold it to the government at a profit. Although DeConcini said he had no knowledge of the government's interest, he was pilloried in the media, including a cartoon by Steve Benson of the *Arizona Republic*, depicting DeConcini's next residence: a jail. DeConcini, formerly a shoo-in for reelection, dropped like a rock in the polls as gleeful Republicans accused him of being unethical and dishonest.

Hatch spoke by telephone with DeConcini to sort out the facts, then issued a press release saying he had served with the Arizonan for twelve years and knew him to be a man of impeccable integrity. Senate Republicans clouded up and rained all over Hatch, with GOP leader Bob Dole bitterly denouncing his "defection."

Hatch had not endorsed DeConcini for reelection; he had simply attested to his honesty. "I probably won't ever hear the end of it, but it was the right thing to do," Hatch wrote privately. "Dennis is a good person. Although we disagree on some things, and I would like to see more Republicans in the Senate, I couldn't stand by and see him treated so unfairly." DeConcini steadied the boat and went on to win by 57-41 percent.

Idaho Republican George Hansen, a charismatic politician but highly controversial maverick, had been in one scrape after another as a congressman representing the Idaho district that borders Utah. By 1984 Hansen had baited the IRS and other federal agencies once too often and it was pay back time. Out of scores of members of Congress who had filed inaccurate financial disclosure forms, the Justice Department selectively prosecuted Hansen, charging him with a felony, while allowing other members amnesty to revise their own disclosure statements without penalty.

Free while appealing his conviction, Hansen continued to campaign for reelection in the summer and fall of 1984. Hatch saw him as a friend who was being treated unfairly, and campaigned in Idaho for Hansen. Many Idahoans agreed that Hansen was being persecuted, and in spite of his pending jail term, he lost the election by fewer than 200 votes. Hatch paid a high price, with Utah Democratic leaders blasting him for supporting a "convicted felon." Pollster Dan Jones said the furor cost Hatch ten points in opinion polls. "Nonetheless," Hatch wrote privately, "we have to do what we believe is right."

A postscript to the Hansen-Hatch controversy came years later when the Supreme Court ruled that filing inaccurate financial disclosure statements was not a felony punishable by prison. By then, Hansen had already been incarcerated at a federal facility in Virginia, and his professional life continued to be problematic.

In 1995, Oregon Republican Bob Packwood became the second senator since the Civil War forced to resign his seat. The Senate Ethics Committee, after a two-and-a-half-year investigation, charged Packwood with making unwanted sexual advances to nearly a score of women, and trying to obstruct its probe by "withholding, altering, and destroying relevant evidence. . . . "

Perhaps no Republican was less like Hatch than Packwood, who often voted with liberal Democrats and had once helped defeat Hatch for a Senate leadership position. But on September 7 when Packwood stood in the Senate chamber and tearfully bade his colleagues farewell, Hatch typically dwelt on Packwood's good points and gave him an emotional hug. As Packwood's colleagues started to stand and tell him goodbye in that session, the Democratic leadership turned tails and briskly walked out. When Majority Leader Dole asked that Packwood be given a reasonable time to wrap up his affairs of twenty-six Senate years, California Democrat Barbara Boxer threatened to try to strip Packwood of his pension if he didn't leave in four days.

California's other senator, Dianne Feinstein, showing the class Boxer lacked, offered a summary strongly endorsed by Hatch: "My father said, 'Don't let a man be known for the last thing he did but for the best thing.'"

Most often it has been everyday people benefitting from the Utahn's benevolence. For many years the guard station outside Hatch's corner suite in the Russell Building was manned by a gregarious African American police officer named C. J. Martin. A devoted Christian, Martin used his vacations to do humanitarian work in Uganda, with Hatch among those helping to finance it. When the Hatches' son Jess married Mary Alice Marriott–granddaughter of the founder of the multi-billion-dollar Marriott Corporation–among those attending the lavish wedding reception as the

Senator's guest was C. J. Martin.

"At the end of one day I was leaving the building and walking by that guard station," recalls Hatch staffer Kris Iverson. "I noticed a tie just like the one Orrin had worn that day, lying on the police officer's desk. I mentioned the coincidence, and the officer just grinned. 'That *is* Senator Hatch's tie,' he said, 'I told him I really liked it, and he took it off and gave it to me.'"

Heather Barney of the Utah staff says "In traveling with Orrin and Elaine I have often been struck by how he seems to prefer the company of common people to that of the rich and powerful." Barney accompanied the Hatches to the 1996 Republican National Convention in San Diego. While most GOP officials hit the convention party circuit to butter up fat cats, Hatch spent the great majority of his time with Utah delegates and his staff.

Hatch often says "I love you" to staff members, male and female alike, along with many other acquaintances. He also has a penchant for hugging people of both genders, despite occasional warnings from aides that his friendliness might be misconstrued in an age of "political correctness." The Senator shrugs off the concern: "If the time ever comes when I cannot express honest affection for people, that will be the time for me to hang it up."

Even those close to Hatch are sometimes taken aback by his innocent boldness. Paul Matulic, his bright, capable foreign affairs aide, was in Budapest with Hatch in 1995 as Salt Lake City was awarded the winter games for 2002 by the International Olympic Committee. That evening, at an elegant reception, the Senator spotted Britain's Princess Margaret in the crowd and offered to introduce Matulic.

"No thanks," answered Matulic, a bearded, no-nonsense guy not given to small talk. "I'm not big on foreign royalty."

The next day, as they chatted at the Frankfort airport, Matulic asked his boss if he had talked with Princess Margaret. "Yes," said Hatch, "and I did what I always do when I meet British royalty."

"Oh, what's that?"

"I kiss them on the cheek!"

Matulic was aghast. Well-versed on protocol, he knew this was not in any diplomatic textbook. Hatch, reveling in his aide's astonishment, then added the crowning touch. "I once kissed the Queen in Buckingham Palace," he crowed. "It's simple: You take them by the hand, you bend down, they pull away, then you swoop in for the kiss!"

While the Senator occasionally mingles with royalty, he does not live like royalty. Frugality is a watchword for him and Elaine, both of whom grew up in modest circumstances–he in the city and she on the farm. Hatch's family and staff had a belly laugh in June 1999 as he was about to throw his hat into the presidential ring. New Hampshire's leading newspaper, the Manchester *Union Leader*, editorialized that Hatch was driven by ego and "will be embraced by voters impressed by $1,000 suits and Italian shoes."

With his tall, slender build, Hatch just *looks* as though he's wearing designer suits. In truth, he buys almost all of them–size 42 long–off the rack at Mr. Mac's in Salt Lake City. Its owner, Mac Christensen, is a personal friend who runs one of Utah's least exclusive men's clothing chains and hawks his suits on TV with frequent two-for-one specials. A typical suit at Mr. Mac's runs about $199. Christensen also keeps Hatch supplied with the latest designer ties that have helped put the Senator on various best-dressed lists.

As for those "Italian shoes," Orrin's unusually narrow feet are shod in shoes–size 12AA–from Land's End of Hingham, Massachusetts. A company catalogue lists them at $75 to $100 a pair. His crisp, high-collar dress shirts–a staple for political cartoonists–used to come special-order directly from the Orient. He now gets shirts–size15-by-35–out of a Paul Fredrick catalogue for $20 to $40 each. Once purchased, they are rarely sent out to be laundered and ironed: Elaine routinely does that at home, finishing them off on an ironing board set up in their second-floor master bedroom. When Hatch needs shoes or shirts, he marks up the respective catalogues and places the orders by phone.

The Hatches' four-bedroom red-brick home in Vienna, Virginia, where they reared six children, was bought a month after his first election to the Senate in 1976, and is modest by Washington-area standards. Its double garage rarely has held a brand-new car; the Hatches usually buy their autos used. During Washington's suffocating summers, most residents who have air conditioning run it full-tilt. But, as one house guest found, given the faintest breeze or break in a heat wave, the air conditioning goes off at the Hatch house, windows go up, and room fans come on.

Utah's restaurant equivalent of Mr. Mac's is a chain of eateries called Chuck-A-Rama. Adults can get a bounteous buffet dinner there for $7.99–the best bargain in town. Not surprisingly, it is one of Orrin's favorite restaurants.

Another trait that sets the Senator apart is his insatiable appetite for work and the productivity that results from it. The *Almanac of American*

Politics puts it this way: "Hatch's Senate career has been shaped by two impulses which are sometimes in tension with each other: a strong conservative philosophy and a sense of responsibility for the superintendency of legislation." In threading his way between those impulses to accomplish the nation's business, the Senator often has been criticized by either the far left or far right–especially the latter on social issues impacting the daily well-being of people.

In the summer of 1996, Hatch found himself assigned to five different conference committees–representatives from the House and Senate who meet together to iron out differences in similar bills passed by their bodies–in addition to his daily duties. "It is almost impossible to do one conference committee, let alone five," he wearily wrote to a friend. "I have been running from one place to the other each and every day. I have not gotten home until 10 or 11 p.m. at night."

During two days alone in that period, he appeared on "Larry King Live," "the McNeil-Lehrer News Hour," CBS News, CNBC, CNN, and Fox Television, while also meeting with print reporters.

During the two-year 104th Congress, ending late in 1996, the Senator played a major role in fashioning new laws impacting terrorism, crime, child pornography, health insurance, immigration, small business taxes, welfare reform, and unfunded mandates. Washington correspondent Lee Davidson of the *Deseret News* wrote that Hatch had pushed 58 pieces of legislation into law during the session. "That's much more than the 37 enacted by the rest of the Utah delegation combined–and a good many of [the latter] were 'softballs,' or relatively easy to pass." Davidson added that "Hatch ranked as the delegation's heaviest hitter by any legislative batting records figured by the Deseret News."

Most members of Congress consider Washington's busy social scene part of the job, but not Senator Hatch. When he's not on the road campaigning he spends most free evenings at home, studying issues, reading for pleasure, writing, or watching sports on television. One reporter some years ago noted that guest lists in "Embassy Row functions or stuffy Georgetown dinner parties" rarely included the names of a handful of powerful locals, including the Senator. All of them, he wrote, "appreciate the use of power here and all exercise their influence while shunning the social circuit."

He also conserves time and energy by rarely shopping and by eating a salad or soup at his desk most weekdays, washed down with water or fruit juice: Hatch avoids tea, coffee, and carbonated drinks.

"The frustrations and demands on Orrin's time are phenomenal," says personal assistant Montoya. "I'm the one who has to keep after him to try to keep him on schedule. No one likes to be continually prodded, and sometimes in frustration he'll bark at me, saying 'I can't get there' or 'I can't do this,' but it's never personal and he's so kind otherwise that I just let it roll off my back."

Hatch usually sleeps fitfully, in part because of chronic back pain. But he almost always arises well before dawn on weekdays, throws down a quick breakfast and handful of vitamin tablets, and is at his office by about 6 a.m, after driving forty minutes to Capitol Hill. On most days he won't be back home until 8 p.m. Many times his work day has begun as a guest on some TV talk show.

At his desk he begins the day by reading ten pages in the scriptures, then scanning a stack of newspapers, including papers from Utah as well as the *Washington Post, Washington Times, New York Times, Wall Street Journal, Los Angeles Times,* and several periodicals including *CQ* (Congressional Quarterly) *Weekly, the Weekly Standard, Time,* and *Newsweek.*

In part because of his work ethic, Hatch is a senator of historic proportions in terms of the sheer volume of legislation that bears his imprint. He has been one of the nation's premier political players during the last quarter of the twentieth century, and has been pivotal in many of the public battles fought during that time.

In 1997, *George* magazine named him one of a half-dozen living "Legends of the Senate." It quoted veteran Washington columnist Art Buchwald as saying, "Hatch is the least frightening of all the senators. When he asks a question, it is like a father asking his son why he took the car out without his permission. I would prefer to testify in front of him than anyone else."

Buchwald hit on a key to Hatch's effectiveness: He is tenacious on the issues but tender with people. Friendship and principle count more with Hatch than does partisanship, and he has been uniquely effective in working across party lines to conduct the people's business. Hatch is a mainstream conservative with a maverick bent. Unlike some doctrinaire politicians on the far right or far left, he believes in the traditional view of politics as the art of compromise–so long as a bedrock principle is not sacrificed.

One national publication called Hatch "an independent-minded and enigmatic politician whom Washington, with its penchant for pigeonholing, is ill-equipped to understand." But Hatch is in good company, said *Parade* magazine columnist Walter Scott, who included this question and answer about another independent-minded politician in his weekly column in 1994:

Q *I just read the wonderful biography "Truman," by David McCullough. I wonder if you can name any current member of the U.S. Senate who is in Harry's class as far as integrity and guts are concerned?*

A In this play-it-safe age of instant sound bites, it is true that few U.S. Senators have the grit and guts of Harry Truman. However, when Washington veterans are pressed to identify the members of the current crop on Capitol Hill who display the most integrity, they name the following Senators: Bill Bradley (D., N.J.), Ben Nighthorse Campbell (D., Colo.), Orrin Hatch (R., Utah), Nancy Kassebaum (R., Kan.), Herb Kohl (D., Wis.) and Harry Reid (D., Nev.).

Kassebaum has since retired, leaving Hatch and Campbell–who later switched to the GOP–as the only Republicans on that elite list.

Following the impeachment and trial of President Clinton early in 1999, Garrison Keillor wrote that "civility" no longer was likely in Washington, and "The best we can do is systematize the cruelty." He suggested giving "a Democratic prosecutor $50 million to see what he can come up with about a Republican "sacrificial victim...of unquestioned high reputation–no going after easy prey like [prominent GOP House members] Henry Hyde or Dan Burton." The perfect target, said Keillor, would be "Senator Hatch...a fine Christian gentleman."

Even Hatch would have a hard time surviving a $50 million investigation, said Keillor, who suggested what such a probe might reveal. Videotapes of security cameras in stores where the Senator shops might show "if he ever scratched himself in public...[or] was undercharged for a pack of hair curlers once and neglected to tell the clerk about it." Perhaps, added Keillor, former secretaries "had to correct his grammar on the letters they typed, the neighbor...had to deal with the leaves from the Hatch maple tree. Search his home. Maybe he has a secret fondness for donning embroidered platform shoes and elephant bells and lip synching to Barry Manilow. Why shouldn't the nation know about this?"

Indeed it should.

2

The Early Years

I remember going up to Orrin when he was about three and patting him on the head and telling him "You're going to be President someday."

—Big sister Nancy

ORRIN DESCENDED FROM a tough, determined bloodline. His great-grandfather, Jeremiah Hatch, was an Indian agent and one of the first white settlers in Utah's Ashley Valley, a verdant nook in the northeastern corner of the state near both the Colorado and Wyoming borders. He led settlers in fending off marauding Indians as well as outlaw gangs.

Jeremiah's children included Josephus, a rancher and coal miner whose thirteen children included Orrin's father Jesse. Josephus died when Jesse was eleven, leaving him and a dozen siblings in the care of their mother, Martha Luella Thomas Hatch.

Six years later, at the age of seventeen, Jesse, gentle and barrel-chested, moved to the tiny mining town of Hiawatha, where he roofed new housing for miners and boarded with the John Bernard Kamm family. Kamm was a welder from Illinois whose family included a very pretty sixteen-year-old daughter, Helen. At the first sign of attraction between Helen and Jesse, her alarmed father whisked Helen back to Illinois and hid her on a relative's farm, far away from the rough-hewn young man.

Jesse, at first resigned, went to work as a wildcatter in Wyoming's oil fields. But he was haunted by the memory of Helen, a spirited brunette with a beautiful figure, warm oval face, and sparkling dark eyes. Within weeks, Jesse had borrowed train fare and headed for Illinois. A taxi driver, for a set fee, agreed to take him on a search for the farm. They crisscrossed Rural Route 7 all day, the driver begging Jesse to give up the search.

"Just one more," Jesse promised. As they approached the last farm, Jesse saw a young woman strolling up a path with a basket of freshly picked berries on her arm. It was Helen. Before the sun set, Jesse had borrowed a suit and they were married at the local courthouse.

"Our marriage was a surprise to both of us," Helen would recall many years later. "He didn't ask me and I didn't ask him. We just did it. I guess I married Jesse because he was the kindest man I ever knew." Their earthly union would last until Jesse's death sixty-nine years later at the age of eighty-seven.

The penniless young couple moved to Pittsburgh in November 1923, a few months after the wedding, where Jesse landed a union card and a job as a wood lather. He would become known as a master craftsman. They made a down payment on a small frame house in a working-class section of Homestead Park, and their first child, Jesse Morlan (Jess) was born. He was followed by four more over the next eight years, but two died within months of birth, leaving surviving sisters Marilyn, known as "Nubs," and Nancy.

Then ripples from the stock market crash reached their doorstep. The housing industry halted in its tracks and, with it, the family income. Their home was now half-paid-for, but they lost it to foreclosure. The Hatches lingered just long enough for Helen to give birth there on March 22, 1934, to their sixth child and second surviving son. They named him Orrin Grant–over the protests of older brother Jess who argued hard for "Samson" or "Moses." Later the family would grow to include three more sisters, Chloe, Frances, and Jessica.

Jesse and Helen borrowed $100 from Minnie Moran, an elderly Scottish friend, and bought a heavily wooded acre of land in Baldwin Borough. They built a modest home with their own hands, using secondhand lumber scrounged from a partially burned building. Before it was eventually painted over, the outside of the house advertised "Meadow Gold Ice Cream."

There were no utilities for the first year, and nature's call was answered at an outhouse. Helen cooked outside over cinder blocks. They planted apple and cherry trees and a large garden that the children were required to help weed–a chore Orrin often tried to duck. Breakfast invariably was oatmeal or eggs from the chickens Orrin raised, and dinner often a thin soup of vegetables from the garden.

As a tot, Orrin had a wooly profusion of white locks of hair which his sisters delighted in running their fingers through, much to his irritation.

The more he protested, the more Nancy and Nubs did it. One cold January morning Orrin had had enough. He appeared at his parents' bedside, a stick slung over his shoulder hobo-style with a red bandana tied to the end, holding a few personal things. "Mom, I'm leavin' home," he announced. "Dem girls are mean to me." With that he was off, before Helen could rouse herself enough to realize he might be serious.

Orrin was gone throughout the morning as snow began to fall. By afternoon the storm had intensified as neighbors joined the family's frantic search for Orrin. Finally, as night fell, the front door creaked open and Orrin shuffled in. He had hiked a ways, then doubled back to the chicken coop behind the house, where he had spent most of the day in a barrel of feed. When the chickens went noiselessly to sleep, his fear of the dark overcame his stubbornness.

While Nancy and Nubs relished teasing him, they also grew up believing he was special. "I remember going up to Orrin when he was about three and patting him on the head and telling him 'You're going to be President someday,'" Nancy told a reporter. "I never told anyone else, but I never forgot it."

Their home was poor in material things but rich in love. Helen and Jesse tried to shield the children from their frequent worry over finances, but Orrin felt deeply their concern. He was unusually quiet, thoughtful, and serious.

When he was five, Orrin and a few friends hiked to Brentwood, two miles away, to buy candy at a dime store. "Orrin had sixty cents," recalled his mother. "When they returned, the other children all had big bags of candy. But Orrin had spent his sixty cents to buy me a 'diamond' solitaire engagement ring. He handed it to me and said, 'Now you will look like the other mothers.'" She kept the ring as a prized keepsake for decades.

The Hatch children walked to McGibney Elementary School, a half-mile from home, where Orrin was an exceptional student. He had an amazing memory and excelled, especially in history and English, but intensely disliked math. Orrin was self-conscious about his patched and worn clothes. The family's social and financial status made an indelible impression on him.

He felt close to both parents but had a particular bond with his mother. Helen was fun, spirited, optimistic, and, in Orrin's mind, righteous without being self-righteous. She quietly lived her own convictions and was utterly nonjudgmental of others. "Only God is in a position to look down on anyone," Helen told her children.

The Hatches were devout Christians–members of the Church of Jesus Christ of Latter-day Saints, commonly called "Mormons." Jesse had belonged to the church since boyhood in Utah and Helen was baptized several years after moving to Pittsburgh. Both were stalwarts in the congregation, making a fifteen-mile round-trip twice each Sunday to attend services. The family read the scriptures and prayed together daily.

Helen had played the violin as a girl and instilled a love of music in her offspring. Somehow she saved enough money to buy an old upright piano, and most of the children learned to play. Orrin sang from the time he could talk and–under protest–also took violin lessons. All the Hatch children also played the organ for congregational singing.

His only brother, Jess, ten years older and strikingly handsome, was as sunny and gregarious as Orrin was serious and reflective. Orrin tagged after him with an affection bordering on worship.

When World War II broke out, Jess volunteered for service in the Army Air Force. He was assigned to the Fifteenth Air Force in Europe as a nose gunner in a B-24 Liberator, and was decorated as one of the relatively few airmen to shoot down a German jet from that exposed position. Jess sent his family a photograph of his ten-man crew, and Orrin kept it on a dresser in the bedroom he had shared with Jess. The family prayed daily for Jess's safety and an early end to the war.

Then, in February 1945, ten-year-old Orrin was playing in the woods across the road when he sensed something was wrong. Racing to the house, he saw a uniformed serviceman standing on the porch with his parents. Helen was sobbing. Jess's plane was missing in action in Austria and he was presumed dead.

Orrin was inconsolable. For days he stayed home from school and couldn't force food down. Virtually overnight a white streak appeared in his hair above the right side of his forehead–a permanent distinguishing mark. In coming years, he would credit some of his keen drive to the need to live two lives–one for himself and one for Jess.

In the following months, Orrin redoubled efforts to assist his grieving parents, shoveling coal, helping his father build a new chicken coop, feeding the chickens and selling eggs.

Orrin still excelled in school. A "B" in arithmetic during the last six weeks was all that marred an all-"A" report card from his sixth grade teacher, Mildred Weyand. As a teenager, his most serious interest was competitive sports, despite an embarrassingly slight build. His legs were so skinny that he sometimes wore long pants even when playing games calling for shorts.

Orrin's self-consciousness over his physique was compounded one day when a big, tough kid from another school tormented him, pushing him all over the schoolyard. Orrin didn't fight back and went home feeling humiliated. "I made up my mind from that point on that nobody would ever do that to me again–nobody," said Hatch decades later.

He began a regimen of calisthenics and running, and took up boxing, filling a duffle bag with sand and rags and hanging it on a mulberry tree outside the kitchen. Donning ordinary garden gloves, he began walloping the bag. In time he came to pack a jarring punch for his size.

"I got so that I had about as good a right cross and left hook as you could have," he recalled. "I never backed down from a fight from that point on." Orrin was no rowdy but was known as a tough kid who, in a fistfight, would never admit he was beaten.

At the age of twelve, Orrin decided basketball would be his standout sport. For months he practiced dribbling and shooting baskets through a crude hoop mounted on a neighbor's tree. Shortly after enrolling at Baldwin High, a school that included grades seven through twelve, Orrin tried out for the seventh-grade team. "That's the first time I ever knew there was a difference between a volleyball and a basketball," he remembers. Orrin had been practicing all those months with a volleyball. Unable to handle a real basketball, he was soon cut from the team.

Doggedly determined, he borrowed a scruffy leather basketball and began shooting again. As a ninth grader Orrin was named captain of his junior high team. He reached his full height of six-feet-two that year, a frame supporting just 118 pounds of sinew and muscle. A scrappy competitor, Orrin fouled out or was thrown out of fifteen games that season.

He was the only junior to start on the Baldwin High varsity, but the team lost twenty-one straight games. The next summer, Orrin and several other promising players joined a summer semi-pro league and began to hone their skills in earnest. Joining them was a new kid in town, Paul Wilcox, later a professional player for Cleveland.

The result was a dramatic turnaround for Baldwin, a perennial patsy. With Wilcox averaging about twenty-four points a game and Hatch feeding him the ball and pouring in another fourteen, Baldwin won the Triadic Conference championship for the first time. In the process they twice beat defending champion Carrick High, with Orrin guarding Carrick's All-City six-foot-eight center, "Meatball" Clark, holding him to four points in each game.

Joyce Strong, who now lives in Bethel Park, Pennsylvania, went all through Baldwin High with Orrin, and was a cheerleader for the basketball team. "He was a great basketball player," she remembers. In addition, she says, Orrin was a student leader. "He was studious, in fact he was a very good student."

In later years Mrs. Strong coordinated most of Baldwin High's reunions, attended occasionally by Orrin. "He, of course, was the hit of the night," she says. "He spent time with everyone....He hadn't lost his charm."

One day in class a teacher called on Orrin to read from the blackboard. He couldn't. That was when his parents and teachers learned a secret of Orrin's fabulous memory: Over the years he had learned to retain everything said in class because he was too near-sighted to see what was written on the board. He began wearing glasses. They also helped on the basketball court–"being able to see the rim of the basket instead of just an orange blur seemed like the most wonderful thing in the world," he recalls–but his hard-nosed play often resulted in broken glasses.

He gained a reputation for rising to other tough challenges. Another student was supposed to play a solo on a string bass in a music festival, but fell ill the day of the performance. The music director, named McElroy, talked Orrin into substituting for him–even though Orrin, a violinist, had never played the bass. McElroy coached Orrin for about an hour, and that evening he played the solo flawlessly–receiving a standing ovation from the audience for his pluck.

Orrin also loved attending performances of the Pittsburgh Symphony Orchestra, sitting high up in "peanut heaven" at the Syria Mosque. Helen and Jesse sacrificed $18.75 a year so Orrin could attend concerts, and he honored their sacrifice by almost never missing a performance. Afterward he would visit nearby museums and galleries, developing a deep love of art and musing on how wonderful it was that such beautiful things were publicly displayed for the enjoyment of both rich and poor people.

When Orrin turned sixteen in 1950, he became an apprentice in the AFL-CIO's Wood, Wire & Metal Lathers International Union. He was a loyal union man, like his father who served for many years as president of Local 33L. Orrin worked at the trade each summer, eventually becoming a journeyman lather. At his father's side, he learned to make elliptical and gothic arches, plaster molding, suspended ceilings, suspension floor lathing, and partitions.

He also was becoming politically aware. The Hatches, like most blue-collar families, were Democrats. "We thought President Roosevelt was the biggest hero that ever lived," recalled his mother. That view was widely shared by American laborers, especially in Pennsylvania where attempts to pass progressive measures desperately needed by workers before and during the Depression had been smothered by a Republican political machine that ruled the Commonwealth.

As a teenager Orrin studied the injustices suffered by laborers in his state and elsewhere, reinforcing his growing loyalty to the Democrats. "I read books about the lives and times of Clarence Darrow, Samuel Gompers, and other great labor lawyers and leaders," he recalled. "I was appalled at how the men were bullied and pushed around by some of the great industrialists."

In a senior class poll, published in the school newspaper, the *Purbalite*, Orrin was voted "most likable" boy. Reflecting on the school year, the paper asked: "Can you imagine...Orin [sic] Hatch without a basketball?" Next to his senior photo in the school yearbook was a thumbnail sketch:

> Basketball whiz...hardworking union man...quite a musician...great sense of humor. Balthi, Orchestra, Key Club, Boys Leaders, Senior Class Officer, Hi-Y, Varsity Letterman, Football, Basketball, Intramurals.

Also that year, Orrin was a candidate in Baldwin High's mock presidential election, held to heighten awareness of the 1952 U.S. presidential campaign. In the first balloting, another classmate was ahead of Orrin, a student senator, but failed to win a majority. "Because he did not have the majority vote of 66, the delegates had to vote again," reported the *Purbalite*. "Senator Hatch won the election. Congratulations."

Nearly fifty years later he would again be hoping for the same headline he saw in the *Purbalite:* "Hatch Wins Presidency." By then he would be one of the nation's most respected U.S. senators seeking to become president of the United States.

3 Molding the Man

"I'm going to blow your head off," he growled, aiming the gun squarely in Hatch's face.

In the fall of 1952 Orrin enrolled at Brigham Young University in Provo, Utah. Later to become the nation's largest private, church-owned university, the school had about 6,000 students when Orrin arrived on the squeaky clean campus in the shadow of the Rocky Mountains.

As a union card-carrying Democrat, Orrin was an oddity at the conservative school. His arrival coincided with the presidential election pitting Republican war hero Dwight Eisenhower against Democrat Adlai Stevenson. In a campus opinion poll weeks before the election, 41 percent of students identified themselves as Republicans, 21 percent as Democrats, and 38 percent as independents. Four years later, on the eve of the second Eisenhower-Stevenson vote, a whopping 84 percent of students preferred Eisenhower and only 14 percent Stevenson.

Orrin maintained a solid "B" average as an undergraduate, while spending a lot of time in intramural basketball and amateur boxing. He starred on a basketball squad which took first place out of seventy-three campus teams. Orrin also fought about ten three-round boxing matches his freshman year, winning most of them by technical knockouts. He hung up the gloves after walloping one opponent with a Kid Gavilan "bolo" punch, a complete-circle uppercut–to the knee.

After working as a lather in Pittsburgh the following summer, he returned for his second year, taking a job as a janitor. "No one wanted a janitor for a roommate except my friend and fellow janitor, LaVar Steel,"

Hatch quips. Steel's family was as poor as his. The two students lived in an old army barracks that had been converted into a dormitory, and ate frugally. When Steel's family sent home-canned tomato juice, Hatch remembers, "we would scrape enough money together to buy some soda crackers, and have a feast of tomato juice and crackers fit for kings."

Occasionally they got on each other's nerves. One time Steel, who outweighed Hatch by about forty pounds, insisted they go down to the boxing room and have it out. They pulled on gloves and climbed into the ring. The fired-up Steel quickly stunned Hatch with an overhand punch. Hands at his side, Steel advanced on his apparently helpless roommate, still clinging to the ropes. Then Hatch's head cleared. He catapulted off the ropes and hit Steel with a hard right-cross. Steel's knees buckled and he slumped to the canvas, eyes glazed. Hatch helped him up. They threw their arms around each other and never argued again.

Hatch had two dates during his first two years on campus, both to girl's-choice events. "There were so many beautiful girls there," he mused, "but I couldn't bring myself to ask any of them out. I felt ashamed because I didn't have any money or good clothes." But thanks to alphabetical seating in astronomy class, pretty, blonde Elaine Hansen sat next to Hatch. She was pleasant and helpful and they struck up a classroom friendship. Elaine was from a farm family in northern Utah's beautiful Cache Valley, and was studying to be a teacher.

It was at BYU that Orrin's spiritual bent came to full flower. He immersed himself in religious instruction and activities sponsored by the Latter-day Saint congregations (called "wards" or "branches"). "It was exciting to see people living Christian lives, and I really felt at home with them," he remembers. "Most of the students were pretty sincere, but the occasional classic pious phony really turned me off."

Hatch had held the Mormon priesthood since he was twelve, and had always planned to serve a full-time mission. Most LDS missionaries serve at their own or their family's expense, and Orrin saved hard to support himself. "I had found the Lord at the age of seventeen" in reading and praying about the scriptures, he says, and "my commitment was total." In October 1954 he dropped by Elaine's dormitory to tell her goodbye–they agreed to write–then entered a missionary training center in Salt Lake City. An intensive week of instruction followed, including practical topics on personal care, how to lead music, and tips for finding "investigators" and teaching them the gospel of Jesus Christ.

Mormons get their nickname from the Book of Mormon, which they consider another witness for Christ–not a replacement for the Bible, which they also revere and follow, but a companion to it. They believe the book is a translation of a historical record of God's dealings with peoples on the American continent. The record was abridged onto metal plates by an ancient prophet named Mormon, whom the book is named for, and later buried in a hillside in what is now upstate New York.

Centuries later, a local farm boy named Joseph Smith said God the Father and His son Jesus Christ appeared to him in a vision in 1820, followed several years later by an angel who gave him the metalic record. The young prophet translated it into the Book of Mormon and, in 1830, established the Church of Jesus Christ of Latter-day Saints. From then until now, Mormon missionaries have circled the globe proclaiming the "restored" gospel.

Twenty-year-old Orrin was assigned to the Great Lakes Mission and, for the next two years, was known as "Elder Hatch." His mission president was a Utah dentist named Lorin L. Richards, assisted by his wife Florence, who had been "called" by church leaders to preside for several years over the mission. They developed a close bond with Hatch, who was unusually dedicated and hard-working. "When Elder Hatch first got there he told us he was going to fill two missions during the two years–one for himself and one for his brother who was killed in the war," Florence Richards told a reporter.

Hatch and his various companions–Mormon missionaries always travel in pairs–served in a number of communities in Ohio, Indiana, and Michigan, packing a lifetime of experiences into two years. One door they knocked on in Springfield, Ohio, was answered by a large man waiting for them with a revolver in hand.

"I'm going to blow your head off," he growled, aiming the gun squarely in Hatch's face.

Hatch, heart racing, looked coolly at the gunman. "We represent the Lord Jesus Christ," he gulped, "and if you pull that trigger, your gun will explode and kill you."

The man slowly lowered his pistol as Hatch and his companion backed away. Reaching the sidewalk, they took off running. "I wasn't about to see if my prediction would come true, and we sure weren't going to give him another chance!" says Hatch.

Missionary work, Hatch decided, was "a life of opposites–good and evil attacking each other, with us missionaries caught in between." He found laboring among the poor "far more rewarding" than among the self-assured rich. Hatch saw miracles in the lives of believers. He witnessed "the blind see, the lame walk, the barren have children, the bitter and disillusioned gain hope, sickness of all types healed, the poor gain success, the ignorant become wise, and peace come into troubled lives for the first time."

His fervor was tempered by a wry sense of humor. Serving in heavily Catholic Sandusky, Ohio, and dressed in dark suits, overcoats, and hats, the youthful missionaries enjoyed walking city streets. "People would wave to us and say, 'Good morning Father,'" recalls Hatch. "I would reach my hand out to them and say, 'Bless you.'" At one home, a Catholic woman asked Hatch to take her confession. He defused the moment with a Mormon-style joke: "I told her I had graduated from being a priest and was now an elder."

Despite such occasional irreverence, Hatch was earnest in the work of teaching, baptizing, organizing congregations, and offering compassionate service. Few missionaries came close to Hatch's exacting standards, and most were far below. Near the very bottom was a tall, muscular missionary among those Hatch was assigned to supervise.

"He was one of the great detractors around and had never worked more than twelve hours a week since entering the mission field," recalls Hatch. When Hatch and his companion, an Elder Olson, first met Elder "Muscles," the latter stuck out his hand in a friendly gesture to Olson. As Olson did the same, Muscles hit him hard in the stomach. Olson doubled over in pain. "Oh Elder, did I hurt you?" asked Muscles with mock concern.

That evening, after helping Muscles and his companion find a new apartment and stock it with food, Hatch and Olson asked to have prayer with the other two before retiring for the night. Elder Muscles, grinning broadly, reached out his hand to Hatch in agreement. When Hatch responded, Muscles hit Hatch in the stomach. Hatch now saw before him not a missionary but an old punching bag hanging from a mulberry tree back in Pittsburgh.

"I wound up and hit him right in the stomach with everything I had," Hatch remembers. "I think my fist went all the way to his backbone." Muscles' face turned beet-red and he fell to the floor gasping. "Oh Elder, did I hurt you?" asked Hatch. "I was just joking."

The missionary lay on the floor for nearly an hour. When he finally pulled himself together, the four elders knelt and prayed. Then Hatch said,

"Let's go to bed because we have to get up at six o'clock."

"I'm not getting up at six!" announced Muscles.

"You sure as hell are," promised Hatch.

When the alarm rang at six the next morning, Muscles stubbornly refused to budge. Hatch, already irritable from spending the night on a cold concrete floor, grabbed Muscles' bedding and deposited it on the floor–with him in it. Squaring off, Hatch announced grimly, "Elder, you're going to get ready, you're going to leave here by nine o'clock, and you're going to work with me all day." The terrified missionary offered no argument.

As they left the apartment at nine o'clock sharp, Hatch offered to knock on every door, give every prayer, and teach every lesson if his reluctant partner would just accompany him. "That week we held sixty-five meetings in homes throughout the city," recalls Hatch. "I believe we did more work in that one week than that missionary had done during his whole mission." By midweek Elder Muscles was no longer just going through the motions. He was carrying his share of the load–and continued to do so throughout the rest of his mission. Years later he met Hatch on Temple Square in Salt Lake City. Now a Mormon bishop–head of a local congregation–he thanked Hatch for a lesson learned long ago in Indiana.

Florence Richards, in a hand-written letter to Helen Hatch in Pittsburgh, reported that "your wonderful son" was then at mission headquarters in Fort Wayne, Indiana, helping to instruct newly arriving missionaries. "President Richards thinks he is the best of the best of our missionaries," she wrote. She continued:

> Now, Sister Hatch, I am going to let you in on a little bit of special news, and at the same time tell you something I hope you will not take offense at. We have known for a long time that Elder Hatch was a natural born leader and an example of integrity for all missionaries to follow. Soon now he will be one of our leaders, and be given a responsibility that will require the best from him. He far excels everyone in every way, but I've noticed lately he could use a new suit. He always looks neat and clean, meticulously so, it's just his suit is sort of faded and thin and worn looking....Elder Hatch is so thrilled with life and his work that he never gives it a thought. Please don't tell him I told you....

Hatch got the new suit. Wherever he was assigned, invariably he helped strengthen the local congregation with newly baptized members and greater dedication to Christian service.

The two years passed quickly. When it ended, Hatch's mission president and his wife called Hatch "the most wonderful missionary the church ever had." Lorin Richards later told audiences back in Utah that Hatch literally had fulfilled his pledge to serve the equivalent of two missions–one for himself and one for his late brother Jess.

Much of that success had come through sheer will. Working past his physical limits to exhaustion, Hatch had endured a headache almost daily during the last eighteen months of his mission. He and his companions had averaged sixty-six hours of proselyting and thirty-nine meetings a week.

Decades later, as a sitting member of the U.S. Senate, Hatch termed his mission experience "the most important two years of my life."

Returning home to Pittsburgh in October 1956, Hatch went back to construction work and took up lathing again to earn money for college. At Christmas he drove to Newton, a Norman Rockwell kind of town nestled in northern Utah, to visit Elaine Hansen and meet her family. Elaine, he concluded, "was everything I expected her to be: decent, clean, intelligent, spiritual, desirous of a big family, and lovely in every way." She had graduated from BYU that spring and was teaching elementary school.

The following summer she visited his family in Pittsburgh. They exchanged wallet-size photos, Elaine writing on hers: "To the most wonderful fellow I know. I love you," and Orrin writing on his: "Too bad I couldn't send ya somethin [sic] better than a picture of this jerk. Love, Orrin."

On August 28, 1957, they were married in the Salt Lake Temple, in a covenant rite of enormous meaning for Mormons, who believe marriages performed in temples potentially bind families together for eternity as well as for mortality. During the wedding reception afterwards, Elaine's friends decorated the honeymoon car with shaving cream letters: "Amateur Night." Says Orrin: "Little did they know how true that was."

That fall he returned to BYU while Elaine taught at a nearby elementary school. Hatch majored in history but his favorite subject was philosophy. He began getting almost straight "A's" and set the goal of becoming an attorney. A surprise diversion in the summer of 1958 foreshadowed his future in politics. On a lark, he reluctantly agreed to enter the race for summer student body president, and won.

Their first child, Brent, was born in October. Two months later Hatch graduated and they headed east to Pittsburgh, where he again lathed to save money for law school. He and Jesse remodeled the chicken coop behind his parents' house into a tiny two-room cottage, added a toilet and small stove, and his little family moved in.

In the summer of 1959, Hatch took the law school entrance exam at the University of Pittsburgh. "My hands were cracked and sore from lathing. I looked around me and saw well-dressed and very intelligent people. I wondered if I really belonged in that elite group." As he finished the exam and was about to leave the building, apparently looking discouraged, a kindly law professor named Jack Rappaport asked if he could help. Rappaport heard Hatch out and encouraged him to apply for a scholarship. Two weeks later Hatch received a full honors scholarship to the law school, which paid his tuition for all three years.

He and twenty-seven other would-be lawyers attended classes in the Cathedral of Learning. In his second year he made *Law Review*, the school's legal periodical staffed by top students selected by the faculty. The next year he graduated near the top of his class. Labor law especially interested him. Still a card-carrying union man and sometime lather, he hoped to use his legal skills to assist fellow workers.

Marcia and Scott were born to the Hatches during law school. Now five of them lived in the dank, uninsulated chicken coop cottage, whose walls turned black from humidity each winter and were repainted by Orrin and Jesse each spring. During his last year in school, Hatch worked as a desk attendant at a girls' dormitory from 11 p.m. to 7 a.m. He attended classes until two or three o'clock in the afternoon. Hatch survived on about four hours of sleep most nights and was perpetually tired.

Elaine worked two or three days a week as a substitute teacher, with Orrin's mother Helen caring for the children. Despite school and financial pressures, Hatch scrupulously avoided studying on Sunday, when he and Elaine took the children to church and volunteered time to the local congregation.

Hatch's political views had changed considerably since he was a youth. He explains: "As a union worker, I heard only one side of things. Almost all the people I knew were working people and Democrats. But I found out later that some of the things I was proud of as a union man were wrong. The Democrats wanted to spend more, raise taxes, and force more government regulations on business. They believed in central control and less personal responsibility. It gradually dawned on me that Democrats were really compassionate, not to the poor, but mainly to union leaders who would help them stay in power."

His political transformation had begun at BYU, and his mission had opened his eyes to exploitation of the poor themselves. "I went on my mission believing that anyone who was poorer than we were in Pittsburgh should have everything given to them. But I saw the difference in the lives of people who counted on handouts to keep them going, and those who struggled to stay independent and maintain their self-respect."

Finally, Hatch says his political views came full circle in law school as he saw how an intrusive government can harm individuals and businesses. In his turn to the right, however, he developed a healthy suspicion of political extremism and was determined not to turn too far. An acquaintance invited him to join the far-right John Birch Society, but he refused.

He graduated from law school in 1962 and in October passed the Pennsylvania bar exam–then one of the toughest in the country. Shortly before graduation he was hired by the city's oldest law firm, Pringle, Bredin, and Martin, whose handful of attorneys–fewer than a dozen–were reputed to be among the toughest but most ethical trial lawyers in Pittsburgh. Hatch apprenticed by taking small claims cases to county court–sometimes as many as eight in a day, frequently on behalf of insurance companies.

With a regular paycheck at last, the Hatches moved out of the chicken coop and bought a home on Orchard Drive in Mt. Lebanon, a middle-class community several miles south of Pittsburgh. Their fourth child, daughter Kimberly, was born on New Year's Eve in 1964.

Hatch was made a partner in the firm within four years, at the age of thirty-two. A year later he received the highest rating possible for ethics and ability for an attorney with that amount of experience–a "bv" rating by Martindale-Hubbell, a national legal organization, based on confidential evaluations by peers. Later, after ten years of practice, including three in Utah, his peers there would give him the "av" rating–again the highest rating possible. Only about 5 percent of attorneys ever achieve the "av" rating.

Hatch's legal success was at last buying the good life. There were hunting and fishing trips with his partners and, early in 1969, a spectacular new home in fashionable Ben Avon Heights–a seven-bedroom French Normandy mansion, purchased for a song in a depressed market. While there, their fifth child, daughter Alysa, was born. Hatch tended to be a workaholic but usually made it to the children's special activities, including the boys' baseball and football games. Elaine anchored the family. She was a highly skilled homemaker and, like Orrin's mother Helen, handled most of the family discipline.

Every other summer they drove to Utah to visit Elaine's family–an uncomfortable trek, as Orrin insisted on driving the eighteen hundred miles straight through to save money on lodging. Orrin and Elaine never forgot what it was like to survive on bare essentials, and they continued to live frugally. They were practical in even the smallest ways. On Christmas Eve, each child was allowed to open one gift–so long as it was the annual pair of new pajamas, to be worn for photos around the Christmas tree next morning.

After they had enjoyed the new house for only six months, an old friend from BYU invited Hatch to join his Utah company. He was president of an oil and gas drilling firm and offered Hatch a position as senior vice president and general counsel.

Hatch had been with his law firm seven years, trying about five hundred cases in court and settling another two thousand out of court. His win rate was extremely high and his legal services much in demand. Hatch and his family could have continued to live comfortably in Pittsburgh on a six-figure income for the rest of his career–the prospect that Elaine initially preferred. But Orrin had long felt drawn to the Beehive State as his ancestral home and the best place to rear their family. In October 1969 he left Elaine and children behind to sell the house and headed to Utah.

The tug of Orrin's family roots in the West had trumped his hard-won affluence in the East.

4

Into the Arena

I enthusiastically endorse Orrin Hatch...a man of quality, courage, discipline, and integrity; a man who believes in individual freedom and self-reliance.

–Ronald Reagan

THE HATCHES ADJUSTED EASILY to Utah, buying a home on Salt Lake City's fashionable east bench and making friends in the neighborhood. Orrin made some small lifestyle changes. He began taking vitamin supplements and exercising more vigorously to cope with a regimen even more demanding than the one left behind in Pittsburgh. More than two-thirds of Utahns also belonged to the LDS Church, a complete way of life for devout members, easing the Hatches' transition. Orrin and Elaine pitched in as church and civic volunteers.

In May 1970 Elaine's brother Ramon died. The following month, when the Hatches' last child was born, they named him Jess Ramon in honor of their two late brothers. They now had six children–three sons and three daughters–ranging from eleven-year-old Brent to baby Jess.

Major change marked Orrin's professional life during the next several years. The drilling company was not going in the direction he wanted. After two difficult years, he left to form a legal association with V.L. Kesler and Dick Gordon. Less than a year later, he left that firm and, with Lowell Summerhays and Dick Landerman, formed Summerhays, Hatch, and Landerman. Again Hatch found that he had different goals than the others, and this partnership also lasted less than two years.

Hatch's most satisfying time as an attorney began in 1975 when he formed a partnership with a bright young lawyer named Walter Plumb, who had been an associate in the last firm. Plumb, who was nearly a head shorter than Hatch, was aggressive and upbeat, always encouraging Hatch and helping to build his self-confidence. Hatch was content at last in being able to call the shots as the most experienced partner. They focused largely on the trial work he relished, specializing in tax fraud, personal injuries, and contract disputes.

Early in his Utah legal career, Hatch tried a case before Willis Ritter, chief judge of the U.S. District Court for Utah and one of the most colorful characters in the state's judicial history. Short, barrel-chested, and snowy-haired, the crusty judge was staunchly anti-government and anti-establishment. Not surprisingly, Ritter was often overturned by the conservative Tenth Circuit, which he despised. Occasionally, after a ruling, he would say, "Now let's see if those dumb bastards in Denver can overturn this." Many attorneys feared or hated him, not without cause.

"Ritter was brutal to any lawyer he thought wasn't good enough to try a lawsuit," recalled Scott Savage, an attorney with VanCott Bagley Cornwall & McCarthy, the state's largest and most prestigious firm. "As a result, he only had to try cases with the best lawyers. It was very common for a lawyer to get assigned a case before Ritter, then call some other attorney acceptable to Ritter to take the case to court."

Hatch first stepped into Ritter's courtroom in the early 1970s to represent a man who had lost two fingers in a train coupler. The case was settled after two days of trial for $62,000, one of the highest verdicts of its type at that time. As Hatch was bantering with the bailiff afterwards, Ritter swept down majestically and announced, "Mr. Hatch, you are one of the finest trial lawyers I have ever had in this courtroom. I like you and I like the way you try a case. You're welcome in this courtroom any time you want to come back." Hatch, for his part, considered Ritter "one of the brightest as well as one of the most cantankerous men I have ever known."

Ritter was good to his word, even after learning Hatch was three things he disliked: a Republican, a conservative, and a Mormon bishop. "One reason Orrin got along well in front of Ritter was that he often represented the little guys that Ritter really liked," said Scott Savage.

Hatch tried another case before Ritter, defending a client indicted with others for running a cookie factory in which federal food inspectors had found rodent droppings. The U.S. Supreme Court had recently ruled that such suits were automatic criminal liability cases, even for company executives who had no hands-on responsibility for food processing.

The trial was a donnybrook, and it looked bad for Hatch's client, a Las Vegas businessman. Hatch appealed to the jury to consider the unfairness of holding criminally liable a man who lived nearly five hundred miles away from the Utah factory. But even more effective was Hatch's scorching cross-examination of a Food and Drug Administration witness. Suddenly Ritter himself turned on the hapless witness and demanded: "Where's the mouse?"

"The mouse?" stammered the startled witness. "What mouse?"

"You know, the *mouse,* the *mouse,*" Ritter shot back. "I'm sure there has to be a mouse here somewhere for you federal boys to make such a fuss about it."

The agent, of course, couldn't produce the mouse that left his calling cards in the cookie factory. The trial fell into disarray and Ritter called a recess and left the courtroom. When he returned, Hatch moved for his client's dismissal, which Ritter granted.

Also before Ritter, Hatch represented a Hispanic railroad worker who had slipped and fallen inside a gondola car, injuring his back and neck. In part because the man spoke almost no English, doctors had failed to pinpoint his injuries until months later when he was totally disabled. The Denver & Rio Grande Railroad Company refused to pay the man a dime.

Two lawyers from VanCott Bagley defended the case, bringing in a railroad doctor who said the plaintiff was a malingerer. They offered to settle for fifteen thousand dollars. On Hatch's advice, his client refused. The jury ended up awarding the man $140,000, a very high figure at that time.

Hatch often represented clients who couldn't pay his usual fees. One who couldn't pay anything was Thure Carlson, a Swedish immigrant who owned a small dry cleaning shop. The diminutive Carlson and his wife routinely toiled sixteen hours a day, making about seven thousand dollars a year. He had bought cleaning equipment and, instead of depreciating it over time, by mistake had written it off as an expense in one year.

The Internal Revenue Service insisted on its pound of flesh, claiming that Carlson over several years had avoided paying income taxes of about $35,000–five times his annual income. The IRS usually prevailed in such tax fraud cases, but Hatch was dogged, using Carlson himself as his best weapon. In one poignant moment on the witness stand, an emotional Carlson turned to the jury and, in his thick Swedish accent, said simply, "I am an honest man."

Jurors retired to deliberate, then streamed in and announced their verdict: "Not guilty" on all counts. The Carlsons hugged each other, then Carlson and Hatch embraced, tears rolling down both men's cheeks.

"Orrin was a tough competitor," said VanCott Bagley's Scott Savage, who tried one case against Hatch and settled about ten others out of court. "He would take advantage when he could get an advantage, but he was fair."

By 1976, Hatch had a lucrative law practice and his family had sunk firm roots in Utah's genial soil. But a new challenge was tugging. Since his years at BYU, Hatch had become increasingly conservative in his political views. He followed current events closely and was disturbed by what he saw. He itched to do something about it.

The nation was still healing from another presidential scandal, in which Richard Nixon resigned from office in August 1974 after the House Judiciary Committee voted three articles of impeachment against him. His successor, Gerald Ford, crippled his own political future a month later by pardoning Nixon. In April 1975 Communist North Vietnam rolled over South Vietnam, stripping away any veneer of victory for democracy and handing America its first wartime defeat. Meanwhile the economy was in a slump, with 9 percent unemployment–highest rate since 1941–and inflation above 5 percent.

The 1976 presidential year seemed a good time for outsiders, and two improbable ones eyed national office: a little-known governor in Georgia, Jimmy Carter, whose sights were on the White House, and Hatch, an even more anonymous Utahn, who began to dream of the Senate. Hatch believed Utah's liberal senior senator, Frank Moss, who was up for reelection that year, was part of the problem rather than part of the solution in Washington.

Hatch's growing sense of urgency hardened into conviction. Sharing and feeding it was his close friend and fellow Salt Lake attorney Grey Nokes. "I was constantly moaning and groaning about what was happening around the world and in Washington," recalled Hatch. Nokes challenged him to put up or shut up. "Why don't *you* run against Moss?" he asked.

Almost no one else gave Hatch any encouragement. In January 1976 he casually mentioned the idea to a neighbor, Frank Madsen. "I'm thinking about getting in the Senate race against Moss," Hatch told him.

"You're crazy!" said Madsen. "Nobody knows you, you're not known as a Republican, and you don't have any money. It's crazy."

Orrin and Elaine took the children to Disneyland over Easter vacation. During the drive to California he gingerly broached the idea of running for the Senate with her. Elaine was adamantly opposed and didn't want to discuss it further. She and both of his parents considered politics nasty business.

The idea of running against Moss did seem preposterous. The Senator was solidly entrenched after three terms in which he had risen to chairman of the Senate Space Committee–important to Utah's defense-dependent economy–and majority secretary, the number three spot in Senate leadership. But Moss's influence in Washington masked a vulnerability back home, where he was out of step with most Utahns on a host of issues. He won his first Senate race in 1958 in a fluke election, taking only 37 percent of the vote in a three-way contest, and had relatively easy races the next two times.

During seventeen years in Washington, Moss increasingly aligned himself with the national Democratic agenda. He strongly supported organized labor and its threat to Utah's right-to-work law. He voted for federal funding of abortion, federal land use planning, and many government social programs considered wasteful by critics.

The ranks of Utah Republicans already challenging Moss looked almost as daunting to Hatch. They included a former four-term U.S. congressman, a former White House aide and longtime Utah political operative, a Washington lobbyist, and–the odds-on favorite to win the GOP nomination–an impressive former assistant secretary at the U.S. Department of the Interior, Jack Carlson.

By contrast, Hatch's name had yet to appear in Utah newspapers. With one month to go before filing deadline, he had no financial reserves and no idea how to raise the substantial amount it would take to run a credible campaign.

Judge Ritter unwittingly played a key role in aiding Hatch. In mid-April, Hatch and dozens of other attorneys appeared before Ritter to hear his calendar for the next month. The docket had twenty-nine cases on it, including twelve of Hatch's toughest cases. Ritter, now the nation's oldest chief judge at seventy-six, smiled disbelievingly as the brash forty-two-year-old Hatch reported "ready" on all twelve.

Ritter knew that no lawyer could possibly be prepared to try a dozen important cases within thirty days. Yet by the time each one was called up, Hatch was ready. Within the month all twelve had been settled, bringing more than a hundred thousand dollars in fees–equivalent to more than four hundred thousand dollars in 2000 and far more than Hatch had ever earned in a single month. It was enough to keep the law firm going through the 1976 election.

Ritter didn't know that by burying Hatch in work, he had provided the financial means for climbing a political mountain–and that when Hatch arrived at the summit, he would push one of Ritter's best friends, Frank Moss, over a cliff.

No doubt Ritter laughed along with other Utahns at the brash political novice. Hatch's campaign resume suggested why. The qualifications he listed for what is often called the world's most exclusive club, the U.S. Senate, had "amateur" stamped all over them:

HIGH SCHOOL
- Voted Most Outstanding Senior Boy
- President, Leaders Club
- Vice President, Senior Class
- Named in "Who's Who in American High Schools"
- Outstanding in Student Activities, Athletics and Fine Arts

COLLEGE
- Summer Student Body President, Graduating with Bachelor of Science Degree in 1959

The list continued with his good record in law school, said he "Was Partner in One of Pittsburgh's Most Respected Law Firms," and gave his bar and other legal associations. It had no trace of government or political experience in the real world.

While such lightweight credentials had everyone else laughing, Elaine wept. After her husband officially threw his hat into the ring, "I cried for three days," she recalled. "I didn't like politicians and didn't trust them. I wanted nothing to do with it."

But Orrin plowed on, publicly releasing a written statement that included a litany of conservative complaints against the federal government–too wasteful, too oppressive, too encroaching on states' rights–plus a few flourishes of his own including opposition to "the deterioration of morals and ethics in our society."

"I am here," he told onlookers after filing, "to ask your support by reason of the fact that I believe I have the courage and capability to campaign successfully against Senator Moss."

Before getting to the main bout with Moss, however, Hatch had to convince other Utah Republicans–to whom he was entirely an unknown quantity–that he was for real. That meant slugging it out with his four Republican opponents in appearances across the state, and somehow influencing the 2,500 GOP delegates who would choose the party's Senate nominee at the state convention that summer.

Knowing he could not individually meet all the convention delegates in the little time remaining, Hatch hit on a novel idea: He would send his voice instead. He recorded a fourteen-minute cassette tape, glued on a red, white, and blue label with his picture, and mailed it to each delegate, accompanied by a parchment bearing the same message.

"For all of Senator Moss's seniority record," Hatch said on the tape, "I have not seen that many of a long list of accomplishments. As a matter of fact, I've seen some things that have been very detrimental to Utah....And if I go back there, I'm going to...represent Utah in such a way that no longer are we considered the laughingstock of the country."

The tape, which included endorsements by several Utahns he had defended in court, dramatically boosted Hatch's name recognition.

Once Elaine knew her husband was in the race for keeps, she adjusted to the idea of being involved in politics. Later, in fact, she remembered the campaign as a highlight of their family's life–a time when the family grew closer. All eight of them drove in a green Ford van to most of Utah's twenty-nine county conventions, the children wearing T-shirts printed with Orrin's name as they passed out campaign literature. Meanwhile, Orrin's parents, who had followed their son to Utah and bought a home nearby, also pitched in. Jesse made "Hatch for Senate" signs and, with the help of Orrin's sisters and their spouses, posted them along highways across the state.

At each county convention, Senate candidates were allotted three minutes. Hatch's courtroom experience served him well under the rigidly enforced time constraints. He gave spirited, rapid-fire presentations, blasting Washington and promising reform.

But his polished rhetoric masked inner uncertainties. "Even though I knew I could speak well, I was really lacking in self-confidence, as I had been all my life," recalled Hatch. "I tried to cover it up by acting self-assured, but I was hurting inside all the time. Some people thought I was arrogant because of this. But I didn't feel arrogant; I felt terribly deficient and most of the time inferior."

Bitter feelings developed between the Hatch and Carlson camps. Jack Carlson, until recently an official in the Ford Administration, waffled publicly on which Republican he supported for president–Ford, his former boss and personal friend–or former California Governor Ronald Reagan, a political demigod in Utah. Hatch had no such ambivalence: He idolized

Reagan, who would speak at the Utah Republican Convention on July 16.

By the eve of the convention, Republican candidates had erected a circus-like arena in the Salt Palace in downtown Salt Lake City. Some had spent thousands of dollars on sophisticated campaign booths in a last-ditch effort to attract delegates. Then there was Hatch's hut. With no money to hire professionals, he relied on an enthusiastic volunteer who patched together a ramshackle booth plastered with red, white, and blue banners. While other candidates offered tasty *hors d'oeuvres,* Hatch's people handed out popsicles labeled "Lick Moss, Vote Hatch."

From morning until evening, Hatch stood in front of his booth pitching passers-by. Among ardent volunteers was an unplanned secret weapon–an attractive and well-endowed woman who passed out campaign brochures wearing a "Hatch for Senate" T-shirt and no bra. "More than one male thought our booth was the hit of the conference," recalled Hatch. "I was mortified. It worried me to death, but she was a nice person and a dear friend, and I didn't want to hurt her feelings."

The next day, each candidate spoke for three minutes. Hatch was introduced by the feisty former president of BYU, Ernest Wilkinson, who said Hatch was "of our culture"–an attempt to blunt the argument Hatch had lived in Utah only six years. Hatch told delegates "Give me your support and I *promise* you I'll beat Senator Moss in November." Despite the huge odds of doing so, 778 delegates voted for Hatch, who came in second to Carlson with 930 votes. They prepared to square off in a campaign ending on primary day in September.

Carlson was considered a moderate, Hatch a far-right conservative, though he rejected that label, insisting he was an "eclectic" who welcomed good ideas whatever their source. In fact their differences were more style than substance. Both opposed national health care insurance, the Humphrey-Hawkins full employment bill making the federal government the employer of last resort, and a common-situs picketing bill–supported by Moss–enabling one striking union to shut down an entire project. Both favored a right-to-life constitutional amendment, Hatch explaining, "I oppose abortions except to save the life of the mother." Hatch repeatedly challenged Carlson to debate, with Carlson largely ignoring him and running against Moss.

In mid-summer, Hatch was invited to Washington by a recently formed coalition of activist conservatives known as the New Right, whose intellectual leader was Paul Weyrich. They liked what they saw in Hatch and talked some donors into contributing several thousand dollars to his campaign–not a huge amount but very timely and helpful given his shoestring budget. For his files, Hatch wrote that, while some of those he met "were much farther right than they needed to be, most were dedicated, conscientious people who wanted to do what was right for this country." He added, perceptively, that Weyrich "is extremely witty, is very bright, and so long as you don't disagree with him, is very charming."

Wilkinson and Cleon Skousen, another prominent Utah conservative who also had recently met Hatch for the first time, continued to marshal support for him. Skousen, a prolific writer on religion and government, sent a fund-raising letter on Hatch's behalf "to the people I know who love the Constitution and want to see it preserved." He said he had spent many hours with Hatch and considered him "a Constitutionalist in the tradition of the founding fathers."

"Without being abrasive," Skousen continued, "Orrin is a fighter. He prepares his cases well. He has a reputation among little people of helping when nobody else will....He has an exceptionally sharp mind and expresses himself as well as anyone I have met in a long time. In other words, he is a born advocate. And on the right side. His conservatism is well-balanced and highly responsible."

As the race entered the final weeks, the lead seesawed between Carlson and Hatch. Although Carlson had spent nearly two decades away from the state as a military officer or federal civilian employee, he reminded audiences that Utah had never been represented by a senator who was not a native son. When a letter to the editor of the *Deseret News* made the same point, Helen Hatch, Orrin's mother, answered in a warm and ingenuous letter of her own:

> I feel so badly that I am the culprit–the reason Orrin Hatch was not born in Utah.
>
> His father and I met in Hiawatha, Utah, where I had been living with my father and stepmother. Orrin's father is of old pioneer heritage. His great-grandfather was sent to colonize Ashley Valley near Vernal, Utah. His other great-grandfather marched with the Mormon Battalion in the war with Mexico. My mother wrote for us to come to Pittsburgh as there was a building boom. Always my husband, a native Utahn, had a deep longing to return to Utah, but by the time Orrin was born we had a large family and the depression was so severe we even lost our home. I am now thinking of Utah's early greats–how they came from New York State, Vermont, Pennsylvania, Canada, and overseas....Orrin has had

> many hard knocks–he struggled to gain an education. He was a history major and loves this country and Utah very much. I would not wish my boy to win without merit.

Brainstorming for an eleventh-hour shot in the arm, Hatch came up with the improbable idea of asking Ronald Reagan for his endorsement. Although Hatch had been one of the earliest candidates in the country to support Reagan for president, it would be almost unprecedented for a Republican of Reagan's stature to take sides in a primary contest. But a Hatch aide contacted Michael Deaver, Reagan's longtime assistant, and Deaver agreed to do what he could. Deaver talked to Reagan's pollster, Richard Wirthlin, a former Utahn, who said he would find out what he could about Hatch.

Wirthlin contacted his nephew, a Mormon bishop in Salt Lake City whose congregation shared the same building where Hatch was bishop of another ward. The nephew told Wirthlin that "you couldn't do better than Orrin Hatch," explaining that his fellow bishop was known for integrity and decency. Wirthlin relayed that character reference to Deaver, and also reported that Hatch was leading and starting to pull away in recent polls. His advice: Reagan would be wise to give the endorsement, helping to cement Hatch's victory as well as a friendship that could be valuable down the road.

Two days before the primary election, the endorsement ran in several Utah daily newspapers:

> THE TIME HAS COME FOR ME TO DO EVERYTHING I CAN TO ENDORSE A MAN OF QUALITY, COURAGE, DISCIPLINE, AND INTEGRITY; A MAN WHO BELIEVES IN INDIVIDUAL FREEDOM AND SELF RELIANCE. WITH THESE QUALITIES IN MIND, I ENTHUSIASTICALLY ENDORSE ORRIN HATCH FOR U.S. SENATOR FROM UTAH. ORRIN HATCH HAS THE QUALITY OF LEADERSHIP, THE FORTHRIGHTNESS OF PURPOSE, AND THE PERSONAL HONESTY NEEDED TO TURN THIS COUNTRY TO A PROPER COURSE.
>
> THIS IS RONALD REAGAN ASKING YOU TO ELECT ORRIN HATCH TO THE UNITED STATES SENATE. GOOD LUCK.

The endorsement sealed Carlson's political fate. Utah Republicans went to the polls on Tuesday and voted almost two to one for Hatch–104,000 to

57,000.

Now it was on to the 1976 general election against Senator Moss, a national political figure considered unbeatable by most pundits.

Frank E. (Ted) Moss was a U.S. senator straight from central casting. Completing his third six-year term at age sixty-five, the native Utahn and former judge tooled around Washington in a yellow Mustang convertible, hair slicked back and flashing a million-dollar smile. The amiable Moss was the bane of conservatives but had risen steadily in Washington with strong labor support, chairing the Space Committee and the consumer subcommittee and holding a leadership position among Senate Democrats. He had anticipated a traditional contest against a fellow Washington insider, Jack Carlson, and was gleeful at Hatch's primary victory. "Hatch was completely a blank page to me" before that, said Moss years later. Moss's former press secretary, Dale Zabriskie, was with his old boss on the day of the Utah primary vote, and tried to tell him that Hatch might be more difficult than he figured because he had no record to attack. However, recalled Zabriskie, "Senator Moss just didn't take Hatch seriously."

A public opinion survey by pollster Dan Jones one day after the primary vote showed Moss in trouble among virtually every demographic group except staunch Democrats. But Moss, in an interview, recalled thinking, "There was just no way I could be beaten by a carpetbagger who was unknown."

Carpetbagger. It was a dog the Democrats would sic on Hatch for the next twenty years, but the mutt always refused to hunt. Hatch was a descendant of Utah pioneers, a son of devout Mormon parents, and had sacrificed hard-won privilege in the East to follow his heart west to Utah. He had been reared in the ideals and traditions of the Beehive State if not on its soil.

While Moss toasted his good fortune at the coming cakewalk, Hatch rocketed out of the starting blocks. Three days after the primary, BYU's Wilkinson, famed for his own work ethic, wrote in his diary that "One thing I have to concede to [Hatch], he certainly gets around everywhere. I have never known anyone who works as hard as he is working."

Hatch's case against Moss rested not on the fact he had been in Washington nearly eighteen years, but on the reality that, while there, he did not faithfully represent the views of most Utahns. Moss was beholden to big labor, routinely voted to expand the federal bureaucracy, and was out of step with Utahns on key social issues including federal funding of abortion.

During their first debate, before eight hundred Rotarians at the Hotel

Utah, Moss asked scornfully: "Who is this *young....upstart...attorney...*from Pittsburgh? The deliberately drawn-out question was calculated to destroy Hatch in as few words as possible. Utahns didn't like young upstarts, were very antagonistic toward attorneys, and generally distrustful of outsiders.

Hatch, sitting tensely on the platform, felt that most Rotarians were staring at him with disdain. He wondered if he had already lost. By the time it was his turn, however, Hatch had calmed himself and his adrenalin was flowing.

"Senator," he began, nodding politely at Moss, "my great-grandfather, Jeremiah Hatch, founded Vernal and Ashley Valley in Eastern Utah. My great uncle, Lorenzo Hatch, was one of the founders of Logan and Cache Valley in Northern Utah, and my great uncle, Abram Hatch, helped to found Heber City and Heber Valley in Central Utah. They were all three polygamists, and everywhere I go, people come up to me and say, 'You know, I think I'm related to you.' If you keep denigrating my Hatch family background, the Hatch vote alone is going to rise up and bite you in the ass."

The Rotarians came apart with laughter. By the time they were back in order, Moss seemed discombobulated and had difficulty getting back on track. He had taken his best shot and missed.

During another debate, Hatch said Moss voted correctly for Utah only during election years. "Now wait a minute," responded Moss indignantly, "you're attacking my integrity!"

"That's right!" answered Hatch.

In a traditional luncheon debate before Utah clergy, Hatch said Congress must clean up its act and return to Judeo-Christian principles so voters can "look up to our senators and representatives." Senator Moss is sincere, conceded Hatch, "but sincerely wrong in his approach to our country."

Moss defended himself and his colleagues, saying "we apply fairly high standards of ethics to ourselves." He emphasized the value of his seniority several times, noting that he wouldn't "be starting at the bottom of the totem pole on the minority side" when Congress opened. Hatch was undaunted. "That's my life, all my life, starting at the bottom."

Three weeks before the November 2 election, a poll published in the *Salt Lake Tribune* showed the two candidates dead even.

Money continued to be extremely tight for Hatch. Although he reported spending about $570,000 on the race, nearly $500,000 went to cover the costs of direct-mail solicitations, leaving less than $100,000 to get his message out through radio spots, newspaper ads, brochures, and posters.

Moss reported spending less than Hatch, but in reality almost certainly far outspent him. One-third of Moss's money officially came from organized labor, but the Senator also benefitted from tens if not hundreds of thousands of dollars in "soft" campaign contributions in union organizing efforts–a huge loophole in campaign finance laws.

But Hatch enjoyed an advantage that outweighed Moss's entrenched special interests: The help of Ronald Reagan, free to campaign since narrowly losing the GOP presidential nomination to incumbent Gerald Ford. Hatch flew to California and cut TV spots with Reagan for the Utah campaign. Then, six days before the election, Reagan interrupted his nationwide stumping for Ford and made a quick stop in Utah to further aid Hatch. Reagan, with Hatch by his side, delivered a stemwinder to ten thousand wildly cheering partisans, giving Hatch's campaign a huge boost as the race headed for the wire.

On election day, Orrin and Elaine and their families drove to the Hilton Hotel to await returns with other Republicans. Utah tied with Alaska in giving Gerald Ford–the state's *second* choice for president, after Reagan–his largest popular vote, 64 percent, in a losing battle with Jimmy Carter.

Early returns showed Hatch in the lead. The trend held firm throughout the night, as 287,000 citizens, 54 percent, pulled the lever for Hatch. His "unbeatable" opponent Frank Moss won about 240,000 votes, 45 percent.

The election gave Democrats the White House for the first time since 1969, along with huge majorities in the House and Senate. The party lineup in the new Senate–which had been in Democratic hands for a quarter-century–remained precisely the same as before the election: 62 Democrats and 38 Republicans. But a political revolution had swept Moss and eight other incumbent senators out of office, with another nine voluntarily retiring, leaving Hatch's 18-member freshman class unusually large and promising rapid rise for those who shined.

Hatch vowed he would shine.

5

Labor Law 'Reform'

If labor law changes were approved by the Senate . . . an estimated 50 percent of all American workers would be forced into unions . . . more money would be poured into welfare-type social programs, and there would be nothing left over for strengthening America's military. The Soviet Union thus would not be forced to develop a more open society and end the Cold War, and the course of history would be quite different.

SENATOR HATCH HIT THE ground running from the moment he was sworn into office by Vice President Nelson Rockefeller on January 4, 1977.

His reputation as a political prodigy preceded him to Washington, with *Congressional Quarterly* observing that the Utahn "was expected to be one of the most intriguing new figures in the Senate ... a born campaigner, with unusual stage presence and oratorical skill." *CQ* added that some conservative groups "were even talking about him as a possible presidential candidate in 1980."

To his chagrin, the first conservative conference he attended as a senator sold "Hatch-Simon 1980" campaign buttons, touting him and former Treasury Secretary William Simon for the future GOP ticket. It was a compliment that surprised the Senator as much as anyone, as he had done nothing purposely to encourage it.

Hatch and newly elected President Jimmy Carter, formerly a governor little known outside his native South, symbolized the political significance of the 1976 election. Both were outsiders who thumbed their noses at the Washington establishment and won. But the Utahn was decidedly in the minority: Along with the White House, lost by Republican President Gerald

Ford, Democrats now controlled the House by a lopsided 291 to 144, and the Senate by 62 to 38.

Hatch was assigned to three committees–Joint Economic, Judiciary, and Labor and Human Resources. He worked prodigiously, and eventually would chair the latter two. He quickly gained a reputation for taking on all sorts of other causes as well. "Back then, Orrin was a lot like Ronald Reagan," said Nevada Senator Paul Laxalt. "He just didn't know how to say 'no.' It was a damn good thing he was a man–otherwise he would have been pregnant all the time."

He tended to make alliances with senators less concerned with political labels and more concerned with the real impact of their work on the daily lives of people. Some of the senators he liked most were not political conservatives like himself but noted liberals, including former Vice President Hubert Humphrey, with whom Hatch developed a warm relationship. "Although we differ on many political matters," wrote the Utahn privately of Humphrey, "I can't help but say that this man has had a profound impact on my life. He is so optimistic, so sincere, so loving....I have learned from him."

Freshman senators were expected to be seen but not heard, a notion Hatch refused to swallow. One older Democratic committee chairman approached him, explaining "Sonny, we want you to sit back and wait a couple of years before offering your views."

Thank you, sir," Hatch answered, "I know you're trying to be helpful. But the people of Utah elected me to do a job here, and I owe it to them to get about it."

For all his brashness, Hatch knew he could accomplish little without the help of veteran colleagues. Several senior Southern Democrats, notably James Allen of Alabama, saw an ally in the young Utahn and trained him to help thwart liberal initiatives. Allen was the bane of liberals and the master of Senate filibusters. He and Senate Majority Leader Robert Byrd of West Virginia, a no-nonsense legislator, were acknowledged as the two men who best knew the Senate's arcane rules and procedures, critical to passing or killing controversial legislation.

Allen was Hatch's mentor, befriending him and teaching him how the Senate really operated. "Orrin, spend time on the floor and learn the rules," the tall, strapping Allen advised. "It will give you power and help you stop some of these things that are ruining our country."

While carrying a full load in Washington, the Senator returned to Utah nearly every other weekend, going to great lengths to tend to constituent needs. *Utah Holiday* magazine liked what it was seeing in the state's new senator, calling Hatch "bright, articulate, unafraid to beard liberal lions in their own dens" and "the most persuasive, tireless defender of the conservative cause to emerge from Utah in several decades."

Meanwhile, across town from Capitol Hill in 1978, powerful labor leader George Meany wanted a pen for his eighty-fourth birthday–the pen President Jimmy Carter would use to sign into law the most sweeping changes in labor union rules in more than forty years. Improbably, all that stood between Meany and his pen was Orrin Hatch, still wet behind the ears as a novice senator with all of sixteen months' experience.

Meany, the crusty leader of the AFL-CIO, and his associates had spent tens of millions as a down payment on labor "reform." For years big labor had given nearly all its congressional campaign donations to Democrats, and it was time for them to deliver. Along with huge Democratic majorities in both houses of Congress, the final piece of labor's power puzzle was put in place with the defeat of Gerald Ford and installation of Carter in the White House.

The price would be worth it: Overhauling America's labor laws would help reverse a sharp decline for unions, whose membership had gone from 35 percent of nonfarm workers at the end of World War II to around 20 percent thirty years later. During 1975-77, more than half of union elections held among U.S. workers had ended in union defeats. Big labor's solution was not to change itself but to change the rules, amending the National Labor Relations Act of 1935, which had been passed to protect workers seeking union representation.

Also near the top of labor's agenda was strangling the despised Section 14-b of the Taft-Hartley Act, the right-to-work provision under which twenty states, including Utah, had outlawed contracts that forced workers to join unions to keep their jobs.

The House, right on schedule, overwhelmingly approved Labor Law Reform and sent it on to the Senate, where the Labor and Human Resources Committee rubber-stamped it on a vote of 16-2. The two dissenters were Hatch and fellow Republican freshman Sam Hayakawa of California. It was a foregone conclusion by virtually everyone that the full Senate would shortly follow the House's lead and pass the bill.

Stakes were momentous. "If labor law changes were approved by the

Senate in the form passed by the House," explained Hatch, "an estimated 50 percent of all American workers would be forced into unions–more than double the rate at that time. More and more money would be poured into welfare-type social programs and there would be nothing left over for strengthening America's military. The Soviet Union thus would not be forced to develop a more open society and end the Cold War, and the course of history would be quite different."

Hatch had been a card-carrying member of the AFL-CIO as a tradesman in Pittsburgh, and by no means was anti-labor. But he had come to believe that unions were in good part responsible for the surge of federal social spending that helped put the nation deeply in debt. "Democrats played union workers for chumps, always calling for more taxes on the rich to fund social programs, even though the taxes always hurt union members the most, including many in the middle class."

Labor Law Reform, among other things, would require companies to hold "quickie" elections for union representation after employees requested them, giving employers little time to defend themselves; give unions the right to come onto company property at the employer's expense before elections to unionize employees during work hours, and add two members to the National Labor Relations Board–an invitation to the Democratic White House and Congress to stack the board with pro-labor members.

Hatch believed laws already on the books tilted the organizing process slightly in favor of unions. "I didn't find that repugnant, having read many books about the terrors of early unionizing attempts by courageous men and women who wanted working people's rights in a society slanted in favor of powerful businesses. However, a delicate balance had emerged which worked quite well, and I didn't think it should be upset by slanting the process completely in favor of one side or the other–the unions in this case."

Whatever Hatch thought seemed of little consequence in May 1978 as Senate Bill 2467, Labor Law Reform, was rolling toward the Senate floor. Leading President Carter's forces to pass it was Majority Leader Bob Byrd, master of Senate rules who was named that year by *U.S. News & World Report* as the fourth most influential man in America.

As the date drew near for the momentous battle, all the generals were in place except one: a leader for the Senate opposition. Business representatives tried to recruit a number of senior senators. All said no.

They were convinced the bill was unstoppable and weren't about to throw their bodies before a rushing locomotive.

Finally, almost by default, they turned to the senator who was ninety-eighth in seniority out of 100 members: Hatch. Reluctantly he agreed, asking fellow GOP freshman Richard Lugar of Indiana to assist him. Their only chance to stop Labor Law Reform was through a filibuster. Such talkathons, while not allowed in the House, had a long tradition in the Senate. Cloture–ending debate and proceeding to a vote on the measure at hand–took sixty votes.

As a counterweight to Byrd, Hatch banked on the help of his good friend James Allen, D-Alabama, a veteran filibusterer who had coached Hatch since his first days in the Senate. Recently Allen and Hatch had led Senate opposition to the Panama Canal Treaties, and the protracted fight had left Allen on the Senate floor for many hours at a stretch, exhausting him and finally breaking his health. On the eve of the battle, Allen invited Hatch into his office.

"You're going to have to take the baton, Orrin," said Allen, "because I'm not going to be around much longer."

Hatch laughed nervously, eyeing his robust, six-foot-four friend. "Jim, you just won your last election by 90 percent. You're going to be here for a long time."

Allen looked down and shook his head.

Lobbyists on both sides pulled out the stops in one of the heaviest efforts at persuasion ever to hit Capitol Hill. "Mail being received in the Senate is beyond counting," reported *U.S. News & World Report.* More than a month before the bill reached the Senate floor, the National Right to Work Committee had generated some 3 million postcards against the bill–an average of 30,000 for each of the 100 senators. The AFL-CIO had generated 2 million for the bill–20,000 per senator, with another 700,000 postcards held in reserve.

In addition to Lugar, key senators on Hatch's team included Democrat Ernest F. (Fritz) Hollings of South Carolina and Senate Republican leader Howard Baker of Tennessee. Their southern region of the U.S. had been particularly inhospitable to organized labor, and was a special target of Labor Law Reform. In the months leading up to the decisive fight, Hatch traveled the country, giving hundreds of speeches to fire up opponents and help bring pressure on key senators from their home states.

Labor interests were a Goliath. The Senate included sixty-two

Democrats, most elected with union help, and thirty-eight Republicans, including a number who voted routinely with the Democratic majority on labor issues. Facing Goliath was a youthful Hatch, with Richard Lugar at his side. Each had been in the Senate less than a year and a half. The only stone in David's sling, and it seemed pitifully small, was to keep pro-union forces from gaining the necessary sixty votes to end the filibuster and proceed to an up or down vote on the bill.

The Senate had voted on cloture only 127 times in history, never more than four times on a single issue. The outcome this time likely hinged on five undecided Democrats: Lawton Chiles of Florida, Dale Bumpers of Arkansas, John Sparkman of Alabama, Russell Long of Louisiana, and Edward Zorinsky of Nebraska. Zorinsky had been a Republican until switching parties to run for the Senate, which he entered with Hatch's freshman class.

Democrats were so confident of victory that their worst fear was crushing Hatch and Lugar too quickly and arousing public sympathy for the two young, inexperienced senators. Byrd decided to let the two freshmen win the first two cloture votes, then kill the filibuster on the third and pass the bill into law.

May 16, Tuesday

The battle opens on the Senate floor. The U.S. Chamber of Commerce says "freedom is at stake." George Meany of the AFL-CIO calls it a "holy war." President Carter says the bill is a top priority and promises to personally lobby key senators.

Democrat Harrison Williams of New Jersey, floor leader for the bill, says it is simply designed to "end delay and bring an end to the growing number of violations of employee rights" in organizing unions. Jesse Helms, R-North Carolina, says its real goal is to "unionize the South by federal force." Hatch holds the floor for two hours in the afternoon.

May 18, Thursday

Byrd announces he will not attempt to end the filibuster until senators return from the Memorial Day recess early in June.

Hatch delivers floor speeches, helps draft remarks for others, conducts daily strategy sessions, and pores over the arcane Senate rules with James Allen, all while attending to other Senate duties. He swims daily to increase his stamina and is up to fifty laps. His workdays now are routinely eighteen hours long and he is chronically tired.

June 1, Thursday

Memorial Day recess week. Hatch works in his neglected yard in Vienna, Virginia, until dark. He is summoned to the telephone where an aide delivers devastating news: James Allen has just died of a heart attack in Alabama. That evening Hatch writes:

> I've had very few things hit me as hard as this news did. Senator Allen was not only my best friend in the Senate, but one of the greatest men I've ever known. He was a spiritual man who...beat himself into the ground filibustering and stopping so many of the detrimental things that really were hurting the country....I've often said that, if a Republican ran against him, I would go down to Alabama and campaign for Jim Allen, because there couldn't be a Republican any better than Jim Allen.

June 5, Monday

Senators start the day by eulogizing Allen. In his tribute, Hatch quotes from two favorite poems: "Thanatopsis," by William Cullen Bryant, ending "...approach thy grave like one who wraps the drapery of his couch about him and lies down to pleasant dreams," and "Ode: Intimations of Immortality," by William Wordsworth:

> Our birth is but a sleep and a forgetting:
> The Soul that rises with us, our life's Star,
> Hath had elsewhere its setting,
> And cometh from afar:
> Not in entire forgetfulness,
> And not in utter nakedness,
> But trailing clouds of glory do we come,
> From God, who is our home.

Then it was back to the filibuster, with Hatch and Jesse Helms–who has been enlisted as Allen's replacement to tutor Hatch on Senate rules–helping to kill two amendments by pro-labor senators, aimed at softening small business opposition to the bill.

June 7, Wednesday

The first cloture vote, at 5:15 p.m. Illinois Republican Charles Percy, torn between union and business supporters, votes against cloture. As he walks by, Hatch thanks Percy, who forces a grin and says, "Well, as you know, I'll leave you before it's all over." Percy, no profile in courage, is promising Illinois businessmen he will oppose labor reform but is clearly planning to vote with big labor when the chips are down.

Cloture is easily defeated, forty-two senators voting for it and forty-seven against. The outcome is no surprise–even Bob Byrd had predicted he'd lose on the first couple of votes.

June 8, Thursday

The second cloture vote. Opponents of the bill again defeat cloture, but this time the numbers have tipped: forty-nine votes for cloture, forty-one against. The votes for cutting off the filibuster are creeping up toward the necessary sixty.

Byrd announces revisions to the bill in an attempt to win enough votes to invoke cloture on the third attempt, scheduled for Tuesday. Hatch says the concessions are not enough. He and other opposition leaders divide up the five wavering senators, including John Sparkman of Alabama who, in his late seventies, is becoming slightly senile and is being exploited by both sides.

June 12, Monday

Crafty Russell Long of Louisiana, one of the five fence-sitters and under enormous union pressure from back home, buttonholes Hatch for the second time with a compromise proposal. Hatch, hesitant to tell Long "no" outright and lose him for certain, puts him off.

Labor's forces have now gotten to John Sparkman. Hatch approaches him and the aging senator confirms that he's going to vote for cloture "because of all these good amendments."

Hatch doesn't mince words. "You come from a right-to-work state, John, and most of your people oppose this bill. If you vote for cloture, it will be a terrible black mark against your long and distinguished career in the Senate." Sparkman looks as if he's been punched in the face.

June 13, Tuesday

The third cloture vote. Hatch drives to the office in a downpour, arriving late at 7:30 a.m., and is on the floor throughout the day, carrying some of the debate. His side beats the third cloture vote, but pro-labor forces pick up five votes and it's now 54-43. Byrd and the White House predict victory tomorrow.

June 14, Wednesday

The fourth cloture vote. Both sides call it "crucial." As the 4 p.m. vote nears, Hollings sits with Sparkman, applying gentle persuasion. Byrd approaches Sparkman's desk. The old man, greatly agitated, barks, "Get away from me!" and shoves Byrd. Sparkman will hold.

Labor Secretary Ray Marshall, who has been assured of victory, makes an unusual appearance in the visitors' gallery to be on hand for the celebration. But the final vote is 58-41, two short of the magical 60. No corks popping today.

June 15, Thursday

The fifth cloture vote–unprecedented in Senate history. Hatch tosses all night, waking at 3:30 a.m. and going over every contingency in his mind. He reaches the office at 7 a.m. and goes to Baker's office for a strategy session. If they win today, they believe, Byrd will be forced to withdraw the bill.

Senators are assigned to keep track of the fence-sitters; Hatch continues to take Ed Zorinsky. Alabama's Maryon Allen was appointed to fill the seat of her late husband, and Hatch gives her a tape of the last speech Jim made on the Senate floor. She tells him that Bob Byrd, trying to peel her away from labor law opponents, has threatened to remove her from her late husband's committees.

Hatch learns that three of his supporters will be away on personal business, missing the afternoon vote. The vote begins at 1:45 p.m. and ends at 2:30. Hatch's team wins again, 58-39. The Senate has conducted almost no other business since the filibuster began a month ago. Nonetheless Bob Byrd, outwardly calm, schedules a sixth vote for Tuesday.

June 20, Tuesday

Byrd postpones the cloture vote until Thursday; he can't get his forces lined up. Lugar writes in the *New York Times:* "The majority leader's duty to the Senate, its rules, its traditions and the country was to withdraw this bill last Friday, secure in the knowledge that he had done his best for the President and for George Meany. Regrettably he has chosen to proceed."

Before retiring at 11:30 p.m., Hatch writes in his personal papers, "I sense that we have had extra help from the Lord. There is no other way we could have held out this long against Bob Byrd with all his power. The only way we can beat them is if the Lord is kind enough to continue to help us.

I think He will be."

June 22, Thursday

The sixth cloture vote. Tossing fitfully all night, getting even less sleep than his usual four to five hours, Hatch reaches his office early. This week's *Kiplinger Washington Letter* arrives. It says: "In all our years covering Congress this is one of the most effective jobs of business lobbying we have seen." But ABC's "Good Morning America" predicts Hatch's side will lose today.

Opponent leaders meet in Hatch's office. Later Hatch goes to Baker's office. Hatch has a nagging worry that Baker, who wants to run for president, will compromise rather than risk a permanent rupture with big labor. Louisiana's Long, blood in his eye, is leaving Baker's office as Hatch arrives.

"Orrin, you know you're going to lose today?" says Baker.

"Not if we can hold onto those five votes," answers Hatch.

"Well, they now have Long and all they need is one more vote and we're whipped," says Baker. "They want to send the bill back to committee, change it enough to void all your amendments, then report it forthwith as the pending business. If you object, Byrd will claim it's a procedural vote and his people will feel that they have to vote with him. They'll have enough votes to win."

Hatch faces a no-win choice. He has prepared some 500 amendments as a backup for a post-cloture filibuster if necessary. But Byrd hopes to take the bill off the floor and rearrange how it is written, so that the amendments won't match it and therefore they will be valueless to Hatch. If Republican Hatch objects, Democrats will feel obliged to support Byrd, their Senate leader, and the filibuster will be defeated. If Hatch doesn't object, the bill will go to committee and be changed just enough to win a couple of wavering votes. Byrd will get cloture. The filibuster will be dead and the bill passed into law.

"Let me know what you want to do," says Baker. "I'll back you, but I think you ought to take the offer."

Hatch returns to his office and sinks wearily into an armchair. Dimly he recalls that Jim Allen once faced a similar challenge. How did he handle it? The Utahn digs through Senate records–and strikes gold. During an earlier filibuster, Allen made sure the Senate adopted a rule that a procedural vote to stop a filibuster could be amended, if the amendments were introduced *before* the vote was called for. If Byrd threatened to win on a procedural vote,

Hatch and Lugar would force the Senate to vote on amendments to that motion–*700 amendments*–in a post-cloture filibuster.

Hatch swings into gear. In a flurry of activity, with paper flying everywhere, all his staff members and other allies become instant amendment writers. They draft 200 new amendments and alter the language on the 500 already waiting as a second line of defense, changing the language slightly on each one so they can now be used to help thwart Byrd's call for a procedural vote.

Five minutes before the 3 p.m. vote, Hatch enters the Senate chamber, clutching the thick stack of amendments, and deposits them with a clerk. Byrd nearly has apoplexy. He has been fairly warned of the latest Hatch-Lugar nightmare that awaits if he pushes the procedural vote.

But Hatch's immediate concern is to make sure the amendments are never needed. He and Robert Thompson, a close ally and officer of the U.S. Chamber of Commerce, retire to Baker's inner office. "Maybe they've got us, Orrin," says Thompson. "What do you think?"

"I would rather lose it straight up and go down fighting, so that all America could see who did it to them, than cave in to these guys," answers Hatch.

"I agree," says Thompson.

They join Baker in his outer office. "Howard, we've come too far to give in now," says Hatch. "Let's beat 'em today."

Baker, leaning against a fireplace, looks sick, perhaps seeing his political dreams vanishing up the flue. But he is true to his word. "I'm with you. Let's do it."

They go to the Senate chamber where Fritz Hollings of South Carolina approaches Hatch. "Orrin, I don't know if we can win. Russell Long is gone." But Hollings is confident he can hold onto Chiles, Sparkman, and Bumpers, if Hatch can corral Zorinsky.

"Are you going to object to Byrd's motion?" asks Hollings.

"If I object to it as a Republican, there's no doubt your fellow Democrats will feel it necessary to follow Byrd on a procedural vote," answers Hatch. "A Democrat has to object."

"Who?" asks Hollings.

"You!" says Hatch.

Hollings, a handsome, white-haired man, pauses. The personal political costs could be enormous. He asks Hatch if fence-sitter Zorinsky is with them; Hollings does not want to fall on his political sword only to lose in the end. Zorinsky, a former retailer and tobacco wholesaler, has been fearfully browbeaten by Byrd and other fellow Democrats, including in a marathon session the night before in which they "promised me everything" to vote with them. But the moderate Nebraskan entered the Senate with Hatch and the two have developed a warm friendship that Hatch counts on as a counterweight to Democratic pressure. As Hollings ponders, Zorinsky enters the Senate chamber, three minutes before the vote. Hatch catches Zorinsky's attention and raises his eyebrows questioningly. Zorinsky nods "yes."

Hatch hurries back to Hollings. "Zorinsky's with us!"

"Then *I'm* going to object!" says a grinning Hollings.

With a confident flourish, Byrd makes the motion to recommit the bill to committee. He glances toward Hatch, waiting for him to object. Instead, a big booming Carolinian drawl fills the chamber from the other side of the aisle: "I object!"

Caught totally unaware, Byrd explodes. Russell Long, maneuvering for weeks for an excuse to cross over to Byrd's side, jumps up from his desk and joins in Byrd's barely controlled tirade, raging about how unfairly opponents are preventing an up-or-down vote on the labor law bill itself, which a simple majority clearly would win. He is obviously angling for at least one more senator to cross with him, giving Byrd and big labor the votes to kill the filibuster.

But Hollings, in a brilliant stroke of psychology, says, "Well, the distinguished senator from Louisiana has always been the *fifty-ninth* vote for cloture and we have always known it."

Everyone fills in the blank. The next senator to crossover will be the *sixtieth* vote–carrying the onus of killing the filibuster and foisting forced unionism on America. The chamber is momentarily silent as Hollings' words sink in.

Then Republican Ted Stevens of Alaska, who deserted Hatch's team long ago, rises. "If Senator Long is going to cross over and vote for cloture, I am going to cross back and vote *against* it."

Pandemonium breaks out in the chamber. Bob Byrd knows that he, President Carter, and the union leaders are sunk.

Byrd's last maneuver is an attempt not to save the bill but to save face. He announces that he too is going to vote against cloture–hoping to fool history into believing the vote is meaningless–and advises other senators to do the same. No one is listening to Bob Byrd anymore. The final vote is fifty-three for cloture and forty-five against.

Labor law reform is dead.

The hoopla on the floor is surprisingly muted. Earlier today, Hatch told his team, "If we win today my union friends are going to be devastated. Let's not shove it down their throats. Let's not cheer or go out of our way to talk to the press. Let's just quietly walk off the floor and thank God we've won."

That is exactly what they did.

The historic debate filled the *Congressional Record* with *8,515* lines delivered by Lugar, *15,789* lines by Williams of New Jersey, floor leader for big labor, and *24,485* lines–highest of anyone–by Hatch.

Accolades poured in from across the country. Months later, *National Journal* labeled Hatch one of five first-term Republican senators "most often named as leaders of the future." The article explained: "Orrin Hatch does his homework–and then some. He set a new model for Senate advocacy when he led the battle against labor law reform legislation." It quoted a Democratic aide as saying, "There's no question he is at the top of the list of conservatives. He's brighter and harder, and he won't cave."

Big labor continued to spiral downward to the end of the century, as U.S. productivity shot upward. In 1999 just 13.9 percent of American workers belonged to unions. A decade after Hatch stuck his thumb in the dike in 1978 and saved the nation from being flooded with union power and prerogatives, U.S. economic and military strength forced the Soviet Union to sue for peace, ending the forty-year Cold War. And shortly afterwards the United States sailed into its strongest economy ever, whose unprecedented expansion was still going strong as 2000 dawned.

6

Growing into a Giant

Imagine Mark McGuire slamming twice as many hits as the rest of the St. Louis Cardinals combined–or Karl Malone scoring twice as many points as all other Jazz members combined. In legislative terms, Sen. Orrin Hatch did that for Utah's all-Republican congressional team this year.

–Lee Davidson, *Deseret News*

BY 1980, AFTER FOUR YEARS OF President Carter, America was in a funk. Fifty-two Americans were held hostage in Iran, and the economy hit its worst slump since the Depression–8 percent unemployment, 13 percent inflation, and an unprecedented 21 percent prime interest rate. Ronald Reagan swamped the hapless Carter to win the White House, with voters for the first time in a half-century turning out of office a president they had elected four years earlier.

Hatch campaigned for Reagan in thirty-six states, playing a "major role" in getting him elected, said Senator Paul Laxalt, campaign chair. Hatch also helped engineer the Reagan Revolution, including deep tax cuts and a determined military buildup, changing the face of the global political landscape. Republicans captured the Senate for the first time in nearly three decades and, improbably, Hatch–barely four years after his first foray into politics–was named chairman of the powerful Labor and Human Resources Committee.

The Utahn had one of Washington's busiest portfolios, sitting on four additional committees and ten subcommittees, and energetically picking up other irresistible causes. As a committee chairman, he helped new majority leader Howard Baker set policy for the entire Senate.

Utah Democrats, underwritten by the AFL-CIO which swore vengeance for Hatch's pivotal role in defeating labor law reform, dismissed his record of achievement as a fluke largely unrelated to the state's core interests. Their weapon of choice for unseating him was Salt Lake City Mayor Ted Wilson–handsome, highly popular, and with a down-home demeanor befitting his background as a former high school teacher. One minute into his January 1982 announcement speech, Wilson threw down the same gauntlet thrown by Frank Moss: You're not one of us.

"My candidacy brings an opportunity for our state to elect a senator who was born and raised in Utah, knows Utah, and would represent Utah first in the United States Senate," said Wilson, summarizing his campaign themes. Hatch was too confrontational, added Wilson, pitting "labor against management, rich against poor" and opting for "spectacular headlines" over real solutions.

Mike Leavitt, a bright, earnest young insurance executive, managed Hatch's campaign. A decade later he would become the state's governor. Wilson's camp included Democratic Governor Scott Matheson, popular former Governor Calvin Rampton, who chaired his campaign, and former Senator Moss, still smarting from Hatch's licking six years earlier and anxious to help even the score.

Despite Wilson's star power–which also included Utah actor Robert Redford, a strong supporter–most Utahns agreed with Hatch's stand on the issues. Sensing that reality, Wilson downplayed policy differences and emphasized Hatch's style. Wilson called his opponent a "show horse" and not a workhorse once too often, and in a debate in Logan, Hatch pounced.

"*Nobody's* outworked me in six years, not one senator," said Hatch testily. "I have authored and supported legislation that has cut taxes, reduced federal spending, decreased government fraud and waste, strengthened the nation's economy, and encouraged American industry." He noted that labor leaders and the Democratic National Committee had made him their number one target for defeat, "so I must be doing something right." He also defended his record for Utah: "My behind-the-scenes efforts may not have landed me on the headlines of every Utah newspaper, but they have landed me at the forefront of every battle."

Polls showed Hatch leading Wilson from start to finish. His victory was all but sealed the Friday before the election when Air Force One landed in Salt Lake City and President Reagan came down the ramp to a sea of cheers. Speaking at the Salt Palace, Reagan gave Hatch and his GOP colleagues credit for helping to rescue the economy from the shambles left by Jimmy Carter. Four days later Utahns gave Hatch a landslide: 58-41 percent.

Wilson had fought a hard, clean campaign and was gracious in defeat. Six years later, after losing a tough race for governor, he told Bill Loos, a fellow staff member at the University of Utah and former Republican operative, that Hatch was "a very fine senator" who had always treated him with respect. Added Wilson: "The next time Orrin runs, I would be honored to head the Democrats for Hatch organization."

Other Democrats likewise tossed in the towel after the 1982 election, conceding Hatch was here to stay. When no one with a prayer of beating him stepped into the ring in 1988 and again in 1994, Democrats ran sacrificial lambs against Hatch. In 1988 it was Brian Moss, small businessman, former government bureaucrat, and son of Hatch's old foe Frank Moss. From the start, labor leaders and the national Democratic Party abandoned the race as unwinnable, leaving Moss to his fate. Hatch crushed him 67 to 32 percent.

In 1994 Hatch's opponent was Pat Shea, a lawyer and state Democratic Party chairman. Shea got into the race just hours before the filing deadline, after three other prominent Democrats–including incumbent Representative Bill Orton–had seriously considered it and backed away. "You'd think holding the honor of challenging Hatch would be fought over," wrote *Deseret News* political editor Bob Bernick. "Instead, it's like root canal work–do it only when you absolutely have to."

Shea said his new approach to government would be the main issue: "We need a fresh look at the problems. We also need someone who has some pull with Washington, with this administration." Shea had been a Rhodes Scholar at Oxford University and later went to Harvard Law School. Despite those blue-blood credentials, he tried hard to paint himself as a commoner and Hatch as out of touch with Utahns. Shea cut a series of TV ads showing him tooling around the state in a camper. But the camper sputtered and rumbled off the road when his campaign ran out of money a month before the vote, forcing him off TV. From there Shea essentially became invisible. Hatch swamped him 69 to 28 percent.

By January 2000–twenty-three years after arriving in Washington–seasoned observers considered Hatch a legislative giant of historic proportions.

"Imagine Mark McGuire slamming twice as many hits as the rest of the

St. Louis Cardinals combined–or Karl Malone scoring twice as many points as all other Utah Jazz members combined," wrote Lee Davidson, award-winning Washington correspondent for the *Deseret News*, at the end of 1999. "In legislative terms, Sen. Orrin Hatch did that for Utah's all-Republican congressional team this year."

Davidson added that Hatch "passed 41 bills through at least the Senate. The rest of the delegation [four other members] combined passed only 20 bills through at least one house. Hatch also hit for a higher average than the rest of the delegation at the halfway point of the two-year 106th Congress. He batted .631 (passing 41 of 65 bills and floor amendments he introduced through at least one house)....Hatch not only moved a lot of legislation, but much of it was major."

The legislation represented a withering array of topics, including the most important crime-fighting bill before Congress–a comprehensive juvenile justice bill to toughen penalties against gangs; the most important patent reform bill in a half-century; a bill to compensate Utah and other downwind cancer victims of the government's atomic testing in Nevada decades earlier; and one of the most important high-tech bills in decades, allowing satellite TV to carry local broadcast channels and offering the new wave of high-definition television to all of rural America.

Other Hatch bills passed by the Senate in 1999 would increase law enforcement against methamphetamines, an alarming growth industry in Utah; toughen software piracy law; ban "cyber-squatting," the unauthorized use of patented names on Internet sites; begin a study of how to fight "date rape" drugs; create new drug-treatment programs; ban counterfeit aircraft parts, and create a visitors center at Four Corners–the point at which Utah, Arizona, Colorado and New Mexico meet.

Hatch did all this–and more–in 1999 alone. Not only did he guide forty-one bills through the Senate, amazingly he was on the Senate floor for 98 percent of roll-call votes in 1999 while also running for president the last half of the year. At the end of the year there were six major high-tech bills before Congress; five of them were written by Hatch and the sixth one, a Y2K (Year 2000) bill dealing with potential computer malfunctions at the start of the new millennium, was largely written by him. His Utah colleague, Senator Bob Bennett, was America's Paul Revere on Y2K, and helped prepare the U.S. and world for what resulted in a largely smooth transition into the new millennium.

One secret to Hatch's success is that, from his earliest days on Capitol

Hill, he has tried to follow this motto: There is no limit to what you can accomplish if you don't care who gets the credit. The Utahn's colleagues like to partner with him because they know he will share the kudos for whatever they accomplish together.

Much of Hatch's work relates to his committee assignments, and is done behind the scenes. Senators and their staffs collect information, including through public hearings; draft legislation; fight for its passage by the committee itself and then by the full Senate, and hope that a parallel process in the House produces a similar bill. Senate and House conferees then meet to iron out differences and write a common bill to be presented to both bodies for final vote.

Over the years Senator Hatch has played these roles numerous times on some of the Senate's busiest and most important committees. For many years he served on the Labor and Human Resources Committee, including as its chair. The committee's name was changed in 1999 to reflect its major concerns: the Health, Education, Labor and Pensions Committee.

Today the Utahn is on the Intelligence and Indian Affairs committees, and is a high-ranking member of the Finance Committee, chairing its taxation and IRS oversight subcommittee. The Finance Committee also plays major roles in fashioning laws on health care, international trade, debt and deficit reduction, and Social Security and family policies.

Hatch's most important assignment is chairing the Judiciary Committee, also serving on three of its subcommittees. Best known for screening nominees to the Supreme Court and lower federal courts, the committee also deals with immigration, technology, terrorism, youth violence, the Constitution, federalism, property rights, and antitrust issues.

Senator Hatch is considered one of the nation's leading authorities on terrorism, and introduced the Anti-Terrorism and Effective Death Penalty Act, along with former Senate Majority Leader Bob Dole.

Also in the Judiciary Committee, Hatch recently played a pivotal role in holding colossus Microsoft to account for breaking antitrust laws and stifling competition. Although Hatch received tremendous heat from Microsoft and its powerful allies for his tough cross-examination of company leaders in several hearings, Hatch was vindicated in April 2000 when a federal judge found Microsoft guilty of waging a campaign to crush threats to its Windows monopoly.

U.S. District Judge Thomas Penfield Jackson gave the U.S. Justice Department and nineteen states, including Utah, almost total victory in their lawsuit against the software giant. He said Microsoft put an "oppressive thumb on the scale of competitive fortune," using illegal methods to smother rivals and protect its monopoly. Two months later, on June 7, Jackson ordered Microsoft split in two–the most significant antitrust decree since those against AT&T in 1982 and Standard Oil in 1911.

Meanwhile, as the Clinton-Gore Administration sent mixed signals of its view toward Microsoft, Hatch stiffened the Justice Department's backbone in pursuing the case by telling its anti-trust officials he would ensure they did not face retaliation.

Hatch's heroics in pursuing Microsoft provided a rare public glimpse of his longstanding leadership in issues critical to the high-tech industry. His wide-ranging work resulted in a coalition of the world's leading software developers giving Hatch its highest award in spring 2000 for his tireless efforts to protect intellectual property. The Business Software Alliance presented Hatch with its Cyber Champion award.

BSA president Robert Holleyman said they honored Hatch "because he recognizes that strong copyright protection for creative works such as software is a principal reason why the high-tech industry is one of the fastest-growing and highest job-creating industries in America."

Some of Hatch's legislative achievements through the years have caused no little heartburn among political extremists and some single-issue groups. Hatch is a principled conservative pragmatist, citing Thomas Jefferson's dictum that in matters of style, swim with the current; in matters of principle, stand like a rock.

Flexibility is essential in politics to solve real-world problems, and is honorable so long as one does not compromise core beliefs. But compromise of any kind is anathema to extremists on both ends of the political spectrum, and Hatch often has found himself fighting lonely battles from the right, to carve out and hold middle ground rather than allow the left to win it all or allow a critical national need to go unmet.

A case in point is Hatch's defense of the Second Amendment–the right to keep and bear arms–which he emphasizes is an enumerated right specifically granted in the Constitution. Gun control is one of the most contentious issues in the nation, and Hatch has long been in the middle of the issue as chair of the Senate Judiciary Committee, which writes crime laws. He sees up close what havoc guns can cause in the wrong hands, and has helped pass bills to keep them out of those hands. But he also is a westerner, and appreciates how important guns are to sportsmen.

Hatch is a leading defender of Second Amendment rights, at the same time seeking reasonable ways to keep criminals from acquiring guns and children from being accidentally shot.

Repeatedly he has challenged the Clinton-Gore Administration on its empty anti-gun rhetoric. While calling for more gun laws, the Administration has largely refused to enforce the thousands of laws, rules, and regulations already on the books, including going after felons who illegally try to buy guns or others who knowingly supply them with guns. Hatch has also fought hard to see that legitimate Second Amendment rights are protected. For all his efforts, though, the Senator gets scorn instead of credit from Gun Owners of America (GOA), a group that makes the National Rifle Association look moderate by comparison.

Located in Springfield, Virginia, and directed by one Larry Pratt, GOA has been noticeably missing at the table over the years as gun-control issues have been thrashed out in hearing after hearing on Capitol Hill. Instead it fits a definition of critics–those who ride in after the battle and kill the wounded. In spring 2000 GOA distributed a flier calling Hatch "an enemy of your Gun Rights." At that same time, GOA's own Internet website graded the Senator "B-" for his gun votes–scarcely what you'd give a failed record. (Utah's other senator, Bob Bennett, got a "C.")

Since even the National Rifle Association says Hatch in fact has an excellent record in defending Second Amendment rights, the real point of GOA's anti-Hatch campaign is probably found on a two-page broadside sent to members, dated February 20, 2000. At the bottom of the missive, right under his name, Pratt says "...if you can help with a contribution of $15, $25 or even $50 to spread the word to other concerned Utahans [sic], it will be put to use in this critical fight."

First make Hatch a bogeyman, then use him to fatten your wallet: It's a formula other special interest groups have also employed through the years.

Hatch's efforts to find solutions to such vexing national issues, while fending off critics, recalls an analogy by Abraham Lincoln in 1864, as his administration faced withering criticism in waging the Civil War. Lincoln compared the situation to French tightrope walker Jean Francois Gravelet, popularly known as Blondin, who captivated the world by crossing Niagara Falls three times in the years just before the war:

> Gentlemen, suppose all the property you were worth was in gold, and you had put it in the hands of Blondin to carry across the Niagara River

> on a rope, would you shake the cable, or keep shouting to him–"Blondin, stand up a little straighter–Blondin, stoop a little more–go a little faster–lean a little more to the north–lean a little more to the south?" No, you would hold your breath as well as your tongue, and keep your hands off until he was safe over. The Government [is] carrying an immense weight. Untold treasures are in their hands. They are doing the very best they can. Don't badger them. Keep silence, and we'll get you safe across.

Lincoln, the first Republican president, also said "The true rule in determining whether to embrace or reject anything is not whether it [has] any evil in it, but whether it [has] more of evil than of good. There are few things wholly evil or wholly good. Almost everything, especially of governmental policy, is an inseparable compound of the two; so that our best judgment of the preponderance between them is continually demanded."

Senator Hatch once explained that "I believe in doing the best we can within the framework of what we have to work with. All too often conservatives have fought great battles only to go down in flames of glory. I want to win. I want to be on the offensive and not perpetually on the defensive. I want to turn excesses around and, if I can't get 100 percent of what we want, I will get whatever we can."

Early in his Senate career, the Utahn read William Rusher's *The Making of a New Majority Party* and saw himself in Rusher's description of a "social conservative." Hatch defined his emerging political identity as "one who wants economic conservatism but who has a great deal of respect for the rights of people and the sufferings they go through." He added "I am trying to be constructive in my conservative beliefs rather than just finding fault all the time."

He views the Senate as he views life. To him it is not a zero-sum game in which one side has to win everything and the other side lose everything. He typically has sought a way for *both* sides to win what they legitimately deserve, believing that only then would the nation truly win.

That gentlemanly yet principled approach has helped Orrin Hatch become a giant in the Senate.

7
The Club

It's wonderful to work with (Senator Hatch), because his word is his bond. If he says he's going to do something, put it in the bank.

–Wyoming Republican Senator Alan Simpson (ret.)

During a Republican presidential debate in December 1999, with George W. Bush far ahead of the pack and Senator Hatch far behind, the Texas governor lobbed the Utahn a softball question. Hatch hit it out of the ball park:

"Just think, Ronald Reagan picked your father [for vice president] because he had foreign policy experience. Somebody suggested the other day that you should pick me because I have foreign policy experience. They got it all wrong. I should be president; you should have eight years with me and boy, you'd make a heck of a president after eight years."

The feisty, funny response even had Bush grinning. It also earned headlines–including a page-one story in the *New York Times*, by a media corps that had pegged Hatch as stiff and straitlaced, and were forced to think again. Liberal columnist Mary McGrory wrote in the *Washington Post* that Bush had been a fall guy for "Utah Sen. Orrin Hatch, the high-collared Mormon elder who provided the laugh riot of the evening by offering to make Bush his vice president....George W. could not think of a rejoinder."

Humor is prized in Washington, especially on Capitol Hill where matters both great and small are hotly debated every day. Legislators such as Hatch who can take issues but not themselves too seriously tend to accomplish the most in a complex process that requires a lot of give and take before any bill is ready to be signed into law.

President Clinton and Vice President Gore have provided considerable humorous fodder for Hatch and numerous others. Speaking to the American Legion in March 1999, the Senator lampooned Gore's penchant for greatly exaggerating his accomplishments. "I know Vice President Gore came to speak to you earlier," Hatch told the Legionnaires, "but, contrary to what he may have told you, he did *not* design the first flag."

Hatch also has repeated a quip by a TV interviewer: "Al Gore is so stiff that racks buy suits off him."

In a speech to a GOP group, Hatch said "You probably saw the story in the newspapers about Al Gore climbing to the top of Mt. Rainier...14,000 feet with 65 pounds of gear on his back. Pretty impressive. But all I can say is, if he thought that was heavy, wait until he campaigns for the White House carrying a 235-pound president on his back!"

The Senator occasionally cites these reported quotes from former presidents:

- Richard Nixon, while attending Charles De Gaulle's funeral – "This is a great day for France."

- Gerald Ford – "President Carter speaks loudly and carries a fly spotter, a fly swasher ... It's been a long day."

- Ronald Reagan to the Lebanese Foreign Minister, during a briefing on the Middle East conflict – "You know, your nose looks just like Danny Thomas's."

- Reagan, while testing a microphone he wrongly thought was off before a broadcast – "My fellow Americans: I'm pleased to tell you today that I've signed legislation that will outlaw Russia forever. We begin bombing in five minutes."

In a GOP debate in Iowa, wealthy candidate Steve Forbes said he was nervous to take a question from Hatch and was tempted to hold onto his wallet. "Steve," Hatch deadpanned, "I couldn't even *lift* your wallet."

The *Salt Lake Tribune* said "Comedian Scotty Kowall called that line 'funny and spontaneous.' Ranking Hatch second to Bush in the overall debate, Kowall said: 'I would give Senator Hatch a '9' on the funny meter.' The comic relief has been welcomed by political junkies fixated on an otherwise dull presidential contest."

The joke in fact was on the media. Those who know Hatch well consider his wry sense of humor one of his strongest assets. But it is a part of his personality usually reserved for friends, staff workers, colleagues, and when addressing outside groups.

In October 1999 he spoke at the Western Republican Regional Conference in Jackson Hole, Wyoming. The Senator told governors that years earlier when he first got into politics the Republican National Committee asked him to help out in rural districts in the South that were overwhelmingly Democratic. "I remember stopping by this one place where this farmer asked me to stay right where I was," recalled Hatch. "He said 'I want to run in and get Ma. She's never seen a Republican before.'

"And so he came back and Ma kind of looked me over. Finally they asked me if I would mind giving a speech. Well, I said 'sure.' And I looked around for a place I could stand, and I found a wagon that spreads that stuff that gets piled pretty high and deep on most farms. So I stood right up there and made my pitch. And when I was through, the farmer thanked me and said, 'Well, son, that was just fine....That's the first time Ma and I ever heard a Republican give a speech.'

"Well, that's OK," I answered, "because that's the first time I ever stood on a Democratic platform!'"

Hatch also told governors about President Clinton dying and approaching the Pearly Gates, where Saint Peter appears and asks, "Who goes there?"

"It's me, Bill Clinton."

"And what do you want?" asks Saint Peter.

"Lemme in," says Clinton.

"Soooooo," ponders Saint Peter. "First, what bad things did you do on earth?"

Clinton thinks for a moment, then answers. "Well, I smoked marijuana, but you shouldn't hold that against me because I didn't inhale. I guess I had an affair or two, but you shouldn't hold that against me because I didn't have 'sexual relations.' And I lied, but didn't commit perjury."

After deliberating for several moments, Saint Peter says, "OK, here's the deal. We'll send you someplace where it's very hot, but we won't call it 'Hell.' You'll be there an awfully long time but we won't call it 'eternity.' And don't spend a lot of time waiting for it to freeze over."

Hatch told his fellow westerners: "I heard a story that when Bill Clinton was just a young boy, his mother prayed he would grow up and become president...so far, half of her prayers have been answered."

As an attorney, Hatch rarely lost a case. While esteeming the nobility of the law, Hatch is impatient with some aspects of today's legal profession, including frivolous lawsuits that land plaintiffs and their lawyers huge sums of money, invariably at what becomes the public's expense. He has gathered and occasionally uses a large store of lawyer jokes, including this favorite:

"Santa Claus, the tooth fairy, an honest lawyer, and an old drunk are walking down the street together when they spot a hundred-dollar bill at the same time. Who gets it? Why the drunk, of course. The other three are mythical creatures."

A staple in Hatch's funny bag involves his wife Elaine. "When we met at BYU I was a janitor," says Orrin. "I progressed from there to all-night dormitory attendant....After I was elected to the Senate, I made the mistake of commenting on our new circumstances.

"We were walking downtown in Salt Lake City when we saw a window washer at work on the ZCMI building. I said to Elaine, 'See, aren't you glad you married me instead of him?' Without missing a beat, she said 'Orrin, if I had married him, he'd probably be a United States senator, and you'd probably be a window washer.'"

On December 4, 1999, Hatch regaled the national press corps. The occasion was the annual Gridiron Dinner in Washington. The Gridiron Club is comprised of the creme de la creme of Washington journalists, and exists solely to put on one riotous, black-tie evening of off-the-record satire each year, shared by official sources they usually cover.

The U.S. president, vice president, many cabinet officers, Hollywood stars, and assorted other VIPs routinely attend. It was there that First Lady Nancy Reagan, facing severe media criticism for being a spendthrift, especially on designer gowns, once brought down the house and resurrected her public image by donning rags and belting out "Second-Hand Rose."

An invitation to speak at the Gridiron probably is the most coveted ticket in town for a politician. In December it was presidential candidate Hatch's turn.

> My friend Ted Kennedy has been campaigning in New England all his life. He knows New Hampshire in the winter, so he gave me his flask

...I really appreciated it, because it's so hard to get my warm milk in a motel at night. I have a reputation for being straitlaced, but actually I come from a very tough state. In Utah–you think it's easy raising money from people who are all sober?...

Is it me, or is Al Gore trying too hard? You got to know that back in high school, Al was the kid who reminded the teachers that they had forgotten to give out the homework assignment. But let's face it, those pop quizzes they put to candidates are really unfair. They should ask general-interest questions, like:

"Who founded the Mormon Church?"

"How many points did Karl Malone score last year?"

"What kind of a name is 'Orrin'?"

Those are the kind of questions that give the American people a real well-rounded sense of a candidate. Look at the facts. When I entered the presidential race–OK, I admit it, I was a long shot–tenth out of ten candidates. But since this campaign started I've been clawing, scratching my way to the top, and I think the results are pretty clear. Within one month I moved to number nine. A few weeks later, I was number eight. In October I moved to number seven, and then weeks later, number six. Some point to the fact that Lamar [Alexander], Dan [Quayle], Liddy [Dole] and Pat [Buchanan] quit, but I see a trend....

You know, I started my campaign late and I haven't gotten much publicity, but apparently things are looking up. My wife said to me this morning, "I hear you're running for president." ...

Speaking of the First Couple, I understand President Clinton went to a mall today to Christmas shop. When Santa asked him a question, the President answered "It depends on what you mean by 'Good.'"

...It's just great to see Vernon Jordan here–the President's "First Friend." I told Vernon how I'd like him to stay on as my First Friend....And I said "Of course, Vernon, there won't be any lobbying when we get together.

And there can't be any drinking beer and stuff like that. And no dirty jokes. No horsing around. And no caffeinated beverages. And we won't be smoking those big fat cigars. And no playing cards....Yep, just a bunch of guys getting together for some good, clean fun." And Vernon said "What other jobs you got?" ...

You know, when the campaign gets too exhausting, I can always turn to my music. Music, they say, speaks to the eternal truths. Lately, when the New Hampshire polls are announced, I'm reminded of the moving words of Three Dog Night: "One is the loneliest number that you'll ever do. Two can be as bad as one, but the loneliest number is the number one." And when the campaign trail gets lonely, many's the time I've found solace in the words of Neil Diamond: "I am, I said/ To no one there/ But no one heard at all/ Not even the chair." ...

Well, who knows what will happen in this presidential campaign. Win or lose, I just hope the American people see me for who I am. Just a wacky kid from Utah trying to get ahead in this crazy mixed-up world.

Hatch's speech was a smash-hit with the media, including Katie Couric of NBC's "Today," who invited Hatch to be on her show.

Such self-deprecating wit helps oil political machinery. "Politics is one of the great sources of tensions," wrote former longtime Congressman Brooks Hays, D-Arkansas. "Humor can become a cohesive force, and laughter a healing exercise...this precious quality of humor may be our saving grace. It may strengthen our faith and enable us to enjoy companionship, even with those who are on opposing sides."

Often quoted on Capitol Hill is an answer by former Senate Chaplain Edward Hale when asked "Do you pray for the senators?"

"No," said Hale, "I look at the senators and pray for the country."

The Reverend Gerald Mann is said to have opened a session of the Texas legislature with this prayer: "Lord, help these senators to remember that making laws is like a love affair: If it's easy, it's sleazy. Amen."

Perhaps nowhere is humor more important than in the U.S. Senate, often called the world's most exclusive club. There, 100 men and women go toe-to-toe on issues of crucial national importance, day in and out. Those senators able to take issues seriously without taking themselves too seriously tend to be the most effective members.

Senator Hatch has that ability. It is something he has acquired over time, to balance an ardent manner he brought to the Senate as a freshman.

When Hatch first arrived in 1977, said Senator Paul Laxalt, R-Nevada, "I thought he had a save-the-world complex. He wasn't malicious, just very ambitious. He was like other new senators who hadn't held office before....He rode pretty roughshod and I was put out with him at first." In 1978 when Laxalt was asked to support Hatch for a GOP Senate leadership post, the Nevadan declined, saying "Orrin is not a member of the club." An aide told Hatch that "He meant you don't drink and carouse with them."

"Then I'll never be a member of the club," answered Hatch flatly, "because I'll never do that."

Later that year, after watching Hatch campaign tirelessly throughout the country for Republicans, Laxalt approached with an olive branch. His early impression, said Laxalt, was that "I thought you were willing to walk on other people to get to the top. I now know I was wrong." The two became close and Laxalt, Ronald Reagan's best friend in Washington as well as his campaign chair, made sure that Hatch stumped the country in 1980 to help put Reagan in the White House.

In January 1982, during Hatch's reelection campaign, Laxalt wrote a fund-raising letter that called Hatch "a true leader in the United States Senate" who "played a major role in helping to elect Ronald Reagan President of the United States."

Reagan returned the political favor, campaigning for Hatch's reelection in 1982 and 1988. At a Washington fund-raiser the latter year, Reagan called Hatch "Mr. Balanced Budget" for his persistent efforts to pass a constitutional amendment forcing the government to drain the red ink from its books. "If every member of the Senate were like Orrin Hatch, we'd be arguing over how to deal with a federal surplus," said Reagan. A decade later the Gipper's vision of a balanced budget became a reality–probably too late, sadly, for the Alzheimer's-struck Reagan to appreciate it.

"If I could ask the people of Utah, my fellow Westerners...to stand with me one last time," said Reagan, "it would be in support of Orrin Hatch's reelection to the United States Senate."

One who hadn't made it to the fund-raising bash, held at the Washington Sheraton Grand Hotel, was Republican Senator Alan Simpson, a lanky Wyoming cowboy who had perfect pitch when it came to humor. His written apology to Hatch:

You may come to my office at S-243 at which location upon the mantel

> is a whip which you may remove, uncoil and [use to] administer six lashes! Of course, I shall be clutching at your bony hand while you try this exercise! I'm sorry to have missed it, my friend....You are a superb colleague in this arena and we desperately need your good services and your sharp and incisive intellect. Oh, what the hell, just list me as a fan! I always have been and I always will be.

Former Utah Senator Jake Garn, who served beside Hatch, said "Orrin Hatch is effective because of his intelligence and his ability to understand the Utah issues; but along with that, his integrity is very important."

Because of his squeaky clean lifestyle, Hatch's Senate colleagues save their bawdier jokes for when he isn't around, occasionally stopping themselves in mid-sentence, only half-joking, by saying "Whoops, I can't tell that one; Orrin is here."

Most Senate humor is spontaneous.

The most caricatured member of Hatch's Senate freshman class was S. I. Hayakawa, at seventy the oldest freshman senator elected in eighteen years. The bespectacled, diminutive semanticist had faced down student protesters in the late 1960s as president of San Francisco State College and parlayed that fame into an election victory over liberal Democrat John Tunney, who had been hurt by a playboy image.

Hayakawa had been criticized in the national media for snoozing during meetings. While traveling in San Francisco, Hatch was asked about his colleague's habit. "One Hayakawa asleep is worth two Tunneys awake," Hatch answered.

Hayakawa dozed off next to Hatch during a joint session in the House chamber to hear President Ford's last State of the Union address. As a television camera began panning the crowd midway through Ford's speech, minority whip Ted Stevens of Alaska yelled to Hatch in a panic, "Wake him up! Wake him up!"

Hatch forcefully grabbed Hayakawa's arm. "Sam, wake up!" Hayakawa leaped out of his chair. "I'm awake, I'm awake," he insisted, sheepishly sitting back down. He was, for the rest of that evening.

South Carolina Republican Strom Thurmond, the Senate's Energizer Bunny, turned ninety-seven a few weeks before 2000. He attracts respect and an occasional chuckle or two.

In 1988 Thurmond, then eighty-five, was the ranking Republican on the Judiciary Committee and Hatch was number two. But Hatch often took the lead on tough issues before the committee and full Senate, including the landmark Fair Housing Bill of 1988. Hatch surprised many of his colleagues by supporting an amended version of the bill on the Senate floor, prompting Thurmond and almost all other senators also to vote for the civil rights measure.

As soon as the vote was over, Ted Kennedy, who had introduced the bill, walked over to Hatch. "I have really done you a favor," said Kennedy in a low, conspiratorial voice. "The *New York Times* wants a picture of us in the President's Room. I suggested you should be there, rather than Strom, because you were the one who made it possible to pass this bill."

Kennedy, Hatch, and Arlen Specter, R-Pennsylvania, stole from the Senate chamber. As they entered the ceremonial room, there was Thurmond, waiting for them.

Kennedy, resigned, arranged the group for the photographer: Hatch on Kennedy's right, Specter on his left, and Thurmond on the other side of Specter. Just as the *Times* photographer started to snap the picture, Thurmond's face suddenly appeared between Kennedy and Specter.

"Strom, what are you *doing*?" asked an exasperated Kennedy.

"I'm the ranking minority floor manager of the bill," explained Thurmond, "and I thought I ought to be able to stand next to the majority floor manager." With that, Thurmond put a shoulder into Specter, nearly thirty years his junior, and muscled him out of position. Hatch and Kennedy burst out laughing, but Specter muscled his way back in. The tussle between the two men continued until Thurmond stopped and eyed Kennedy.

"Well," he said, "then I'll get on the *other* side of you." Thurmond started to nudge Hatch, who good-naturedly stepped aside.

Next morning, the *New York Times* carried an article on the fair housing bill, accompanied by a picture of the four senators laughing. Left to right: Hatch, Thurmond, Kennedy, and Specter.

Often the wit, wry and dry, comes during Senate debate. There was, for example, a colorful if esoteric exchange between Hatch and Robert Byrd, D-West Virginia–two of the Senate's brightest and most well-read members–over Hatch's proposed constitutional amendment to balance the budget. It came two decades after their momentous struggle over labor law reform, but now the tables were turned as Byrd successfully led forces to defeat a Hatch proposal.

Byrd called the constitutional amendment "gimmicky," while still complimenting Hatch as "a man after my own kidney, as Shakespeare would say." They duked it out verbally as Hatch stood beside a tall stack of twenty-eight consecutive unbalanced budgets.

Hatch: I just wish my colleague from West Virginia were on our side on this, because I think it would be a much easier amendment to pass. But I understand why he is not, and I know how sincere he is. But, like Paul of old–

Byrd: Like who?

Hatch: Like Paul of old, who held the coats–

Byrd: A great Apostle.

Hatch: The man who held the coats of the men who stoned the first Christian martyr, he is sincerely wrong.

Byrd: Paul was?

Hatch: Paul was, yes, for holding the coats of those who stoned the first Christian martyr, Stephen. Paul was sincere. He meant what he said....But he was wrong....

Byrd: Moses struck the rock at Kadesh with his rod. He smote the rock twice and water gushed forth and the people's thirst and the thirst of the beasts of the people were quenched. The waters of a balanced budget are not going to flow from that piece of junk. I say that with all due respect to my friend.

Hatch: Let me say this. Moses also struck the rock at Meribah, and gave water and was forbidden from entering the promised land after forty years of traveling in the wilderness....He was following, in a sense, the same pattern, but without God's will. And I am tired of following the same pattern which I cannot believe is God's will....I am sorry that we have twenty-eight years of unbalanced budgets in a row, and we are looking at twenty-eight more because we are unwilling to do what is right.

[Next morning]

Byrd: Let us all remember that "the devil himself can quote scriptures for his purpose." My purpose here is to strip away the hype and rhetoric and examine the manner in which this constitutional amendment will actually work....If an excess of outlays over receipts were to occur, Congress can require that any shortfall must be made up during the following fiscal year. Now that is a loophole that, if adopted by Congress...would be big enough for Hannibal to take his 46,000 men and his 37 elephants, with which he crossed the Rhone River in 218 B.C., through. Of course, he had 80 elephants at the Battle of Zama in the year 202 B.C. But you could just take all those elephants, all 80 of them, through the loopholes created by those words.

Hatch: My friend talks about Hannibal crossing the Alps. If my historical background is correct, the discussion of Hannibal in the Alps was by Livy, who wrote the *History of Rome*. I think it was a little unfair to bring in 37 elephants. Actually, as I recall the estimate there were at least 100 donkeys [Hatch nearly said "jackasses"] which, if Hannibal was alive today, as the good Democrat that he was, would be trampling all over the balanced budget amendment with all of those donkeys–not [GOP] elephants. I think the elephants would be nudging him forward to try to do what is right.

Hatch and Massachusetts Senator Ted Kennedy are a political odd couple, with voting records at oppose ends of the spectrum in nearly every area. But, while disagreeing 95 percent of the time, they have also linked arms to pass landmark legislation, pulling each other toward the center on key issues that fit Hatch's definition of one proper role of government: to help those who cannot help themselves but would if they could.

The two share concerns for people on the lowest rungs of society–"He has a very strong sense of justice," says Kennedy–and a friendship well-oiled by humor. Most Republicans simply plow around Kennedy. But not Hatch. Months after first arriving on Capitol Hill, Hatch had a hot debate with him on the Senate floor over foreign aid to Latin America–Kennedy literally screaming his arguments, as he was wont to do. Afterwards, as a gesture of goodwill, Hatch walked over to Kennedy, who introduced Hatch to his staff, about ten people sitting on a couch behind him.

"You folks all owe me," Hatch told them.

"We owe you?" one asked.

"Yes, sir," Hatch explained, "because I'm keeping your boss's blood rushing through his body so that this dissipated sop will probably live longer than he would otherwise, and you fellows will continue to have jobs."

They roared with laughter, joined by Kennedy. That evening Hatch wrote a note to himself: "I have to admit that I enjoy the guy but believe him to be almost a total demagogue."

Over the next two decades, they became friends despite sharp political and lifestyle differences. In the process, Hatch helped rehabilitate Kennedy–no longer the "dissipated sop" of twenty years ago–and Kennedy helped loosen up the straitlaced Utahn. They have been there for each other in the highest and lowest times in their personal lives, and have forged a friendship rare for two people so opposite in so many ways.

But neither has abandoned his political moorings. "Orrin has not changed his philosophy in the years I've known him" said Kennedy in an interview. "Orrin has a defined political philosophy, which is a rudder that guides his political actions. It suits him temperamentally and in his soul. That's impressive at a time when many put their finger to the wind to find out which way the winds are blowing, and sort of adjust accordingly."

How has Hatch been so effective in the clubby Senate despite his refusal to party with fellow members? "He understands and I think is fundamentally committed to the concept of civility, which is an essential element to be an effective legislator," explained Kennedy. "It's been said that after reaching the Senate, some people blow and some people grow. Orrin has grown. He learned to fight for what he believed in and still maintain a sense of humor and decency."

Hatch has also proven he can take it as well as dish it out. One of his favorite television shows was "Murphy Brown," with Candice Bergen in the title row. Former Vice President Dan Quayle tangled publicly with Bergen over her portrayal as an unwed mother. But Hatch took a different tack when Murphy had a dartboard in her fictional newsroom office, with a bumper sticker above it that said "I love Orrin Hatch."

In response, Hatch mounted an "I Love Murphy Brown" inscription above his office dartboard and sent Bergen a photo of him throwing darts at it. Bergen loved it, and invited Hatch to be a guest performer in a "Murphy Brown" sequence. He accepted, appearing on November 8, 1993.

In April 1997, Marie Woolf, a premier graphic designer and political cartoonist–one of only a handful of nationally successful women cartoonists in a male-dominated field–sketched a cartoon of Hatch throttling Attorney

General Janet Reno, as Reno gasps "Anita [Hill] warned me about this." When the syndicated cartoon appeared in a Utah newspaper, Hatch contacted Woolf for a copy. The Californian sent him the original, which now hangs on his office wall in Washington, and secured him as keynote speaker for a national cartoonists' convention.

When Hatch ran for president, Woolf was one of the first people he hired, to create and administer his presidential web site, considered the most original, comprehensive, entertaining, and user-friendly in the 2000 presidential election.

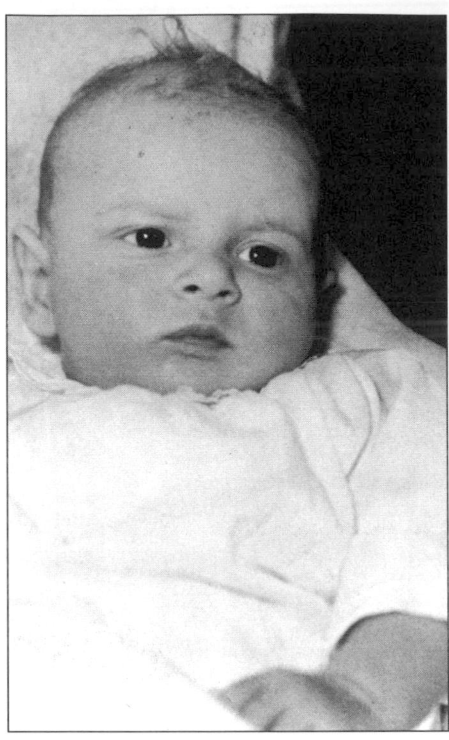

Family home in Pittsburgh built with used lumber.

Orrin as a tot in 1934.

Playing baseball at home.

An all-American boy.

The family in 1939: (from left rear) Jess, Helen, Jesse, (front left) Orrin, Frances, Chloe, Marilyn and Nancy.

Jess Hatch (standing third from right) with B-24 crew before the crew was shot down over Europe in 1945.

The Hatch family in 1947: (from left) Orrin, Jessica (being held), Jesse, Helen, Marilyn, (front) Chloe and Frances.

Hatch's first campaign speech, high school, 1952.

BYU Intramural basketball champs, including a bespectacled Hatch, receive award from varsity coach Stan Watts, 1953.

Elder Hatch (kneeling second from left) with other new LDS missionaries in Ohio, 1954.

Elaine, pregnant with first child Brent, as Orrin picks the tune, June 1958.

Senator and Mrs. Hatch in the U.S. Capitol.

Elaine and their six children visit Orrin in his Capitol Hill office: (children from left) Alysa, Marcia, Scott, Kim, Jess, and Brent, 1981.

In 1957 Elaine Hansen writes on back of photo: "To the most wonderful fellow I know. I love you."

He writes back to Elaine, "Too bad I couldn't send ya somethin [sic] better than a picture of this jerk. Love, Orrin."

Elaine Sharon Hansen and Orrin Grant Hatch begin married life, August 28, 1957.

With
Ronald Reagan
in the Oval
Office, 1982.

Double hand-shaking with
President Reagan, flanked
by Republican Senators
(from left)
Robert Dole,
Dave Durenberger,
Jesse Helms,
and Jake Garn.

The Hatches'
dream home
in Ben Avon
Heights,
Pittsburgh,
left behind
to move to
Utah in 1969.

Family home
in Vienna,
Virginia.

Giving the famous Hatch hug and an award to a Special Olympics participant.

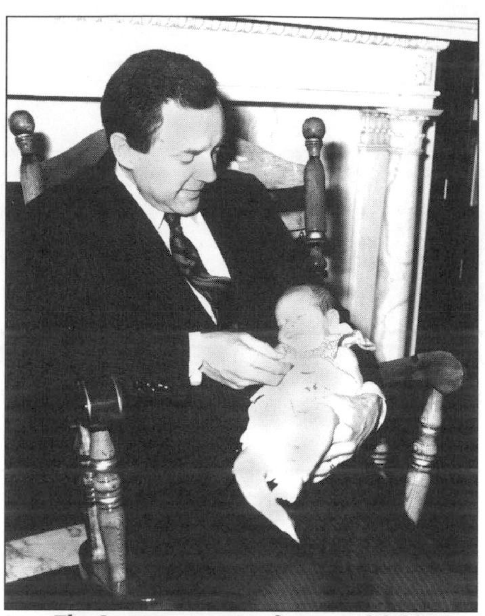

The Senator caressing first grandchild Stephanie Hatch, 1982.

Outside his office, Senator Hatch is lobbied by children and teachers on a bill.

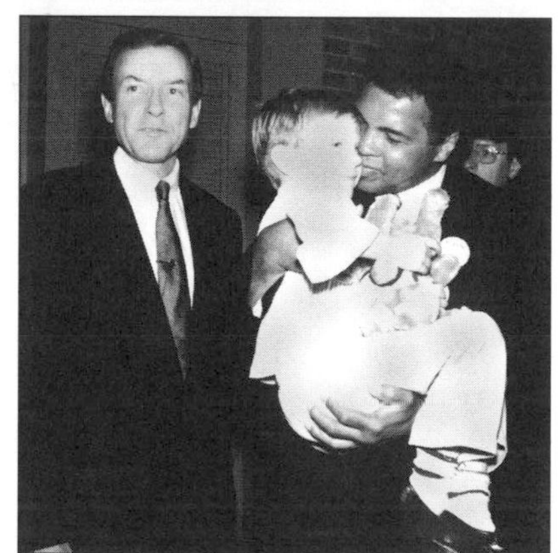

With Muhammad Ali hugging a friend, 1990.

Convinced that "the future is in very small hands," Hatch makes friends at a northern Utah day-care center.

Senator John Warner, R-Virginia, in 1986 pens, "To Orrin– One of the Senate's true leaders."

Actress Rita Moreno signs photo, "For Orrin Hatch– How fortunate for the children of the United States that they are ever present in your heart!"

With Utah's Debbie Fields of Mrs. Field's Cookies, 1992.

The Hatches and Jake and Kathleen Garn welcome President Bush to Utah in 1992.

Part II

8

Suffer The Children

I know that some people will ask why I am doing this....
The answer is simple: It is the right thing to do. The lack of health insurance for children is a nightmare for parents. For a sick child, it is perhaps the most horrifying experience of all. This legislation will provide a more comforting night for millions of parents... and for their children as well.

"THE FUTURE IS IN VERY SMALL HANDS."

Senator Hatch offers that simple sentiment to explain his work for children. A father of six and grandfather of nineteen, his concern has been manifest in many small ways and some very big ones that have profoundly helped youngsters. He has emerged as perhaps the nation's leading political figure in fashioning laws of major importance to the health and well-being of children.

Kristine Fawson, head of Utah's Legislative Coalition for People with Disabilities, met with Hatch in his office, bringing her husband and their developmentally disabled son, Shane. Once the business of the meeting had ended, Hatch chatted with Shane about his job, the Utah Jazz, and other topics. Shane mentioned that he liked Hatch's tie.

"I've got one you'd like even better," said Hatch, disappearing into a closet and coming out with a tie that had the Pink Panther all over it. Shane returned to Salt Lake City with his new favorite tie, and wears it often, says his mother.

Another young beneficiary of Hatch's extensive tie collection is Jimmy, an elevator operator at the U.S. Capitol who has Down's syndrome. Hatch has given him more than a half-dozen ties, according to an aide, and reportedly is the only senator Jimmy knows by name.

Utah press secretary Heather Barney remembers Hatch stopping by her office in Salt Lake City a few years ago. "I knew my baby sitter was dropping off my children to me at any moment, and I was praying they wouldn't arrive until Orrin had left." No sooner had they got down to business, however, than "I heard the footsteps of my son Alex–who was about four then–running down the hall, yelling at the top of his voice 'Mommy, Mommy where are you?'

"Orrin's reaction was priceless. Instead of being at all irritated, a huge smile spread across his face and he was delighted to meet my children." Hatch struck up a particular friendship with Alex, sitting him on his lap a few years later for a photo. Barney had eight-by-ten copies made for each of them. Alex signed his "I love you." Hatch signed his back: "To my friend Alex, I'm so proud of you. Always listen to your parents and do what is right. I love you too! Orrin, U.S. Senator Utah. P.S. I'm counting on you."

Millions of children and their parents have also counted on the Senator, and he has come through time after time. He has done so often while fending off political retribution from the far right and sometimes criticism from Republican colleagues.

Hatch helped establish a national commission to reduce infant mortality. He has cosponsored legislation to ensure safe, affordable immunizations for children, noting that for every dollar invested, ten dollars are saved in future medical costs. He was the principal co-sponsor and promoter of the Missing Children's Act, authorizing the Attorney General to work closely with state and local law enforcement agencies to list and help locate missing persons.

He has fought for stronger laws to protect children from sex crimes, and helped develop the Child Protection and Sexual Predator Punishment Act. Among other things, the measure includes stricter provisions against interstate commerce in child pornography–including on the Internet–and more severe penalties for convictions.

The Utahn is a longtime champion of Head Start, the preschool education and social program providing services to millions of disadvantaged children since 1965. It has been very successful: Studies show Head Start children are less likely to need remedial or special education, drop out of school, commit crimes, or go on public assistance. As a member of the Labor and Human Resources Committee, Hatch repeatedly increased funding for the program, enabling enrollment to more than double. In addition, he helped add new services, required literacy and child development training for parents of Head Start children, and performance standards which must be met for programs to continue to receive federal funding.

He is also a leading supporter of the Women, Infants and Children (WIC) program, which provides fortified food supplements to low-income women. A federal study shows one dollar spent on WIC's prenatal program saves up to three dollars in Medicaid costs in the first two months of a child's life. WIC also saves in potential special education costs down the road.

In January 1986 Hatch was especially concerned about one very sick little girl. Eight-month-old Keile Burrell of Roy, Utah, was dying of biliary atresia, a malfunction of the bile duct, at Salt Lake City's famed Primary Children's Hospital. Keile (pronounced "key-lee") urgently needed a liver transplant to survive. Although she would be their youngest transplant patient ever, the University of Nebraska Medical Center agreed to attempt the operation–but only with a guarantee of full payment.

With Keile sinking fast, Primary Children's called Hatch for help on Friday, January 16. Hatch immediately called President Reagan, who ordered a medical jet from Utah's Hill Air Force Base to stand by to transport the tiny girl to Omaha. The President also guaranteed that the money would be made available to cover costs, probably through Medicaid. That evening Keile went into a coma. By the next afternoon a donor had been found and Keile was flown to Omaha. She was still comatose when she arrived. Doctors were dubious but operated anyway.

Four months later, Hatch walked into an anteroom in the west wing of the White House. Waiting to enter the Oval Office with him to greet the President were Wayne and Rochelle Burrell, holding their daughter Keile, now a healthy one-year-old.

Hatch's two largest monuments to children were built a decade apart: the nation's first child care program, in 1989, and child health insurance, in 1997. Both were fashioned by Hatch as block grants–a fiscally conservative approach he insisted on to give states maximum flexibility in meeting local needs. Both times, Hatch went through political purgatory to push his proposals into law.

A decade ago, when Hatch ventured into the minefield of child care, one of every two women with children under three worked outside the home, and millions of "latchkey" children returned from school to empty houses. Many Americans saw the need to help provide care for such children, and policy-makers periodically studied the issue. But for decades social conservatives had successfully blocked a national program, arguing it would lead to a Soviet-style state takeover of parental responsibility. As the nation dawdled, a generation of youngsters grew up on mean streets and America was paying a fearful price in crime, drugs, school dropouts, teen pregnancy, and other problems.

"We are cannibalizing our children," said Dr. Edward Zigler, a child psychologist and leading advocate of organized child care. "When you see thirteen babies in cribs and one adult caretaker who can do nothing but change diapers and pop bottles, you see children who are being destroyed right after birth." Zigler, a Yale professor, got Hatch's ear while speaking at the Senator's annual women's conference, which he started in 1985.

In addition, Hatch's Utah women's advisory group repeatedly told him that child care was the leading social problem in the state and nation. Utah had the nation's largest families and its youngest population. It included 150 thousand children under age thirteen who needed child care, with only 30 thousand slots available in licensed facilities.

"I believe it is far preferable for parents to care for their own children," said Hatch when introducing his child care bill in September 1987. "But I have been persuaded by the facts...." The trend toward two working parents and single-parent families would continue, and "whether these changes are good or bad is not the issue. It is time to face reality." Time would prove Hatch right: By 1995, 55 percent of U.S. women giving birth the previous year returned to their paying jobs–up from 31 percent two decades earlier in 1976.

Hatch proposed to help states subsidize essential child care for low-income families. His plan turned heads. Columnist George Will wrote that "Since the 1950s, when the conservative movement coalesced out of many exasperations, conservatism has been on a long march, transforming itself from an ideology of protest to a philosophy of governance. Another small step in that direction is Sen. Orrin Hatch's decision to act on the fact that Ozzie and Harriet are as gone as tail fins."

Another pundit wrote that "Some conservative [politicians] predict that Sen. Orrin Hatch of Utah will need a neck transplant before the year is over, to replace the one he's sticking out on the issue of day care."

That prediction was on the mark; Hatch was castigated by the far right and faced intense pressure from fellow Republicans to abandon his plan. Instead Hatch wedded his bill to one sponsored by Senator Christopher Dodd, D-Connecticut, after talking Dodd into major changes. Hatch insisted on greater state and local controls in setting health and safety standards, and on giving parents greater choice of care, including use of religious providers, grandparents, or adult aunts and uncles.

With Hatch as its major co-sponsor, the Act for Better Child Care (ABC) was passed by the Senate in June 1989 and signed by President Bush, providing $2.5 billion over three years to help states furnish child care for low-income families. Once implemented, many of those who initially had opposed ABC acknowledged that it was working well to stem the child care crisis, increase the choices available to parents, and improve the overall quality of care.

As the final vote was taken, Senate Majority Leader George Mitchell rose in the chamber to praise Hatch for "the remarkable independence of judgment and political courage that have marked his political career....Often [we] find ourselves on different sides of an issue. But as always, he has conducted himself with intelligence, with dignity, with vigor and genuine courage."

Also in 1989, Elizabeth Glaser, wife of actor Paul Michael Glaser, who played detective David Starsky on "Starsky and Hutch," came to see Hatch. She was steered to him by one of the Senate's leading liberals, Ohio Democrat Howard Metzenbaum.

Elizabeth Glaser, as the entire nation would soon come to know, was living a nightmare. Eight years earlier, when she was nine-months pregnant with their first child, she hemorrhaged and was given seven pints of blood. Their daughter, Ariel, was delivered successfully, and seemed healthy. But in 1985 Ariel became mysteriously ill, and only then was it discovered that both the daughter and mother had the HIV virus, precursor to AIDS. Elizabeth had been infected by the blood transfusions and Ariel from Elizabeth's milk. A son, Jake, born later, also had HIV.

After baby Ariel died, Elizabeth and two friends, Susan DeLaurentis and Susie Zeegen, met around a kitchen table in 1988 and founded the Pediatric AIDS Foundation. Its mission: "To identify, fund and conduct critical pediatric AIDS research that will lead to the prevention and treatment of HIV infection in infants and children."

Elizabeth tried to interest the Reagan Administration in the cause, setting up meetings with Ronald and Nancy Reagan, Barbara Bush, and Surgeon General C. Everett Koop. She concluded, however, that the Administration was not interested. Then she approached Senator Metzenbaum, who told her to see Senator Hatch because "Hatch knows more about the Food and Drug Administration than anyone else."

"But he's a conservative Republican," protested Glaser.

"You go see Hatch," Metzenbaum insisted. "He has a heart."

Glaser made an appointment and dropped by the Utahn's office. He immediately offered to help. Hatch not only opened doors for her at the FDA, but suggested they organize a private sector fund-raiser to get the foundation off the ground. Shortly afterward Hatch and Metzenbaum co-sponsored a huge dinner in Washington, with Hatch putting the bite on many of his high-level contacts, especially in the pharmaceutical industry. They raised $1.3 million and the foundation was in business.

Elizabeth Glaser became a national figure when she electrified the 1992 Democratic National Convention with her story, suggesting only Democrats cared about those with AIDS. "For me, this is not politics. It's a crisis of caring," she told delegates in Madison Square Garden, many of them weeping. "My son and I may not survive four more years of leaders who say they care–but do nothing."

After the convention, she telephoned Hatch to apologize for not crediting him in her speech. "I couldn't very well mention your name at a Democratic convention," said Glaser. "Oh sure you could," laughed Hatch.

Two and a half years later, in December 1994, Glaser died of AIDS.

At the time of her convention speech, about 200 thousand Americans had died from the disease; by the time Glaser joined that grim list, 50 thousand more had died as well. In 1999, Susie Zeegen and others who carried on Glaser's work went to Hatch and asked if he would host the group's ten-year anniversary dinner. He readily accepted, co-sponsoring the event with Senator Barbara Boxer, D-California, and raising $2.5 million–the largest amount ever raised for what by then was called the Elizabeth Glaser Pediatric AIDS Foundation.

Hatch and Madeline Stone of Nashville wrote a song especially for the event, sung by Santita Jackson, daughter of Jesse Jackson, and another friend of Hatch's, tenor Chris Willis, both backed by a young inner city chorus. The name of the song: "We Are the Innocent."

Polls showed Republican control of Congress in serious jeopardy heading toward the 2000 elections, in good part because many Americans felt Republicans didn't care about their most basic concerns. One of those worries was health insurance for the working poor, especially children in those families.

Hatch had long been concerned over children's health. Early in his first term, a Utah mother brought her twelve-year-old son, suffering from fatal cancer, to see Hatch. He invited the boy, Bill Ficken, to join him on the dais in a Senate hearing room, which was awash with TV klieg lights. Bill was reluctant to remove his baseball cap and reveal a head shiny from chemotherapy. To help put him at ease, Hatch fetched another cancer "baldy," former Vice President Hubert Humphrey, who warmly welcomed the boy and offered encouragement, though Humphrey would lose his own fight to the disease within a year.

When Mrs. Ficken's camera failed to work, the two men stood head to head fussing with it as if it were on an operating table. Finally giving up, they promised to send individual photos. The Fickens returned to Utah with a boy who had made two powerful new friends.

"It's one thing for an older fellow like myself to have this dread disease," Humphrey said in a handwritten note to Hatch. "But what a pity–how sad–to see a 12 year old boy suffering so much and his all too brief life snuffed out–What a pity."

In following years, Hatch witnessed the anguish felt by families with sick children who could not afford medical care. He could not square the fact that such families lived in the wealthiest nation on earth, yet the United States stood almost alone among industrialized countries in not ensuring health care for its most vulnerable citizens.

Even routine health concerns give such families sleepless nights. "I had two women from Provo, Utah, come in and see me," Hatch wrote to a friend in 1997. "Both of them work part time and both husbands work full time. Neither family earns more than $20,000 a year. They don't know what to do. Their children have the same problems as other children–hearing problems, colds, pneumonia, asthma, poor vision, broken arms and legs, cardiovascular, respiratory, and other problems that are matters of great concern to these families."

For thinking, feeling Americans, the lack of health insurance for fellow citizens, especially children, is a serious issue. Although Medicaid covers health care for the poorest citizens, in 1997 forty million others were without insurance, including about ten million children. An estimated three million of those children apparently were eligible for Medicaid, but had slipped through its safety net.

Nearly 90 percent of the remaining seven million children belonged to families in which at least one parent worked. They were the working poor–too well-off to qualify for Medicaid but too poor to afford insurance. Half a million of the uninsured were less than a year old.

In Hatch's Utah, more than fifty thousand children had no health insurance, despite living in a family-oriented state that had one of the nation's most robust economies.

While many politicians gave lip service to the need, solutions had always foundered on the shoals of special interests and ideology. Private industry and local and state governments resisted any new federal mandates, warning especially against open-ended entitlement programs. A central pillar of conservative ideology is opposition to federal social-spending programs, which conservatives view as socialistic and wasteful. Washington had recently gone through a bruising battle over universal health coverage–led and lost by Bill and Hillary Clinton–and few national politicians were willing to fight another battle over the issue.

An exception was the irrepressible Ted Kennedy, longtime scourge to some Americans and hero to others. In the mid-1990s, Kennedy had introduced a child insurance bill flying all the red flags conservatives loathed: It called for a huge entitlement program of $50 billion over five years; created a huge new bureaucracy to administer it; would have raised cigarette taxes seventy-five cents a pack to pay for it; and would have tied the hands of states receiving the money with many strings and mandates.

From that moment, Hatch and Kennedy–close personal friends but fierce foes on most issues–tangled over child health insurance. Over the previous twenty years they had become the most powerful legislative duo in the Senate, finding common ground to forge landmark legislation in a variety of areas, notably health care. On child insurance, Kennedy knew he could not prevail in a Republican-controlled Senate without Hatch's assistance. But Hatch, despite a strong desire to help children, was unwilling to join with Kennedy on the latter's terms.

"We negotiated, fought, and screamed at each other, and our staffs had numerous battles as we tried to fashion an approach we both could live with," explained Hatch. What emerged was their Children's Health Insurance and Deficit Reduction (CHILD) Bill, introduced in March 1997.

CHILD pulled the fangs from Kennedy's bill while preserving its value. The Hatch-Kennedy bill called for $20 billion in child health insurance over five years and $10 billion for reducing the federal deficit. It provided no entitlement to insurance if funds were lacking. State participation would be entirely voluntary, with participants required to match federal funds by 40 percent–the same as Medicaid–to assist more children. The money would flow as essentially no-strings-attached block grants to states, eliminating the need for a new federal bureaucracy. The tax on cigarettes would increase 43 cents a pack to pay for it.

"We chose the cigarette tax to fund the bill because tobacco use generates so many of our society's health care problems," explained Hatch. "If the smoking revenues go down as a result of this added tax, I'd love to have that problem."

Hatch took delight in having Kennedy cosponsor a bill that would directly reduce the federal deficit–a goal Kennedy had previously resisted. Kennedy was also forced by Hatch to accept the most conservative approach to providing funds to states–directly through block grants, leaving final decisions, with reasonable parameters, to the states themselves. This approach usually is anathema to dedicated liberals like Kennedy, who act as though governors are either too ignorant or too untrustworthy to properly use such funds.

"What is unmistakably clear is that, despite our philosophical differences, Senator Kennedy and I share a common belief in a government by the people and *for* the people–a government that will help those who are most in need and cannot help themselves," explained Hatch in a private letter at the time the bill was introduced.

> I know that some people will ask why I am doing this–and with Ted Kennedy no less. The answer is simple: It is the right thing to do ...Children are our nation's most precious resource. But unfortunately, too many parent couples and single parents in our country go to sleep at night worrying about their child's health and what would happen if their child became terribly sick. The lack of health insurance for children is a nightmare for parents. For a sick child, it is perhaps the most horrifying experience of all. This legislation will provide a more comforting night for millions of parents across our great nation–and for their children as well.

Child advocates hailed Hatch's decision to fight for child health care. He also struck a chord with other citizens, who told pollsters that health insurance was their fifth-highest concern. As the Hatch-Kennedy bill was introduced, the Census Bureau reported that nearly 14 percent of children–one in every seven–had no health insurance. The lack ranged from nearly 27 percent among Hispanics to 13.4 percent among whites.

But even after cajoling Kennedy into accepting a far more conservative approach, Hatch faced withering criticism. Fellow conservatives compared him to Karl Marx, Benedict Arnold, and Brutus. Some of the sharpest attacks came from Republicans, led by Senate Majority Leader Trent Lott, who wanted to offer a feeble measure providing some political cover for the GOP while doing little to provide insurance for children.

Also complicating the effort was a tentative agreement among congressional Republicans, Democrats, and the Clinton White House, to hold down spending to produce a balanced budget by the year 2002. Many feared the CHILD bill would undo the fragile budget compromise.

Lott and other Republicans regarded Hatch as an apostate, doubly so for teaming up once more with their nemesis Ted Kennedy. Lott frankly despised Kennedy and vowed that no new social-spending bill sponsored by Kennedy would pass the Senate on his watch.

Seasoned observers, however, saw a familiar freight train coming: the Hatch-Kennedy Express. "There may not be two more relentless legislative advocates than the Utah Mormon and the Massachusetts Democrat," wrote Al Hunt of the *Wall Street Journal*. "They are an awesome one-two punch." Their bill, said Hunt, "is driving Mr. Lott and Oklahoma Sen. Don Nickles, the Senate GOP whip, crazy. They demagogue it as big government and tax-and-spend, misrepresenting what it would do. And they are strong-arming every Republican in sight to oppose it."

Hatch's fellow Utah senator, Bob Bennett, did in fact jump ship, removing his name from the bill after initially co-sponsoring it.

Movement conservatives, noted Hunt, were trying to derail the measure by portraying Hatch as a pawn of Kennedy: "It doesn't make sense to them that a straight-laced Mormon supports raising sin taxes to help kids. In fact, the final measure unmistakably bears the Hatch imprimatur. Mr. Kennedy wanted to increase cigarette taxes by 75 cents a pack from the current 24 cents; they settled on a 43-cent increase. Mr. Hatch insisted the program be run by the states and be strictly voluntary. Therefore, it would not be an entitlement. And one-third of the $30 billion the measure would raise over five years would go to deficit reduction, an unfortunate sop to the Utah Republican. The need is undeniable."

His colleagues' criticism stung but did not stop Hatch. As opposition mounted, he turned, as he often does, to the scriptures for guidance. Among Bible passages that seemed pertinent was Psalms 41:1 "Blessed is he that considereth the poor. The Lord will deliver him in time of trouble."

And trouble there was. In spring 1997 a Washington, D.C.-based group called Citizens for a Sound Economy began spending $30,000 a week on radio ads in Utah to belittle Hatch. A voice imitating Ted Kennedy thanked Hatch "on behalf of the citizens of Massachusetts" for cosponsoring the "liberal" child insurance bill. Later it was revealed the group received funds from tobacco giant Philip Morris–which would be gouged by the new tax. Then, in May, Hatch's fellow Utah Republicans piled on at their state convention, passing a resolution voicing the party's opposition to his bill.

The nation's governors–including Hatch's good friend, Mike Leavitt of Utah–almost unanimously opposed it. They feared it would establish yet another budget-busting entitlement program, and would lead to another federal mandate that states were in no fiscal shape to handle.

But one of Utah's leading commentators helped balance the scales. Don Gale, then the voice of KSL Television, blasted the citizens' group for its "mean-spirited" attack ads. Said Gale:

> The issue involves a substantial increase in federal cigarette taxes. The object is to discourage people–especially young people–from smoking. Certainly it's a worthwhile goal. But Senators Hatch and Kennedy know the added revenue would soon be swallowed by the federal government if it is not directed to specific purposes. In the best tradition of political bargaining, they decided to dedicate part of the revenue to child health care and part of it to deficit reduction ....
>
> Utah voters know Senator Hatch makes up his own mind about issues. He always has, and he always will....Senator Hatch should be applauded, not criticized by a campaign of well-financed and offensive commercials.

Despite Republican doubts, Hatch saw the child insurance bill as both good policy and good politics. He compared it to the minimum wage issue. There are excellent reasons to oppose raising the minimum wage: It inevitably leads to fewer entry-level jobs as employers fire low-level workers and don't hire new ones–an outcome especially hurtful to youths seeking their first jobs. Hatch strongly opposes raising the minimum wage for those reasons. But politically the issue has long been a loser for Republicans, as Democrats successfully have demagoged the matter, accusing them of being heartless toward workers.

Given this reality, Hatch, an opponent of increasing the minimum wage, often has pleaded with GOP leaders to offset minimum wage bills by getting something for them that Republicans want, knowing they inevitably will pass Congress, and that when they do Democrats will receive all the credit and Republicans all the blame for trying to stop them. Such reasoning usually has fallen on deaf ears. Most recently, then-Senate Majority Leader Bob Dole insisted he had the votes to simply kill the minimum wage bill. He was wrong: Enough GOP members defected to pass the measure. Just as Hatch predicted, Democrats were hailed as the worker's friend and Republicans as the enemy, further threatening the GOP's tenuous control of Congress. (In 1998, the minimum wage was stopped for one of the few times, with Hatch leading the fight.)

Hatch feared history was about to be repeated, this time over health care, and he was determined not to let it happen. He was concerned about his party's political position–but more concerned about the well-being of millions of families and their children. "Child health insurance is a problem that society needs to solve," he said in a letter to a friend as criticism rained down on him. "I believe we can [pay for it] by getting the cigarette companies to become responsible for all the damages and health problems they cause, and I believe it's the right thing to do."

In Senate debate, he argued that the health of children was far more important than the principle of not raising cigarette taxes. "When it gets to the point when we are so ideologically constipated that we place the preservation of cigarette excise taxes above the welfare of American citizens, we then need to rethink our philosophy," he said.

Meanwhile Hatch worked tirelessly behind the scenes on Majority Leader Trent Lott and others to soften opposition to the bill. He helped persuade colleagues to include $16 billion in the overall budget package for child health care. But, although the budget resolution did not specify how it would be apportioned, senators intended most of it for Medicaid to treat the poorest of the poor, with only $2 billion going to children of the working poor whom Hatch was especially trying to help. The $2 billion would have been enough to help only about three million of the ten million children from poor working families.

The issue came to a head in a decisive political battle behind closed doors at night on June 19, 1997. With the entire federal budget package at stake, the Senate Finance Committee, including Hatch, met to finalize an overall tax-and-spend agreement. When several other committee members suddenly suggested they slap a new tax on cigarettes–but use it to pay for several corporate programs, not for child health care–Hatch saw red.

"Look," he told senators firmly, "we simply cannot raise a 20-cent tax on cigarettes to give to airlines and other wealthy beneficiaries and do nothing for child health insurance." Hatch added that "Everybody knows this money was intended for the children, and if you take a bill to the floor that gives it to corporate welfare instead, Kennedy and I are going to clean your clock!" Hatch suggested that, in the interest of comity, "I will accept an additional nine, ten, eleven or twelve billion dollars on top of the sixteen billion, and that'll end the problem."

At that point, New York Republican Alfonse D'Amato–one of the Senate's shrewdest politicos–jumped in. Leaning over to Hatch, he said "Orrin, you're saving the Republicans. They are so doggone stupid that they don't realize that this issue is going to kill them. If they don't follow your advice, we're going to lose control of both the Senate and the House." D'Amato then spoke up to the entire committee, saying Hatch's compromise was reasonable, and urging the panel to accept it.

Two other Republicans–Frank Murkowski of Alaska and Charles Grassley of Iowa–echoed D'Amato, causing two GOP conservatives, Phil Gramm of Texas and Don Nickles of Oklahoma, to seethe. "They were very offended," recalled Hatch. "If looks could kill, I would have been burned to a crisp." Finally Hatch turned to ranking minority member Daniel Patrick Moynihan of New York. Already sure of the answer, Hatch asked: "Where are the Democrats on this?" Moynihan, grinning, promptly said "All who are in favor, raise your hands." Every Democrat's hand shot up.

Gramm and Nickles began to argue vehemently against any more money for children, but were steamrolled into silence. Finally, Hatch agreed to reduce his bottom-line demand for additional funding from $9 billion to $8 billion, a concession accepted by committee chairman Bill Roth of Delaware. Added to the $16 billion already in the budget package, that meant child health insurance would receive a total of $24 billion over the next five years–$4 billion *more* than in the original Hatch-Kennedy CHILD Bill. It was not enough to cover all poor children, but it was a great start. The committee then voted eighteen to two to accept the package–with all Democrats voting yea, along with all Republicans except Gramm and Nickles who voted nay.

It was now late into the night, but lobbyists swarmed around senators as they emerged from their closed-door session. "The children are clearly the winners tonight, make no mistake about it," Hatch said. That weekend, the *New York Times* reported: "At the insistence of Mr. Hatch, who argued that the proceeds of the tobacco tax should not go to special interests, most of what was left of the $15 billion–about $8 billion–went to increasing health care coverage for uninsured children. The result was to give enough members of both parties a reason to vote for the bill."

The landmark legislation accomplished three major things: (1) provided insurance to millions of needy children; (2) increased taxes on cigarettes to pay for it; (3) provided the glue that held Republicans and Democrats together to pass the first balanced U.S. budget in twenty-nine years and the first major tax cut in sixteen years. The legislation also preserved state decision-making by providing funds without heavy-handed control from Washington.

Accolades poured down on Hatch from child advocates. Marian Wright Edelman, head of the Children's Defense Fund, wrote him that "Yet again you have proven that deep commitment and hard work will prevail at the end of the day! Were it not for your leadership, there would be no children's health initiative of 1997....At every turning point you were there to keep the issue alive. Against all odds, you succeeded."

In summer 1999 Hatch was talking with New York's Republican governor, George Pataki, about the program, now called CHIP–the Child Health Insurance Program. "How do you like CHIP?" asked Hatch. "That is the single greatest bill I have seen that shows the appropriate relationship between the federal and state governments," said Pataki. Funds were flowing to states as block grants, giving them both the means and flexibility to meet critical health care needs of poor children. By then Pataki and virtually all other governors, including Utah's Mike Leavitt, had warmly embraced a program they had fought tooth and nail just two years earlier.

Savvy Republicans also credited Hatch with helping to keep their party's hand in the national political game. Veteran House member Marge Roukema of New Jersey, for example, wrote:

July 30, 1997

Dear Orrin,

Three cheers for you and for expanded children's health care and the cigarette tax!!! You were great for giving this leadership. The Republican Party should thank you for saving it from itself. God in His heaven is surely smiling down on you.

Most sincerely,
Marge R.

9

Women and Families

That you would take the time to be so thoughtful speaks to what I believe is ultimately important and enduring: caring for others regardless of any philosophical differences.

–Feminist opponent in a note to Hatch

IT WAS A MEETING BY CHANCE in the small exercise room of a Los Angeles hotel. Patricia Cornwell, blond, thirtyish, and soon to become very rich as one of the world's best-selling novelists, was burning up calories on a Stairmaster. Nearby on another Stairmaster was a slim, handsome, graying man who looked familiar.

"Don't I know you?" asked Cornwell in her slight North Carolina drawl.

"You may," grinned Orrin Hatch, who was at the hotel to give a speech. "But I'm not sure you'd want to tell anyone."

Cornwell laughed knowingly. He recently had become every liberal's prey in cross-examining Clarence Thomas and Anita Hill as she tried unsuccessfully to block Thomas's Senate confirmation to the Supreme Court. Cornwell, an independent-minded Democrat whose chilling murder mysteries reflect meticulous forensic research–she has attended hundreds of autopsies–was convinced along with most feminists that Hill was right and Thomas was wrong. Cornwell later sent a couple of her books to Hatch, a voracious reader of both fiction and nonfiction, who now calls himself "her biggest fan." He has promoted her books, including to Bill and Hillary Clinton who subsequently invited Cornwell to the White House.

Along the way, Hatch sat Cornwell down with Clarence Thomas, challenging her to use her extraordinary intuitive skills to judge his character for herself. Afterwards, the Senator wrote this note for his files: "As of yesterday, upon meeting Justice Thomas, she is totally convinced that

Justice Thomas is everything I have told her he is." Hatch and Cornwell have also teamed up to find federal resources to combat real-world crime.

While Cornwell and Hatch continue to disagree on some issues, she is a strong supporter. Cornwell dedicated her smash 1995 bestseller *The Body Farm* to "Senator Orrin Hatch, for his tireless fight against crime." She tells interviewers "he's a truly good man."

Kay Scarpetta agrees. Millions of fans know Scarpetta as the savvy heroine of Cornwell's novels. The plot of *The Body Farm* includes a Senator Frank Lord, who sounds suspiciously a lot like Hatch. Lord "was a distinguished man with thick gray hair, and deep blue eyes. He was quite tall and lean, and had a penchant for elegant silk ties...." It doesn't take a pathologist to identify Senator Lord as Senator Hatch, especially given this tell-tale dialogue:

Senator Lord: "NOW's picketing, and my opponent remains very busy painting me as a woman hater with horns and a pointed tail."

Scarpetta answers that it isn't fair: "You've done more for women than anyone I know."

Cornwell's conversion is typical. Those who come to know Hatch–as opposed to the image drawn by pundits and political enemies–invariably are taken with him as a human being, even if they disagree with his views. Over the years, the Senator's candor and kindness have won him numerous admirers among people representing a broad range of the political spectrum. Nadine Cohodas of *Congressional Quarterly* wrote that "The main ingredients of Hatch's senatorial style seem to be his willingness to work hard, his intelligence, and his outwardly sincere manner."

Hatch's respect for women comes naturally. All his life he has been surrounded by competent, caring women who have helped guide and temper him. In 2000 his top Senate assistants in both Washington and Utah were highly capable women–Patricia Knight and Melanie Bowen, respectively, leading staffs that had many other women in key policy-making roles.

The Senator's wife of four decades, Elaine, is a bright, personable former school teacher, model homemaker, church and community volunteer, and exemplar of traditional values. Born to hard work in a Utah farm family, she is modest and unassuming. Elaine initially resisted Orrin's entry into politics, but long since has adjusted to the demands of public life. Her warmth and sensitivity win hearts wherever they go, and she is an integral part of his political success. "She gets me a lot of votes," Orrin is fond of saying.

Elaine largely reared their six children, successfully instilling in each of them solid values and skills, as Orrin traveled the world on the people's business. They have been totally loyal to each other, and there has been no hint of infidelity or other deep discord in their marriage, which seems stronger today than ever.

Each year they ride together in Utah's Pioneer Day Parade, a big holiday on the 24th of July. In 1994, however, Elaine sprained her back and was unable to attend. "I've called her morning and night to make sure she's all right," Orrin wrote his mother. "I felt bereft as I rode in the parade without her." Early in 1997, Elaine spent six weeks in Los Angeles helping a daughter following the birth of a new grandson. Orrin joined her in March, noting in a letter to a friend that "It was great to be reunited with Elaine.... This was the longest we had ever been apart in our marriage. I surely did miss her."

Orrin has co-written and dedicated three songs to Elaine for three recent wedding anniversaries. For their thirty-ninth it was "All Because of You," written with Peter McCann, whose credits include "Take Good Care of My Heart" and "It's the Right Time of the Night." For their fortieth Orrin produced "Sacred Love," written with Madeline Stone, and for their forty-first it was "I Put My Trust in You," written with McCann.

The remarkable woman who more than anyone else shaped Hatch was his mother, Helen Kamm Hatch. As a teenager, she had followed her heart and not her parents' advice in marrying Orrin's father, Jesse, a gentle but rough-hewn young man with little formal education. Together, over the next sixty-nine years, they built a legacy of faith, hard work, and integrity that were passed on to a posterity that included, by 1995, five living children–Orrin and four sisters–thirty-nine grandchildren, ninety-two great-grandchildren, and three great-great-grandchildren. Helen died in 1995 at the age of eighty-nine, three years after her beloved Jesse.

Growing up in their family home in Pittsburgh, Orrin got along well with both parents. But he had a particular bond with his mother, an attractive, delightful woman who was both the family sparkplug and disciplinarian. She kept Orrin and his siblings moving forward by example, encouragement, and the natural consequences of their decisions. Though day-to-day challenges of providing for their working-class family kept Jesse and Helen from enjoying many privileges that affluence affords, Helen held a mirror of a wider world and greater possibilities before her children, and helped them see their reflections in it.

Helen was fun, spirited, optimistic, and in Orrin's eyes saintly without being self-righteous. While living a strict moral and ethical code, Helen did not judge others–or allow her children to do so.

In her eightieth year, Helen was attending the annual women's conference sponsored by her son at the Salt Palace in Salt Lake City, and went to the restroom. Inside was a tall, husky man dressed as a woman. She quickly exited and security guards raced to the room, locked it from the outside, and summoned police. As officers removed and led away the transvestite, Helen remained wide-eyed and perfectly calm at Orrin's side. "Well," she said finally, "he certainly had on a beautiful pink dress."

Orrin reached the Senate well versed in the ways of traditional American women but was less prepared to understand movement feminists. His attempts to deal with them the same way–through mutual respect and understanding–have met with mixed results.

When former Oregon Senator Bob Packwood was in Congress, he and Hatch often were on opposite sides of women's issues–on abortion, the Equal Rights Amendment, and various civil rights bills. Despite scandalous personal behavior with women that eventually cost him his seat, Packwood was a highly effective legislator. One person who made him so was an ardent feminist on his staff named Sana Shtasel. Although she had helped her boss fight Hatch time after time, when Shtasel announced she was leaving Packwood's staff, Hatch dropped by to tell her good-bye, leaving a letter and a poem he had written:

The sharp eyes blazing, the fulgent mind churning,
The fire shooting out, with fierce determination....
This one believes and lives her scenario
[As] very few others do who really make a difference,
Or count for something in the end.

Shtasel, deeply touched, returned a note thanking Hatch for his "incredible kindness," adding "That you would take the time to be so thoughtful speaks to what I believe is ultimately important and enduring: caring for others regardless of any philosophical differences."

A prominent feminist who came to know and support him was Betty Southard Murphy, former chairman of the National Labor Relations Board, who raised campaign contributions for him. During one difficult set of hearings on the Equal Rights Amendment, which she supported, Hatch was sharply criticized by other feminists. In response to an unflattering article in *People* magazine, Murphy wrote to *People:* "Although [Hatch] opposes the ERA as written, he is a tireless worker for equal rights for women and has a proven track record."

He has bucked a trend on Capitol Hill by quietly setting an example of equality on his own staff. A Gannett News Service study of 11,500 congressional staffers found a gender pay gap between "highly paid men who hold most of the power, and lower-paid women whose careers can be stunted by an institutional glass ceiling."

The *Salt Lake Tribune* ran the story with a sidebar titled "On average, Hatch Pays Women More Than Men"—the only member of Utah's congressional delegation to do so at that time. Hatch's staff then included twenty-six women paid an average of $30,300, and fourteen men, paid an average of $29,400.

Observers have been struck by the difference between Hatch and many other conservatives. He does not gloat in ideological victories, and cautions staff and colleagues not to rub salt in defeated opponents' wounds. One national reporter noted Hatch's demeanor after the Senator helped defeat a civil rights bill he considered extreme. Immediately after the vote, he left the Senate chamber and circulated among disappointed proponents, promising to come up with an approach he could support. "That took gall, guts, and an awful lot of sense," said a labor lobbyist.

The Utahn's gentlemanly approach and penchant for seeking middle ground obviously have not endeared him to all opponents, and he has been attacked by both the extreme right and extreme left, whose partisans bitterly oppose compromise. Sometimes they use below-the-belt tactics, demonizing Hatch for thwarting their wills and as a way to fatten their organizations' coffers by describing him in blackest terms to gullible contributors.

If liberal opponents have their way, the Utahn will forever be fixed in the public mind as one of the Senate bullies who attacked poor Anita Hill as she leveled implausible charges against Clarence Thomas in 1991. The historic truth is that the overwhelming weight of Hatch's effort was directed not at destroying Hill but saving Thomas. While Hatch uncovered damaging evidence against Hill's veracity, he said almost nothing to her during her highly dubious testimony before the Senate Judiciary Committee. In fact, on behalf of the committee Hatch apologized to Hill for the unethical leak of an FBI report that resulted in her being dragged before the panel.

"I wish you well," he told Hill, who had hoped to kill Thomas's confirmation by ambush from the shadows, but instead was dragged into the limelight. Lacking credible evidence to the contrary about a man he had known personally and professionally for a decade, Hatch saved Thomas in the conviction he was a person of integrity who would serve the nation well. Hatch played a key role in putting Thomas on the Supreme Court, but paid a high political price.

The Thomas-Hill saga added fuel to the fire of radical feminists, who had been targeting Hatch for years. In a scorched-earth speech at the National Press Club in 1985, for example, Eleanor Smeal, then president of the National Organization for Women, blasted "right-wing bigotry" that threatened NOW's agenda in civil rights, birth control, and abortion. "We must wrap [bigotry] around the neck of the right wing as we fight for liberty and justice for all," she said. "We don't take our right-wing fascist opponents seriously enough."

Asked to name the "fascists," Smeal reeled off a list of noted conservatives, including Hatch. "When they stop calling us leftists and communists and pinkos, I'll stop calling them fascists," said Smeal.

Hatch issued a press release that afternoon:

> I can't speak for the others she mentioned, but I have never referred to Ms. Smeal as a Communist or a "pinko." Ms. Smeal and I have had occasional differences on some issues...[but] I believe I've given her, or her associates, every opportunity to air her views at my hearings. And although we haven't agreed on every issue, I hope never to resort to name calling.

On another occasion, during hearings before the Senate constitution subcommittee, Hatch and other members were subjected to an intemperate broadside by a proponent of the Equal Rights Amendment. Jane O'Grady, representing her boss, labor leader George Meany, head of the AFL-CIO, accused opponents of the ERA of "misinformation, emotional rhetoric, and distortion." Here is how Hatch answered her:

> Hatch: I would think that the federation would want to make the best case it could that it does not discriminate against women and had not in the past. The statement is such a strong statement here today. How

many women are on the governing board of the federation?

O'Grady: There are thirty-three vice presidents of the AFL-CIO.

Hatch: How many of them are women?

O'Grady: I think you know the answer to that, Senator. There are no women on the executive council of the AFL-CIO.

Hatch: Yes, I did know the answer....I have no further questions.

The Senator also takes his lumps from ultraconservatives, who falsely claimed him as one of their own when he first arrived in the Senate, and have never forgiven him for marching to the drum roll of his own conscience.

When he became the chief Republican sponsor of a national child care bill a decade ago, Phyllis Schlafly, head of the Eagle Forum, sent him a scathing letter, also released to the media for maximum embarrassment. "Dear Orrin," it began, "To echo the famous cry of one who was betrayed by a man thought to be a friend, '*Et tu*, Orrin!'" Schlafly's letter went downhill from there, asking why he had "abandoned the pro-family cause" by "co-sponsoring such a thoroughly bad bill."

The Senator has gone far out of his way to give conservative as well as liberal women's groups considerable opportunity to air their views before Congress. And their concerns have not fallen on deaf ears: He has been a tireless champion and leading sponsor of legislation to help women where it counts the most to most of them–in enhanced personal growth, in their families and homes, in the workplace, and in their special health-care needs.

In 1981, as the Reagan Revolution returned the Senate to Republican control for the first time in three decades, Hatch took the reins of power as chair of the Labor and Human Resources Committee–just four years after first arriving in Washington. "Asked about his priorities," wrote Al Hunt of the *Wall Street Journal,* "the new Labor Committee chairman talks first about combating sex discrimination."

During January, the Utahn held hearings on the general topic of sex discrimination in the workplace. Three months later, he held one of the nation's first hearings specifically on harassment, with one federal official testifying that 42 percent of federally employed women told surveyors they had been victims of sexual harassment. He was ahead of his time in shining a spotlight on the issue: Clarence and Anita were still a decade away, and Bill, Paula, and Monica nearly two decades.

The Senator has championed many measures to help women balance work and family. Early on, he voted to overturn a Supreme Court decision that held women were not entitled to company disability benefits in cases of pregnancy. He also encouraged flextime–flexibility in work hours, which especially benefits women with families. He repeatedly sponsored legislation to amend the Fair Labor Standards Act to guarantee the right to work at home, and introduced the American Family Protection Act to offer preferred rehire rights and retention of benefits for any employee taking up to six years leave after the birth or adoption of a child or up to two years to care for a seriously ill family member.

He also was the chief Republican sponsor of the nation's first child care bill, pushing it into law in the teeth of threats of political retribution from the far right. Today even many former opponents admit the law works well, distributing block grants to states to help low-income women provide proper care for their youngsters when they must work for pay.

Hatch has been a leading sponsor of legislation to help women succeed as entrepreneurs and in non-traditional jobs. He asked the Small Business Administration to provide incentives for lending institutions to issue smaller loans for small enterprises–many of which are female-owned–in return for SBA-backed mini-loans of under $50,000. The Senator also cosponsored legislation, and helped push it into law, to provide more training for women in higher-skilled, often higher-paying nontraditional occupations. These are particularly important to single mothers, making it possible for more of them to support families without outside assistance.

In 1997 Hatch, a member of the Senate Finance Committee and chair of its tax subcommittee, was an active proponent of the Taxpayer Relief Act–a package of IRS tax reductions that were signed into law by President Clinton. They included, notably, child tax credits–$400 per child for 1998, rising later to $500 per child–and expanding the availability of full individual retirement accounts (IRAs) to nonworking spouses.

In addition, he sponsored legislation to restore the tax deduction for a home office–especially important for those who have home-based businesses, such as real estate agents or caterers, but who have been penalized by court decisions that define "principal place of business" to exclude a home office if work is performed anywhere else.

Abortion has divided America ever since the Supreme Court's *Roe v. Wade* decision in 1973 legalizing it. Hatch finds the practice abhorrent but would not throw a blanket prohibition over it, believing abortion may be justified in the relatively rare cases when a pregnancy endangers a woman's life or results from rape or incest. Surprisingly, and despite a quarter-century of feminist propaganda, by 1999 a majority of American women would be at least as restrictive as Hatch, according to two polls that year. The feminist Center for Gender Equity and pro-life Christian Coalition both found that 53 percent of women favored prohibiting abortion totally or only with the exceptions of rape, incest, or to save the life of the mother. If these were the only exceptions, over 95 percent of abortions would be banned.

Kathryn Crosby, widow of singer Bing Crosby, was one person who helped Hatch understand another side of the issue. In a private conversation, she told Hatch how she and Bing used to visit Baja, California, a vacation paradise where she spent her time working with poor Mexicans instead of socializing. She told of watching innocent Mexican children being battered and neglected by parents who didn't want them to begin with. Crosby provided appointments with her own gynecologist for some of the women to get intrauterine contraceptive devices.

Hatch left Crosby with a stronger belief that all views should be heard, and a better appreciation that there were well-intentioned arguments on both sides of the abortion issue.

He studied abortion carefully, held an exhaustive set of hearings on it in 1981 to listen to all sides, and wrote a booklet about abortion in 1984. The Senator also introduced a constitutional amendment to give states "concurrent power to restrict and prohibit abortion," specifying that state law would take precedence over federal law where a state law was more restrictive. Many observers considered Hatch's approach ingenious–allowing traditional family-oriented states greater leeway in restricting a practice their residents opposed. But consensus did not exist in Congress for such action, and the amendment finally was shelved.

After a later hearing, Gloria Feldt, president of Planned Parenthood, sent Hatch this hand-written note: "Thank you for your courtesy and decorum at this morning's hearing on a difficult issue. I appreciate the opportunity to testify. Though we disagree on this issue, I hope we may someday work together to prevent the need for abortion."

As national polls in the 1980s showed increasingly fewer Americans wanting to overturn *Roe v. Wade*, Hatch dove into a new cause: making adoption easier and safer. "I realize that not every child is greeted with the joy Elaine and I felt over the arrival of our six unique, challenging, and rewarding children," said Hatch. "But every child is special and capable of making a contribution to their family, community, and nation that no other individual can make. Many thousands of couples pray every day that they will be able to adopt children. Those contemplating killing their unborn infants instead could help answer such prayers."

He began in 1984 by cosponsoring an anti-fraud bill making it a federal offense to conceal any material fact in connection with an adoption, and making it unlawful for a person to solicit or receive money for arranging an adoption.

Hatch also chaired two days of hearings which revealed that some 50,000 children in the United States were legally free for adoption, yet remained unplaced. Adoption across state boundaries, for example, was frustrated by the need of many children for extensive health care. Medical costs which were covered by Medicaid in the home state were not chargeable in the adoptive state, and adopting families could not always afford to pay the needed expenses. Hatch sponsored a bill specifying that once a "special needs" child is deemed Medicaid eligible, the new state must assume continued Medicaid liability.

In another bill he addressed the sheer cost of the process, which ranged up to $15,000 for domestic adoptions and $20,000 for foreign adoptions. His Fairness for Adopting Families Act proposed removing the dollar limitation on the income tax deduction for adoption expenses, and expanded the list of eligible expenses. Hatch introduced versions of his bill in six different congresses. His modified proposal finally was signed into law in 1996, giving citizens a tax credit of up to $5,000 in qualified adoption expenses.

"When a child is adopted into a loving family, everyone wins," noted Hatch, "including couples who desperately desire children, the children themselves who want to belong to a family of their own, and our society as a whole which desperately needs stronger family units."

He has also fought to require parents to financially support their children. According to the 1990 census, about 50 percent of noncustodial parents who owed child support failed to meet the obligation. Unpaid child support has been a leading contributor to the growing number of single-parent families on welfare. Hatch helped pass tougher child support enforcement legislation, and supports efforts to garnish the wages of employees to pay outstanding child support debts.

The Senator, who was a fine athlete himself, has helped assure equal access to sports for women. Title IX, which became law in 1972, has given many a college athletic director heartburn. It mandates that schools receiving federal funds provide equal opportunities in sports for women–a very tall order for those with traditional, expensive all-male programs such as football. "I remember when legislation was pending to remove funding under Title IX for women," said Jan Bennett, a longtime Hatch aide. "Orrin got to work and saved the funding."

Early in his Senate career he cosponsored congressional resolutions supporting parity for women's track and field events in the Olympics. Later he cosponsored a joint resolution calling for a national "Women in Sports Day" to highlight the contributions and achievements of women athletes, and to recognize the positive effect that such participation has on girls and young women. The resolution passed Congress and was signed by President Reagan.

Hatch has used his congressional clout to fight for numerous other measures to assure the personal health and safety of women. He crafted a plan that helped guarantee block grant funds for rape crisis centers, was prime co-sponsor of the Violence Against Women Act, which became law in 1994, and later supported allocating additional resources for shelters and other programs to aid victims of domestic violence. He also hosts a charity golf tournament in Utah each year, with much of the proceeds funding women's shelters throughout the state.

He is a cosponsor of the Patient's Bill of Rights–congressional legislation to protect consumers of managed care health plans by establishing federal standards regulating HMOs and similar health programs. Standards include a new appeals process to protect both consumers and providers from managed care practices thought to undermine access to and quality of care. Provisions of specific interest to women include requirements that HMOs allow patients to have access to obstetricians and gynecologists without referral from a primary care doctor, and that the Centers for Disease Control and the National Institutes of Health study women's health issues, such as osteoporosis and other bone disorders, various types of cancers, and heart disease.

The bill imposes a mastectomy care mandate on all types of health plans and health insurance. The length of hospital stay can only be determined by the physician in consultation with the patient, and health plans must cover all stages of reconstructive surgery.

Such provisions are part of Hatch's longstanding efforts to fight breast cancer, a nightmare disease that killed an estimated 43,000 American women in 1999–one every three minutes. It will affect one out of nine women who live to age 85. The good news is that breast cancer death rates have declined about 2 percent a year since 1989, in part because of earlier detection with mammography. The American Cancer Society says the five-year survival rate for localized breast cancer is 96 percent, compared to only 22 percent after it spreads to other organs.

Hatch has worked hard to encourage early screening. A Senate committee adopted his amendment requiring that all federally funded family planning clinics provide instruction to low-income women in breast self-examination. A law signed in 1992 included a provision cosponsored by Hatch to help ensure that a woman receives accurate mammography services. He cosponsored legislation requiring Medicare to cover the patient costs for individuals enrolled in cancer clinical trials, and in 1998 joined a number of colleagues to request an additional $175 million for a Department of Defense breast cancer research program.

The Senator is also the leading voice in Congress supporting the vitamin and mineral industry. There is a growing body of evidence on the benefits of these products, such as the use of folic acid by pregnant women to prevent birth defects in their babies. The federal Centers for Disease Control had concluded that a certain percentage of folic acid taken by women could prevent neural tube defects–spina bifada–in their babies. But for more than a decade the FDA stubbornly and stupidly refused to allow the claim to be made. Today most cereals routinely include folic acid.

Hatch also was the chief Republican sponsor of three major bills that were signed into law to fight AIDS, the third leading cause of death among African American women aged twenty-five to forty-four, and a scourge that has infected thousands of babies born to victims of the disease.

Many such initiatives have arisen from the women's conferences Hatch has sponsored annually since 1985. The conferences, a fixture each fall in Salt Lake City, attract several thousand women, and were an outgrowth of another Hatch innovation: his own women's advisory group, established shortly before the first conference. The group included some thirty Utah women leaders representing a wide range of approaches. "I wanted all views represented," explained Hatch, "so I made certain that Democrats and independents were included along with Republicans."

"He started these conferences long before such things were fashionable," said Jan Bennett, who cochaired the event. "He was thinking about the broad range of women's needs and genuinely wanted to find the best solutions."

Conferences have featured top keynoters–from former U.N. Ambassador Jeane Kirkpatrick to pop psychologist Dr. Laura Schlessinger–and have offered a wide range of workshops on such topics as property and other legal rights; child-rearing; training, education and employment; surviving in a male-dominated workforce; women's health; home-based/cottage industries; homemaking as a career choice; combating stress; and women as policymakers.

The women's conferences helped open Hatch's eyes. He realized that the concerns of women appearing before his committees in Washington were also major issues in Utah, despite the state's strong emphasis on traditional family patterns and lifestyles. In the mid-1990s, divorce ended half of all Utah marriages and over half of Utah women worked outside the home, including 45 percent of mothers with preschool children.

As the powerful chairman of the Senate Judiciary Committee, Hatch has helped assure women equal access to the nation's judicial benches. He has worked to maintain a single standard of qualifications and judicial fitness for all nominees. In 1998 alone, the Senate confirmed twenty-one women as federal judges who had been approved by Hatch's committee. Another seven women had been approved by the panel and were awaiting Senate action.

Supreme Court Justice Ruth Bader Ginsburg personifies Hatch's commitment to helping women reach the top of the legal profession. In 1993 Hatch was widely credited as the key person who talked President Clinton into bypassing several male candidates in favor of nominating Judge Ginsburg to the high court. In the 1970s Ginsburg had been a trailblazer in gender-discrimination law, arguing six women's rights cases before the Supreme Court and winning five of them. But as a judge on the D.C. appellate court for thirteen years, she had earned a reputation for being restrained and nonideological.

In 1996 Ginsburg sent Hatch a note on Supreme Court letterhead, saying "Your April 15 letter is one more example of what you told me at our first meeting–that you and I agree on the great contributions women can and do make to the good and welfare of society, though our path to recognition of women's dignity and stature is not always the same." She enclosed an article she had recently published, with a hand-written notation, "For Orrin, with respect and appreciation."

10

Health and Longevity

Senator Hatch is father of the modern generic-drug industry, which some experts call the biggest consumer victory of the 1980s....Generic drugs–less costly, safe alternatives to brand names–usually enter the market at prices 30 percent lower than brand names.

THE LONGEVITY OF SENIORS AND and the quality of their lives are key, longstanding issues for Utah and Senator Hatch. That concern is manifested in practical ways for most seniors in the state. A Harvard University study in 1997 found that men in Utah's Cache and Rich counties lived longer than anywhere else in the United States.

On March 22, 1999, Senator Hatch got another reason to continue his decades-long work for senior citizens: he became one, turning sixty-five that day.

"We talk about new visions on aging," he told his twelfth annual seniors conference two months later. "Each year that theme takes on added significance for me. Which is to say the term 'vision' seems less and less to do with grand plans and more and more to do with the strength of my new bifocals! It gets to the point, doesn't it, that when we lose our glasses, we can't look for them till we find them. Go figure!"

That was how the Senator welcomed a thousand attendees to the seniors conference he has sponsored in Salt Lake City for the past dozen years. The late Lawrence Welk's "Champagne Lady," Norma Zimmer, spoke and sang at this one, and workshops were offered on such things as learning to use the Internet ("Widening our World"), Alzheimer's, reverse mortgages, grandparenting, humor, and safe driving for the older driver.

The last topic, said Hatch, "reminds me of a hundred-year-old man who was driving down I-15 when his car phone rang. Answering it, he heard his wife's urgent voice warning him: 'Herman, I just heard on the news that there's a car going the wrong way on I-15. Please be careful.'

"'Heck,' said Herman, 'It's not just *one* car. It's *hundreds* of 'em!'"

Hatch said, "Lest you think I'm making fun of my elders, remember that I'm now officially a senior citizen myself." He added that "The very fact that so very many of us are here today in good health bears powerful witness to the twentieth century strides in health science and longevity research. What a marvelous time to be alive."

As the twenty-first century settles in, Hatch notes, there is considerable challenge as well as opportunity for America's older citizens. In the fall of 1999, the U.S. Department of Health and Human Services released its annual "report card" on the nation's health, which says that in thirty years, one of every five Americans will be over age sixty-five. Life expectancy for older Americans has continued to increase. A person sixty-five-years old in 1997 could on average expect to live to be nearly eighty-three; an eighty-five-year-old in 1997 could expect to live to be over ninety.

There has been a substantial long-term decline in mortality, especially from heart disease. Death rates from heart disease among persons sixty-five to eighty-four have been cut nearly in half since 1970; among those aged eighty-five or older, death rates have dropped more than 20 percent.

Despite added years of life, most older citizens are not severely limited in their daily activities, even though living with chronic conditions. Most noninstitutionalized persons seventy years or older suffer from arthritis, and about one-third have hypertension, according to the report. Diabetes was reported by 11 percent.

As of 1995, fewer than 10 percent of noninstitutionalized individuals seventy or older were unable to perform one or more routine daily activities such as bathing, dressing, or using the toilet. Disability rates increased with age, from about 5 percent among persons seventy to seventy-four, to nearly 22 percent for those eighty-five or older.

Seven out of ten non-disabled persons sixty-five or older participated in some form of exercise at least once in a recent two-week period, including walking, gardening, and stretching.

"Many older people are in good health and leading active lives in the community," said Jeffrey Koplan, director of the Centers for Disease Control which helped produce the report. "However, a significant number of persons over age eighty-five still have chronic illnesses and disabilities that limit their ability to fully participate in everyday activities. As life spans increase we must help all of our citizens prepare for a healthy old age. People of all ages should be tobacco-free, eat right, and keep physically active so their golden years will be healthy years."

Senator Hatch says "While we have made huge strides in health and longevity, our goal must be for every individual to have access to proper health care and other resources essential for a high quality of life." The Senator has taken many solid steps to help senior citizens live happier, healthier, less-stressful lives.

Early in 2000, with Hatch's strong support, a law was passed to let Social Security recipients collect their full benefits no matter what they earn. The measure is retroactive to December 31, 1999. Previously Hatch had cosponsored legislation that became law in 1996 to increase the amount that seniors could earn up to $30,000 before being penalized with deductions.

Greater longevity requires greater income to continue to have a good quality of life to the end. At the same time longevity has been increasing, however, savings have been dwindling. "Retirement security is a topic on everyone's mind these days," said Hatch at a Senate hearing on pension legislation. "The average American today will spend one-third of their lifetime in retirement."

"The savings rate in this country has sharply declined in the last twenty-five years," he said. "In 1974, when we created IRAs [individual retirement accounts], the average American saved 9.5 percent of their income. In 1998, that same American saved only one-half of 1 percent of their income, the lowest level since the Great Depression of the 1930s." Inadequate savings today, the Senator emphasized, "will lead to a retirement crisis later down the road."

Among other factors, Hatch blames the impossibly complex IRS Code for the low savings rate. The code's rules discourage individuals from taking advantage of tax laws for retirement. In addition, the IRS "penalizes savings and investment. This is the wrong message to send to the American people. We should be enacting simple laws with few restrictions to encourage everyone to save as much as possible." Hatch, who chairs the Senate taxation and IRS oversight subcommittee, seeks to reform the tax code and shrink the Internal Revenue Service itself, calling the agency a "monster" that needs to be overhauled.

"We should repeal the estate tax altogether," says Hatch. "It is inefficient, costing sixty-five cents [to administer] for every dollar that we collect, and unfair because it is a second tax on the same earnings. The wealthy hire lawyers and advisors to create trusts and do complex estate planning to minimize the amount of tax they will pay. It is the families of small business owners, family farmers, and Great Aunt Edna who are hit hardest by this tax. We must find a way to remove this crushing burden from their backs."

Hatch has long been the leader in Congress in pushing for a balanced federal budget, repeatedly introducing a constitutional amendment mandating a balanced budget. He also has been a leading voice in Washington for two decades to simplify and lower the capital gains tax rates, which plague all seniors who were foresighted enough to save and invest. The Hatch- [Joseph] Lieberman capital gains bill became law in the 1990s, reducing the capital gains tax rate from 28 percent to 20 percent and providing a critical boost to sustain the nation's high-flying economy through the decade. Hatch continues to fight to lower capital gains taxes even more.

"Cutting the capital gains tax has often been labeled as a tax cut for the rich," says Hatch. "This is not true. Millions of Americans are becoming investors. They purchase stock and mutual funds directly or they invest directly through stock options, employee stock ownership plans, or 401(k)s. Roughly half of American households now have some sort of stock ownership, and the number grows every year."

Senator Hatch has worked in many other ways to make the tax code more fair to older Americans and their families. Among tax and finance efforts, some of which were signed into law as the Taxpayer Relief Act of 1997, have been these:

- He cosponsored the Senior Citizens Home Equity Act to rein in excessive fees being charged to seniors who participate in the Home Equity Conversion Program sponsored by the U.S. Department of Housing and Urban Development.

- He has cosponsored bills to completely repeal the estate and gift taxes, increase the unified credit and lower the estate tax rates, and allow a bigger exemption from the estate tax for family businesses and family farms.

- He cosponsored a bill to expand IRAs and create the recent Roth IRA.

Decades ago, most workers spent their entire careers with one or two companies, which in turn provided pension benefits to help see them through retirement. As of 1999, however, only one in five Americans working for small business had access to pension plans through their employer. Reasons include both a highly mobile workforce and cumbersome pension rules that act as a disincentive for businesses to offer pension plans.

Hatch is a cosponsor of the Pension Coverage and Portability Act. Among other things, the bill would help pension plan participants keep more of their retirement savings and make it easier to roll over one type of pension plan into another type, notably when changing jobs. He also has opposed proposals by the Clinton-Gore Administration to raise taxes on certain life insurance products, including policies used by many seniors to supplement their incomes.

As a member of the Senate Finance Committee, Senator Hatch has worked effectively to safeguard Social Security. "Among my biggest priorities is ensuring the solvency of Social Security," says Hatch. "We need more than the Band-Aid approach that President Clinton has offered. We need sound reform to keep this program on a secure financial footing." He also supports the "Social Security lockbox" to prohibit Congress from spending the Social Security surplus. The measure sequesters all FICA funds not currently needed and preserves them intact until they are needed.

In 1999 Senator Hatch again cosponsored a bill to repeal the 1993 increase in the tax on Social Security benefits. After 1993, Social Security benefits that were subject to taxation went from 50 percent to 85 percent. Repealing the increase would help provide financial security for seniors.

The Senator has used his clout on the Finance Committee to protect and improve Medicare, the nation's health insurance program for the elderly and disabled. He introduced a bill to create a commission that would make recommendations to the president and Congress on long-term changes needed to keep Medicare financially solvent for the foreseeable future. Although his proposal was enacted, the approach became deadlocked because of the Clinton-Gore Administration's lack of cooperation.

"Medicare reform should be led by experts in that area, not politicians," says Hatch. "The Administration made the choice to use Medicare reform as a political issue by scaring seniors and poisoning the environment for reform. I want to bring the best minds together to develop a comprehensive reform for Medicare. The issue must transcend partisanship." In any reform, says Hatch, he would guarantee that benefits would not be cut for current enrollees or those nearly eligible for Medicare.

Hatch supported a number of provisions to the Balanced Budget Act (BBA) of 1997 which provided for the most sweeping reform of Medicare since its birth three decades ago. Provisions included steps to ensure the financial solvency of Medicare–needed because it was on the verge of going broke–and new and enhanced health care preventative benefits. Among benefits are coverage for annual mammograms for women age forty and over; coverage for pap and pelvic examinations every three years, or annually for women at high risk; coverage of certain annual prostate cancer screening, and colorectal screening tests for men over age fifty.

Passage of the BBA in 1997 assured the financial solvency of Medicare for another ten years. However, it also created some problems for Medicare recipients that Hatch has worked successfully to rectify. In November 1999 a bill he introduced the previous summer was signed into law as part of an omnibus budget bill, restoring $2.1 billion in new Medicare spending in nursing homes and helping to ensure continued beneficiary access to nursing home care.

The measure was needed after the BBA created a new nursing home payment system to save Medicare dollars. "Unfortunately," Hatch explained, "the total amount of projected savings appears to have been greatly exceeded."

In addition, he explained, the Health Care Financing Administration (HCFA), the agency overseeing Medicare, "has not properly developed a payment formula that accurately reflects the costs of providing nursing home care to patients with complex medical conditions." As a result, nursing homes are being asked to provide some services that cost more than Medicare pays. "This is particularly true for medically complex patients, such as those needing treatment for cancer, hip fracture, or stroke," he said.

Hatch's bill proposed increased funding for fifteen specific payment categories under the nursing home payment system. Without congressional action, warned Hatch, some nursing homes would have been forced to close their doors.

A month after introducing his measure (S. 1500), which had thirty Senate cosponsors, Hatch welcomed hundreds of nursing home operators to Washington to a "Save Our Seniors" rally in support of his bill. Addressing visitors on the steps of the Capitol, Hatch assured them that "Today the Medicare program is on more solid financial ground, although clearly long-term reform of this program remains a top priority in Congress.

"We also know today that some of the payment policies we approved in 1997 are creating severe, yet unintentional hardships for skilled nursing facilities in their ability to provide quality health care for medically complex Medicare patients....Protecting beneficiaries' access to quality, skilled nursing care is the fundamental goal for all of us here today. The most vulnerable should not be the most forgotten."

Senator Hatch has also cosponsored legislation to improve another part of the Balanced Budget Act, to ensure that Medicare beneficiaries are allowed to "privately contract" with the physician of their choice without any penalty to the physician who provides the health care services. In addition, the Senate has approved Senator Hatch's proposal to make sure that beneficiaries who wish to select a managed care option under Medicare will be able to know that they are picking a plan which allows them to choose their own doctor.

Provisions of another Hatch bill (S. 1626) signed into law in November 1999 help ensure that Medicare patients have access to the latest health care advances, such as BRACHY therapy for prostate cancer, coronary stents, and new generations of pacemakers. Previously, Medicare did not always reimburse adequately for such new medical technology and pharmaceuticals, putting them out of reach of most seniors. Hatch's measure helps assure Medicare beneficiaries access to these advances by allowing more reasonable reimbursement rates.

Hatch also was the prime sponsor of a home health care bill–now a law–to authorize the use of public funds to provide seniors essential care in their own homes when appropriate. There, friends or family can assist with giving the care, in a setting more psychologically soothing to the recipient, and at a cost much cheaper than in an institution.

Senator Hatch is an original cosponsor of the Patients' Bill of Rights Plus Act, passed by the Senate in July 1999. It would provide new consumer protections, enhanced health care quality, and increased access to health services for up to 124 million Americans enrolled in employer-sponsored health care plans. In 1998, according to the U.S. Department of Health and Human Services, about 12 percent of Medicare enrollees were among those in managed care plans.

Senator Hatch chaired the Labor and Human Resources Committee in the 1980s when it had jurisdiction over about 2,000 federal programs. During Hatch's six years as committee chair, administration was streamlined and total outlays of these programs were reduced in real terms by 25 percent–even as *more* money than ever before was going to those who needed it.

The high cost of medicine is a serious concern for many Americans, especially senior citizens. "Too many citizens on fixed incomes are forced to choose between food and drugs," says Hatch. Medicare provides generous benefits for hospitalization but nothing for prescription drugs.

While Medicare provides payments averaging $5,000 a year per beneficiary, average older Americans spent another $2,400 out of pocket for health care in 1999, according to the American Association of Retired Persons (AARP), the nation's largest organization of senior citizens. The out-of-pocket amount included $413 in prescription drugs, a monthly premium, as well as co-payments and deductibles. Medicare does not pay for many expensive services and products including routine physicals, eyeglasses, and most dental care.

While many Medicare beneficiaries have other means to pay for drugs–such as retiree benefits from former employers–about one-third of seniors, more than 13 million, have to pay out of pocket. About 4.5 million seniors spend $1,000 or more a year for their medicines, and at least 1.3 million spend more than $2,000.

Senator Hatch is father of the modern generic-drug industry, earning the unofficial title while helping to rein in soaring drug prices. As former chairman of the Senate Labor and Human Resources Committee, he engineered a major law creating the industry, which some experts call the biggest consumer victory of the 1980s. It resulted in greatly reducing the price of many current drugs and, through extending patents on some other drugs produced by pioneer firms, helped attract the investment needed to develop the next generation of life-saving drugs.

The landmark legislation was the Hatch-[Henry] Waxman Drug Competition and Patent Term Restoration Act of 1984. The measure allowed makers of generic drugs–less-costly, safe alternatives to brand names–to use faster new application procedures in seeking approval by the Food and Drug Administration. Generic drugs usually enter the market at prices 30 percent lower than name brands. Generic drugs have saved consumers between $8 billion and $10 billion a year since 1984–a cumulative savings approaching $150 billion.

Recently Hatch has been working to get the FDA to speed up its review of applications for generic drugs. Although the law requires the FDA to approve such applications within 180 days, in 1998 the agency was meeting that deadline only half the time. Such delays are costly to consumers.

The Senator also is involved in the current debate over whether prescription drugs should be covered as a benefit under Medicare, and is considering viable alternatives.

Many studies show that vitamins and minerals have a significant protective effect on the health of older citizens, who often do not eat adequately. Hatch has been the leading voice in Congress in making vitamins and minerals widely available to all Americans. One Hatch initiative, for example, would allow participants in the food stamp program to buy vitamins and minerals with their stamps.

He authored the Dietary Supplement Health and Education Act, which became U.S. law in 1994. Although the federal government had pressed for more restrictions on the industry, a *Salt Lake Tribune* editorial on the final bill said it "balances the interests of dietary supplement users like Utah Sen. Orrin Hatch, who do not want the industry to be hamstrung by Food and Drug Administration regulations, and the concerns of consumer advocates, who do not want the public to be duped by snake-oil health claims. Those on both sides of the issue feel they got a reasonable deal."

In 1998, the Senator received the "Lifetime Achievement Award" from the National Nutritional Foods Association for his work to promote the availability of dietary supplements and consumer information on their advantages.

Another Hatch bill provided federal incentives that led to the development of some fifty "orphan drugs"–pharmaceuticals critically needed by 200 thousand or fewer people, not enough of a user base to make their development attractive to drug companies under normal procedures.

Senator Hatch has been involved in many other health issues important to seniors. He cosponsored an amendment to the budget resolution for fiscal year 2000 to increase funding for veterans health care. He also introduced–and the Senate passed in 1999–a bill to amend the Radiation Exposure Compensation Act, to recompense many Utahns who were exposed to radiation as a result of government tests during the Cold War. The Senator was working with his House colleagues in 2000 to help ensure that the bill is passed by the House of Representatives and signed into law.

As chairman of the Senate Judiciary Committee, Senator Hatch has also led efforts to fight many types of crime, including those that especially target seniors. Telemarketing fraud, for example, bilks its victims of $40 billion every year, with experts testifying that more than 60 percent of fraud victims are age sixty-five or older. Senator Hatch helped fashion the Telemarketing Fraud Prevention Act, which toughens jail sentences for those convicted of such crime, and requires a stiffer sentence if the victim is a senior.

11

The AIDS Crisis

I do not agree with [gays'] sexual preferences. But that does not mean I do not have compassion for them; that I am just going to write them off and tell them to forget it, go ahead and die, because they differ from me.

AT THE START OF THE NEW MILLENNIUM, the scourge of AIDS (acquired immune deficiency syndrome) has receded as a fear for most Americans. But the nation's graveyards still tell a chilling tale. Through December 1998, at least 410,800 citizens had died of AIDS–more than the 405,400 Americans killed in World War II.

Horrific as that cumulative figure is, earlier in the decade experts predicted it would be far worse in the United States. And meanwhile, in the developing world, where an estimated 95 percent of those dying from AIDS live, the disease is still spreading unabated.

AIDS is caused by a virus, HIV (human immunodeficiency virus) which ravages the body's immune system, leaving it vulnerable to destruction from other diseases. U.S. deaths from AIDS have declined some 70 percent since 1995, including an unprecedented 48 percent from 1996 to 1997, and another 21 percent to 1998. While the incidence of new infections remains steady and high, HIV mortality has dropped out of the fifteen leading causes of death after being the eighth leading cause in 1996.

Analysts and health experts routinely credit Orrin Hatch high among those who have made possible the breakthroughs in research and treatment that are prolonging the lives of thousands of individuals suffering from HIV infection. As a strictly monogamous, heterosexual man who has been faithfully married to the same woman for four decades, Hatch seems an unlikely candidate for such accolades. But the record speaks for itself.

Hatch's role began in the wake of a series of AIDS milestones. AIDS did not register as a serious concern to most Americans until the mid-1980s. While the epidemic was cutting a swath through the gay community starting in 1980–leading some scientists initially to call it Gay-Related Immune Deficiency Syndrome (GRIDS)–it was not until the illness and AIDS death of screen star Rock Hudson in 1985 that the disease came to be widely feared by many citizens, and recognized as a potential threat to the general population.

Along with promiscuous gay men–the largest single group of sufferers–victims also included male and female sexual partners, intravenous drug users using the same needles, babies born to infected women, and individuals receiving tainted blood.

"In those early years, the federal government viewed AIDS as a budget problem, local public health officials saw it as a political problem, gay leaders considered AIDS a public relations problem, and the news media regarded it as a homosexual problem that wouldn't interest anybody else," writes Randy Shilts in his definitive book on the early years of AIDS, *And the Band Played On*. "Consequently, few confronted AIDS for what it was, a profoundly threatening medical crisis."

Shilts blames all these groups for waking up too late to the enormity of the peril, starting with Reagan Administration officials who "ignored pleas from government scientists and did not allocate adequate funding for AIDS research until the epidemic had already spread throughout the country."

Scientists at the Centers for Disease Control (CDC) first noticed the new pattern of illness in 1981 and early in 1982 recognized it as a syndrome–a specific disease. Senator Hatch was then chairman of the Senate panel that deals most directly with health issues–the Labor and Human Resources Committee. "Although he was a conservative Mormon from Utah," writes Shilts, "Senator Orrin Hatch...was committed to not letting health become a partisan issue, particularly in regard to AIDS." Hatch was one of a relatively few people praised by Shilts.

"Hatch's committee, however, included some of the looniest, raving New Right homophobes in the Senate....Thus, when [California Congressman] Henry Waxman's Public Health Emergency Act went to Hatch's committee [in 1983], he made the unusual parliamentary move of holding the bill at his desk and allowing it to go straight to the Senate floor without a hearing. Hatch figured it was better to have no hearing, than one in which health issues would get mixed up with the fringe Moral Majority politics. These were the legislative acrobatics that AIDS would routinely demand on the Hill for years to come."

Later that year Hatch was instrumental in having Dr. James Mason, formerly public health director for Utah, appointed director of the CDC. Although gay leaders initially were dubious about the appointment, writes Shilts, Mason "proved an unusual ally for researchers" and "had an ingrained American sensibility about fairness and couldn't see the sense in letting a horrible epidemic rage through the nation, even if he personally objected to the sexual proclivities of the people it largely struck." Mason later became head of the Public Health Service.

In 1984, researchers at the National Cancer Institute (NCI) in Bethesda, Maryland, and at the Pasteur Institute in Paris independently but almost simultaneously identified HIV as the probable cause of AIDS. The following year, American virologist Robert C. Gallo at the NCI developed a test kit approved to screen blood for the virus.

Testing became a national issue, however, with some people fearing reprisals if it were known they carried the virus. Hatch was the chief proponent in Congress of legislation to ensure the confidentiality of test results, reasoning that gay men and others at high risk would not submit to testing unless they were assured it would not ruin their lives.

In September 1986, the drug AZT was found to be effective in retarding the progress of HIV. Two months later, in the November elections, Democrats wrested control of the Senate from Republicans, relegating Hatch to the top-ranking minority member on the Labor and Human Resources Committee, with Democrat Ted Kennedy of Massachusetts replacing him as chairman.

One of the most critical questions facing the committee was what to do about AIDS. Kennedy and Hatch's answer was the first comprehensive national proposal offering policy outlines for dealing with the epidemic. It was part of an omnibus package that included various other health provisions. Among AIDS components it:

- Established the National AIDS Commission to promote the development of a national consensus on AIDS policy and map out a coordinated approach to the disease. It would take up where a commission appointed by President Reagan left off.

- Approved a three-year authorization of $270 million for AIDS education.

• Appropriated $400 million for anonymous counseling and testing and services for AIDS patients.

• Directed the hiring of nearly 800 new federal AIDS researchers.

Considerable opposition arose to the proposal–from within the Reagan Administration and from conservatives in Congress and elsewhere. During floor debate in April 1988, tempers flared. When Senate Majority Leader Robert Byrd of West Virginia tried to temporarily set aside consideration of the AIDS bill (S. 1220) to consider two veterans' bills, Republican Lowell Weicker Jr. of Connecticut came unglued.

"I find it strange that we can pass veterans' legislation so speedily and so cleanly, but somehow we cannot address the greatest threat that has been posed to this nation since World War II," said Weicker. Shouts of approval echoed from the visitors' gallery, which was filled with supporters of the bill.

"What can be more important than 1.5 million people infected with the AIDS virus, many of whom are going to die?" asked Weicker.

As North Carolina's Jesse Helms sought to attach a killer amendment to the bill, Hatch faced down his fellow conservative. "Let us quit judging and let us start doing what is right," said Hatch. "This bill is not a homosexual rights bill, but a public health bill. It is to help people who need help, and that includes homosexuals." He noted that, while homosexuals and intravenous drug users were the largest groups of AIDS sufferers, others had contracted it through contaminated blood and heterosexual relations.

Helms: "The point is, we should not allow the homosexual crowd to use the AIDS issue to promote and legitimize their lifestyle in American society. And that is what is going on."

Hatch: "I do not agree with [gays'] sexual preferences. But that does not mean I do not have compassion for them; that I am just going to write them off and tell them to forget it, go ahead and die, because they differ from me."

Hatch's side prevailed; the bill passed the Senate on an overwhelming vote of 87 to 4, and also passed the House by a wide margin. Although President Reagan was urged to veto the measure, Hatch lobbied him hard to sign it. "I think this is not only the best we could get, it's a darn fine bill and it's going to save a lot of lives," said Hatch. Reagan signed it into law on

November 4, 1988.

The Reagan Administration itself was deeply divided over AIDS, with Education Secretary William Bennett siding with Helms and squaring off against Surgeon General C. Everett Koop, who argued that moral judgments about homosexuals and drug abuse were beside the point in a public health debate. Bennett and other conservatives favored mandatory testing and reporting requirements, while Koop argued that those at greatest risk of AIDS would be forced underground if faced with such tests.

Koop's strong stance made him a pariah among many conservatives. When a dinner was held in his honor, far-right leaders Paul Weyrich and Phyllis Schlafly sent Hatch and others letters, telling them to withdraw as sponsors. They succeeded in scaring off some sponsors, including several Republican presidential aspirants, but not Hatch, who not only attended the event but gave a speech paying tribute to Koop for his dedication to saving lives.

In June 1987, Reagan had appointed a special commission to study AIDS and make policy recommendations to the Administration. After initial turmoil that reflected national divisions, late that year the panel, under retired Admiral James D. Watkins, began its work.

In thirty-nine days of hearings, Watkins said later, nearly 800 witnesses "made clear to us that if the nation does not address the [discrimination] issue squarely, it will be very difficult to solve most other HIV-related problems. People simply will not come forward to be tested, or will not supply names of sexual contacts for notification, if they feel they will lose their jobs and homes based on an HIV-positive test."

The Watkins' panel released its final report in June 1988, which surprised many observers by generally siding with the Kennedy-Hatch approach. It urged anti-discrimination protection for those who tested positive for exposure to HIV. That same month, the National Academy of Sciences (NAS) released its own report also calling for federal anti-discrimination laws to protect those carrying the virus.

Public health officials cheered the recommendations of the NAS and Watkins commission, while many conservatives blasted them. Led by Jesse Helms in the Senate and GOP Congressman William Dannemeyer of California in the House, conservatives sought routine, mandatory testing of large groups of people, with public health authorities given the names of those who tested positive.

The White House initially refused to accept its own panel's

recommendations on anti-discrimination, as President Reagan turned to his drug-abuse advisor, Dr. Donald Ian Macdonald, to implement AIDS policy. Macdonald said most of the commission's 340 recommendations had been or would be implemented, but not the critical anti-discrimination measure because some people in the White House had expressed what he called an "unwillingness to reward the behaviors that cause AIDS."

While Supreme Court decisions chipped away at the Administration's position, the impasse was not finally resolved until 1990 with passage of the Americans With Disabilities Act–passed in good measure because of Hatch–which included people with AIDS and HIV among those given federal protection from discrimination.

The next major legislative action came in 1990 with a bill sponsored in the House by Henry Waxman and in the Senate by Hatch and Kennedy. By mid-summer of that year, the Public Health Service reported there had been more than 143,000 known cases of AIDS in the United States, including nearly 90,000 people who had died. Another one million Americans were infected with HIV.

Although steps had been taken by then to protect the nation's blood supply, they came too late for some citizens, including Ryan White, an Indiana youth who put a public face on the dread disease. White was a hemophiliac who contracted HIV through tainted blood-clotting products. He was barred from attending school, and his court fight to be reinstated drew wide public attention. White died in April 1990 at the age of eighteen.

Since AIDS was primarily a disease of young males and others not adequately insured or eligible for Medicare, health facilities in hard-hit areas were swamped with charity cases–often in hospitals when less expensive care would suffice if it were available.

In March 1990, fast-track legislation was introduced by Hatch and Kennedy to deal with the emergency. By the first week in April the measure had passed the Labor and Human Resources Committee on a unanimous vote. It allotted funds to hard-hit areas as well as grants to states to develop and operate programs to provide comprehensive care for AIDS and HIV sufferers.

Actress Elizabeth Taylor, at a news conference with Hatch, noted that "Thousands and thousands of lives hang in the balance unless we begin to treat AIDS as a true national emergency."

When the bill reached the Senate floor in May, the arguments mirrored the 1988 AIDS debate, with North Carolina's Jesse Helms again the leading foe. Helms said the crisis was being exaggerated by an AIDS lobby, and was consuming funds needed to fight diseases afflicting many more citizens, including Alzheimer's, cancer, and diabetes. Those Americans, he charged, "are being cast aside, along with common sense, in the headlong rush to feed the appetite of a movement which will not be satisfied until the social fabric of the nation is irreparably changed."

With that, an angry Hatch threw down his prepared text and once more took on his fellow conservative. "Should we just let the disease run rampant because we do not agree with the morals of certain people?" asked Hatch. "I do not condone homosexual activity, but that does not have a thing to do with this bill. AIDS is a public health problem....There are a lot of good people who are infected with the AIDS virus who make contributions to our society. We should provide them compassion and care."

During the heated debate, Hatch glanced up at the visitors' gallery and saw Mrs. Jeanne White, mother of Ryan White who had died the previous month. She looked dejected, as the debate was not faring well that day. Suddenly Hatch made a motion to change the bill's title to the "Ryan White Comprehensive AIDS Resources Emergency Act of 1990." The full Senate, on a voice vote, agreed. White's name was about to pass from newspaper headlines into public law.

On May 16 the Senate passed the bill on a vote of 95 to 4. Early in August, following a Senate-House conference, a compromise bill that included $900 million in emergency funding for fiscal 1991 and other unspecified funds over the next four years, was sent to President George Bush. Like Reagan, Bush considered a veto. Again Hatch lobbied the President hard to approve it. On August 18, Bush signed into law the Ryan White Act.

For Hatch, another human face on the AIDS saga was that of Terry Beirn, a top Labor Committee assistant to Senator Kennedy. Beirn had helped staff seven Labor Committee hearings on AIDS between 1987 and 1989. A native New Yorker, Beirn was an honors English graduate of Yale University and had been a radio reporter in New York and San Francisco. In 1984 Beirn, suffering from AIDS-related symptoms, returned to the East, where he helped found the American Foundation for AIDS Research (AmFAR).

Actress Elizabeth Taylor also was instrumental in starting the organization. She came to Hatch's office personally to thank him for supporting the foundation, which later gave the Senator its "man of the year" award.

In July 1991, Nancy Taylor, a Labor Committee staffer, told Hatch that Beirn was in a New York hospital with AIDS and a probable melanoma on the brain. Expecting to die, he asked to talk to Hatch before the surgery. Hatch called immediately. Beirn thanked the Senator for his compassion and work on behalf of AIDS patients and asked for his prayers. Hatch assured him of them. When Beirn died days later, Hatch, against the advice of his political advisors, co-hosted a memorial service held for Beirn in the Labor Committee room. Among other things, Hatch said:

> I am honored to say a few words about the legacy he left upon this earth. I had the privilege of talking with Terry while he was desperately ill. He faced his illness with guts, courage, and a strong, abiding faith.
>
> This country owes a great debt of gratitude to Terry. Over 100,000 Americans have died because of AIDS. Terry worked diligently to find cures and treatments for these and other Americans who are infected. Legislation that Senator Kennedy and I worked on to expand research, treatment, and prevention efforts will help resolve the AIDS issue. Terry was a large part of that effort....Terry also recognized that AIDS affects every American, regardless of belief, regardless of sexual orientation, regardless of lifestyle or community....In [AmFAR] he hoped to make people aware all over this country of the problems related to AIDS. To Terry's father, his sister, and brother, Chris, who is here, I want you to know that Terry has left the world a better place.

The following month, the Terry Beirn Act was signed into law. It amended the Public Health Service act to require that clinical trials be designed to encourage participation by existing HIV primary care providers. The intent was to bring such trials closer to the patients. It required federal health agencies to work collaboratively with pharmaceutical companies and local health providers in designing and conducting clinical trials.

The pioneering act provided the model adopted by other disease groups, including breast cancer patients, to get the latest and best research to the most patients as quickly as possible.

Other advances against AIDS have followed on other fronts. Notably, during the early 1990s, before perinatal preventive treatments were available, an estimated 1,000 to 2,000 babies with HIV infection were born each year in the United States. These numbers have been reduced dramatically, through counseling and voluntary testing of pregnant women and use of AZT by infected women during pregnancy and delivery, and for the infant after birth. Between 1992 and 1997, perinatally acquired AIDS cases declined 66 percent in the United States.

At the dawn of a new century, it may be difficult for most Americans to even recall that for much of the last two decades, AIDS was the nation's number one public health concern. But self-satisfaction is dangerous. While AIDS has dropped out of the leading causes of death for Americans as a whole, it continues to devastate other populations.

Consider these sobering numbers at the end of 1998:

AIDS was still the fifth leading cause of death for Americans between the ages of twenty-five and forty-four. Among African American men and women in this age group, it was the leading cause of death. While African Americans of all ages represent 12 percent of the total U.S. population, they made up nearly 37 percent of reported AIDS cases.

Hispanics represented 13 percent of the population but accounted for 20 percent of reported cases. The AIDS incidence among Hispanics was 28 per 100,000 population–nearly four times the rate for whites.

While recent advances have gone far to protect infants in the United States, AIDS has afflicted more than 6,500 children under the age of five; 1,900 from age five to twelve, and 3,400 from thirteen to nineteen.

Meanwhile, though the United States has taken strong measures to combat AIDS, prodded by Hatch and other leaders, little has been done to halt the worldwide epidemic. An estimated 95 percent of AIDS sufferers live abroad. The U.S. Centers for Disease Control and Prevention estimates that worldwide, some 33 million people–43 percent of them women–are living with HIV/AIDS, including 1.2 million children under age fifteen.

The United Nations estimates that 16 million have died from AIDS since the epidemic began, more than half of them in eastern and southern Africa, leaving some 10 million AIDS orphans on the continent. The disease is so devastating in Africa that in January 2000 the U.N. Security Council took up the issue for the first time, calling AIDS a threat to peace because high death rates among Africa's elite government, police, and armed forces leaders jeopardize the ability of some countries to govern effectively. In 1998, wars in Africa killed 200 thousand people. AIDS in Africa killed an estimated 2 million people. During 2000, Senator Hatch was working to get more money for African AIDS initiatives.

In October 1999, the fifth International Congress on AIDS in Asia opened in Kuala Lumpur, Malaysia. "AIDS has never posed a bigger threat to development than it does now," said Malaysian Prime Minister Mahathir Mohamad, calling upon pharmaceutical companies to lower the cost of AIDS drugs for poor countries. About 7 million people in the Asia-Pacific region are living with AIDS or HIV, he said.

Echoing the U.S. debate on AIDS, Mahathir criticized conservative authorities for seizing slogans instead of solutions: "For too long, many religious officials have hidden behind a veil of denial, condemning those who have been infected while doing little to prevent others from suffering the same fate."

That same month, in Indianapolis, Jeanne White-Ginder announced she was closing the doors of the Ryan White Foundation, named for her son, because of dwindling donations. Foundation leaders attributed the drop in funds to a general belief that the AIDS crisis was over.

In fact, said the group's chairman, Mark Maddox, "the AIDS epidemic is in the midst of one of its worst crises yet–the crisis of complacency."

12

Education

Of all the occupations in America, teachers may deserve their own "appreciation day" the most. Perhaps no occupation influences the future of our country more.

IN FEBRUARY 1999 THE UTAH State Legislature was rushing toward the close of its annual forty-five-day session. Among programs about to be abandoned for lack of funds was one establishing the Center for the School of the Future at Utah State University. The center, which was praised by many Utah educators, would facilitate teacher interaction and improve primary and secondary education through identifying, testing, and publicizing "best practices" found in schools throughout the nation.

After the center failed initially to win legislative support, a USU official telephoned Senator Hatch in Washington, carefully explaining the promising program. Hatch immediately saw the center's potential. Within an hour, he had contacted Utah Governor Mike Leavitt, urging him to use his influence with legislators on behalf of the center. The Governor, prodded again by Hatch in a second telephone call a few days later, met with legislative leaders and struck an agreement to give the center $250,000 a year. The center was saved, and has since begun to soar.

Hatch's quick and effective response was typical of his strong support for education. For a decade and a half he played a key role on the Senate committee that handles education–the Labor and Human Resources Committee (whose name was changed in 1999 to the Committee on Health, Education, Labor and Pensions). Hatch chaired the panel from 1981 to 1986 and was its ranking minority member from 1987 to 1992. He played an important role in every education bill considered by the Senate during that period, and, though no longer assigned to the committee, continues to work hard for America's teachers and students.

While the primary policy role in American education comes at the state and district level, the federal government also plays a vital role, both through the power of the purse strings and through federal mandates that filter down to every public classroom.

Individual teachers will benefit financially from a measure principally cosponsored by Hatch and passed unanimously by the Senate in March 2000. The amendment, sponsored by Hatch along with Senator Susan Collins, R-Maine, gives educators an enhanced tax deduction on money spent to keep themselves current in their fields of knowledge.

The amendment to the Affordable Education Act also allows teachers a $100 tax credit for materials they supply for their classrooms out of their own pockets. Under current law, such expenses are deductible only when they exceed 2 percent of the taxpayer's adjusted gross income. The amendment exempts teacher development expenses from the 2 percent floor, making it easier to deduct the costs.

"Many Americans may be unaware that many teachers subsidize their schools out of their own pockets," explained Hatch. He noted they purchase items for classrooms ranging from extra worksheets, art supplies, tablets, and pencils to library books and educational games. "These dedicated teachers incur personal expenses for materials for their classrooms because they love teaching and care about their students. This tax change is justified because teachers, unlike many other professionals who may take deductions, are engaged in nonprofit public service."

Hatch, who chairs the Senate subcommittee on taxation, explained that the $100 credit for classroom supplies represents a dollar-for-dollar reduction in tax liability. "This amendment will provide modest tax relief for teachers who, for too long, have been footing the bill themselves for improving the quality of teaching. It is time we helped out by getting our tax policy in sync with our goals for education."

Hatch has had a reverence for teachers and the teaching profession since he was a small boy growing up in Pittsburgh. He sometimes had feelings of inferiority, in part because of humble family circumstances that forced him to attend school in worn, second-hand clothes. But he recalls fondly that his teachers made him feel equal in every way to other students, and helped Orrin reappraise himself and gain the confidence to succeed in life.

Knowing that a warm welcome awaited him at McGibney Elementary, Orrin relished walking the half-mile to school on even the iciest winter days. At McGibney he became an exceptional student with an uncanny ability to memorize lesson material. He saw, even at that early age, that education is the great equalizer, offering wondrous psychic benefits and, he suspected, even greater rewards down the road for those who excelled.

Later, at Baldwin High School, English teacher Eleanor Smith had the greatest influence on him. "She gave me a love for English literature which has been with me all my life," says Hatch. "She was able to get across the idea and concept that English study creates lifelong benefits." He continued to correspond with Smith for decades, and her inspiration has borne considerable fruit, as Hatch has authored several books as well as hundreds of poems, song lyrics, public statements, and Senate speeches.

Hatch is also proud that his wife, Elaine, holds a college degree in elementary education, was teaching school when they married, and, as a substitute teacher, helped support their young family as Orrin earned his undergraduate and law degrees.

"Of all the occupations in America, teachers may deserve their own 'appreciation day' the most," Hatch said on the Senate floor during national Teacher Appreciation Week in May 1999.

"Perhaps no occupation influences the future of our country more ....Teaching is not just a job, it's a calling. It is a calling to impart knowledge, to mete out discipline, to inspire, to motivate." He then told of "one special teacher who made a real difference" in his life, a Mr. McElroy:

> When I was a young boy, I played my violin in the school orchestra. On the day of one of our most important performances, the student who was supposed to play a solo on the bass got sick and was unable to perform. My music director, Mr. McElroy, came to me and convinced me that, even though I had never played the bass, I could perform the solo.
>
> I had terrible doubts about my ability to step in and do the job. But Mr. McElroy had confidence in me, even if I didn't. And he worked with me and encouraged me and coached me for most of that afternoon. That night I was able to play the solo without making a mistake.
>
> As I think back on it, this was one experience that taught me that if I applied myself I could meet a challenge. When, in 1976, everyone believed I was a long shot to win the nomination and, indeed, the election to become Utah's senator, I should have told them about Mr. McElroy.

Hatch also paid tribute to Utah's 1998 teacher of the year, Diane Crim, who taught math at Salt Lake City's Clayton Intermediate School, and Dave Sanders, the Littleton, Colorado teacher who was brutally slain a week before Teacher Appreciation Week while trying to protect students during the massacre at Columbine High School.

"Mr. McElroy, Diane Crim, and Dave Sanders all represent the best of the teaching profession," said Hatch. "There are thousands of others we could mention who have helped our children learn the keys for living such as reading, math, science, and history. But, more than that, they have helped reinforce values like hard work, perseverance, team work, and integrity."

The Senator is a strong supporter of the Title VI flexible block grant program, whose funds are used by teachers for a variety of needs, including professional development. He also has been a major advocate for math and science programs that provide resources for advanced education, workshops, and in-service training for teachers in those subjects.

Congress overwhelmingly passed a bill co-sponsored by Hatch in 1999 to permit all fifty states to waive certain education regulations that prevent programming and educational reform. The approach, popularly called "Ed-Flex," would free states or individual school districts within them from many federal regulations so long as they were progressing toward improving student performance. "Education should be governed at the local and state levels, in effect providing fifty state laboratories from which everyone can look for better ideas," said Hatch.

"It will help de-bureaucratize our schools," said Hatch. "For too long our school boards, principals, and teachers have not been able to think in terms of doing the best things for education, but rather the things prescribed by regulations," he said. "I have heard repeatedly from citizens in Utah that education is among their top concerns. But they want the federal government as a partner, not as the ultimate authority on educational policy and maker of decisions that should rest with their own elected school boards." Hatch said the measure tells state and local educators "We trust you and we support you."

At the same time, Hatch believes no child should be stuck in an underperforming or unsafe school, and that low-income families should have the same ability as affluent families to choose better schools. He supports vouchers for students wishing to escape poor schools.

The Senator is acutely aware that teacher salaries and other educational resources–largely state rather than federal issues–are not as strong as they should be, notably in his own state of Utah, which has the nation's highest percentage of school-age children and the lowest percentage of working-age adults. Utah has a strong education tradition, and spends a relatively high proportion of state funds on education. But because of its unusually high ratio of children, Utah's spending per student is the lowest in the nation, though its students typically test better than national averages on standardized exams.

Hatch is working hard to change the inherently unfair formula of Title I of the Elementary and Secondary Education Act (ESEA), under which more federal funds are awarded for students living in wealthy states than for those living in relatively poor states. Years ago Hatch succeeded in changing the reauthorization language of ESEA to help ensure that resources are more fairly distributed among school districts. The Clinton-Gore Administration, however, routinely has refused to fund the equalization section of Title I. Hatch said he will continue to try to amend ESEA to force the federal government "to correct this terribly inequitable funding formula."

The U.S. Department of Education notified seventeen of the twenty-one Utah school districts receiving Title I concentration grants that, based on the department's census data, they are no longer eligible for the grants. Senator Hatch is very concerned about potential loss to the seventeen districts and, early in 2000, was working on a long-range solution. Meanwhile, in the short range, the districts were held harmless for the current fiscal year in an emergency supplemental appropriations bill.

Hatch also is a longtime supporter of the Impact Aid program, which helps compensate school districts that are substantially affected by large federal installations, such as military bases. These federal installations do not have to pay taxes to the state and county, depriving them of needed revenues. Impact Aid helps to make up the difference.

"Anything we can do through tax incentives to help families and the state make education more affordable is important," said Hatch during a March 1999 hearing before the Senate Finance Committee.

"I do have to brag a little about my home state," he said. "While Utah does not fare well under the current formula for federal education funding, Utah does more with less better than any state in the nation. For example, Utah is first in the nation in both advanced placement (taking college classes in high school) participation and performance on a per capita basis. Utah is second in the nation in the percentage of its adult population holding a high school diploma."

Hatch has used his clout as chairman of the Senate Finance Committee's taxation subcommittee to make education more affordable for families. "Wherever I go I hear again and again how the cost of education at today's colleges and universities is going up," he said in the March hearing. "As a father who has put six children through college, I know how parents are sacrificing to provide their children with a college education."

In recent years Hatch helped push into law such measures as allowing Individual Retirement Account (IRA) withdrawals for education purposes, creating education savings accounts, creating tax credits for education, allowing a deduction for student loan interest, and making it easier to use a qualified state tuition program.

The Senator supported the A+ Education Savings Account which, among other things, would have increased the contribution for educational savings to $2,000, expanded the qualified educational expenses to include the costs of elementary and secondary education, and extended the current exemption from gross income for employer-provided education expenses through 2002. Although Congress passed the measure, it was vetoed by President Clinton.

Hatch also supported the 1999 Senate-passed tax reduction measure which included provisions to eliminate the five-year limit on tax deductions for student loan interest and to authorize private universities to have tax-deferred pre-paid tuition plans.

School infrastructure is another critical issue, said Hatch, with more and more districts seeking help to save crumbling, overcrowded facilities. Utah, for example, has 40 school districts and 763 public schools on which the state spends about $350 million annually in new repairs—mostly from district tax levies. The need for new schools in states with high population growth, such as Utah, is also acute. While Utah builds about a dozen new schools a year, as of spring 1999 the high cost of new construction had pushed Utah students into 1,150 portable buildings.

A measure introduced by Hatch and passed by Congress in 1999 enabled the Ogden-Weber school districts in Utah to lease a military facility at no cost. The Hatch bill, called the Surplus Defense Property for Public Education Act of 1999, allows tax-supported public education entities, including school districts and technical institutes, to receive at no cost surplus properties under the Base Realignment and Closure Act (BRAC), provided that the facilities are used for educational purposes.

Hatch has huddled with U.S. tax and education experts in an attempt to strengthen the federal role in funding school infrastructure, thereby freeing up more state and local funds for other purposes. "It seems to me that there could be more creative ways of solving this problem than another big federal direct spending program," he told the Senate Finance Committee. "We certainly do not want federal ownership of school buildings. But there is a federal role in helping to finance the necessary infrastructure for education."

While helping with traditional bricks and mortar, Senator Hatch also is a strong supporter of distance learning–especially important in spread-out Utah, where many students live far away from campuses and would be denied higher education if classes weren't delivered nearby.

Utah State University, in Logan, has one of the nation's leading distance-education programs, involving a number of branch campuses and downlink satellite sites at some eighty locations throughout Utah and into nearby states. USU's off-campus program offers more than a dozen bachelor's or master's degrees, involving thousands of students, including about 500 who receive degrees annually without ever going to the Logan campus.

In April 1999 Hatch brought the federal government's top copyright officials to Utah to meet with representatives of Utah's education, library, and high-tech communities on the subject of distance learning in the digital age. They met with more than a dozen educational institutions and high-tech companies and witnessed Utah's leading distance education technologies. "We saw more in-depth, complex demonstrations than we've currently seen," said MaryBeth Peters, U.S. Register of Copyrights. "We came away with a much better understanding of the way that this is evolving."

The Senator has long been a leading supporter of Boys and Girls Clubs, which work hand in hand with schools to keep youth off the streets and engaged in wholesome activities. In 1996 Congress enacted Hatch's legislation authorizing $100 million in federal funds over five years to establish and expand clubs in public housing and distressed areas. After it was signed into law, he then made certain it was fully funded by House and Senate appropriations committees.

Researchers at Columbia University found that public housing developments that have active Boys and Girls Clubs have a 25 percent reduction in the presence of crack cocaine, a 22 percent reduction in overall drug activity, and a 13 percent reduction in juvenile crime. Club members also do better in school and are less attracted to gangs.

Noted alumni of Boys and Girls Clubs include actor Denzel Washington, former basketball superstar Michael Jordan, and San Francisco 49ers quarterback Steve Young.

In 1997 Hatch introduced a measure providing seed money to enable Boys and Girls Clubs to expand to 2,500 and serve an additional one million youth. "We are providing seed money for the construction and expansion of clubs to serve our young people," he explained. "This is bricks and mortar money to open clubs, and after they are opened they will operate without any significant federal funds. In my view this is a model for the proper role of the federal government in crime prevention."

Hatch said programs such as Boys and Girls Clubs are critical to help fight the rise of gangs and drug use among youth. "By some estimates there are more than 3,875 youth gangs" as of 1997, he said. "They have 200,000 members in the nation's 79 largest cities, and the numbers are increasing." His home state of Utah is not immune, said Hatch. In Salt Lake City, during the four years from 1992 to 1996 the number of identified gangs increased 55 percent, from 185 to 288; the number of gang members increased 146 percent, from 1,438 to 3,545, and the number of gang-related crimes increased 279 percent, from 1,741 in 1992 to 6,611 in 1996.

"Every day our young people are being bombarded with cultural messages in music, movies, and television that undermine the development of core values of citizenship," Hatch explained. "Popular culture and the media glorify drug use, meaningless violence, and sex without commitment. The importance of Boys and Girls Clubs in fighting these trends cannot be overstated."

Hatch is also the Senate's leading voice in seeking other ways to curb juvenile crime. He authored S. 254, a comprehensive youth violence bill, introduced in 1999. A product of some two years of hearings and research by the Senate Judiciary Committee, which he heads, in 2000 it was the most deliberated and sweeping crime bill before Congress. It seeks to deter youth criminal behavior, punish offenders, and to head off anti-social behavior through mentoring and other pro-active programs.

Among other things, the bill includes provisions to fight gangs and discourage teens from joining them; find alternative placement for disruptive students; authorize funds for drug testing and drug treatment programs; facilitate the transfer of disciplinary records among school districts; allow criminal background checks for persons seeking school employment; permit funds to be used by school personnel for crisis preparedness and violence prevention programs, and allow funds for the purchase of security equipment safety improvements.

"Our nation has been riveted by a series of horrific school shootings in recent years," he said in an August 1999 hearing, "which culminated this spring with the tragic deaths of twelve students and one teacher at Columbine High School in Colorado. Sadly, the killings at Columbine were not an isolated event." Hatch said in 1997, juveniles accounted for nearly one-fifth of all criminal arrests in the U.S., committing 13.5 percent of murders, some 17 percent of rapes, nearly 30 percent of robberies, and 50 percent of arsons.

The Senator has spoken out strongly about the impact of media violence on youth, and released a major report by his committee called "Children, Violence, and the Media."

"The report confirms what most of us have suspected for some time: Pervasive media violence leads to real-world violence," said Hatch. "Over the past 40 years more than 1,000 studies have examined the effects of media violence, and the predominant finding has not changed. Exposure to media portrayals of violence increases aggressive behavior in children. As one expert has put it, arguing against the link between media violence and the violent actions of our youth is 'like arguing against gravity.'"

Key recommendations in the report, many of which are in S. 254 or its House counterpart, H.R. 1501, seek national reform to reduce the amount of media violence and limit children's exposure to it. The proposals seek to empower parents and encourage responsible behavior by the media industry, rather than relying on government compulsion or creation of a new federal bureaucracy. Recommendations include:

- Ensure that parents have access to filtering technology that will empower them to block access to Internet content they deem unsuitable for their children.

- Enact a limited antitrust exemption enabling entertainment industries to enforce their existing ratings systems.

- Provide for a national media campaign to educate parents about existing ratings systems, the V chip, Internet filtering technology, and other tools available to parents.

- Encourage the television, motion picture, music, and video game industries to develop a uniform ratings system for their products that would be easier for parents to understand and apply.

The Senator himself personifies lifelong learning. He enjoys art and music and is a voracious reader as well as writer of both fiction and nonfiction. He has long been one of the leading figures in Congress in sponsoring hearings to investigate creative new approaches to national problems in many fields, including education.

Hatch also believes strongly that students should work on developing good character as much as on academic and job-related skills. In a keynote speech when receiving an honorary degree at Dixie College in St. George, Utah, in 1998, he urged graduates "to build on your education and experience at Dixie College to be the best person you can be. Character in our society has for too long been underrated as a virtue–and questionable character for too long seen as a symptom and not as a cause of societal problems."

Greatness, he said, is not defined only in such terms as Olympic medals or Nobel prizes, "but also as raising good families, doing honest work, and being kind to your neighbors."

Hatch added:

> I would rather be remembered for my integrity than the bills I passed. But good character doesn't come automatically. Each of us has to fight a variety of temptations every day. Each of us must work to overcome a weakness of one type or another....Whether you choose to continue your formal education or not, you must never stop learning. Read. Enjoy music and art. Take up a sport–perhaps one you've never played or watched. Visit new places. Try food from a foreign country. Find some new constellations in the night sky. The key is not to get stale. Keep your mind working and your outlook fresh....Do not neglect your spiritual growth. Whatever your religious roots may be, nurture them. Our faith can guide our vision. It can direct our actions. It can be a strong foundation for whatever we choose to build in terms of our career goals, our communities, our families, our government, and our own happiness.

13

Toward a Colorblind Society

I believe in equality of opportunity, but not equality of condition or result ....There is no such thing as reverse discrimination. There is only discrimination, pure and simple, whether it runs forward or in reverse.

LIBERAL COLUMNIST MARY McGRORY, no fan of Hatch, in 1997 conceded: "William T. Coleman Jr., the black man appointed by President Gerald Ford to be secretary of transportation, who is now the Grand Old Man of the remnants of moderate Republicanism, says 'there is not a scintilla of racism in Hatch–I spent five days with him in 1991 talking about the civil rights bill, and there was no trace.'"

That will come as no surprise to those who know Hatch. Those who don't deserve a more complete explanation of where he stands on one of the most divisive issues of our time.

For starters, consider the 1980 Republican National Convention. Senator Hatch ended one convention session with an unscripted prayer that included these words: "Help us to stamp out discrimination, but not by discriminating."

Most listeners probably scratched their heads at that. But one group knew all too well what he meant. They had been denied employment or educational opportunities because of so-called "reverse discrimination"–an attempt to remedy the effects of past discrimination against others at their expense.

The 1964 Civil Rights Act–the most far-reaching civil rights measure in U.S. history–committed America to the proposition that all citizens were to be treated equal under the law. It prohibited discrimination in employment, education, and public accommodations on the basis of race, color, religion, national origin, or sex. Subsequent Supreme Court and lower court rulings, however, went beyond the Act's intent to allow preferential treatment of targeted groups at the expense of members of other groups, opening a Pandora's Box of unfairness.

"I believe in equality of opportunity, but not equality of condition or result," Hatch explains. "Preferences and quotas favoring one group virtually always hurt another. There is no such thing as reverse discrimination. There is only discrimination, pure and simple, whether it runs forward or in reverse."

Occasionally the issue hits the headlines, as in 1978 when the Supreme Court ruled that the UC Davis Medical School had discriminated against Allan Bakke, a white male, by following an affirmative action plan that included a fixed, numerical racial quota. However, the court also ruled in *California Regents v. Bakke* that race may be a *factor* in admitting minority students. In subsequent cases it upheld the lawfulness of giving minorities and women preferential treatment to redress imbalances in the work force.

The result has been government-sponsored discrimination, and has led to results that defy all logic. In California, for example, notes a group of scholars, "Taking into account women, the disabled, nonwhite immigrants, and minorities, nearly 75 percent of all Californians today are members of a protected affirmative action class–in fact everyone except white males."

While white males are the largest single group affected, by no means are they the only ones:

• Jennifer Riel, the daughter of hard-working Filipino immigrants, had been a student officer and class valedictorian at Sweetwater High School in Chula Vista, California in 1991 when she applied to attend UC Berkeley. At least five classmates from Sweetwater who had lower grades and SAT scores were accepted to Berkeley, but Jennifer was not. The reason: They belonged to minority groups "under-represented" in the UC system.

• Janine Jacinto was a 39-year-old single mother of four children and a Phi Kappa Phi honors student in anthropology at California State University, Sacramento, in 1994. She applied for the university's graduate program in social work but was rejected. A stunned professor asked if she had checked the Hispanic box on the affirmative action form. "No, I can't lie about my ethnicity because I'm not Hispanic," she answered. Further investigation discovered the department's confidential rating sheet that awarded as many as 13 out of 38 total points for being an under-represented minority and other aspects related to race or ethnicity.

• Patrick Loen was denied admission to an elite public magnet school in San Francisco because he is Chinese American. Under the district's diversity system, Chinese Americans had to have a higher score of 62, whereas the minimum for whites and other Asians was 58, the minimum for blacks and Hispanics was even lower. Patrick's mother testified before a hearing chaired by Hatch in 1997. "Patrick would have gotten into Lowell if he were white, Japanese, or black," said Charlene Loen. "He was rejected because he is Chinese American."

"The Chinese quota was in effect full," said Hatch. "That is not the promise of America." He added that "The question we all must answer is whether one American's racial suffering should be valued above another's. It is a question that will only become more complicated and more urgent as our population grows ever more diverse." The nation is at a crossroads, says Hatch. "Down one path is the way of mutual understanding and good will; the way of equal opportunity for individuals....Down the other path is the way of mutual suspicion, fear, ill will, and indifference; the way of group rights and preferences."

Hatch supports legislation directing the federal government to do away with quotas and other discrimination on the basis of race, color, national origin, or sex. It would not, however, stop special outreach, recruiting and marketing efforts to these groups–the original intent of affirmative action.

President Clinton, whose political base is rooted in those receiving preferential treatment, has threatened to veto any such move. The Administration and its allies have smeared those who support the legislation, charging they are trying to turn back the civil rights clock and wipe out decades of progress for women and minorities. Clinton and his allies also have not hesitated to play the race card on behalf of specific minority candidates for office–leveling ugly charges against anyone who opposes them, no matter the reasons.

In the longest-running case, Senator Hatch has steadfastly opposed the appointment of Bill Lann Lee, a Chinese American, as the Justice Department's civil rights chief. Hatch and others have opposed Lee on the basis that he went too far as a lawyer for the NAACP in pressuring companies , municipalities, and local governments to adopt racial quotas to avoid court action. However, President Clinton has been just as adamant, making an end run around the Senate confirmation process by naming Lee "acting" civil rights chief–a title he has held while doing the job since 1997.

The imbroglio has been troubling for Hatch precisely because Lee is a minority–opening the Senator to charges of racism, however unfair, and because Hatch genuinely admires Lee. "I believe Mr. Lee is a very fine man, a man of conviction and a skilled lawyer," said Hatch. "I like him personally and would support him for almost any other position in government, but not one that allows him to implement unconstitutional policies."

On October 5, 1999, on a straight party line vote, the Senate defeated the nomination of Missouri Judge Ronnie White, an African American, to the federal bench there. Senator Patrick Leahy of Vermont–Hatch's minority counterpart as ranking Democrat on the Judiciary Committee–suggested Republicans had adopted a "color test" for nominees. President Clinton said the rejection "provides strong evidence for those who believe that the Senate treats minority and women judicial nominees unequally."

The rejection showed no such thing. In fact, White's case was so rare that it proved the rule: Minorities and women have fared exceptionally well before the Hatch-led Judiciary Committee as well as before the entire Senate. Clinton, speaking to the American Bar Association that summer, noted the number of minorities and women he has placed on the federal bench, calling them "the most diverse group in American history."

Clinton can't have it both ways. Each of the judges he points to with pride was confirmed by the Senate, and all with Republican support. The Department of Justice reported that in 1998, about 32 percent of judicial nominees were women, and 21.5 percent were minorities. Hatch's Judiciary Committee staff computed that in 1999, over 45 percent of judicial nominees cleared by the committee and reported to the Senate floor were women or minorities.

Hatch has worked behind the scenes to dissuade the Administration from forwarding some potential nominees whom he considered bad choices. But he nas never done so on the basis of sex or minority status. Hatch's opposition to White was a rare exception. White was strongly opposed by Missouri's two senators and a host of law enforcement officials for his lenient record on death penalty cases.

Among other reasons they opposed White, local and national law enforcement agencies said he had opposed the death penalty three times more often than other Missouri judges. In one particularly egregious case, he reportedly tried to overturn the death penalty of a murderer who stalked and killed a sheriff, two deputies, and the wife of another sheriff.

"Using race as a political tactic to advance controversial nominees is especially troubling," said Hatch in a Senate speech. "I care too much about the Senate and the federal judiciary to see these institutions become the victims of base, cheap, wedge politics. I would urge my colleagues and the President to reconsider this destructive and dangerous ploy."

While such issues deeply divide Congress, and occasionally tempers flare, most of the time there is a surprising amount of good will between opposing sides–in the mutual belief that opponents also are acting honorably.

Occasional humor helps: In 1993, Carol Moseley-Braun, an Illinois Democrat and the only black woman in the Senate (she has since been defeated) stopped the Senate cold and shamed her colleagues into undoing a vote to extend the patent for the emblem of the Daughters of the American Revolution, because it includes a version of the Confederate flag. Among those opposing her was the bane of liberals, Republican Senator Jesse Helms of North Carolina.

Later, Moseley-Braun told a Washington dinner audience, she was riding an elevator with Hatch when Helms stepped on and started to sing "Dixie." Helms turned to Hatch and said "I'm going to sing 'Dixie' until she cries."

Moseley-Braun answered, "Senator Helms, your singing would make me cry if you sang 'Rock of Ages.'"

In 1990 Hatch went far out on a political limb and played a crucial role in passing the Americans with Disabilities Act (ADA), a landmark civil rights measure potentially affecting up to 43 million physically or mentally impaired citizens. After working out most differences with Democrats, Hatch became the chief Republican cosponsor.

He had prepared an amendment to exempt businesses with fifteen or fewer employees from the ADA's more costly provisions. However, during crucial negotiations, John Sununu, chief of staff in the Bush White House, caved in to Democrats and the bill went forward without the Senator's amendment and some other Hatch suggestions. As voting began on the measure, Hatch went up to Ted Kennedy to shake hands. Kennedy, sporting a big grin, gushed, "If Sununu only knew what is in this bill!"

Hatch was not happy with Sununu, but still believed the bill had more good than bad. Hatch led the fight on the floor for passage, and the Senate approved it on a vote of 91 to 6 in July 1990. It bars discrimination against those who are disabled, giving them the same civil rights protections in jobs, housing and other services already given racial minorities.

At about the same time, Senator Hatch also led a fight to establish a Republican Hispanic task force on Capitol Hill, to help open opportunities and give new voice to Hispanics. Several years later Democrats copied Republicans by establishing their own Hispanic task force. He also was the lead Republican sponsor, along with former Democratic Senator Birch Bayh of Indiana, of a measure to protect the civil rights of people in prison.

A decade ago, Hatch was the prime cosponsor and helped write a bill introduced by Paul Simon, an Illinois Democrat, requiring the FBI to gather data on "hate crimes"–those motivated by prejudice based on race, religion, ethnic origin, or sexual orientation. "For persons who are members of minority groups with a history of mistreatment or persecution," he said, "these crimes cause anxiety, unease and concern about their security, a security others may take for granted."

Hatch has continued to support hate crimes legislation, introducing a bill as recently as July 1999. His bill proposed a fund to help states combat hate crimes and allow federal prosecution of such crimes committed across multiple state lines. Hatch's approach didn't go as far as some advocates sought, but went beyond what others wanted. It called upon Washington to provide leadership in combating hate crimes, while leaving the states as primary enforcers of the law. That bill and others like it died, however, in the year-end budget squeeze.

Beyond the public record, there is overwhelming private evidence that the Senator is a true believer in equality. Among African Americans he has hired for his own staffs have been Brian Jones, a lawyer formerly on the Senate Judiciary Committee; Charmaine Kearney, a computer specialist on his personal staff; Brian Williams, a webmaster, and Hispanics John Flores, formerly on the Senate Labor and Human Resources Committee; Anna Cabral, Judiciary Committee deputy staff director, and former staffer Luben Montoya, whose wife Ruth is Hatch's executive assistant.

Hatch has gone far out of his way to assist minorities and give them greater visibility and status. Perhaps most noteworthy about Hatch's efforts is the fact he has had no political incentive to court minorities: As of the 1990 census, his home state of Utah was about 96 percent white and less than 1 percent black.

While already carrying a very full load, a number of years ago Hatch joined the Senate Indian Affairs Committee to assist American Indians, Native Hawaiians and Alaskan Natives with such issues as education, economic development, land management, health care, and legal claims against the United States.

Both times when Supreme Court vacancies arose during President Clinton's tenure, Hatch urged Clinton to consider Jose Cabranes, a federal district judge in Connecticut, to fill them. "Hispanic-Americans would go wild if you chose Cabranes," Hatch told Clinton. "It would really be a feather in your cap to put the first Hispanic on the Supreme Court."

Discrimination is abhorrent to Hatch, whose church suffered severe persecution and is headquartered today in the Rocky Mountains and not in Missouri or Illinois because its members were killed or driven from their homes there by mobs a century and a half ago.

During most of its existence, the LDS Church did not allow blacks to hold the priesthood. However, that was a reality that many members, including Hatch, carried as a cross. On June 9, 1978, Hatch was in the middle of leading a filibuster against the Labor Law Reform bill. He left the Senate floor momentarily to take a telephone call from Neal A. Maxwell, a top LDS official. Elder Maxwell informed Hatch that the church had just issued a statement that henceforth "every faithful, worthy man" in the church would be given the priesthood. That included African Americans, who had been joining the church in increasing numbers.

That night, in a personal note, Hatch rejoiced: "This is really, really wonderful. I had been praying for a long time for this to change. I was so excited and so buoyed up by this event that I floated all day long. I think I could have stood losing labor reform today."

That same year, Massachusetts Republican Edward Brooke–the only African American in the Senate–faced a primary contest against a GOP conservative. Hatch joined others in signing a telegram endorsing Brooke, which helped him narrowly win the primary. The far-right establishment, led by Paul Weyrich, bitterly criticized Hatch, as Brooke sent him a note saying "Your endorsement was perfectly timed and politically potent....I'll always be grateful."

Privately Hatch mused that he had supported Brooke even though the two rarely voted alike. Wrote Hatch: "Ed Brooke is the only black in the U.S. Senate, and a friend, and I would hate to have him lose."

Hatch is personal friends with a number of other prominent blacks, including Muhammad Ali, civil rights leader Jesse Jackson, Supreme Court Justice Clarence Thomas, and Utah Jazz superstar Karl Malone. But some observers suspect Hatch's motives.

"Karl Malone is a bigger fool than I thought if he lends his support to a man who is only interested in 'using' Karl to further his own personal agenda (like most Politicians)," wrote Thomas W. Ladanye of Payson, Utah, in a letter printed in the *Salt Lake Tribune*. "I also wonder when was the last time Hatch and his wife had a non-celebrity black family to their home for dinner, without any political, or other, strings attached."

Hatch in fact has socialized with blacks who were unknown outside their circles in Washington. Among others was an African American police officer in his office building named C.J. Martin. Hatch donated to Martin's humanitarian work in Uganda. When Hatch's youngest child, Jess, was married in 1993, Martin was among the personal friends attending the wedding reception.

Another black friend was another Capitol Hill policeman named Charles Coffer. Hatch's friends in the black community also included one of Washington's little giants, Smallwood Williams, bishop of the Bible Way Church. During the late 1980s, Hatch attended a service there with Coffer, a member of Williams' congregation. Williams, who looked like a black Friar Tuck–short, stout and bald–insisted that Hatch sit next to him in a high-backed chair facing the congregation, and called on him for an impromptu talk. After that, Hatch occasionally returned, and arranged for Williams to serve as Senate chaplain for a day.

When Bishop Williams died at age eighty-two, Hatch attended his funeral. Thirty-five hundred parishioners and guests crammed the church and thousands of other mourners spilled into New Jersey Avenue and nearby streets. Midway through the service, the conducting minister, with no advance warning, announced that Hatch–"one of the bishop's dear friends"–would address them. Hatch did so, offering a short sermon on the resurrection and quoting several scriptures from the Bible.

Several years later, in February 1997, Hatch again was invited to speak at the Bible Way Church. After Hatch's guest sermon, the new pastor, James Silver, took him upstairs to a hall of pictures depicting important events in Bishop Williams' life. Among other photos was one of Williams and his family and Hatch in the Senate dining room.

When Hatch spoke at Bishop Williams' funeral, also in the audience and called on to speak impromptu was Jesse Jackson, who gave a fiery discourse with strong political overtones. As Hatch left the stand, Jackson, seated among scores of other ministers, jumped up and grabbed his hand. "Senator," said Jackson, himself one of the country's premier orators, "you're a preacher!"

Hatch and Jackson often are on opposite sides of public issues. But they share a mutual respect and friendship, strengthened in part through Jackson's children. As Hatch's music-writing career blossomed in the late 1990s, a favorite soloist he chose to perform his songs was Santita Jackson, a gifted mezzo-soprano and Jesse Jackson's daughter. Another favorite is Chris Willis, a young African American male in Nashville, whom Hatch promoted and put together with Santita for joint performances of his and other songs.

On a Sunday morning in August 1998, Hatch was in Utah when Jesse Jackson called, asking for help. Jackson's son, Jesse Jr., a U.S. congressman from Chicago, and his son's wife Sandi, were at the University of Utah Hospital after she had suffered a miscarriage while attending a conference. Jesse Sr. asked Hatch to telephone the young couple to see if they were doing okay, but Hatch did much more. The Senator and an aide, Ron Madsen, bought flowers and a get-well balloon, and went to the hospital.

Jesse Senior's other two sons–Jonathan and Yusef–also flew in. "What wonderful young men," Hatch wrote to a friend. "Jesse and his wife have done a great job with these kids." Sandi, 34, had miscarried twenty weeks into her pregnancy.

While Hatch was at the hospital, Jesse Sr. telephoned him again to say he was flying in later that day to surprise his sons and Sandi. The Senator himself drove to Salt Lake International Airport and picked up Jackson, taking him to the hospital for a surprise reunion with his family. A statement later released by the hospital at the Jacksons' request said Hatch had joined the family in a prayer circle led by Jesse Sr.

14

And Justice For All

The U.S. Constitution, which apportions governmental rights and responsibilities [including selection of federal judges], was a product not only of man's ingenuity but of God's own purposes.

AMERICA'S JUDICIAL BRANCH ALMOST certainly is the least understood of the three branches of government. Yet, given the direct and lasting impact of its decisions on the daily lives of citizens, arguably it is the most important.

"The due administration of justice is the firmest pillar of good government," said George Washington in 1789 when Congress approved the judicial system that has persisted to this day. "I have considered the first arrangement of the judicial department as essential to the happiness of our country and the stability of its political system." James Madison, father of the Constitution, wrote that "in framing a government which is to be administered by men over men, the great difficulty lies in this: You must first enable the government to control the governed; and in the next place oblige it to control itself."

Some 200 years later, the United States continues to wrestle with Madison's challenge. Orrin Hatch probably has spent more time than anyone else in the ring helping to shape today's Supreme Court and the rest of the federal judiciary.

As a 23-year member of the Senate Judiciary Committee, and its current chairman, the Senator has helped confirm more than 1,000 U.S. district and circuit court nominees and has personally presided over some 300 of President Clinton's judicial appointments–nearly one-half the current federal judiciary. In addition, Hatch has had a hand in confirming eight of the current nine members of the Supreme Court, including elevating William Rehnquist to Chief Justice.

The Supreme Court in 2000 had a precarious conservative-liberal balance that hinged on the fall presidential election. The next president likely would appoint at least three new members to the Supreme Court, along with the other half of lower federal courts–who together would affect almost every aspect of the nation's life. "When citizens elect the president they also elect, with rare exception, his judicial choices," Hatch emphasizes.

The possibility that Al Gore might become president and make those choices greatly concerned Hatch. "More than one in five decisions in 1998 were decided 5-4," he explains, "including very important cases in civil rights, crime, criminal procedure, and in one instance on the question of how our census–which determines our political representation in the U.S.–can be conducted."

He predicted, "If Al Gore gets control of the Supreme Court, many 5-4 decisions will go the other way. The death penalty will definitely be overruled. Quotas will be in vogue as he and his liberal elite guard give preferences to one societal group over others. It could lead to even greater animosities and class antagonisms than we experience today."

Hatch emphasizes: "This means that Al Gore and his elite leftists would control two of the three constitutionally separated and coequal branches of government. And they might take over the House of Representatives as well, the body where all money bills originate. How clear can it be? This would spell disaster. It would take twenty to fifty years to get our country back on track, if then."

"Voters should remember that federal judges are appointed by the president for a lifetime," says Hatch. "They are unelected, and by design–in an attempt to insulate them from political pressure–are not directly accountable to the people. The American people do have a voice in the selection of federal judges–that voice is heard every four years in electing the president. While the Senate has a secondary role in the appointment of judges, by far the most important role is exercised by the president, who chooses them."

Section II of the Constitution says the president "shall nominate, and by and with the consent of the Senate, shall appoint...judges of the Supreme Court." Selection of judges for lower federal courts follows the same pattern. That advice and consent begins in the Senate Judiciary Committee. Senator Hatch has encouraged the nomination and appointment of men and women whose records suggest they will faithfully interpret the Constitution rather than attempt to legislate from the bench.

While the formal role of senators is limited to confirming or rejecting a president's nominees, Senator Hatch has directly influenced a number of key presidential selections, including to the Supreme Court, and has played a pivotal role in confirming several current justices.

Justice John Paul Stevens, at 79 the oldest member of the court, was appointed by President Gerald Ford in 1975–two years before Senator Hatch reached the Senate. William Rehnquist was appointed to the high court even earlier than Stevens–in 1972 by President Richard Nixon. But Hatch later played a decisive role in elevating Rehnquist to Chief Justice after President Reagan nominated him to replace retiring Chief Justice Warren Burger in 1986.

Judge Antonin Scalia was nominated to fill the empty seat. Scalia's confirmation was uneventful, but Rehnquist's unleashed a bruising battle on the Judiciary Committee as Democrats tried hard to derail him. When Democratic Senators Ted Kennedy of Massachusetts and Howard Metzenbaum of Ohio insisted Rehnquist was "too extreme" and not "mainstream," columnist George Will noted that the two liberal senators "are not exactly [the] Lewis and Clark team you would send exploring to locate the American mainstream."

Hatch led the defense of Rehnquist even though the Senator was several rungs down the GOP seniority ladder on the committee. He argued that "When it comes to competence, when it comes to integrity, when it comes to faithfulness to the law, I believe you get an A-plus in those areas." Opposition to Rehnquist, said Hatch, was nothing more than "character assassination....It's time we quit hacking at everybody who comes before this committee."

Hatch also coined the phrase "Rehnquisition" to suggest how unfairly Democrats were treating the nominee. In the end, the committee voted to approve Rehnquist's nomination, followed by a 65-33 vote by the full Senate. Scalia–insulated by his Italian roots against opposition from Democrats who feared alienating Italian Americans–sailed through without a negative vote.

Praise for Hatch's efforts came from many quarters. The *Baltimore Sun's* respected legal reporter Lyle Denniston called Hatch "a tall, superbly dressed senator with a made-for-television face, the real leader of the pro-Rehnquist forces and a senator with a conservative record entirely pleasing to Ronald Reagan." Reagan himself said in a note: "Your comments during the committee hearings and your skilled negotiations with your colleagues were key to the committee's approval of my nominees, and I thank you." Rehnquist wrote Hatch: "You have been a tower of strength on the Judiciary Committee during a rather grueling ordeal for me. Thank you from the bottom of my heart."

In 1981 Senator Hatch was one of the first senators outside Sandra Day O'Connor's native Arizona to endorse her as the first woman appointed to the Supreme Court. While O'Connor, like Scalia, reached the high court without a negative Senate vote, six years later the partisanship over President Reagan's judicial nominees had reverted back to the Rehnquist mode.

In 1987, Reagan nominated Robert Bork, a brilliant conservative jurist in the District of Columbia, to replace retiring Justice Lewis F. Powell, Jr. The knives that had been sheathed temporarily were drawn with a vengeance. In one of the ugliest episodes in U.S. judicial history, comprised of equal parts innuendo, outright lies, and character assassination, Senate Democrats and their special interest allies turned justice on its ear.

Millions of dollars were spent in an unprecedented propaganda campaign against a court nominee. Being anti-Bork became a litmus test for political correctness. "We will fight Bork all the way until hell freezes over," said the NAACP, "and then we'll skate across on the ice." Molly Yard, feminist icon and president-elect of the National Organization for Women (NOW), called Bork "a Neanderthal."

Hatch and his conservative colleagues mounted a determined defense of Bork, with Hatch arguing that "By any standard of fairness, the judgment must be rendered in your favor." But special interests, he added, "fear that you would let legislatures legislate....Judge Bork would make Congress, which is accountable to the voters, make the tough decisions....What [special interests] fear is that the people will once again rule America and it might not bring the results they want.

"They fear that their results-oriented activism may not win in a Court ruled by law, not politics." Such arguments were in vain against a tidal wave of opposition. Bork's nomination–called a "DeBorkle" by Hatch–was defeated in the Judiciary Committee and later by the full Senate. He wrote Hatch "to express both my gratitude and my admiration for the masterful way you supported my nomination."

With Bork's nomination dead, President Reagan nominated Douglas

Ginsburg, a judge on the same U.S. appeals court as Bork. Almost immediately that nomination also ran into trouble, notably over Ginsburg's admission that he had smoked marijuana within the past decade. His nomination died before reaching the Senate, and the White House stepped up to bat for the third time with Anthony Kennedy, a federal judge in Sacramento. Kennedy's nomination sailed through the Judiciary Committee, was approved unanimously by the full Senate, and he took his seat on the Supreme Court in February 1988.

In July 1990 President George Bush nominated David Souter, a little-known judge on the First Circuit Court of Appeals, to replace retiring Justice William J. Brennan. Unlike Rehnquist and Bork, Souter had published almost nothing, and his views on most issues were unknown. He was easily confirmed, and went on to establish a relatively liberal record that led President Bush to say he made a mistake. (Bush's lament is reminiscent of President Dwight Eisenhower's. Ike said he made two major mistakes during his presidency, and both of them–Earl Warren and William Brennan–were sitting on the Supreme Court.)

Then came Clarence Thomas in 1991, whose nomination regrettably and unfairly will forever be linked in history to Anita Hill. Thomas, a member of the D.C. appellate court, was nominated by President Bush to replace another African American justice, retiring Thurgood Marshall. Thomas's life was vintage Horatio Alger: born in a broken family in tiny Pin Point, Georgia, reared by his grandparents, educated in Catholic schools and at Yale Law School.

But his conservative views were anathema to liberals, especially his insistence that "Racial quotas and other race-conscious legal devices only further and deepen the original problem," and "I emphasize black self-help as opposed to racial quotas." Liberal special interests were livid at Thomas. "We're going to Bork him," vowed Patricia Ireland, president of NOW.

Hatch and Thomas had been friends for a decade. Thomas had appeared before the Senator's committees for confirmation to various federal posts, and the two occasionally went out to lunch. Hatch believed he knew Thomas well. Thus when Anita Hill appeared late in the confirmation process and leveled ugly charges of sexual harassment at Thomas, with whom she had worked in government, Hatch did not find the charges credible. He took the lead in defending Thomas.

Perhaps the most sensational hearings in Senate history followed, with Hill and friends trying to carve up Thomas, and Hatch and others defending him. In the end, the Senate voted 52-48 to confirm Thomas–one of the closest margins ever for a Supreme Court nominee.

(Feminists demonized Thomas as a sexual harasser, even though, when spun the most antagonistic way possible, Anita Hill's strongest charge was that he had talked dirty to her. Years later, when President Clinton had an illicit, overt sexual relationship with White House intern Monica Lewinsky, leading feminists–including Hill herself–defended Clinton.)

"How important was Senator Hatch to my confirmation?" Thomas asked rhetorically in an interview with the author. "That's easy. I never would have made it without him....He was the one person on the committee who knew me very well, both professionally and as a friend."

In March 1993, the only Democratic nominee left on the Supreme Court, Byron White, a friend of Hatch's, announced his retirement. Hatch issued a written statement: "I hope that President Clinton...will choose someone who appreciates, as Justice White does, that judges are not free to substitute their own policy preferences for the written law."

He added that "In the confirmation process, whether a nominee is politically liberal or conservative is irrelevant. What matters is that we have judges who will neutrally and objectively interpret and apply the laws, not judges who will impose their own policy preferences."

As chairman of the Judiciary Committee, Hatch was besieged by reporters asking whom he thought President Clinton should nominate. The Senator offered a number of names, saying it would be a great idea to put the first Hispanic on the court–something he had pushed for the last three vacancies. Jose Cabranes, a federal district judge in Connecticut, would be an excellent choice, said Hatch. Judge Stephen Breyer, whom Hatch had helped put on the First Circuit Court of Appeals in 1980, was another name he put forward.

Hatch also suggested Ruth Bader Ginsburg of the D.C. appellate court. As a private attorney she had been a trailblazer in gender-discrimination law, arguing six women's rights cases before the Supreme Court in the 1970s and winning five of them.

Hatch respected Ginsburg's keen intellect and the fact that, as an appellate judge for thirteen years, she had been restrained and generally nonideological in her rulings. In fact, Ginsburg's voting record was very similar to those of Robert Bork and Antonin Scalia when all three served together on the D.C. Circuit Court of Appeals.

President Clinton telephoned Hatch and named several possible male candidates, including Interior Secretary Bruce Babbitt, asking Hatch how each would fare before the Senate. Hatch and Babbitt have openly disagreed on many things over the years. The Senator considers the former Arizonan sincere in his devotion to environmental causes, but wrong on too many gut issues for the West.

"You might be able to get him confirmed," Hatch told Clinton, "but there would be blood everywhere.... Mr. President, you're relatively early in your presidency. Do you really want this type of battle, which you might well lose?" Hatch carefully explained that many westerners consider Babbitt an environmental extremist, and some believe him to be unprincipled in his support of the environment over longstanding rights of people.

After giving his opinion, Hatch suggested to Clinton several additional names, including Cabranes, Breyer, and Ginsburg. Hatch then telephoned Ginsburg to tell her she was in the mix–something that took her by surprise. Within a week, Clinton announced his nominee was Ginsburg. Led by Hatch, she sailed through the Judiciary Committee and was confirmed by the full Senate, taking her seat on the high court in August 1993.

In spring 1994 Justice Harry Blackmun retired, giving President Clinton an opportunity to name a second member of the Supreme Court. Again he telephoned Hatch for counsel, as it became clear the President once more was leaning toward nominating Babbitt. Hatch told Clinton that Babbitt may have difficulty being confirmed because of actions he had taken, especially involving the environment and public lands, that were highly unpopular with western senators. Hatch and others worried that Babbitt would attempt to legislate from the bench rather than faithfully interpret the law.

Hatch encouraged Clinton instead to focus on several other potential nominees, including Breyer, a moderate member of the U.S. Court of Appeals for the First Circuit whom Hatch knew personally. Although pundits continued to bet on Babbitt, Clinton took Hatch's advice and nominated Breyer, who was confirmed to become the ninth member of the current Supreme Court.

Some conservatives, still seething over the treatment by Democrats and their allies of court nominees chosen by Republican presidents, have put great pressure on Hatch to exact retribution. Specifically they have urged him to use his powerful position as Judiciary Committee chair to dump President Clinton's court nominees they don't like.

But Hatch argues that "To simply target all nominees who are politically liberal would not be a proper exercise of the Senate's advice and consent power. If we politicize the process by insisting that each side's nominees meet the other side's ideological preferences, we will wind up using the lowest common denominator in choosing judges–and the nation will be poorer for it. We must attempt to keep partisan politics out of the process and still ferret out those who, if confirmed to lifetime appointments on the bench, will be activists more loyal to their own policy preferences than to duly passed laws."

Thomas Jipping, head of the right-wing Free Congress Foundation, regularly has attacked Hatch for voting to seat Clinton's nominees. In August 1999 the group issued a report which said Democrats were more effective than Republicans in advancing their views of the judiciary. Senate Democrats, they said, favor judicial activists "who are willing to change the meaning of statutes or the Constitution to accomplish certain goals," while Republicans favor judicially restrained nominees "who take the law as they see it." Democrats more often prevail, argued Jipping.

Hatch says he takes his judicial cues not from Republicans, Democrats, or pressure groups such as Jipping's, but from the Constitution. He believes strongly in appointing judges who will faithfully interpret the Constitution, and not activists who will try to create new laws from the bench. He has strongly exerted his influence to that end, within constitutional limits. Twice he has derailed liberal activists President Clinton strongly considered putting on the Supreme Court itself, where leverage over the nation's life by nine justices arguably is greater than the leverage of the thousand or so lower federal court judges combined.

The Senator also has played a strong role behind the scenes in discouraging the White House from nominating to lower courts many potential judges whose records indicate they would be activists on the bench. Jeanne Lopatto, spokesperson for the Senate Judiciary Committee, said Hatch has "worked hard to keep politics out" of the confirmation process itself. The record Jipping's foundation dislikes, she added, "is something to be proud of."

In addition to working behind the scenes, Hatch often has spoken out publicly about the dangers of judicial activism, which he says is "equally objectionable when it comes from the political right as when it comes from the left." Early in the twentieth century, he noted, conservative activists on the bench overreached in a number of economic cases. In recent decades, however, activism usually has tried to impose a liberal agenda on society, tending to be pro-abortion, pro-quota, pro-criminal and prisoner, while being anti-family and anti-religion.

While Republican presidents have also appointed activist judges, says Hatch, "on the whole judges appointed by Democratic presidents are invariably more activist and more sympathetic to criminal rights than the great majority of judges appointed by Republican presidents." In a series of speeches, and in a chapter written for a recent book, the Senator cited a number of egregious cases, including the following federal judges, all appointed by President Clinton:

• District Judge Harold Baer, Jr., who suppressed evidence seized by two policemen during the stop of an automobile in New York City in 1995. The officers watched four men rapidly leave the scene after placing two bags in the trunk of a car driven by a woman. The bags turned out to contain eighty pounds of cocaine and heroin. Judge Baer said officers had violated the Constitution's ban on unreasonable searches and the car's driver should go free–despite her detailed, videotaped confession of being a repeat drug-runner. Further, said Baer, local residents didn't trust police and "had the men not run when the cops began to stare at them, it would have been unusual." (After Hatch and others blasted the decision, Baer reversed himself.)

• Judge James Beaty, who–along with a judge appointed years earlier by President Jimmy Carter–overturned the conviction of Timothy Sherman, who had brutally murdered his mother and stepmother in Maryland. The evidence was overwhelming that Sherman had killed them with a shotgun, then hidden the gun in the branches of a large tree. But because a juror had gone to look at the tree–improper though not prejudicial–the two Fourth Circuit judges granted Sherman the right to a new trial. On April 17, 1996, the entire Fourth Circuit upheld Sherman's original conviction.

• Judge J. Lee Sarokin of the U.S. Court of Appeals for the Third Circuit, and Judge Rosemary Barket of the U.S. Court of Appeals for the Eleventh Circuit. Judge Sarokin repeatedly has sided with criminals and prisoners–including overturning death sentences of killers–while Judge Barket has openly voiced suspicion of police and taken a tolerant attitude toward drugs. "These are two of the most activist friends of criminal rights on our federal courts of appeals," said Hatch in a Senate speech. Although Hatch led opposition to the two judges when they were nominated to the appeals courts, the Clinton-Gore Administration fought hard and both were confirmed by the Senate in 1994.

Evidence of judicial activism or a soft-on-crime outlook is not always present in a nominee's record, explains Hatch. Witness the Supreme Court appointments of Presidents Eisenhower and Bush. Since the prerogative of selection belongs to the White House, says Hatch, "every president is able to obtain confirmation of most of his nominees. The general judicial philosophy of nominees to the federal bench reflects the general judicial philosophy of the person occupying the Oval Office. And differences in judicial philosophy have real consequences for the safety of Americans in their streets, homes, and workplaces."

He notes that "Some voices call for such radical countermeasures as the impeachment of sitting judges. However appealing this might seem, the Constitution specifies that federal judges cannot be removed from office unless they have committed 'high crimes and misdemeanors.' For Congress to go beyond that and target judges for removal based on the popularity of their decisions–however repugnant some decisions are–would be decidedly dangerous to our liberties. We must not prescribe a cure worse than the disease."

Following the Democrats' shameful treatment of Supreme Court nominee Robert Bork a decade ago, the Senator said, "The sad truth is that his judicial record was practically ignored. This was the tragedy–and the danger. Federal judges are not politicians and ought not to be judged like politicians."

"After being thrust center stage into these historic battles, and witnessing first-hand the toll on individual lives and the incalculable damage to the independence and integrity of the judiciary," says Hatch, "I vowed that if the tables ever turned, I would not be party to retaliatory partisanship. Otherwise, the entire process would degenerate into an endless cycle of revenge and retribution, damaging the institutional standing of both the Senate and the judiciary."

Explains Hatch:

> Judging a judge by political, rather than legal, criteria strips the

> judicial office of all that makes it a distinct separate power. The framers of the Constitution gave judges life tenure and insulated them from the political branches for a crucial reason. Judges must protect our lives, liberties, and property against impassioned politicians who at times are convinced that economic or social conditions justify extreme measures....
>
> No American would wish his life, liberty, or property to rest in the hands of a judge who is most concerned about what a newspaper headline might say or what some senator might say in a future confirmation debate.

At the root of his philosophy, says Hatch, "is a firm belief that the U.S. Constitution, which apportions governmental rights and responsibilities, was a product not only of man's ingenuity but of God's own purposes." He cites a letter written by George Washington to his friend Marquis de Lafayette that the Constitution "will be so much beyond anything we had a right to imagine or expect...that it will demonstrate as visibly the finger of Providence, as any possible event in the course of human affairs can ever designate it."

15

Patriotism and Foreign Policy

The lush green grass at Arlington/Shimmers in the morning sun
As pure white crosses seem to glow/Sentinels in perfect rows
Everyone who lives and breathes/Wonders at the sight of these
Who gave to us a gift beyond compare/"Thank God
for those who rest in honor there"

IT IS IMPOSSIBLE TO UNDERSTAND Orrin Hatch, who wrote these lyrics, without knowing how deeply he loves America. Hatch's patriotism is not that of a jingoistic sloganeer, but of a deeply grateful citizen who, each morning as he passes near Arlington Cemetery on his way to work, reveres those who made the ultimate sacrifice to keep our country free.

Hatch represents not Samuel Johnson's famous dictum of patriotism as "the last refuge of a scoundrel," but a definition once offered by Democratic presidential candidate Adlai Stevenson:

> [True patriotism] is a sense of national responsibility which will enable America to remain master of her power–to walk with it in serenity and wisdom, with self-respect and the respect of all mankind; a patriotism that puts country ahead of self; a patriotism which is not short, frenzied outbursts of emotion, but the tranquil and steady dedication of a lifetime. These are words that are easy to utter, but this is a mighty assignment. For it is often easier to fight for principles than to live up to them.

A defining experience in Hatch's boyhood came during World War II when he learned that his beloved older brother Jess was missing in action in Europe and presumed dead. The shock of that news profoundly influenced

Orrin's life. In 1949, four years after Jess's plane was shot down, his remains were located in Vienna and returned to Pittsburgh for burial. Fifteen-year-old Orrin's vivid memory of the memorial service was of the casket, draped in an American flag that was then presented to his mother. Today that flag, encased in glass, rests on a mantle in his office.

As a sitting U.S. senator, in 1984 Hatch joined other members of Utah's congressional delegation and Governor Scott Matheson to present medals to the parents or spouses of thirteen Utahns missing in action in the Vietnam War. As one serviceman's name was called, a rough-hewn old rancher and his wife stood to receive a medal, the man sobbing uncontrollably.

When it was Hatch's turn to speak, his own eyes filled with tears. He said in part:

> While a man can have no greater love than to be willing to lay down his life for his friends...the pain of losing a family member who has so laid down his life sometimes seems unbearable. I have never hurt so badly as when I, as a boy, learned of my older brother's death in World War II. Not a day passes but that I reflect upon the loss of my brother. These melancholy moments are filled with so many emotions–anger that he was taken from me; pride that he died honorably for his country; sadness, for I miss him still; solace, in that I will be with him again someday.
>
> But as piercing as my own pain has been, I realize full well that your own sorrow has been augmented by uncertainty....In closing, I am compelled to mention that truth of which I hope you are all aware: These men are not missing in the eyes of God. The God who rules the universe watches over these young men–wherever they might be.

As the meeting broke up, Hatch embraced the ranch couple, telling them he empathized with them. "It almost tore my heart to shreds," he wrote privately that night. As this book was going to press in May 2000, the Senator and Janice Kapp Perry had just written and dedicated a song to his late brother Jess for Hatch's ninth CD. Earlier, with time on his hands between flights at an airport, Hatch had put other thoughts about his brother to paper.

Almost forty years ago my only brother died,
We know not how, but it must have been badly,
For one member of his crew returned, unspeaking,

Never to talk again about the awful end
Which laid my brother down, till brought home again,
Encased in metal, no longer to be seen,
Or touched, or loved, except in absentia
For such future time God provides,
To those who hope, who pray,
Who never go away, in spite of death.

Hatch has tried to keep faith with those who have fought and bled for this country–and with their loved ones, some of whom, like his own parents, have had only an American flag as a reminder of the price of freedom. One way he has honored their sacrifices is by helping to lead a national effort to pass a constitutional amendment protecting the flag from desecration, thus restoring the flag protection that had existed for the first 200 years of the country's life.

It is a jarring sight to see Old Glory in flames–as Americans often did during the turbulent 1960s, and as the author did as a U.S. correspondent in Iran two decades ago, covering the American hostage crisis. In today's prosperous, relatively peaceful times, desecration of the flag is rare, perhaps offering the best possible political climate for calm deliberation of the subject.

The federal government itself–the Supreme Court–raised the issue. In 1984 a man named Gregory Johnson, during an anti-American rally in Dallas, Texas, torched a U.S. flag, chanting "America, the red, white and blue...we spit on you." He was convicted of violating a Texas law against desecration of the flag.

But five years later, in *Texas v. Johnson*, the Supreme Court ruled 5-4 that Johnson was protected under the First Amendment guarantee of free speech. The ruling reversed 200 years of constitutional precedent in which states had prohibited desecration of the flag. In 1989 Congress enacted the Flag Protection Act to undo it. But the high court also struck down that law, leaving the constitutional route the only sure way to protect the flag.

A constitutional amendment requires a two-thirds vote in each house of Congress and approval by three-fourths of the states. By 1995 forty-nine state legislatures–all but Vermont–had voiced support for an amendment, leaving the issue in the hands of Congress. The House three times has passed the amendment overwhelmingly, but the Senate remains unconvinced. While no senator wants the flag desecrated, many express fear that passing the measure will erode free speech. They include Hatch's Utah colleague Senator Bob Bennett, who says a better approach would be simply passing a federal law to prosecute those who destroy the flag. But amendment supporters fear any such law will be struck down again by the Supreme Court.

Hatch is the Senate's leading champion of the amendment, which has just seventeen words: "The Congress shall have power to prohibit the physical desecration of the flag of the United States." In the latest skirmish over it in March 2000, he and Bennett led opposing forces as the amendment was narrowly defeated 63-37, four votes shy of the two-thirds needed for passage.

"I urge the Senate not to tinker with the First Amendment and First Amendment rights," Bennett told their colleagues. Hatch countered that "Destroying property might be seen as a clever way of expressing one's dissatisfaction. But such action is conduct, not speech. Restoring legal protection to the American flag would not infringe on free speech."

Hatch vowed to continue bringing up the amendment in future congresses. "It will pass eventually," he predicts. "The flag amendment reflects the will of the people. I believe passage and ratification of this amendment are inevitable."

Bennett was among just a handful of Republicans voting against it. In the past the opposition has been led by Democratic leader Tom Daschle of South Dakota and Patrick Leahy of Vermont, top-ranking minority member of the Judiciary Committee. They have been strongly backed by the ACLU, People for the American Way, and the American Bar Association. But they are in a minority: Polls have shown most citizens support the amendment. In May 1997, for example, a national poll by Wirthlin Worldwide indicated 81 percent of respondents would vote for a constitutional amendment to protect the flag, with 69 percent calling it "important."

When Hatch introduced the latest amendment in 1999, fifty-eight senators cosponsored it, including Democrat and chief cosponsor Max Cleland of Georgia, who directed the Veterans Administration under President Jimmy Carter. Cleland was grievously wounded in a grenade explosion in Vietnam, losing both legs and an arm.

Retired Army Major General Patrick Brady, who heads the Citizens Flag Alliance, a huge grassroots group pushing the amendment, explains that "A nation is defined by its symbols, its citizens, and its values. We have preserved one special symbol for the ages and by doing so we ensure the next generation is taught the values of respect, service, and sacrifice." Brady earned the Congressional Medal of Honor in Vietnam, where he was an air ambulance pilot. He and five other Medal of Honor recipients testified before Hatch's Senate Judiciary Committee in April 1999, with Brady saying "The importance of the flag in combat is highlighted by the fact that more medals of honor have been awarded for flag-related heroism than any other action."

Opponents also include some certified war heroes, notably Nebraska Democratic Senator Bob Kerrey, who won the Medal of Honor and lost a leg to combat in Vietnam before coming home and later denouncing the war. But an overwhelming number of veterans almost certainly support the amendment.

General Norman Schwarzkopf, U.S. commander in Deseret Storm, in a letter to members of the Senate, said "I regard legal protections for our flag as an absolute necessity and a matter of critical importance to our nation. The American flag, far from a mere symbol or a piece of cloth, is an embodiment of our hopes, freedoms and unity. The flag is our national identity."

Washington attorney Adrian Cronauer, whose often hilarious wartime exploits were the basis for the movie *Good Morning Vietnam!* told Freedom Forum's First Amendment Center that the need to protect "the purity of the First Amendment" is not a reasonable argument against the flag proposal, when restrictive laws already forbid such things as yelling "Fire!" in a crowded movie theater or publishing troop movements during a war. The flag amendment, said Cronauer, is "just another limitation that the American people want, and it's a very narrow limitation. It doesn't lead to anything else."

Hatch argues that "We need not alter the Bill of Rights. Instead, we should restore its meaning as it existed for over 200 years. I know that members on both sides of the aisle have deep feelings on this issue, as I do. Freedom of speech is essential to the proper functioning of our democracy, and the love of freedom, as symbolized by the American flag, is essential to the long-term survival of our democracy."

The Senator adds that "Love of liberty does not reside merely on a battlefield, in a parade, or on a school yard. As Judge Learned Hand said, 'Liberty lies in the hearts of men and women; when it dies there, no constitution, no law, no court can save it.' If the government sanctions the destruction of the flag, the government destroys, little by little, the love of liberty that the flag instills in us all."

For all his tenderness toward the American flag, Hatch is a hard-headed realist on matters of U.S. defense and foreign policy. In September 1999 he followed Vice President Al Gore in speaking to 4,000 veterans at the American Legion's national convention in Anaheim, California. Gore wore the American Legion cap of his Tennessee post and gamely tried to defend the Clinton-Gore Administration's record on defense, but veterans weren't buying it.

Legionnaires were "polite" to the Vice President, reported the *Orange County Record*, "but reserved their most enthusiastic applause for Sen. Orrin Hatch...who followed Gore and didn't hesitate to criticize the current administration."

Hatch accused Clinton-Gore of "eight years of neglect" of military needs and an absence of moral leadership that has damaged military morale. He called the number of military families on food stamps "deplorable," Pentagon health care an "embarrassment," and desecration of the American flag "unspeakable." That brought legionnaires to their feet in a standing ovation.

Hatch is currently serving his second term on the Senate Intelligence Committee–one of few senators granted more than a single term. He has traveled extensively abroad and has examined first hand the threats facing U.S. troops and diplomats. He has worked hard for a strong national defense, to protect vital American interests abroad and to discourage terrorism against the West.

He believes that, as the world's only military and economic superpower, the U.S. must be engaged overseas in a carefully focused way. Overall foreign policy objectives, says Hatch, should be to promote regional stability, prevent conflicts, deter aggression, and reduce threats through diplomacy wherever possible.

Hatch is intimately familiar with terrorist threats to the United States, and has been a leading voice advocating effective action against terrorists who target America. He is a key sponsor of the Anti-terrorism and Effective Death Penalty Act, to strengthen the government's hand in combating terrorism. The American Security Council, a leading private group seeking strategic military superiority for the United States, routinely rates the Senator 100 percent correct in his voting to support defense and foreign policy initiatives that help assure peace through strength.

From the start of his Senate career, Hatch signaled he would not turn aside from any issue he deemed vital to national security. In 1977 President Carter and Panama's leader Omar Torrijos signed two treaties giving the Panama Canal to that country by the year 2000. The treaties were approved by the Senate Foreign Relations Committee and reached the full Senate early in 1978 to muster the two-thirds vote required for ratification.

Although Senator Paul Laxalt, R-Nevada, formally led Senate opposition, most of the floor arguments against the treaties were waged by Alabama Democrat James Allen and his freshman GOP protege Hatch. The Utahn offered amendments and argued against the treaties as the debate stretched from days into weeks. Hatch also made a quick trip to Panama for a firsthand look at the canal, and traveled throughout the U.S. speaking out against the treaties. In the end, the two treaties were barely ratified, on identical Senate votes of 68-32, one more than the required two-thirds.

As the canal was handed over to Panama on the eve of 2000, an amendment Hatch helped attach to the treaties more than two decades ago is looking better and better. It was introduced by his colleague Dennis DeConcini, D-Arizona, and stipulated that the United States could intervene militarily in Panama after the turn of the century if the vital choke-point were shut down for any reason. Although Panama will control the canal itself, port facilities apparently will be leased to and operated by China–a fact the Pentagon, in a secret report, has called a significant security threat.

Hatch was a strong advocate for restoring America's military power after it dipped dangerously under President Carter. By 1980, Carter's last year in office, analysts said U.S. military forces were no longer adequate to deter aggression.

Skilled military personnel, discouraged by low pay and lack of other support, were leaving the armed forces in droves. Shortages of technicians as well as spare parts had grounded many Air Force and Navy fighter planes. Six Army divisions were judged unfit for combat. America's weakness was symbolized late in 1979 when Iran took 52 Americans hostage–holding them throughout the remainder of Carter's term–and Russia invaded Afghanistan, placing Soviet troops next door to vital Middle East oil fields.

President Reagan replaced Jimmy Carter in January 1981 and, strongly supported by Hatch and other key congressional leaders, set about to rebuild America's defenses. That October, Reagan unveiled the most sweeping overhaul of U.S. strategic forces in history. The $180 billion program to expand military defenses, said Reagan, would close "a window of vulnerability" to nuclear attack by the Soviet Union.

Despite cries of critics that the program would ignite a new arms race with Russia, history proved otherwise: Within a decade Russia sued for peace, an ugly wall was torn down in Berlin, and the four-decades-long Cold War was over.

Senator Hatch did more than speak and vote to support Reagan's foreign policy initiatives; he personally went abroad to further them. In November 1982 he traveled to Europe, visiting the sites of four different arms-control talks in which the U.S. was then engaged. One stop was in Madrid, where Hatch and U.S. arms negotiator Max Kampelman had a meeting with a group of Russians who proved wholly unresponsive to U.S. concerns.

As the disappointing meeting was breaking up, Hatch displayed the personal diplomacy that is a hallmark with him. The head of the Soviet delegation, a man named Dubinin, had unusually thick, wavy hair that stood about five inches off his head–in contrast to most members of the Soviet delegation who were bald. The Senator suddenly turned to Dubinin and said "I would like to get some of the vitamin pills that Yuri Vladimirovich Dubinin used to get all that hair."

When it was translated, the other Russians howled with laughter as Dubinin smiled. Then Hatch added: "And it looks like the rest of your delegation could use some of those vitamin pills, too." This time Dubinin doubled over laughing.

The ice was broken–and it continued to melt. Several years later Dubinin was assigned as Soviet ambassador to Washington, where he and Hatch renewed their acquaintance as Dubinin helped guide his country into the post-Cold War era.

The Utahn was first appointed to the Senate Intelligence Committee in January 1985. During the next two years he took an active role in shaping U.S. foreign policy. He championed freedom fighters on three continents and insisted that the United States should not just help them survive against vastly superior forces, but help them punish and, if possible, defeat oppressors. A key tool in Hatch's diplomatic pocket was the Stinger–a five-foot-long, thirty-five pound, heat-seeking missile, fired from the shoulder by one man. Its specialty was destroying low-flying enemy aircraft. In 1986, Hatch flew to southern Africa and met with Angolan rebel leader Jonas Savimbi, whose group, UNITA, was fighting a communist-backed group, the MPLA, that included thousands of Cuban troops armed with Russian equipment. Returning to the U.S., Hatch pressed the Reagan Administration to arm UNITA with the Stinger.

"The battle for Angola is...a battle over ideologies," wrote Hatch in an article printed in a number of U.S. newspapers. "Soviet totalitarianism vs. freedom, self-determination and democracy." Hatch, backed by other concerned Americans, succeeded in persuading the Administration to arm Savimbi's rebels with Stingers and other modern weapons. The weapons helped force the Cubans out of Angola in 1991.

When not traveling to meet with foreign leaders or freedom fighters, Hatch used his powerful pen in their various causes. Among other initiatives, he called on Washington to support a democratic resistance group in Ethiopia against its Marxist leader, Mengistu Haile-Mariam, whose brutal policies had helped lead to mass suffering and starvation.

Hatch also was a strong supporter of contra rebels fighting the Sandinista regime in Nicaragua, which was backed by Cuba and the Soviet Union. "The United States has a very clear-cut choice: either support the resistance forces now or end up making a military commitment ourselves later," wrote Hatch.

The Reagan Administration's secret support for the contras gave the Administration its worst black eye. In a complex scheme, U.S. operatives had sold weapons to Iran, America's arch-enemy, and used some of the proceeds to covertly assist the contras at a time when Congress had barred such aid. President Reagan said he was not "fully informed" about the diversion of funds, and heads began to roll, including that of Marine Lieutenant Colonel Oliver North, fingered by superiors as the only person in government with "precise knowledge" of the cash transfers.

Hatch and twenty-five other members of Congress were named to a special Senate-House joint committee to investigate the Iran-contra affair. In the nationally televised hearing, held in the ornate Senate Caucus Room above Hatch's office, North continued to take most of the heat for the Administration. Democrats hoped to nail President Reagan instead, but those hopes were dashed by his former national security advisor, John Poindexter, who insisted he alone had authorized the secret diversion of funds, and Reagan was kept out of the loop to protect the presidency. "The buck stops here, with me," testified Poindexter.

Senator Hatch knew what had happened was against the law. But he also knew it was motivated by a worthy purpose: to stop the spread of

Marxism through Central America, toward the U.S. doorstep. During his cross-examination of a parade of witnesses, Hatch put on public record the strange on-again, off-again history of Congress's assistance to the contras. He also made certain that witnesses had a full opportunity to explain what was at stake in Nicaragua.

A key witness was Robert McFarlane, who had preceded Poindexter as the President's national security advisor. Among other questions, Hatch asked McFarlane: "Isn't it a fact that President Reagan...was sincerely committed to a position in Nicaragua what would ultimately lead to peace and stability in our region of the world?"

Many of Hatch's colleagues did a slow burn as the Utahn called the hearings a "public media show" that was helping America's enemies by publicizing U.S. documents, methods, and secret plans. "Mistakes have been made," Hatch said to Colonel North, "but...we don't have to beat our country into submission, or people like you, just because mistakes have been made."

Following McFarlane's appearance at the hearing, he and his wife Jonny took a two-week trip to Japan and China. Upon their return, McFarlane wrote to Hatch expressing "desperation" that the ongoing hearings were not considering such vital issues as "How *are* we going to deal with Soviet efforts to subvert and establish control over developing countries ever closer to vital U.S. interests?"

> Throughout our trip....Jonny and I kept coming back to your courage in going against the tide of unrelieved negativism and superficiality. Neither were you soporific, playing on people's sympathy for me or anyone else. You pounded home several fundamental truths–that Iran is important, that stopping the [Iran-Iraq] war is important, that sharing such an initiative broadly is infeasible, and that losing in Nicaragua holds untold costs for us as a nation. But you sure were alone....Someday it will be my responsibility to write about this period....When it comes, Orrin Hatch will have a place of distinction as one who, when principle was involved, was deaf to expediency.

In November 1987, after ten months of work, the joint Iran-contra committee released a stinging, highly politicized 450-page report. All six Republican House members on the committee and two of the five Republican senators, including Hatch, refused to sign it. Instead they issued a 150-page report of their own, maintaining that President Reagan and his aides were guilty not of criminality but of errors of judgment.

While Oliver North would continue to be verbally pummeled by critics, many national security authorities in retrospect believe that the $3.5 million he transferred to the contras kept them alive as a viable force and resulted ultimately in democracy in Nicaragua with the election of President Violeta Chamorro in 1990.

Senator Hatch has long been one of Israel's strongest supporters in Washington, convinced Israel is a bulwark of strength and stability in the volatile Middle East. When President Clinton nominated Strobe Talbott to be deputy secretary of state–number two position at State–Hatch voted against confirmation in 1994, largely on the basis of Talbott's negative views toward Israel.

Talbott, once a college buddy of Clinton's and later an editor at *Time* magazine, repeatedly had criticized Israeli defense policy and questioned Israel's strategic importance to the United States. During Senate confirmation hearings, however, Talbott recanted some past views of Israel and was confirmed on a vote of 66 to 31.

Hatch has had close ties to a number of Israeli leaders, including Anatoly Sharansky, a world symbol of freedom who was imprisoned for nearly a decade by the Soviet Union for agitating for human rights for Jews. Finally released to emigrate to Israel, Sharansky formed a new political party to press Israel to step up its immigration and absorption of Soviet Jews. He served as Minister of Industry and Trade, and was appointed Minister of the Interior–foreign affairs–in July 1999. Hatch met with Sharansky and, by wire and telephone, has worked with him over many years on behalf of other Soviet Jews.

Hatch also developed a personal friendship with former Israeli Prime Minister Benjamin Netanyahu. They have visited each other in their respective countries, and corresponded on various issues. After the Senator sent him a CD of his music in 1998, Netanyahu responded with a letter saying "Your songs are simply beautiful. Sara and I have enjoyed them immensely....Such warmth and fine artistry are rare, and they make me prouder than ever of your friendship."

Hatch has been honored by a number of Jewish groups. In April 1996 the Anti-Defamation League gave the Senator the Leon Klinghoffer Award for his leadership on an anti-terrorism bill. Klinghoffer was the disabled New Yorker who was shot in his wheelchair and thrown off the cruise ship Achille Lauro by Palestinian hijackers in 1985.

In September 1997, in a ceremony in Jerusalem, Hatch received the prestigious Theodor Herzl Award for his support of Israel and his "unwavering commitment to justice."

Perhaps Hatch's most important foreign policy achievement was in Afghanistan, whose people the Soviets had been unable to conquer or pacify despite using vastly superior firepower after marching into the country to support a puppet regime in 1979. Opposing them were fiercely determined but poorly equipped Mujahedin rebels, headquartered across the border in Pakistan.

In May 1985, Hatch led a U.S. delegation around the world in a diplomatic effort aimed especially at gaining support for aiding the Mujahedin. The plane they flew signaled the unmistakable importance of their mission Air Force Two, usually assigned to Vice President Bush and emblazoned in blue with "UNITED STATES OF AMERICA."

A member of Hatch's delegation, New Jersey Senator–and later presidential aspirant–Bill Bradley, graphically described their visit to refugee camps inside Pakistan near the famed Khyber Pass. The camps were filled with Afghan women and children fleeing south to escape such Soviet atrocities as giving children toys that exploded. In his memoir, *Time Present, Time Past*, Bradley wrote:

> After a tour of the camps, we sat at a table under an open-air tent before three hundred active and former Mujahedin freedom fighters in turbans and flowing pants. As Hatch, our delegation leader, was introduced, the guerrillas began chanting, the chant growing into a roar. Men whose legs had been lost to Soviet land mines sat in the front row, next to men who had only one eye and no patch over the bad one. Some of them held rifles. We told them that America was committed to helping their cause, and they listened to us through an interpreter, cocking their turbaned heads to the side as if they were birds on a perch.

They met with Pakistan's president, Mohammed Zia ul-Haq, and other world leaders, securing support for arming both Pakistan and the Afghan rebels to drive out the Russians.

"Orrin Hatch, on the same 1985 trip, had put into motion steps that would lead to giving the Mujahedin handheld Stinger missiles, which could shoot down Soviet helicopter gunships and fighter bombers," wrote Bradley. "That action stopped what [President Zia] feared would have been the easy advance of Soviet forces through Pakistan to the long-desired Russian and Soviet dream, a warm-water port."

That outcome, however, did not come easily. While the U.S. sent Stinger and Sidewinder air-to-air missiles to Pakistan itself about six months after the Hatch delegation's mission, it took considerable lobbying by Hatch and others before the Reagan Administration would agree to arm the loosely organized Mujahedin with Stingers for fear the high-tech weapons might fall into the wrong hands.

Near the end of 1985 Hatch received a green light to lead another group to Asia to sound out key power brokers and secure support for more military aid to the rebels. Among stops was one in Beijing, where Hatch, accompanied by two senior CIA officers, huddled with the chief of China's intelligence service. Hatch asked China's top spy master if his country would support greater U.S. involvement in Afghanistan. His answer: "Yes." Hatch then asked if China would support the U.S. in supplying the Mujahedin with the Stinger missile. Although some U.S. analysts believed China would refuse, again the spy master said "yes."

The jubilant U.S. delegation returned to Washington near the end of January 1986, and Hatch relentlessly pressed the Administration to give the Stingers to the Mujahedin. Finally, by summer, a shipment of 150 Stingers arrived in Pakistan. A missile at a time, they were distributed to rebel units that had been trained to use them. They apparently entered rebel arsenals for the first time in October. Two months later the State Department reported that the Mujahedin had been shooting down an average of one Soviet or Afghan government aircraft each day since October.

By the following spring, Pentagon sources said the Soviets had stopped flying both helicopters and fixed-wing aircraft over some parts of Afghanistan because of the Stingers. The Soviets had no answer for the new weapons, and they finally sent a white flag up the pole. By the following February, all Soviet troops were out of Afghanistan.

Hatch's pivotal role in the drama remained concealed until the *Washington Post* broke the story in 1992. Its investigative reporter concluded, "In retrospect, many senior U.S. officials involved see the decision [to arm rebels with the Stinger] as a turning point in the war and acknowledge that Hatch's clandestine lobbying played a significant role." The *Post* added that "Today, some involved in the Afghan program say they believe the Soviet defeat was one of several decisive factors that helped discredit Soviet hardliners and encourage Mikhail Gorbachev's reforms."

In coming years, analysts would credit the end of the Cold War to at least four factors: Reagan's military buildup, the deployment by NATO of Pershing II nuclear missiles in Europe, America's pursuit of the "star wars" Space Defense Initiative (SDI), and the Stinger decision which led to the Soviet defeat in Afghanistan, unmasking the USSR's vulnerability to its Eastern bloc allies.

"Today, under President Clinton and Vice President Gore, our nation's military strength once more has eroded," says Senator Hatch. A slimmer military was expected after the end of the Cold War, but analysts say it has shrunk far beyond what is prudent to meet U.S. commitments and emergencies. Military spending dropped from 26.5 percent of the federal budget in 1989 to 14.6 percent in 1999. Many military units lack equipment and readiness, tens of thousands of armed forces personnel are on food stamps, and enlisted men and junior officers are leaving the military in record numbers.

Hatch was a strong supporter of the Soldiers', Sailors', Airmen and Marines' Act, passed in 1999 to provide a badly needed boost in pay and benefits for those who serve the United States in uniform. He also supported expansion of a program to include Medicare-funded demonstration projects for military retirees over the age of 65, pharmacy benefits to all active and retired personnel, and expanded coverage under existing dental programs for these groups.

Under the Clinton-Gore Administration, funding for Operation and Maintenance (O&M) got so low that backlogs at military depots kept entire units from operating safely. Hatch strongly supported Pentagon O&M increases in 1999 above the Clinton-Gore request, as well as increased funding for military hardware.

The Senator also has pushed efforts to get the Department of Defense more focused on promising new military technologies. He has supported, for example, improved pilot training through greater use of night vision and advanced simulation; a technology research and development road map; a National Missile Defense system; and a space-based defense system with laser technologies to destroy missiles before they enter the atmosphere.

While working to strengthen the military, Senator Hatch consistently has urged the White House to act more decisively to head off potential threats and face real ones. "As we look back on the Clinton foreign policy, I must sadly conclude that he missed the moment" to advance American interests and values at the end of the Cold War, Hatch said in January 2000. "Clinton missed the moment because he came into office believing that he could ignore foreign policy. He made policy without a hard-headed belief in the national interest as the North Star of U.S. foreign and defense policies.

"He believed he could make deals with dictators like Slobodan Milosevic of Serbia and Kim Jong-il of North Korea. He missed the moment because he believed in fashioning 'strategic partnerships' with states like Russia and China that had not yet fully made the choice to play by the rules of the international community."

Hatch listed five major challenges facing the U.S. abroad: (1) preventing destructive major-power rivalries, notably involving China or a resurgent Russia; (2) the threat of extremist regimes and terrorists; (3) the rise of "gangster states" bankrolled by such things as Colombian cocaine or Russian insurance fraud; (4) expanding the American-sponsored sphere of peace and security; and (5) promoting democratic political change around the world.

"The twentieth century was the century of American sacrifice and triumph; they are not separable," said Hatch. "The sacrifice was ours; the triumph was shared by freedom-loving people around the world. We took no possessions, we liberated. We expected no tribute, and we donated more than any country in the history of man. We required of the world no obeisance, but promoted the dedication to principles that dignified the individual without prejudice to society or class."

A decade ago Hatch foresaw the trouble brewing in the Balkans, and personally has been involved in the troubled region since then. Hatch visited Croatia in 1990 on the eve of that country's first free elections, and helped talk its president into allowing international election observers, who helped assure a fair vote.

A year later Hatch was the first senator to call for lifting the U.S. arms embargo on Croatia, in the face of threats from the Serbs. Then, in 1992, he successfully helped urge the Bush Administration to recognize the Croatian government. "We must think more broadly," Hatch said at the time, "to deal with refugee and security issues in the Balkans."

During the Clinton-Gore Administration the Serbs, goaded by their murderous leader Milosevic, continued to cut a swath of destruction through the Balkans. Hatch was one of the strongest voices urging the Administration to lift an arms embargo against the Croatian-Bosnian federation to allow those peoples to defend themselves.

In April 1994, Hatch wrote that "The Clinton Administration has no idea of what it wants to do or how to do it. It has hesitated, vacillated, and equivocated. As a result, the United States and the world community have been outfoxed and outwitted at every turn." By then, Serbia had given the world a chilling new phrase–"ethnic cleansing"–in a vicious war against its neighbors that led to 200,000 deaths and four million refugees. NATO bombing helped end the war and led to an uneasy peace agreement, signed late in 1995 by Milosevic and others.

The following April, Senator Hatch was part of a small congressional delegation flying to the Balkan region to assess the situation. The group covered seven countries in nine days, meeting with leaders in each one. The most intense session was in Belgrade with Milosevic. Other members of the delegation treated Milosevic gingerly, but Hatch regarded him as a war criminal responsible for attempted genocide, and gave him no quarter.

Later, describing his impressions of Milosevic to a friend, Hatch wrote that he "is a bland-faced man who looks like a hoodlum but was trying to convince us he is a reasonable person. He appears to me to be a person of no conscience....He was almost pleading with us to accept him (without saying so), but...it is difficult to respect a person like him."

According to another participant in the tense meeting, Hatch peppered Milosevic with tough questions about his intentions in Kosovo. Milosevic insisted there would be no problem, but Hatch showed he didn't believe it, and left the meeting shaking his head. Three years later, Kosovo exploded.

16

Religious Freedom

For if any be a hearer of the word, and not a doer, he is like unto a man beholding his natural face in a glass: For he beholdeth himself, and goeth his way, and straitway forgetteth what manner of man he was ....Pure religion and undefiled before God and the Father is this, To visit the fatherless and widows in their affliction, and to keep himself unspotted from the world.

–James 1:23-24, 27

ORRIN HATCH HAS NOT FORGOTTEN what manner of man he was when he moved to Washington some two decades ago, and his life continues to reflect James' definition of a pure, practical faith. The Senator is a devout, Sunday School-teaching Christian. While holding fast to his faith, he has encouraged others to follow the tenets of their own belief systems.

"Do not neglect your spiritual growth," Hatch advises on an Internet site. "Whatever your religious roots may be, nurture them. Our faith can guide our vision. It can direct our actions. It can be a strong foundation for whatever we choose to build in terms of our career goals, our communities, our families, our government, and our own happiness."

In 1995 Hatch received a letter from a woman in Amherst, Virginia. She had read the author's first book on Hatch and said "When I [first] wrote you I did not know if you believed in God or to what degree. It is a great joy to know that there are saints (saved by the blood of Jesus) in leadership in our country–we are so blessed....It is very comforting to have 'met' you and know your Godly stand and your fearlessness of man."

Hatch answered that "If only I were worthy of your title, 'saint.' Then I could really work wonders on Capitol Hill that could be felt across this nation. We are at a desperate time in our nation's history when attributes such as faith in God, honesty, and the pure love of Christ are severely lacking in our society. I am very concerned that we may never recover from the absence of these and other values in our lives, and I am dedicated to doing everything I can to prevent this from happening....Please take care, and may God bless you."

Religion is important to most Americans. Aggregate polls by the Gallup organization from 1992 to 1999 asked 40,000 adults "How important would you say religion is in your own life...?" Those who answered "very" or "fairly" important ranged from 84 percent among 18- to 29-year-olds, to 91 percent among those 65 or older. In May 1999, 9 out of 10 respondents told Gallup they prayed–a figure that hasn't changed in a half-century–including 3 out of 4 who pray on a daily basis. "Most adults say they pray to a supreme being, such as God, the Lord, Jehovah, or Jesus Christ," reported Gallup.

The Supreme Court historically has vigorously protected Americans' First Amendment freedoms. State and local governments, for example, could not impede religious expression unless their laws were tightly written to protect a compelling government interest.

That view took a U-turn in 1990 when the Supreme Court ruled (*Employment Division v. Smith*) that churches are subject to all generally applicable and civil laws as long as the laws were not passed specifically to suppress religious expression. The Smith case involved use of a drug in an Indian religious ritual. Protection of religious liberty–the first freedom guaranteed in the Bill of Rights–was a "luxury" the nation could no longer afford, said the high court.

Because of the ruling, within a few years lower courts overrode religious liberties in more than fifty cases. "The potential impact of the Smith case is frightening," said Representative Sue Myrick, a North Carolina Republican. "Now police can arrest a Catholic priest for serving communion to minors in violation of a state's drinking laws. Local officials can force an elderly lady to rent her apartment to an unwed or homosexual couple in violation of her Christian beliefs. Our law enforcement officials can conduct an autopsy on an Orthodox Jewish victim in violation of the family's religious beliefs." Local governments were also restricting churches from locating in residential areas, and were dictating church construction.

Senator Hatch, on the heels of the Supreme Court's Smith decision, introduced the Religious Freedom Restoration Act to overturn it. He persuaded Ted Kennedy to cosponsor the bill. Nearly three years later, in 1993, the American Civil Liberties Union, on behalf of Hatch and Kennedy, sent a letter to all their colleagues in the Senate urging support for the legislation. Hatch and the ACLU rarely agreed on anything, but they agreed that religious freedom was at risk.

By then the coalition pressing for the law had expanded to include a wide range of liberal, conservative, and religious groups. Included were the National Council of Churches, National Association of Evangelicals, Southern Baptist Convention, American Jewish Congress, National Conference of Catholic Bishops, the Church of Jesus Christ of Latter-day Saints, and the Traditional Values Coalition. The coalition called the proposed law the most important blow for religious freedom in the United States since adoption of the Bill of Rights.

The Supreme Court ruling stirred memories of the Holocaust and alarmed leaders of the LDS Church, whose early members had suffered severe persecution, often at government hands, during the nineteenth century–including an "extermination" order issued by Missouri's governor that resulted in Mormons being violently driven from that state in 1838.

"The Act does not affect any of the issues that fall under the rubric of separation of church and state," wrote the ACLU, "but simply restores the previously prevailing legal standard"–meaning that government had to show a "compelling" state interest that justified the restriction. A companion bill was introduced in the House, and Hatch and Kennedy, backed by nearly seventy faiths and civic groups, shepherded the legislation through Congress.

In November 1993, in a ceremony on the South Lawn of the White House, President Clinton signed the Hatch bill into law. "We all have a shared desire to protect perhaps the most precious of all American liberties–religious freedom," said the President. Some 200 people representing many faiths witnessed the signing, including Hatch's guest, M. Russell Ballard, a member of the LDS Church's Council of the Twelve.

Their rejoicing proved premature, however. Just months later, when the new law was tested in a federal appeals court, the Clinton-Gore Administration weighed in against it. The issue involved $13,500 in tithing paid by a Minnesota couple, Bruce and Nancy Young, the year before they filed for bankruptcy in February 1992. A bankruptcy court ruled that their cash donations were "fraudulent" and ordered their Protestant church to return it to a government bankruptcy trustee.

Leaders of the Youngs' church in suburban Minneapolis refused, saying the government was infringing on the couple's constitutional right to free religious expression. They appealed the decision to the 8th U.S. Circuit Court of Appeals–one step below the Supreme Court. Among those with a special interest in the case was the LDS Church, whose members also follow the Old Testament tenet of donating 10 percent of their earnings to their church.

After the Justice Department filed a brief supporting the decision against the Youngs' church, Hatch appealed to President Clinton and Attorney General Janet Reno to reverse that position, which Hatch called "a slap in the face" to the nation's churches. Clinton, at the eleventh hour, blinked, ordering the Justice Department to reverse itself and side with churches rather than with loan collectors. The department did so, backing out of the case just thirty minutes before its attorney was scheduled to make an oral argument in court.

Hatch hailed the decision as "a tremendous step forward in our efforts to protect the fundamental rights of the citizens of this nation–the free exercise of religion."

That victory also proved ephemeral, however. Government infringements on religious liberty continued, capped by a Supreme Court decision in 1997 that partly overturned the Religious Freedom Restoration Act authored by Hatch. Among those encountering problems during the following year:

- Orthodox Jews in Los Angeles, barred by zoning laws from meeting in the home of a member. They met there because of a religious belief against riding in cars on the Sabbath, which they would have to do to reach their distant synagogues.

- A Jewish youth who had to file a lawsuit to stop his school's crusade to prohibit his wearing of a Star of David.

- Catholics, forced to go to court to protect the right of prisoners to practice confession without fear of their words being revealed to police.

- Jehovah's Witnesses, denied jobs because, in following their faith, they refused to take an oath.

Brigham Young University law professor W. Cole Durham found through research that minority religions were five times more likely than large religious groups to have zoning action taken against them to prevent their building of churches. "The differences are so staggering that it is virtually impossible to imagine that religious discrimination is not playing a significant role," Durham told a House hearing in 1998.

Durham, for example, cited the case of an Islamic Center whose application for a building site was long delayed, and repeatedly changed, because of opposition. After a site was finally approved, the city ordered services stopped because of complaints–even though there was a residence next door used for worship by Pentecostal Christians, who, said Durham, "caused more noise, provided less parking and in general seemed less deserving of a zoning exception than the Islamic Center."

During the same hearing, Rabbi David Zeibel, representing an Orthodox Jewish group, said restrictions allowed by Supreme Court action made it hard for Jews to wear yarmulkes at school and work because of dress standards, hard to get kosher foods because of government food processing rules, and hard to prevent autopsies that violated their faith.

In June 1998 Hatch introduced a bill aimed at restoring religious liberties struck down the year before when the Supreme Court gutted much of the first law he wrote. Joining Hatch on Capitol Hill to give his bill a rousing ecumenical send-off were some eighty groups–Christians, Jews, Muslims, and ideologies ranging from the ACLU to the Christian Coalition.

Under Hatch's bill, government could interfere with religion only when it showed an overriding, compelling reason to do so, such as protecting public health and safety. "We believe we have constructed legislation that can merit the support of all who value the free exercise of religion, our first freedom," said Hatch. His chief co-sponsor, Senator Ted Kennedy, explained the bill was needed because "the complex rules used to govern our modern society and economy unnecessarily, and often unintentionally, interfere with religious freedom."

When hearings on the bill opened before the Senate Judiciary Committee, Hatch, the committee chair, called his bill a "second-best situation" to the Supreme Court returning to its historic protection of religious liberty.

> These protections are necessary, not because there are systematic pogroms against certain sects now as there had been earlier in our

> history. No. Hostility to religious freedom comes more subtly from the blind, bureaucratic behemoth of the regulatory state. As it imposes its arbitrary rules into every corner of our lives, it seems unable somehow to cope with the infinite variety of religious experience in America....So, perhaps the Mormons, for example, are no longer driven from state to state, and their extermination is no longer an explicit state policy, but they are still told they cannot build their temples in certain towns.

Although Hatch's 1998 bill did not make it into law, he sponsored a similar bill, the Religious Liberty Protection Act, which was before Congress in 2000. "Passage of this measure remains one of my highest priorities," he said.

While continuing to lead the fight to protect religious liberty at home, Hatch has also been deeply involved abroad, notably in Russia. In June 1996 Alexander Lebed, a former paratrooper general-turned-politician blasted foreign-based religions, pointedly calling Mormons and some other non-Russian faiths "mold and filth which have come to destroy the state," and vowing to banish them from his country. He also said Russia had only three traditional religions–Russian Orthodox, Islam, and Buddhism–alarming his country's 1.5 million Jews, who have suffered considerable persecution during Russia's history.

Lebed's intemperate comments were especially noteworthy given their timing–one week before a presidential runoff in which he had thrown his support to Boris Yeltsin, assuring Yeltsin's victory while placing himself in a position potentially to become president of Russia one day.

Faced by a storm of protest, Lebed backtracked somewhat a week later. "I didn't want to offend anyone. I apologize," he said at a news conference. Lebed laughed when asked about the LDS Church, saying "the poor Mormons," and acknowledged that Judaism was a reality in Russia. But he stuck to his call to ban foreign religions. "Regarding 'strangers' on our territory....I'm categorically against them," he said, this time only singling out the Aum Shinri Kyo, the Japanese sect blamed for a nerve gas attack in 1995 that killed a dozen people in Tokyo.

Lebed, appointed by Yeltsin as his national security chief, set off alarm bells around the world, including in Salt Lake City, home of the Church of Jesus Christ of Latter-day Saints. Following the collapse of the Soviet Union, the church in 1991 received approval by the Russian government to engage in religious activities. Within five years it had built up six different missions in Russia and had about 5,000 members and 300 missionaries.

LDS Church spokesman Don LeFevre said "We have noted and appreciate General Lebed's apology, but we still feel that he may not be fully aware of the fact that the Latter-day Saints in Russia are law-abiding citizens and that the Church has been and is involved in numerous humanitarian projects benefitting the Russian people."

Those who hoped in 1996 that Lebed and his sentiments were a passing phenomenon were to be sorely disappointed. The gruff Lebed, regarded by some Russians as their best bet to bring the country back to respectability in the world community, has proved as tough and resilient in politics as in war. Before resigning his army commission in 1995, he had fought with distinction in most of the former Soviet Union's and Russia's military conflicts of the previous fifteen years, ending as commander of the Fourteenth Russian Army, based in Moldova.

After serving a stormy tenure as Yeltsin's national security chief, in 1998 Lebed, a barrel-chested former boxer, declared his candidacy for governor of Krasnoyarsk. The bleak region four times the size of Texas stretches from Mongolia to the Arctic Circle. Though early polls gave him little chance against the incumbent governor, Lebed was not to be denied. He traipsed doggedly through the snow and permafrost, visiting more than a hundred towns and villages by plane. Against all odds, Lebed, forty-eight-years-old, won. People throughout Russia and the world took notice.

Lebed was invited to the U.S. by Congress and was the only Russian politician at President Clinton's second inauguration in 1997. Where would Lebed take Russia if given the chance? His own words are not reassuring. In his autobiography, *My Life and My Country*, he says flatly that democracy does not fit Russia. "It doesn't completely suit our historical experience, our traditions, our national character," he wrote, adding that "One of the fundamental miscalculations of Russian reform is that we simplistically, one-sidedly accepted the democratic idea and everything connected with it."

As Lebed's political star rose in the last half of the 1990s, it became ominously clear that he spoke for many of his countrymen who also were weary of Russia's painful experiment with democracy. Trouble for foreign-based religions in Russia also rose.

In June 1997 the Duma, Russia's parliament, passed a bill called "On Freedom of Conscience and Religious Association." Strongly pushed by the

Russian Orthodox Church and a large majority of Russian lawmakers, it blatantly discriminated against most other religions. Among onerous provisions, to be deemed a religious organization, a religion had to demonstrate that it had officially existed in Russia for at least fifteen years–dating to Communist dictator Leonid Brezhnev, when the Soviet Union was officially atheistic and repressive to religion.

The proposed law was contrary to the Helsinki Treaty of 1989, which barred "discrimination against individuals of communities on grounds of religion," and flew in the face of the Russian constitution itself. Article 19 of the constitution says "The state guarantees the equality of rights and freedoms regardless of...attitude to religion, convictions, membership in public associations, as well as other circumstances. Banned are all forms of limitations of human rights on social, racial, national, language or religious grounds."

Once more Hatch helped lead the fight against the latest threat to freedom of religion. Initially supporting an amendment introduced by Senator Gordon Smith, R-Oregon, to cut foreign aid to Russia if the restrictive bill became law, on July 16, 1997 Hatch rose in the Senate to warn that "U.S. assistance is not an entitlement. It is a demonstration of our support for the emergence of democracy in a land cursed by communism for most of this century. If Russia turns back to the night of authoritarianism, we should not squander our resources."

Along with that stick, Hatch offered Russia a carrot, praising Boris Yeltsin's support for democracy and pinning hopes on his veto of the Duma's bill. "I will stand and applaud him when he vetoes this bill," said Hatch. "But if this bill becomes law in Russia," he added, "our support for democracy in Russia has been dealt perhaps a fatal blow. We should not waste our funds promoting democratic development on a government that turns away from democracy. And if President Yeltsin signs the bill against religious rights...I will pray for Russia."

Hatch, realizing the proposed law was aimed especially at faiths such as the LDS Church that actively proselyte for new members, lobbied mostly behind the scenes to avoid the appearance of undue parochial interest. Instead he got Ted Kennedy–considered the best-known senator in Russia–to lead Senate denunciation of the proposed law.

Back home in Utah, some of Hatch's constituents believed he and others were unwisely mixing religion and diplomacy. One letter printed in the *Salt Lake Tribune* said Congress's "intent to 'punish the offending countries' is a modern-day version of the Crusades and the Spanish Inquisition: 'Accept our religion, or be burned at the [financial] stake.'"

Within a week after Hatch and others publicly denounced the bill, Yeltsin vetoed it. It was not an easy move, said Yeltsin, because the bill was strongly supported in Russia. Nonetheless, he added, "Many provisions of the law infringe on constitutional rights and freedoms of individuals, establish inequality between different confessions, and violate Russia's international obligations."

World religious leaders let out a collective sigh of relief, reflected in a letter to Hatch from Jeffrey R. Holland, a member of the LDS Church's Quorum of the Twelve Apostles, who oversaw church efforts in Russia. By then the Mormons had about 7,000 members, seven missions, and 500 missionaries there. Wrote Elder Holland:

> I can't adequately express my appreciation to you for what you did to help the United States...during the recent freedom of religion debacle in Russia. Furthermore, you blessed our faithful members in Russia who have been fasting and praying that they would not lose their beloved missionaries there. We know the battle is not over, but this is a marvelous victory in the early going...we are grateful that as citizens of this nation our interests are protected by the Senate along with all other Americans.

Although the most onerous bill was vetoed by Yeltsin, that fall he signed another law creating separate categories of religions and placing restrictions on faiths that could not show they had been operating in Russia for at least fifteen years. Foreign-based religions continued to function in Russia, looking nervously over their shoulders, waiting for the government to clarify their status.

While they waited, Hatch, a member of the Senate Intelligence Committee, and Gordon Smith, chairman of the European affairs subcommittee of the Senate Foreign Relation Committee, went to Russia the following April, 1998, to review various issues in bilateral relations. Issues included strategic weapons proliferation, NATO expansion, sales of nuclear weapons to Iran, and especially religious rights. Hatch had been to Russia many times; Smith, an Oregon Republican and fellow Mormon, was going for the first time.

They were briefed by U.S. State Department officers in Moscow and St. Petersburg and, among many other sessions, met with representatives of various faiths, including Russian Orthodox, Catholic, Baptist, Pentacostal, Jewish and LDS. Representatives described the difficulties of operating in Russia, especially in areas far removed from Moscow, where local bureaucrats often enjoy considerable autonomy in interpreting rules and regulations coming from the capital. Problems included obstructions to registrations, visas, and the importing of religious literature.

The head of one large Catholic parish told the visiting senators that "The Catholic Church has had problems in Russia for 600 years. I cannot imagine the problems religions are having that have only been here six years!" Among key Russian figures meeting with them were Aleksandr Kudryavtsev, the top Ministry of Justice official responsible for religion law, and Andrey Loginov, President Yeltsin's top political advisor on religion.

Hatch and Smith also paid their respects to the head of the Russian Orthodox Church, Alexy II, in a one-hour audience. Since 1990 the grey-bearded patriarch has led the largest ecclesiastically independent church in the commonwealth of Eastern Orthodox churches, currently including more than 120 dioceses and a membership estimated at 60 million. Russia's traditional religion dates to the tenth century, and its fortunes have waxed and waned under various tsars.

Following the Communist revolution of 1917, the Soviets nationalized all church-held property. Wholesale destruction of churches and the arrest and execution of many clerics followed. The church's historic headquarters compound in Moscow, the Danilov Monastery, was used as a detention colony for juvenile criminals before being restored to the church with the breakup of the Soviet Union a decade ago. Today many observers believe the church has strongly encouraged the government to impede the progress of competing religions on Russian soil.

"The patriarch was very kind, very decent," said Hatch in an interview. "He talked about Russia's difficult times under a formal ideology of atheism, as well as the social upheaval and anomie that currently plagues the country, especially its young people. We expressed our sympathies with these concerns." A new religious law was intended to shield Russia from groups that had "terrorist intentions" or were "trying to buy souls," Alexy told them.

While voicing some displeasure with the presence of foreign faiths in Russia, suggesting they contribute to Russia's social unease, the patriarch told Hatch and Smith he believed the religious rights law should be implemented fairly and without discrimination. That general view was echoed by government officials Kudryavtsev and Loginov.

"I returned from Russia moderately reassured that central government officials there do not wish to see official discrimination against any religion," said Hatch. "More problems will remain in the regions, as they have existed for quite some time. We need to accurately track the status of freedom of faith in Russia on all political levels, and to carefully watch for any signs of official or systematic discrimination against any faiths. The United States must seek to support the remarkable, historic development of Russian democracy across the board. One fundamental measure of progress will continue to be freedom of conscience and faith."

In May 1998, a month after Hatch and Smith returned home, Russia officially recognized seven more churches–Roman Catholic, LDS, Baptist, three Pentacostal groups and the New Apostolic Church. Their status thus was clarified under the new law and, in the case of the Mormons, gave them the green light to continue humanitarian and missionary efforts and provide meeting places for members. Russia's action removed Washington's threat to withhold as much as $200 million in foreign aid.

Hatch came to believe the threat to withhold aid might be counterproductive, cutting off assistance to Russia and other countries that could be used to develop legal structures which, over time, could be the ultimate guarantors of democracy. "There is a conceptual problem whenever we seek to apply serious diplomatic and economic sanctions to worldwide problems," he said in a Senate speech supporting a more flexible U.S. approach to dealing with countries that restrict religious freedom.

"On the one hand, you risk over seventy cases of unintended consequences. I use that number because recent estimates are that at least seventy nations violate, abuse or proscribe outright religious freedom. One legislative solution mandating tangible and serious sanctions applied to over seventy cases can have a myriad consequences we don't intend."

He noted that some democracies likewise abuse freedom of religion. "I have met communists who believed, and believers who countenanced oppression of other faiths," said Hatch. "The varieties of personal faith and its expressions are countless, but the fundamental political right to personal conscience is indivisible, and universally desired...the pursuit of this political right must be a conscious, vocal, activist, and determined part of our foreign policy."

The distinguished Senator from Utah mingles with the "Founding Fathers."

In Salt Lake City with the Reverend France Davis of Calvary Baptist Church.

Being sworn in for a fourth Senate term by Vice President Al Gore, January 1995.

With entertainer and former teen idol Pat Boone.

Appearing with the Reverend Jesse Jackson on CBS's "Face the Nation," June 1997.

Pope John Paul II greets Senator and Mrs. Hatch at the Vatican.

With Gordon B. Hinckley, when the president of the Church of Jesus Christ of Latter-day Saints addressed the National Press Club, Spring 2000.

With the Reverend and Mrs. Billy Graham.

With good friend Rabbi Baruch Korff, 1990.

With Mother Teresa at a national right to life convention.

As chairman of the Senate Republican Hispanic Task Force, Hatch meets with actor/ director Edward Olmos.

Hatch's Democratic counterpart on the Senate Juciciary Committee, Senator Patrick Leahy of Vermont, exchanges neckwear and writes, "Orrin– You are a special friend notwithstanding your taste in ties or politics!"

Honoring some staff members on National Secretaries' Day in the Senate Dining Room. Pictured are (left to right) first row: Mary Anderson, Linda Jepsen (deceased), Senator Hatch, Charmaine Kearney, Donna Day, back row: Jenny Ward, Steve Bergstrom, Ruth Montoya, Kerry Hinton, and Chanda Smith.

Receiving the Surgeon General's Medallion for contributions to health care from C. Everett Koop.

Hatch, the "father" of the generic drug industry, chats with actor, health enthusiast, and fellow Republican Arnold Schwarzenegger.

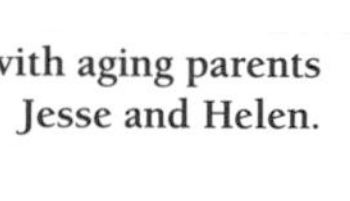

Orrin with aging parents Jesse and Helen.

The growing Hatch clan.

Hatch and Angolan rebel leader Jonas Savimbi point to a plate bearing Cyrillic letters, on a Soviet rocket launcher captured from Cuban troops during Angola's "civil" war.

In Beijing with Deng Xiaoping and fellow senator Edward Zorinsky, D-Nebraska, 1986. Hatch headed a U.S. delegation that won China's support for giving high-tech weapons to guerrillas fighting the Soviets in Afghanistan.

With Lech Walesa, Poland's "George Washington."

With British Prime Minister Margaret Thatcher.

Senator Hatch, in a border enclave near Pakistan's famed Khyber Pass, addresses Mujahedin leaders fighting to drive the Soviet Union out of Afghanistan. His determined effort would help end the Cold War.

With FBI Director Louis Freeh.

On the day of the signing of Hatch's Religious Freedom Restoration Act, the Senator introduces President Bill Clinton to Elder M. Russell Ballard, member of the LDS Church's Council of Twelve Apostles, 1993.

Part III

17

Clinton and Gore

The Clinton-Gore Administration may one day be remembered as the most deceitful and corrupt in our nation's history.

WILLIAM JEFFERSON CLINTON, like Orrin Grant Hatch, has a consistent report card in the subject of character. Unlike Hatch, America's forty-second president consistently has flunked.

Hatch is widely regarded as one of the most honorable men in government–a reputation painfully reinforced in the early 1990s by a thorough two-year investigation of him by the Justice Department and Senate Ethics Committee. At issue, based on the flimsiest of grounds, was Hatch's alleged activities involving the Bank of Credit and Commerce International (BCCI).

In November 1993 the Ethics panel concluded that "there is no credible evidence which provides reason to believe that Senator Hatch engaged in any conduct which would constitute a violation of any law of the United States or of any rule of the Senate, nor any reason to believe that the Senator engaged in any improper conduct."

Then there is Bill Clinton. Where does one begin? Just to list in detail all the significant charges against him–some shared by his wife–during his public life is a daunting task. The profusion of bad news on Clinton coming out of Arkansas during the 1992 presidential election–draft dodging, pot smoking, suspicious financial deals, and especially womanizing–was no surprise to insiders. "We made a serious mistake back then by not listening more to the reporters in Little Rock who really knew him," says the *Washington Post's* David Broder, one of the nation's most respected political journalists.

Another *Post* reporter, Pulitzer prize-winner David Maraniss, probably understands Clinton better than anyone outside the First Family. Maraniss's biography, *First in His Class,* is regarded as the authoritative source on Clinton. In a thin follow-up book, *The Clinton Enigma*, Maraniss wrote that early Clinton traits included a tendency "to block things out, to compartmentalize different aspects of his life, to deny reality and create a fantasy life,...and to feel a constant hunger for love and affirmation."

Other traits came later, including "a sex drive so powerful that some psychologists would classify it as an addiction...a lack of normal standards of self-control, an abuse of the privileges of public office, and a reliance on aides, friends, and family to shield him from the public consequences of his behavior."

Nobody has shielded him better than First Lady Hillary Rodham Clinton. Even after the sordid Lewinsky affair that almost cost them the White House, she was making excuses for his behavior. "He was so young, barely four, when he was scarred by abuse that he can't even take it out and look at it," she told an interviewer in 1999. "There was terrible conflict between his mother and grandmother. A psychologist once told me that for a boy being in the middle of a conflict between two women is the worst possible situation."

How did Hatch and Clinton arrive at such opposite extremes on the character scale? One obvious clue is their dissimilar parentage and upbringing, which for Clinton was problematic well before the mother-grandmother conflict. Deceit and philandering marked Clinton's family, while accountability and moral rectitude characterized Hatch's. Measured by nature or nurture, Hatch clearly had a far straighter start in life than did Clinton.

Clinton's father was William Jefferson Blythe III, a fast-talking traveling salesman who died before Bill was born. Before marrying Bill's mother, Virginia Cassidy, in 1943, after a whirlwind courtship, W.J. had previously married a seventeen-year-old girl, Adele Gash, and divorced her a year later; been listed on a birth certificate as the father of Adele's baby two years after the divorce; married another woman that same year, 1938, and divorced her nine months later; and married Adele Gash's little sister, Faye, for a few months in 1940, apparently to avoid having to wed another young woman who said she was carrying his baby.

Virginia Cassidy apparently knew none of that history before marrying Blythe a few weeks before he was shipped off to World War II. He survived the war and returned home, but was killed in a car accident three months before Bill was born in 1946 in Hope, Arkansas. Four years later Virginia wed Roger Clinton, a good-time guy nicknamed "Dude," who was already married and had two stepsons when they began dating.

Like Virginia's first husband, Clinton was a notorious womanizer. He was also a gambler and an abusive alcoholic who sometimes terrorized Virginia and her sons, Billy and his younger brother Roger, Jr., born to the couple. Although Billy took his last name, his stepfather spent little time with him, not even bothering to legally adopt him.

Clinton's dysfunctional family scarcely could have been more opposite Hatch's. Orrin's parents, Jesse Hatch and Helen Kamm, were callow teenagers when they wed in 1923 in her native Illinois. They were inseparable from then on, struggling together through life's challenges, including the Depression and the deaths of four children. Helen called Jesse "the kindest man I ever knew." Their union, never scarred by infidelity or other abuse, lasted nearly seven decades, until Jesse's death in 1992. Helen died three years later.

When Clinton and Vice President Al Gore took office in January 1993 as the nation's first baby boomer leaders, Hatch vividly recalled his own arrival in Washington sixteen years earlier. On a personal level he empathized with Clinton and vowed to lay partisanship aside in helping him effectively gather the reins of government. During the first weeks of Clinton's tenure, he telephoned Hatch, tracking him down at a Utah restaurant.

"Senator," said Clinton, "I just want you to know how much I appreciate the fair-minded way you have treated our nominees."

"Thank you, Mr. President," answered Hatch. "I'm going to help you all I can and hope you'll continue to choose people I can fully support. I sincerely want you to succeed."

Many of Clinton's nominees came before Hatch's Senate Judiciary Committee. Other conservatives urged Hatch to retaliate for injuries inflicted on nominees of Presidents Reagan and Bush over the previous dozen years. But Hatch refused, determined to give Clinton a fair chance.

Zoe Baird, a Connecticut lawyer and the first woman ever nominated as attorney general, was first up before his committee. Hatch was impressed. "She is clearly intelligent and I think will make a good Attorney General," he wrote. "I also think we could not do any better. She at least has private sector experience and I hope that will guide her in her work there."

Baird, however, was to become a footnote in history. She and her husband had illegally hired two undocumented Peruvians. Although Clinton's transition team had brushed it off, public outcry was loud. Others quickly backed off, but not Hatch. "I do not condone Zoe Baird's hiring of unauthorized aliens to work in her household," he explained. "But this admitted wrongdoing should be put in perspective. She has a fine overall record in the legal profession." Hatch worried that, should Baird not be confirmed, a less competent attorney general might emerge.

Nonetheless, hours after Baird's appearance before the Judiciary Committee, she became the first U.S. cabinet nominee in more than a century to withdraw her name. Other early Clinton candidates likewise had the rug pulled out from under them by a skittish White House because of relatively minor infractions. It was a pattern repeated over and over during the Clinton-Gore Administration: If a nominee became controversial, chances were good that Clinton would cave in to public opinion and Congress rather than go to bat for him or her. One result has been a pervasive weakness in an administration peopled by many second-rate players.

One of those players–Attorney General Janet Reno–replaced Zoe Baird and confirmed Hatch's worst fears. America's "see no evil, hear no evil" top cop received mounds of evidence of wrongdoing by President Clinton, Vice President Gore, and other Administration officials, and routinely ignored it.

Hatch especially was troubled by her refusal to appoint an independent counsel to investigate Clinton-Gore fund-raising in the campaign cycle ending with their reelection in 1996. Those sleazy activities amounted to essentially renting the White House to major donors, including in 103 intimate "coffees," jogging and dinners with Clinton, and hosting 938 overnight guests–big donors and personal friends–at the Executive Mansion from 1993 through 1996. Never before had a president and vice president turned the White House into such a wholesale political money-making machine.

Gore called potential donors from his White House office–apparently a first for a vice president–breaking a rule against using a federal facility for such activities. When pressed on the issue, Gore shrugged it off by saying there was "no controlling legal authority" that would justify an investigation.

Among other flagrant abuses, Gore and Clinton participated in fund-raisers that landed illegal contributions. They included a notorious luncheon attended by Gore in April 1996 at the Hsi Lai Temple in Los Angeles. It netted $109,000, supposedly from Buddhists who were later reimbursed–an illegal dodge. One longtime Gore aide and key Democratic fund-raiser involved with that and other temple fund-raising, Maria Hsia, was indicted by a federal grand jury and, early in 2000, convicted on five felony counts. Gore was roundly criticized for his role in the scheme, including by Democratic opponent Bill Bradley and GOP standard-bearer George W. Bush in the 2000 presidential campaign.

Gore acknowledged "mistakes" in fund-raising–the kind of non-apology apology for which his mentor Bill Clinton is famous–but said he did not realize the temple luncheon was a fund-raiser. Yet six weeks before the event Gore, a habitual micromanager, sent a personal e-mail that recommended turning down a New York event because "we have already booked the fund-raisers" in California. A high Democratic priority in 2000 was protecting him from the 1996 scandals. At this writing Attorney General Reno was still doing her part, refusing to call Gore to account.

Clinton and Gore also have had money ties to two other Asian women–Pauline Kanchanalak of Thailand and Hong Kong billionaire Nina Wang. The two women, along with Maria Hsia, all have connections to Chinese intelligence or to the military arm of the Chinese Communist Party, the People's Liberation Army, according to two congressional investigators whose 1998 book on the White House's tangled web was called, appropriately, *The Year of the Rat: How Bill Clinton Compromised U.S. Security for Chinese Cash.*

Election law prohibits campaign donations from abroad, and specifies that donors must give only their own money. The Democratic National Committee blithely ignored both laws, accepting and laundering millions of dollars in tainted funds.

Most of the money was funneled through three Chinese-Americans–John Huang, Charlie Trie, and Johnny Chung–with close ties to China, raising the possibility that China compromised the very nerve center of America's political system. Records show that, among them, the three men were admitted to the White House scores of times, and given access to highly sensitive U.S. military and trade secrets.

"The fund-raising disclosures have blown up into the biggest political scandal in the United States since Watergate," editorialized the *New York Times*. "It is paralyzing the President, preoccupying Congress and fueling public cynicism about our political system...for an Attorney General of the

United States, blind stubbornness is no substitute for impartial legal analysis, civic-minded leadership and loyalty to the public."

Senator Hatch, who directed the Judiciary Committee to probe many of the misdeeds, said "The Clinton-Gore Administration has used every conceivable means to dissemble, mislead and fool the people as well as to cover up official corruption. Such actions are something new and something terribly dangerous. This routine practice of political deception to hide an inner falsity...the cynical deceit that you've not done anything wrong if you can talk your way out if it, is the real cultural legacy of this Administration."

Hatch's bill of particulars came in a twenty-eight-minute videotaped "fireside chat" he released early in January 2000 while still in the presidential race. The video was shown on prime-time television in the key early primary states of Iowa and New Hampshire, and mailed to thousands of individual citizens in Iowa. It was by far the most comprehensive summary of Clinton-Gore corruption issued by any presidential candidate.

"From its first day, this Administration said it believed in 'the permanent campaign,'" noted Hatch. "Unlike earlier administrations that at least tried to give up politics to run the government, this Administration said openly it believed in politics all the time....This was one promise the Administration kept."

Among Administration activities described by Hatch, in addition to illegal fund-raising:

- Political misuse of federal agencies including the FBI, Secret Service, Immigration and Naturalization Service, and IRS.

- Opening of White House doors "to suspicious characters–despite official warnings–who purchased access to the President and various federal departments with their checkbooks."

- Frequent visits to the White House by a "bagman" for an Indonesian family "tied to Chinese business and government interests, and another Clinton-Gore fund-raiser who was indirectly tied to a high official of the Chinese army."

John Huang, Clinton and Gore's chief money-raiser in the Asian-American community, worked for the Lippo Group, an Indonesian conglomerate headed by James Riady, who had close ties to China. During a limousine ride with Clinton in 1992, Riady promised the future president he would raise a million dollars for him. Huang later testified before a House committee that the money was raised as promised, and he was the conduit for the laundered funds.

In 1994 Huang also arranged a $100,000 payment to Clinton's close friend Webster Hubbell, an ex-law partner of Hillary Rodham Clinton. At the time, Hubbell was under investigation in the Whitewater scandal, and some observers believe the payment was to keep Hubbell from testifying against the Clintons. Shortly after the payment Clinton appointed Huang to a high-level Commerce Department position.

Of Huang, Hatch said, "No administration in our history has ever had a political fund-raiser in such a high position in government who was so closely tied to foreign interests, allowed him not only repeated access to the White House but to CIA briefings and top-secret clearances, and then made him privy to the United States' positions in trade negotiations. The Administration also altered those positions in ways that were favorable to these foreign interests. And finally, all of this occurred as allegations cropped up of missile technology transfers and a massive breach of U.S. nuclear secrets by the Chinese government."

As a result of such abuses, said Hatch, the Clinton-Gore Administration may one day be remembered "as the most deceitful and corrupt in our nation's history."

FBI Director Louis Freeh and Attorney General Reno's hand-picked lead investigator Charles LaBella, reviewed the fund-raising evidence and urged Reno to seek the appointment of an independent counsel to pursue it. But despite the array of alleged wrongdoing–including perjury by Administration officials, damaging missile technology transfers, and even theft of nuclear secrets–Reno refused to pursue the corruption and instead thwarted the work of LaBella and Freeh.

Senator Hatch has led efforts to make Reno accountable, saying she has a "legal and ethical obligation" to request a special counsel "to explore all areas of what can only be described as one of the most questionable fund-raising scandals in history....What is at stake is whether the public's confidence in the rule of law and the integrity of the Department of Justice will be further eroded by this Administration."

But Reno repeatedly rebuffed Hatch and others. Instead the department arranged sweetheart plea bargains with key wrongdoers who might have provided damaging testimony. Seventy witnesses took the Fifth

Amendment against self-incrimination, eighteen fled the country, and twenty-three foreign witnesses refused to be interviewed.

In another critical area, the Clinton-Gore Administration, by example and precept, has shown a cavalier attitude toward drug abuse. Clinton, who acknowledges trying marijuana in his college days but "not inhaling," set the tone. The Secret Service told a House committee that when Clinton-Gore came into office in 1993, the agency found more than forty White House employees who had used illegal drugs, including about two dozen recently. Drugs included cocaine and hallucinogens.

The Secret Service did not want to grant permanent passes to about a dozen of these White House employees. After the White House balked and agreed to require employees with known drug backgrounds to undergo periodic surprise drug tests, the Secret Service relented. But agents continued to express concern that some White House employees could be blackmailed.

A federal study released in August 1996 showed that teen-age drug use had more than doubled over four years, and that one in ten teens now said they used drugs each month. "The statistics confirm an upward spiral of drug abuse across the nation since President Clinton took office," said Hatch.

While violent crime has steadily decreased in recent years, many observers credit a robust economy, the FBI under its excellent director Louis Freeh, and get-tough programs by such local leaders as New York Mayor Rudolph Giuliani. The White House itself has been largely AWOL in fighting crime. It has opted for headlines by supporting the Brady Bill and other contentious gun-control legislation of peripheral value at best, while refusing to enforce laws already on the books against the use of firearms in committing crimes. Criminals cause about 13,000 deaths each year using firearms, and commit another 330,000 violent crimes using guns.

"Law-abiding citizens are being killed and wounded by criminals using firearms, and we have a president who, instead of enforcing the law, seems intent on punishing law-abiding citizens," said Hatch. The Bureau of Alcohol, Tobacco and Firearms (ATF) is the government's regulatory arm for firearms. Perhaps preoccupied working with gun-control groups, it reduced the number of referrals for prosecution of firearms violations by 44 percent from 1992 to 1998.

Senator Hatch's National Instant Check System (NICS) to keep guns out of the hands of those known to be at high risk of misusing them went into effect in November 1998. Over the next year, there were about 100,000 denials of firearms purchases by such individuals as felons or those convicted of domestic violence. Yet as of fall 1999 the ATF under Clinton-Gore had referred only 200 cases for prosecution–one for every 500 violations.

The Senator, as head of the Judiciary Committee, stepped into the anti-crime breach early in the Clinton-Gore years, and became point man in the entire Congress in fighting crime. He and former House Republican leader Newt Gingrich of Georgia led the charge against the 1994 Clinton crime bill, which weakened mandatory minimum sentences for violent offenders, included an assault weapons ban, and contained billions of dollars in social spending boondoggle funding.

The issue became historic: Although a scaled-back version of the bill eventually passed, the Clinton crime bill was the single greatest galvanizing incident for Republicans in 1994, who recaptured the House that year for the first time in decades, with Gingrich becoming Speaker.

Since then Hatch has introduced and pushed into law numerous crime-control measures. They include the Antiterrorism and Effective Death Penalty Act of 1996, passed in the wake of the Oklahoma City bombing. It provided tougher sanctions against terrorists and ways to reduce terrorism, and helped curtail endless frivolous appeals of inmates on death row. Another Hatch measure imposes reasonable limits on the ability of all prison inmates to inundate courts with superficial lawsuits.

Hatch also has taken the lead in passing stronger measures to curb the possession, production and trafficking in methamphetamine, a popular and vicious drug made with easily available ingredients. Despite his successful law-making efforts in Washington, the deadly drug continued to spread like a prairie fire across the country, including in Utah, which in 1999 had the dubious distinction of having more illegal meth labs per capita than any other state.

Among many other initiatives, recent crime-control measures by Hatch:

- Provide for the first time that federal courts must order violent criminals to pay restitution to their victims.

- Strengthen federal penalties for offenses, including arson, against religious property.

• Restore funding for the office of America's drug-control czar, which was slashed by the Clinton-Gore Administration.

• Toughen laws against sexual exploitation of children, including over the Internet.

• Increase funding for a national program to help find and assist missing and exploited children.

While Janet Reno has been a bust as Attorney General, Senator Hatch has high praise for the FBI's Louis Freeh. The two have worked closely on many crime-fighting measures, and their admiration is mutual. Hatch has received a number of letters from Freeh, including one dated October 9, 1996 which began: "Dear Orrin, Once again I must thank you for your extraordinary support of law enforcement." The subject was passage of a bill against economic espionage, which Freeh called "an amazing accomplishment for which I am grateful."

In foreign policy the Clinton-Gore Administration has lurched from crisis to crisis, never formulating a coherent and consistent view of America's place in the post-Cold War world. Clinton's first weak Secretary of State, Warren Christopher, was replaced by another, Madeleine Albright, in 1997.

Albright, the first woman Secretary of State, has been obsessed with her image, and career diplomats say she is a weak presence in policy meetings. She has spoken loudly while carrying a small stick, and her lectures to assorted rogues around the world rarely have been backed up by Administration action. Albright had been a staff member to President Jimmy Carter, responsible for foreign policy legislation, and during her tenure with Clinton the Administration's lack of a global strategy has had all the earmarks of Carter's hapless presidency.

Lacking credible, ongoing diplomatic initiatives–and distracted, in Clinton's case, by recurring scandal–the Administration repeatedly has dallied until pushed to the wall, then often has reacted with military force, the ultimate failure of diplomacy. The recurring knee-jerk violence invites terrorist retaliation the U.S. may well yet suffer. Much of it might have been avoided had the world's only superpower stayed focused and exercised its might effectively on all fronts–diplomatic, economic, and cultural as well as military.

The People's Republic of China (PRC) has benefitted enormously under Clinton-Gore, running up a huge trade deficit with the U.S., improving its high-tech military capability courtesy of the White House and profit-hungry American companies, and having the Administration run interference for its admittance into the World Trade Organization. A disturbing pattern has characterized the relationship: Clinton-Gore have utterly failed to require quid pro quos of the PRC; the more they have given China, the tougher China has been on its dissidents.

The Cox Report, a unanimous bipartisan study released in 1999 by a House select committee–five Republicans and four Democrats–outlines in grim detail China's relentless march toward superpower status at America's expense. Former Secretary of Defense Caspar Weinberger, in the forward to the 374-page volume, says the PRC "will use–and have used–every available means to make Communist China our strategic equal...stealing or buying our technology, opposing and blocking our foreign policy actions, and trying to displace American influence in Asia and the Pacific region."

> The great mystery when we look at the actions of the Clinton-Gore administration is trying to explain why? Why would the administration so cavalierly endanger American security? Is it really a matter so simple, so sordid, so base as campaign contributions? Perhaps. But [whatever the motive] the Clinton-Gore administration stands condemned of some of the worst and most damaging national security decisions of this century.
>
> ...what the Cox Report has uncovered regarding espionage by agents of the PRC is the most serious breach of national security since Julius and Ethel Rosenberg betrayed our atomic secrets to the Soviet Union and Aldrich Ames sold us out for a mess of pottage. For their crimes, the Rosenbergs were executed. The crimes uncovered here by this Report have yet to be redressed.

One unquestioned bright spot in the Clinton years has been the nation's economy. Clinton deserves credit for retaining Alan Greenspan as Federal Reserve Chairman, and for appointing Robert Rubin as his first Secretary of the Treasury. Starting with a solid economic foundation owing in part to major tax cuts under President Reagan, and working with a Republican-led Congress, the two men were remarkably effective in setting policies giving the U.S. economy its longest peacetime expansion in history. Unlike many Clinton appointees, Rubin and Greenspan are greatly admired among

Republican as well as Democratic lawmakers.

When Clinton reached the White House, unemployment was at 6.9 percent, the U.S. budget deficit was $255 billion, and the Dow Jones industrial average was below 4,000. When Rubin, a former Wall Street investment banker, stepped down in the spring of 1999 after six years at Treasury, unemployment was at 4.3 percent, three decades of solid deficits had been replaced with a surplus, and the market had topped 11,000 for the first time–putting new money in the pockets of millions of Americans.

Many observers credit the strong economy–and the fear by many citizens of rocking the boat–with saving Bill Clinton from being thrown out of office by the Senate in 1999 after the House impeached him. Certainly it was not respect that led most citizens to favor his retention. A day after he was impeached by the House in 1998, a national poll found that just one in four Americans believed he had high personal moral and ethical standards. Yet only 33 percent said the Senate should remove Clinton from office.

History likely will say that Clinton had the intellect, the charisma, and the political instincts to be a great president. But he lacked the integrity essential for any effective relationship, beginning with a basic dishonesty so ingrained that some psychologists believe he literally doesn't know when he is telling the truth and when he is not.

Many politicians bow to expediency on matters of national policy, but Clinton has taken the art to new depths in his public as well as private life. From early in Clinton's tenure, Republicans were spared having to call attention to his notorious nature, by Democrats eager to put moral distance between themselves and the head of their party. Representative David Obey, D-Wisconsin: "I think most of us learned sometime ago, if you don't like the President's position on a particular issue, you simply need to wait a few weeks."

Senator Bob Kerrey, D-Nebraska, told *Esquire* magazine that Clinton was "an unusually good liar. Unusually good. Do you realize that?" At about the same time, Senator Ernest Hollings reported that "Clinton's as popular as AIDS in South Carolina." He added that the President's "approval ratings were up to 50 percent now....If they get up to 60 percent, his people tell me Bill can start dating again."

Vice President Al Gore unfortunately has learned well from his mentor Clinton. Gore has blithely changed positions on many hot topics–ranging from abortion to gun control–to suit his 2000 presidential campaign, while refusing to acknowledge the discrepancies with his past until confronted with irrefutable proof.

The morning after the February 1, 2000 New Hampshire primary, Gore corrected Diane Sawyer on "Good Morning America" when she said he had lost the youth vote to Bill Bradley. "We won in every single demographic category," insisted Gore. It was another lie. Bradley beat Gore in New Hampshire among younger voters, aged eighteen to twenty-nine, by three points, and among male voters by four points.

Getting a straight answer from Gore in the presidential campaign has been like trying to hold quicksilver: Just when you think you have it, open your fingers and you'll find it has slipped away. Poor Bill Bradley almost went nuts during the presidential primary season, trying to get his fellow Democrat to own up to the many inconsistencies in his record and his illegal fund-raising, well-documented and widely acknowledged by almost everyone but Gore himself.

As the frustrated Bradley waved copies of newspaper stories headlining Gore's campaign illegalities and demanding the Vice President come clean, Gore was busy blowing still more smoke, savaging Bradley's record and positions. For instance, he blamed the former New Jersey senator for voting for President Reagan's budget–failing to note that Bradley led the fight against the deep tax cuts that were the centerpiece of the Reagan program.

Using a vicious, longstanding Democratic tactic of scaring senior citizens, Gore repeatedly said Bradley's health care plan would end Medicaid and threaten Medicare, putting millions of older citizens at risk. Bradley in fact proposed to replace Medicaid, not end it. Gore also used Bradley's health plan as a weapon to try to turn the gay and lesbian community–a key Democratic voter bloc–against Bradley. In February 2000 Bradley woke up to a front-page story in the *San Francisco Chronicle* in which Gore said his rival's health plan "would devastate tens of thousands of people with long-term debilitating diseases such as AIDS."

Bradley, usually known for cerebral reserve, finally came unglued, accusing Gore of "shamelessly" stooping to "the worst use of scare tactics I have seen in many years." In a debate with Gore, Bradley added that "If you're running a campaign that says untrue things, I wonder if you can be a president who gets people's trust?"

Gore's attempts to inflate his resume are a staple for stand-up comics. To appear more as a man of the people, Gore has stressed his experience as a youth working the family farm in Tennessee. While "Farmer Al" spent some recreational summer time there as a youth, he was in fact reared in comfort and affluence in a Washington, D.C. hotel, family quarters when his father was in Congress. Born with a silver spoon firmly in his mouth, Gore attended an exclusive private prep school before going on to Harvard.

Among other things, Gore has claimed to be the father of the Internet, has said that he and wife Tipper were the models for the three-hanky movie *Love Story*–both claims false–and that he "found" the Love Canal–the area in upstate New York evacuated in 1978 because of chemical contamination. Gore *held hearings* on the Love Canal–months after President Jimmy Carter declared the neighborhood a disaster area.

" . . . at times, when Gore descends to the politics he disdains, he can't find the level beneath which he will not sink," wrote *Time* magazine columnist Margaret Carlson. "A Gore [political] appearance should be closed-captioned with the truth," she added. Lying comes so much more natural to Gore's mentor Clinton, noted Carlson. "Gore is just so obvious. When laying one on us, he tilts his head, goes all syrupy like an infomercial host, and slows his singsong voice even further (picture a teacher's pet whining Good morning, Miss Jones, and you've captured the Gore cadence)....Gore keenly senses he's not perfect and rewrites history to try to make it so."

Gore's character and grating personality aside, there were many substantive reasons in 2000 for citizens to pray he did not become president. Senator Hatch called Gore "a nice man, an earnest man with whom I served for many years in the Senate. But a man who, in the words of one commentator, 'Never met a regulation he didn't like.'" Hatch considers Gore a radical environmentalist and old-line liberal whose administration–especially his appointments to the Supreme Court–would harm the country for decades to come.

A legacy of the Clinton-Gore years has been a further debasement of our language. "Parsing"–separating sentences into their individual words and examining each one–has been common during their tenure. Thus President Clinton famously sought a definition of "is" during his crooked testimony over Monica Lewinsky before a legal panel, and Vice President Gore often tried to weasel out of embarrassments by using tortured semantics.

Opinion polls suggested, regrettably, that they succeeded to a significant degree in confusing citizens on the differences between right and wrong. Pandering to such bedrock Democratic constituencies as gays and establishment feminists, they have tried to all but obliterate the lines between traditional values and the radical social agendas of such groups.

Political columnist Charles Krauthammer, writing more than a decade earlier, seemed to anticipate the Clinton-Gore era:

> "If he does really think that there is no distinction between virtue and vice," warns Dr. Samuel Johnson, "why sir, when he leaves our houses let us count our spoons."...
>
> Perhaps the deepest cause of moral confusion is the state of language itself, language that has been bleached of its moral distinctions, turned neutral, value free, "nonjudgmental." When that happens, moral discourse becomes difficult, moral distinctions impossible and moral debate incomprehensible. If abortion is simply "termination of pregnancy," the moral equivalent of, say, removing a tumor, how to account for a movement of serious people dedicated to its abolition? If homosexuality is merely a "sexual preference"–if a lover's sex is as much a matter of taste as, say, hair color...then why the to-do over two men dancing together at Disneyland? But there is a fuss because there is a difference. One can understand neither with language that refuses to make distinctions.

As Clinton and Gore neared the end of their first term in 1995, here were some reviews:

- Columnist Richard Cohen described a "Full Clinton" as a "back-flipping, buck-passing, dive off the lowest board possible."

- George F. Will wrote that "Plainly put, almost no one thinks [Clinton] believes a word he says. Or, more precisely, he believes everything he says at the moment he emphatically says it, and continues to believe it full throttle right up to the moment he repudiates it. He has the weird sincerity of the intellectual sociopath, convinced that when he speaks, truth is an option, but convenience is an imperative."

- Columnist Joe Klein said "[Clinton] gives the appearance of taking stands–for some sort of tax cut, some sort of welfare reform, some sort of balanced budget–but these are ploys, mirages....He doesn't fight for anything substantive–except, of course, reelection."

Nonetheless, defying political gravity and fortunate to be paired against former Senate Majority Leader Bob Dole and running mate Jack Kemp, who ran a dull, enervating campaign, Clinton-Gore won a second term in 1996. They did so with widespread revulsion in the electorate, reflected in the lowest voter turnout–48.8 percent–since the 1920s. For the second time Clinton and Gore failed to capture half the vote, finishing with 49 percent, as Dole picked up 41 percent and Reform Party candidate Ross Perot got 8 percent.

Women ironically kept Clinton and Gore in the White House. While men split their vote between Clinton-Gore and Dole-Kemp, 43 percent and 44 percent respectively, 54 percent of women pulled the lever for the Democrats and just 38 percent for the GOP ticket–perhaps the largest gender gap in history.

By then Clinton's dark character and habitual abuse of women were common knowledge. Those who voted for him–and those who failed to vote–have only themselves to blame for his second sorry term. Most had heard of Gennifer Flowers, Paula Jones, and various other women dismissed by a Clinton aide as part of the "bimbo eruptions" from his past. They had not yet heard of another young woman who would also be used and discarded by Clinton–star-struck, sweet-faced Monica Lewinsky.

By the time Clinton was elected to a second term in November 1996, he had been having an affair with the former White House intern a full year. Lewinsky began working as volunteer at the Executive Mansion in July 1995, accepting a paying job there on November 13. Two days later, during the government shutdown, she saw Clinton at a White House birthday party, lifted her jacket, and showed him the straps of her thong underwear. They stepped to his private study, kissed, and later that evening had their first sexual encounter.

A Washington psychiatrist compared Clinton to the *Titanic*: "Lots of power. Big. Sexy. Thinks he's invulnerable, like the builders of the ship. And here is this twenty-one-year-old iceberg."

18
Bill and Monica

The American people have been doomed to a guided tour of hell.

–Atlanta Journal-Constitution

BEFORE MONICA THERE WAS Paula Jones. After all the prom queens he had violated with impunity, there was something fitting about Bill Clinton finally being brought to account by a cosmetically challenged woman his surrogates dismissed as "trailer park trash."

Paula Corbin Jones was to Bill Clinton what tax evasion was to Al Capone: Both men were done in not by their weightier crimes but for lying about a relatively small one. It was not small, however, to Jones, twenty-four and a $10,000-a-year state government clerk on May 8, 1991, when working the registration desk of a conference at a Little Rock hotel. A state trooper approached and told her "The governor said you make his knees knock." He conveyed Clinton's invitation for her to visit his room, saying "We do this all the time."

Three years later, in May 1994, after the trooper, Danny Ferguson, apparently leaked a distorted account of what happened in that room to the *American Spectator* magazine, Jones filed a civil suit against the President in U.S. District Court in Arkansas. Stuart Taylor Jr., legal affairs reporter for the *New York Times*, spoke for most of his media colleagues when he wrote that "My guess is she's lying, at least about the more lurid details."

Jones's case was newsworthy, since she apparently was the first woman in history to sue a U.S. president for sexual harassment. But the mainstream media refused to pursue it beyond doing obligatory stories on the legal steps of the suit. Not only did the White House rebuttal sound plausible, but the details of her account were so raw and disgusting that even America's huge anti-Clinton cottage industry had difficulty accepting them at face value.

After entering his hotel room, said Jones, Clinton began with small talk, saying her boss Dave Harrington was his "good friend." Next came compliments: "I love the way your hair flows down your back" and "I love your curves." Clinton then put his hand on her thigh and started sliding it up, while trying to kiss her neck as she ducked away. Jones walked across the room, confused and upset, sat down at the end of a sofa nearest the door, and "tried to distract Mr. Clinton by asking him about his wife and her activities...." Not to be denied, Clinton "then walked over to the sofa, lowered his trousers and underwear," and "told me to 'kiss it.'"

"I was horrified by this," said Jones. "I jumped up from the couch and told Mr. Clinton that I had to go...[he] said 'Well, I don't want to make you do anything you don't want to.' Then, in what she took as a warning that he had ultimate control over her state job, he reportedly said "If you get in trouble for leaving work, have Dave call me immediately and I'll take care of it." Finally, she recalled, "As I left the room, Mr. Clinton detained me momentarily, looked sternly at me and said 'You are smart. Let's keep this between ourselves.'"

Little wonder there was widespread disbelief in her account: It would take someone truly perverted to act that way. Later that year Jones and her husband and son moved to California.

Other legal proceedings followed her initial filing: August 10, 1994–Clinton files a motion to dismiss Jones's suit on grounds of presidential immunity; December 28, 1994–U.S. District Judge Susan Webber Wright rules that a trial cannot take place until Clinton leaves office but fact-finding procedures can proceed; January 9, 1996–an appeals court rules that Jones's lawsuit can go to trial; June 24, 1996–Clinton appeals to the Supreme Court and on this day the court agrees to consider delaying the case until he leaves office. There is rejoicing in the White House, since the move puts the lawsuit on hold until after the November election.

Clinton's largely free ride in the media over Jones came to an abrupt end shortly before his reelection. Stuart Taylor, who had branded her a liar in 1994 when reporting for the *New York Times*, and said he voted for Clinton in 1992, did a painstaking and detailed investigation of the case. Notably, he interviewed six witnesses Jones had talked to soon after her run-in with Clinton, who supplied "impressive" corroborating details. Taylor wrote a thirteen-page analysis, published in the November 1996 issue of a respected legal magazine, the *American Lawyer*.

Paula Jones's evidence of "predatory, if not depraved, behavior by Bill Clinton is far stronger than the evidence supporting Anita Hill's allegations of far less serious conduct by Clarence Thomas," wrote Taylor, adding that "Jones's evidence is highly persuasive."

Most reporters, for all their proclaimed independence, are loath to go out on a limb alone. But Taylor's piece opened the floodgates to the Clinton-Jones story, and the rest of the media swam through. Almost overnight Jones's allegations began to be taken at face value.

Senator Hatch was as unprepared as anyone in 1994 to fully believe Jones's allegations. Despite Clinton's reputation, Hatch's periodic conversations with him gave scant evidence that the President was in fact a Mr. Hyde as well as a Dr. Jekyll. On the evening of July 20, for example, two months after Jones filed suit in Arkansas, Clinton telephoned Hatch to thank him for helping to shepherd new Supreme Court Justice Stephen Breyer through the Judiciary Committee. The President was gracious and expansive.

"I just finished reading *The Body Farm*, and noticed that Patricia Cornwell dedicated it to you for your work on crime," said Clinton.

"Do you know her?" asked Hatch.

"No, but I've read all her books," said Clinton. "I think she's a great writer."

Hatch seconded that opinion about his good friend. "You ought to have her come in and meet her."

Clinton said he was planning to have a dinner for a number of mystery writers, and that he would invite Hatch along too. They also spoke of Clinton's nominees to lower federal courts, and the possibility of detailing some bipartisan attorneys from the Justice Department to help speed up the screening process.

By then Hatch had been appointed to the ad hoc Whitewater Committee to investigate the President and First Lady's controversial land dealings back in Arkansas. "I want you to know that I will do my best to see that you and Hillary are treated fairly," said Hatch. Clinton thanked him.

Afterward, in a private letter, Hatch wrote that "It was a nice conversation and I can easily see why so many people like him. However, there is always an edge there that indicates to me that one should not place too great a confidence in his friendship or his friendly ways."

The delaying tactics of Clinton's legal team succeeded in keeping the Jones lawsuit from coming to an early trial that might have derailed his reelection in November 1996. By the following July, with the clock ticking on his second term and the threat growing that the Jones case would taint his legacy, Clinton and his advisors changed tactics. They filed a petition to have the case thrown out of court or, barring that, considered expeditiously to get it behind the President. Clinton also came close to settling out of court with Jones, but heavy-handed tactics by his legal team led Jones to dig in her heels and press on.

Jones's lawyers had been flooded with the names of other women whose alleged relations with Clinton reportedly would show a pattern consistent with Jones's account. A new name that surfaced was that of former White House intern Monica Lewinsky. Her confidant, Linda Tripp, had secretly tape-recorded Lewinsky's conversations about Clinton, and briefed Jones's lawyers. On January 7, 1998, Lewinsky signed an affidavit declaring she "never had a sexual relationship with the president."

Lewinsky, unlike Paula Jones, was born to a life of privilege, growing up in wealthy Beverly Hills, California, the daughter of a doctor-businessman and a socialite mother. Her parents had a nasty divorce when she was fourteen. Lewinsky attended Beverly Hills High School where she appeared in musicals and was named by the school yearbook as "most likely to get her name in lights."

In May 1995 she graduated with a degree in psychology from Lewis & Clark College in Portland, Oregon, where she made dean's list. She then moved to Washington where her mother was living in the Watergate complex, namesake of the presidential scandal that drove Richard Nixon from office two decades earlier.

Nine days after Lewinsky signed the affidavit, Attorney General Reno approved independent counsel Kenneth Starr's request to expand his Whitewater probe to investigate the possibility of subornation–solicitation–of perjury and obstruction of justice in the Jones case.

The next day, January 17, Clinton was questioned under oath by Jones's attorneys in the Washington office of his lawyer, Robert S. Bennett. First Clinton was asked about Kathleen Willey, who said he had made sexual overtures to her in the White House on the very day when–unbeknown to both at the time–Willey's husband committed suicide. Clinton denied her account.

Then the subject turned to Lewinsky, with Clinton acknowledging he knew her casually, first as a White House intern and then as a paid staffer. Here is a comparison of points, quoting directly from Clinton's deposition and paraphrasing relevant findings in Ken Starr's report the following September:

Q. Is it true that when [Lewinsky] worked at the White House she met with you several times?
A. I don't know about several times ....I saw her on two or three occasions then, and then when she worked at the White House, I think there was one or two other times when she brought some documents to me.

Starr report: Clinton met with Lewinsky many times.

Q. At any time were you and Monica Lewinsky alone together in the Oval Office?
A. I don't recall.

Starr report: They were alone many times.

Q. Have you ever talked to Monica Lewinsky about the possibility that she might be asked to testify in this lawsuit?
A. I'm not sure.

Starr report: A month earlier, on December 17 at about 2 a.m., Clinton called Lewinsky and told her she was on the Jones case witness list. He told her to say she came to the White House to visit his secretary, Betty Currie. On January 5 they talked again, Clinton suggesting she could tell Jones's lawyers that others had helped her obtain a Pentagon job. Two days later she signed her phony affidavit.

Q. Have you ever given any gifts to Monica Lewinsky?
A. I don't recall. Do you know what they were?

Starr report: Clinton gave her many gifts during their affair. Twenty days earlier, on December 28, the two met in the Oval Office, where Clinton gave her several Christmas presents, including a stuffed animal, chocolates, and a pair of joke sunglasses. That afternoon, Currie drove to Lewinsky's apartment, collected a box of gifts given by Clinton, and hid the box under her bed at home.

Q. Did you have an extramarital sexual affair with Monica Lewinsky?

A. No . . . I have never had sexual relations with Monica Lewinsky. I've never had an affair with her.

Starr report: In addition to various instances of "phone sex" late at night, Clinton and Lewinsky had sexual encounters in or near the Oval Office at least ten times from November 15, 1995, to March 29, 1997. (Later he argued legally, though not publicly, that she always performed oral sex on him and he did nothing to her in return, thus it was not sexual relations.)

Clinton's twisted testimony assured that 1998 would be remembered in American history as the year of L'affaire Lewinsky. At a White House event on January 26, Clinton, with Hillary at his side, wagged an infamous finger at the cameras and declared "I did not have sexual relations with that woman, Miss Lewinsky. I never told anybody to lie." Apparently his other hand was behind his back, fingers crossed.

Clinton's apologists, enablers, and spin doctors rallied to his side, as they had always done. The next morning, the First Lady appeared on NBC's "Today" show, charging that the controversy had been fabricated by a "vast right-wing conspiracy." That evening Clinton stepped into the House chamber to deliver his annual State of the Union address, not mentioning the spreading scandal. He dispatched Vice President Al Gore to Capitol Hill to tout his address and rally Democrats. Behind closed doors, Gore told them "It's important that Democrats support the President and his agenda today, tomorrow and in the future."

Weeks later, veteran freelance journalist Christopher Hitchens was lunching at the Occidental restaurant with a woman named Carol Blue and a man named Sidney Blumenthal, a notorious advisor to Clinton. Hitchens, in a sworn statement, said "in the presence of myself and Carol Blue, Mr. Blumenthal stated that Monica Lewinsky had been a 'stalker' and that the President was 'the victim' of a predatory and unstable sexually demanding young woman. Referring to Ms. Lewinsky, Mr. Blumenthal used the word 'stalker' several times...[he] advised us that this version of the facts was not generally understood."

Salacious tidbits from Linda Tripp's tapes were seeping into the media, lawyers for the trapped Lewinsky were trying to cut a deal with Starr–her truthful testimony in exchange for immunity for lying in the Jones case–and

Clinton's presidency was on the line as never before.

Satirists had a field day. Columnist Dave Barry's advice to Clinton: "Do what the people expect of you: lie." Regarding a blue dress of Lewinsky's that apparently was stained with Clinton's body fluid during sex and kept but never cleaned by her, Barry suggested the President "could always say *he* was wearing the dress."

Senator Hatch, asked if he believed the charges about Clinton were true, said "I'm very concerned that they are." He compared the relationship between a president and intern to that between a teacher and student or doctor and patient. "If these allegations are true, then there's been a tremendous abuse of power," said Hatch. "Teachers don't have sex with students; doctors don't have sex with patients; and lawyers shouldn't have sex with clients. Nor should a president have it with young interns."

Hatch also added a new word to the scandal's vocabulary. If all the charges are true, said Hatch, "This president would go down as the greatest canoodler in history." The Dictionary of American Slang says the word dates to 1859 and derives from "canoe." Canoodle has two meanings–to kiss, neck or caress; or to coax by showing affection. Hatch, who loves language, explained that he had sought a term less stark than "adulterer" or "fornicator," and his staff came up with canoodler.

At the same time, Hatch cautioned against a rush to judgment, noting that the charges against Clinton had yet to be proven.

The White House continued to stall Starr at every turn, as the President's propaganda machine railed against the millions of dollars it was costing to pursue Clinton. White House pressure–abetted by a confused media–began to divide even Republicans, with Senate Majority Leader Trent Lott suggesting in March 1998 that Ken Starr should end his investigation and "show his cards."

Hatch, one of Starr's strongest supporters, firmly disagreed. He insisted that justice should take its course, noting that the high cost and long delays were in large part a result of White House stonewalling, including a long string of court room appearances and claims of executive privilege. "They have thrown up roadblocks every step of the way," fumed Hatch. He was particularly incensed that attorneys in the White House had grown from four to eighty-four, primarily because of Clinton's personal problems. "Today, the White House's $24 million payroll happens to have a significant percent of it dedicated to attorneys," said Hatch.

The political climate in Washington was poisonous, with little focus on anything but the scandal. Clinton held only one Cabinet meeting all year–early in 1998 to lie to his Cabinet officers about Lewinsky so that they would go out and lie to others, as they did.

Hatch, a bellwether figure in the drama as head of the Senate Judiciary Committee and frequent guest on TV talk shows, appealed for calm. He called the capital a "vicious, mean-spirited place," that would deter good people from entering politics. He urged Americans to withhold judgment on Clinton until hearing him out.

At the same time, Hatch also had a warning for Clinton, who had ignored requests by Starr to voluntarily provide testimony, leading Starr to issue the President a subpoena. Appearing on CBS's "Face the Nation" July 26, the Senator said Clinton could face impeachment charges if he ignored a grand jury subpoena to testify about his relationship with Lewinsky.

"The fact that he would ignore and violate a subpoena would certainly be grounds to file articles of impeachment," said Hatch. Clinton "has an obligation as the highest official in government, sworn to uphold the Constitution and laws of this country" to respond to the subpoena, emphasized Hatch. The President could fight the subpoena all the way to the Supreme Court, Hatch noted, but if Clinton lost there, it could lead to a constitutional crisis.

Pressure applied by Hatch and others worked. On July 28 Starr granted Lewinsky immunity to testify. The next day Clinton also agreed to testify in response to the subpoena. Several days later the scandal reached a low point when Clinton was asked for a blood sample to test his DNA against the stain on Lewinsky's blue dress.

In a national TV talk show, Hatch put Clinton squarely on the spot. Looking directly into the camera lens, the Utahn said "Mr. President, if you didn't tell the truth in the Paula Jones case, admit it. Period. Say you didn't tell the truth to protect your wife and daughter...then apologize to the American people. *And if that's all you did*, we are a forgiving nation, and you can probably get this behind you."

Hatch tried hard to get Clinton to do the right thing, however belatedly, in the firm belief that, should Clinton be impeached, no Democratic senator would vote to convict him–a prediction that came true. That TV interview prodded some forthright White House staff members to leak to the *New York Times* that the President was going to tell the truth–putting tremendous additional pressure on Clinton to be straight with the grand jury.

Hatch's conciliatory comments did not sit well with some conservatives. Some GOP senators made veiled threats to strip him of his committee chairmanship if he persisted. But more dispassionate observers applauded. The *Washington Post's* veteran Capitol Hill reporter Helen Dewar called Hatch and Democratic Senate colleague John Kerrey of Massachusetts "honest brokers [who] have focused attention on the possibilities for accommodation in what is otherwise a starkly partisan and polarized arena of combat."

"I've spent a lifetime helping people who have difficulties," Hatch told Dewar, "as an attorney, a Mormon bishop" and as a senator. "My heart goes out to anyone in difficulty . . . I believe that everybody can be redeemed. That's how dumb I am."

Hatch, in a style some have dubbed "the mace and the olive branch," also made it clear he would help lead the charge against Clinton if the President refused to come clean about what he had done, and failed to do all within his power to set things straight. Hours before Clinton appeared before the grand jury in mid-August, Hatch gave him another clear public warning: "If the President goes before the grand jury and lies, then there'll be a real call for his impeachment."

On August 17, 1998, Clinton testified to the grand jury for some five hours via closed circuit television–the first U.S. president to face a criminal probe of which he was the target. He emerged to give an infamous four-and-a-half-minute speech summarizing his testimony.

A crush of national media clamored for a reaction by Hatch to the brief speech. The Utahn, seated at an anchor desk at KSL Television, the NBC affiliate in Salt Lake City, watched the speech on a monitor, surrounded by a horde of journalists.

"I kept glancing at Orrin to gauge what he was thinking," says his Utah press secretary Heather Barney. Clinton, pale and weary, began by insisting his earlier answers about Lewinsky in the Jones deposition were "legally accurate." In other words, that he hadn't had "sexual relations" with her. However, he admitted, "Indeed I did have a relationship with Miss Lewinsky that was not appropriate. In fact it was wrong." He gave no indication just what was wrong, leaving an otherwise uninformed viewer to conclude he perhaps forgot to pay Lewinsky overtime or maybe parked his car in her staff parking slot.

Clinton's mea culpa went downhill from there. Much of the rest of his speech was spent deflecting blame from himself and placing it on Kenneth

Starr. "I had real and serious concerns about an independent counsel investigation that began with private business dealings twenty years ago...moved on to my staff and friends. Then into my private life....This has gone on too long, cost too much, and hurt too many innocent people ....It's nobody's business but [my family's]."

Recalls Heather Barney: "When the President started the second half of his remarks and began blaming Ken Starr for his problems, Orrin's whole demeanor changed." By the time the brief speech was over and Tom Brokaw had reached Hatch for a live interview by satellite for NBC Nightly News, the Senator was seething. Hatch, who considered Clinton's statement arrogant, noted that the President had not apologized and chose instead to attack Starr.

As he walked off the set, Hatch turned to KSL anchor Ruth Todd. "Wasn't that pathetic?" he said of Clinton's attack on Starr. They walked down a hallway, flanked by other reporters, and he added, "I'm offended by that. Boy, I'll tell you, what a jerk."

Hatch's intemperate comment–not meant for public consumption but spread far and wide by the media–helped set the tone for other coverage of Clinton's speech. Nonetheless the Senator continued to extend an olive branch to Clinton.

Several weeks later, on September 9, Starr delivered his devastating 450-page report to Congress, citing eleven possible impeachable offenses. Reading it, Hatch's heart sank as he realized Clinton had rejected his advice to be honest with the grand jury. "What I've read is very serious," he said. "It's not good....But I still think that the President of the United States constitutionally deserves...at least the process to be fair."

That evening Hatch was a guest on CNN's "Larry King Live." In discussing Clinton, King also asked about the President's daughter, Chelsea, a student at Stanford University. There were occasional reports that Chelsea's privacy was being invaded, and speculation that her fellow students were giving her a hard time over her father's embarrassing behavior.

"If they give her trouble they'll have to deal with me," warned Hatch. "She's a wonderful young woman and doesn't deserve this. When you look at her, you know the Clintons have done something right." Two days later, Congress made the voluminous report public. It spoke entirely for its X-rated self, including incredibly vile language and descriptions of presidential conduct. House leaders, sobered by opinion polls still showing sizable support for Clinton, cautioned members not to launch personal attacks on the President. But some members weren't listening, including Democrats fearful of fallout in the November elections, less than two months away.

"Last time I saw [Clinton]," said maverick Democrat James Traficant, Jr. of Ohio, "he was swinging on the chandelier in the Oval Office with a brassiere around his head, Viagra in one hand and a Bible in the other, and he was torn between good and evil. I'm going to say what I want to say and I don't give a damn who says what." Traficant's colorful vision likely was inspired by Clinton's habit of entering and exiting Foundry United Methodist Church, large Bible in hand, as press photographers relayed the devout scene to the world.

On the same day the report was publicly released, Friday, September 11, Clinton, in the eye of the hurricane, addressed clergy gathered at the annual White House prayer breakfast. "I don't think there is a fancy way to say that I have sinned," he told them. But Clinton assured the clergy "I have repented."

Two days later, on Sunday, Clinton was still swamped by the Starr report and fighting to come up for air. He skipped church, instead focusing on a thick White House briefing book summarizing news reports about his predicament. Opinion leaned heavily against him. The *Wall Street Journal*: "We are quite prepared to argue that [the Starr report] is quite sufficient grounds for removing a President." The *Washington Post*: "Mr. Clinton's behavior is at the margins of impeachability." *USA Today*: "He should resign because he has resolutely failed–and continues to fail–the most fundamental test of any president: to put the nation's interests first."

Some leading Republicans also called for impeachment.

Early Sunday morning Hatch left his home in Vienna, Virginia, for downtown Washington and the studios of CBS, where he was to appear on "Face the Nation" with Bob Schieffer and Gloria Borger. Forty minutes later he pulled into the CBS parking lot and his Washington press secretary, Paul Smith, approached the car with a message: Clinton had just called the studio looking for Hatch. The Senator reached the White House on his car phone.

"How are you?" came the familiar voice at the other end. "I just wanted to chat with you a little bit about my situation."

"Of course, Mr. President," answered Hatch, fully aware that Clinton hoped to forestall further damage Hatch might inflict momentarily on nationwide television.

"Well, I finally followed your advice last Friday," said Clinton of his meeting with clergy.

"Yes, you did," answered Hatch, "and it would have been better had you done so seven months ago or even a month ago in your speech after the grand jury proceeding."

Clinton asked what Hatch thought of his remarks at the prayer breakfast.

"I accepted it," says Hatch. "I certainly accept your apology, and I've certainly forgiven you. Not that I'm anybody special."

"What do you think I should do now?" asked the President.

"You ought to quit relying on splitting legal hairs and following the advice of your lawyers. You ought to follow the advice of [deputy White House chief of staff] John Podesta, [political advisor] Paul Begala, and some of your other political advisors who want you to just let it all hang out and tell people that you have done wrong, are repentant, and are willing to give everything you have to finish out your presidency."

Clinton reminded Hatch that he told the clergy on Friday he had repented.

"Repentance is more than just saying you're sorry and asking for forgiveness," pressed Hatch. "Just saying you're sorry is not enough. What you need to do is not only recognize that what you've done is wrong, but have remorse for having done so, then refrain from ever doing that offensive conduct again. And, finally, make restitution–to your wife, your daughter, your Cabinet, the others you work with, and the American people.

"The only way you can do that is to humbly quit trying to hide behind legal stratagems....You have this 'Slick Willy' reputation that you're not used to telling the truth. What you need to do is quit criticizing Judge Starr for actions you've done wrong, and start acknowledging you've done wrong and you will do anything to right that wrong."

Hatch told Clinton that nobody bought his argument that he was legally correct in testifying under oath that he and Lewinsky did not have sexual relations. "I used to be a pretty good country lawyer, and that is not believed by anybody. If you tried to make that argument before a jury of your peers, they would throw you out of court....The American people feel the same way."

Clinton told Hatch that during the latter part of his relationship with Lewinsky, he had cut off physical contact and spent the time trying to help her. Later, Hatch wrote privately, "That was the only part of our conversation that seemed totally phony." The President also said he was "trying to do what's right" and make amends with his wife and daughter and the rest of the country. He then mentioned Hatch's defense of Chelsea on TV's "Larry King Live."

"I heard you stuck up for my daughter the other night," said Clinton. "I will never forget your kindness in doing so."

Knowing Clinton feared a criminal indictment if he admitted to having perjured himself in the Jones deposition, Hatch assured him that if he stopped "playing these mindless legal games," and made a clean break with the past, "nobody's going to indict you during your presidency, or when your presidency is over."

But Clinton and his advisors continued to hide behind legalese, attack Kenneth Starr, and dig for mud to fling at congressional Republicans.

Weeks later, Hatch received strong evidence that Clinton had not mended his ways. He and the President happened to be in Los Angeles at the same time, Clinton hitting up his Hollywood pals for campaign funds–his primary pursuit, along with keeping his office, in 1998–and Hatch giving a keynote speech to a state convention. As Hatch prepared to board a plane back to Washington, a young agent assigned to the President's security detail approached.

"I'm a Secret Service agent," the agent said in a hushed voice. "I want you to know that [Clinton] has not changed. He's doing the same things he has always done. He isn't sincere." Agents trusted Hatch, who had tried to mediate between the White House and Kenneth Starr after Starr tried to subpoena them to testify about what they saw while guarding Clinton. The Secret Service feared the precedent would make it more difficult to protect presidents in the future.

Hatch tried to reassure the discouraged agent.

"I'm going to quit the Secret Service because of this."

"How long have you been in the service?" asked Hatch. The agent told him. The Senator encouraged the agent to "hang on, this is only going to be another two years. We need people just like you in the Secret Service."

Hatch then boarded the flight, taking his seat in business class. No sooner had he settled in than another Secret Service agent came up to him.

"Senator," he said softly, "we appreciate all you're doing. We believe in you. I just want you to know from one who has been on the President's detail that he is not a good man. It's just awful." Hatch assured him that the American system was strong and the nation would get through the crisis.

A top national security aide to Clinton also phoned Hatch, warning that the President's affairs had left him wide open for blackmail by a foreign government. "We've got to get this guy out of office," he told Hatch.

The exchanges helped confirm what Hatch had suspected but was reluctant to accept. Bill Clinton still had not learned his lesson.

19

The Impeachment

This great nation can tolerate a president who makes mistakes. But it cannot tolerate one who makes a mistake and then breaks the law to cover it up....President Clinton did more than just break the law. He broke his oath of office and broke faith with the American people.

As impeachment loomed, a law professor who was running for Congress said "I think it's plain that the President should resign and spare the country the agony of this impeachment and removal proceeding." He added that there was "no question that an admission of making false statements to government officials and interfering with the FBI and CIA is an impeachable offense."

The year was 1974, the president was Richard Nixon, and the University of Arkansas professor was Bill Clinton. Now it is 1998 and Clinton is about to eat his words.

Presidential scholar Stephen Hess of the Brookings Institution noted that "A president in his second term really has only his first year–his fifth year in office–to be creative." By the sixth year, Congress is preoccupied with the mid-term election. After the election, the president is a lame duck.

Clinton, in his fifth year in office–1997–cooperated with the Republican-led Congress to enact several major initiatives. A plan to cut taxes and balance the budget–a longstanding GOP goal–was passed, along with an overhaul of welfare to require recipients to work. Another initiative–largely engineered by Senator Hatch–was signed into law by Clinton to allow states to provide millions of children of the working poor with health insurance.

But privately, Clinton still dallied with Monica Lewinsky, and perhaps others, and one can only speculate what else might have been accomplished for the nation if he had been fully focused on its interests.

A visit to the White House by Mexican president Ernesto Zedillo on November 13, 1997, demonstrated how Clinton juggled his public and private affairs. While Zedillo was in the ceremonial front area of the White House awaiting a state dinner, Clinton's secretary Betty Currie sneaked Lewinsky up the back stairs to see Clinton. Lewinsky gave him several gifts, they kissed, and he rushed off for the dinner. The following year, 1998, was almost wholly consumed by Clinton's misdeeds, largely ending his moral authority as America's leader and making him a lame duck a year early. He was kept aloft on a soaring economy, but otherwise risked the nation's interests across the globe, proving the biblical warning that a double-minded man is unstable in all his ways. "Clinton is, in a sense, being protected by his scandals, which distract attention from the disintegration of U.S. interests–from Russia to Kosovo to Iraq to North Korea–as a result of feckless policies that periodically leaven his inattention," wrote columnist George Will.

As most citizens shook their heads in disgust at their rogue president, a huge cottage industry was born. T-shirts, bumper stickers, and clever postcards making light of the scandal blossomed across the country. The mainstream media joined supermarket tabloids in competing for Bill and Monica tidbits. Internet sites featuring the latest raunchy jokes and anecdotes proliferated. David Letterman, Jay Leno, and other comics and talk show hosts mined the scandal for endless hours of monologue.

In March 1998 the annual white-tie Gridiron Dinner was held in Washington's Capitol Hilton ballroom, traditionally bringing together about 600 top government officials, including the President and First Lady, and assorted other VIPs, with national journalists, for an evening of off-the-record satire.

This year the event's main buzz, of course, was Topic A. President Clinton smiled gamely as skit after skit lampooned his affair with Lewinsky. Carl Rowan belted out a song, dressed as a golf-ready Vernon Jordan, Clinton's best friend who lined up a job for Monica Lewinsky at Revlon in New York in an obvious attempt to make her less accessible to investigators. Rowan crooned this number, to the tune of "Deep River":

Dee-ee-ee-eep doo-doo!/ First, Bill calls Vernon Jordan./
Pro-oh bo-no/I take the call out of civic duty.../
Job counseling/ For disadvantaged youngsters.
Thank Revlon/ It's my way of payin' back society.

Douglas Turner, Washington correspondent for New York's *Buffalo News*, played Clinton aide George Stephanopoulos, instructing four giggly, flirty White House interns dressed in green schoolgirl outfits and berets. To the tune of "People Will Say We're in Love," he sang:

> *Why do they think up stories that link young chicks with him?*
> *They'll never understand that no gossip sticks to him.*
> *Nevertheless, the things that you say can raise concerns.*
> *Here is the gist, a practical list, for new interns:*
> *Don't whisper in his ear,*
> *Don't whistle when he runs,*
> *Don't say you admire his buns,*
> *People will say you're in love.*

Clinton, keeping with tradition, addressed the Gridiron crowd. "Please withhold the subpoenas until all the jokes have been told," he began. "I offer my remarks with this caveat: They were a whole lot funnier before the lawyers got a hold of them." Among jokes Clinton said his lawyers suggested for his remarks:

"Knock knock."

"Don't answer that."

Clinton also borrowed material from a new film, "Primary Colors," based on a book of the same name–thinly disguised fiction of his first campaign for president. "This is not the first time John Travolta has modeled a character on me," said Clinton, striking a disco pose from Travolta's 1977 film, "Saturday Night Fever." "That's my theme song–'Stayin' Alive.'"

Five years earlier, in 1993, just two months into his presidency, Clinton had appeared at the Gridiron Dinner wearing a sequined cutaway jacket. He played "Yakety Yak" on his saxophone, and then announced, as the audience howled, that "There's nothing like a little sax to get you out of trouble."

But now it is 1998 and, except for evenings of satire, not many are laughing. The leader of the free world himself has become the joke, with serious and even dangerous consequences for the United States and the many nations who count on the U.S. for global leadership.

Peggy Noonan, former speech writer to President Reagan, caught the essence of America's dilemma:

> In the [Starr] report and in his comments it was clear that the most important thing to Bill Clinton is, now and always, Bill Clinton....He is an actor....He absorbs his lies, and becomes them....
>
> Mr. Clinton seems–and this is an amazing thing to say about a president–to lack a sense of patriotism, a love of country, a protectiveness toward her. He dupes the Secretary of State, who must be America's credible voice in the world, into lying for him to the public and press. He fears his phone is being tapped by foreign agents, opening him to international blackmail. But he does not discontinue phone sex. Instead, he comes up with a cover story....
>
> Jesse Jackson once said, 'God isn't finished with me yet,' and it was beautiful because it was true. God isn't finished with any of us. Maybe He will raise up Bill Clinton and make him a saint, a great one. Maybe He will make Bill Clinton's life an example of stunning redemption. But for now, and now is what we have, Bill Clinton is not wise enough, mature enough, stable enough–he is not good enough–to be the American president.

With the possibility of impeachment looming late in 1998, Clinton and his legal team cleared the decks of one lingering headache: Paula Jones. In November Clinton paid her $850,000, but offered no apology, in return for her agreement to drop the lawsuit against him.

By then the Jones/Lewinsky scandal had polarized the nation and Congress, with few signs of statesmanship on a starkly partisan horizon. Exceptions among Senate Democrats were Daniel Patrick Moynihan of New York, Bob Kerrey of Nebraska, and Joseph Lieberman of Connecticut who, early in September, stood on the Senate floor and skinned the leader of their party.

"The transgressions the President has admitted to are too consequential for us to walk away and leave the impression for our children and our posterity that what President Clinton acknowledges he did within the White House is acceptable behavior for our nation's leader," said Lieberman. The Senator, who had been a close ally of Clinton's, added that the President had "compromised his moral authority" and made it more difficult for parents to instill "values of honesty" in their children.

On the other side of the aisle, Senator Hatch stood out among Republicans. He condemned Clinton's acts and insisted that justice must be served, yet refused to demagogue the issue. Hatch's earlier warnings to Clinton to save himself by telling the truth had fallen on deaf ears. It was now too late: After the Starr report became public in September, events unfolded in a tidal wave of inevitability.

Clinton was trapped in the web of lies he had spun throughout the year, including these three during his videotaped testimony to the federal grand jury: (1) oral sex is not sex; (2) the physical relationship with Monica Lewinsky was only to gratify him, and he did not touch her private parts (essentially making her a sex slave); and (3) the intimate contact began in 1996, not in November 1995 when Lewinsky was still a twenty-two-year-old White House intern.

To cover these and other lies, Clinton repeatedly tried to obstruct justice–concocting stories with Lewinsky in advance to cover their tracks; helping to arrange a job for her in New York through his buddy Vernon Jordan when he knew she might be called as a witness in the Jones case; suggesting to Lewinsky how she could answer questions by Jones's attorneys; concealing evidence, including gifts his secretary Betty Curie retrieved from Lewinsky; attempting to influence Curie's testimony by drumming into her falsehoods about his relationship with Lewinsky; and lying to various potential witnesses, knowing they would repeat the lies to the grand jury.

By Starr's reckoning, Clinton committed eleven offenses that "may constitute" grounds for impeachment. Only one other president had been impeached in the nation's history–Andrew Johnson in 1868, largely on political grounds in the aftermath of the Civil War.

Under the Constitution, the House of Representatives conducts formal inquiries into alleged misdeeds of federal officials, leading to possible impeachment–similar to an indictment in a court of law–by a simple majority vote. The Senate tries all impeachments, which require a two-thirds vote, 67 members, to remove an official from office.

Early in October 1998, the House voted 258-176 to begin the impeachment process. All Republicans voted to do so, joined by 31 Democrats. "All of us are pulled in many directions by our political parties, by philosophy and friendships," said House Judiciary Committee chairman Henry Hyde, R-Illinois. "But mostly we're moved by our consciences." Democratic leader Richard Gephardt, D-Missouri, said "The question today is not whether to have an inquiry, the question is what kind of inquiry should we have." House Democrats tried but failed to limit its scope to something less than impeachment.

Feminist leaders, nakedly hypocritical in their refusal to support Paula

Jones, beat the drums of support for Clinton, whose abuse of women was light years beyond anything ever alleged against Supreme Court Justice Clarence Thomas, who had been demonized by feminists for supposedly talking dirty to Anita Hill. After a House committee passed articles of impeachment against Clinton, Betty Friedan, founder of the National Organization for Women, said Republicans pushing for impeachment were "a bunch of dirty white men" risking the stability of the federal government.

As Congress and the White House prepared for the historic struggle, eyeing each other like two wary boxers in a ring, a phenomenon was occurring beyond the Washington beltway. Despite–or, more likely, because of–the flood of salacious refuse from the massive Starr report that seeped into homes through the media, most Americans were becoming angrier not with Clinton but with Kenneth Starr and Congress.

Throughout 1998 Clinton defied the laws of political gravity. Gallup, for example, took thirteen polls from January through July, asking "Do you approve or disapprove of the way Bill Clinton is handling his job as president?" In January, weeks before he testified falsely in the Paula Jones case, Clinton's approval rating was 59 percent. It rose from there–to a high of 67 percent in April, dipping slightly in July to 65 percent.

During the last half of the year, pundits, pollsters, and politicians alike were certain that public opinion would turn against Clinton as awareness of his misdeeds sunk in. But they were wrong. Early in September, on the eve of the Starr report's release, 59 percent told the *Washington Post* they approved of the job Clinton was doing; a month later, well after the report had oozed into the national consciousness, that figure went *up* to 67 percent–something no one could satisfactorily explain.

Republicans previously had relished the coming midterm elections of November 3, confident that angered voters would rise up and take Clinton's problems out on his fellow Democrats. But as voting day neared, Clinton's stock was holding steady and the GOP's was falling.

Three weeks before the election, a CBS/*New York Times* poll found that approval of Congress had dropped from a high of 56 percent in September to 43 percent in mid-October. Forty-eight percent now disapproved of the job Congress was doing, and a majority could not name a single accomplishment of the just-ending Republican-controlled session. Meanwhile Clinton's job approval rating was 63 percent, with 70 percent approving his handling of the economy.

The most important poll came in voting booths weeks later, as

Democrats picked up five House seats–the first time since the Great Depression sixty-four years earlier that a party controlling the White House gained members in Congress in a nonpresidential year. Republicans managed to hold their own in the Senate and in most statehouses–California the most important exception–but the U.S. House results stunned the GOP and put Democrats just a handful of seats away from recapturing that body in the 2000 elections.

"The Republicans did what they do so often–they assembled a firing squad in the shape of a circle," said Jack Pitney, a college professor and former official at the Republican National Committee. Randy Tate, head of the Christian Coalition, said "The message coming out of this election is that issues do matter, and issues make a difference. Democrats had an agenda, albeit a liberal agenda . . . but some agenda will beat no agenda every time."

Other observers credited the economy, which presidents historically have been given more credit for shaping than they deserve. During the five years between 1992 and 1997, the stock market had risen faster than at any time in history. Many Americans were afraid to rock the boat, and Clinton was the boat.

The midterm election confirmed Republicans' growing fears: Impeachment was a thorny thicket and Brer Rabbit Clinton had led them right into it. The problem was how to get out with the least possible pain.

House Speaker Newt Gingrich walked the plank over his party's failed election strategy, which focused too much on scandal and too little on everyday concerns of citizens. Just four years after leading Republicans to majority status in the House for the first time in four decades, Gingrich was replaced by Representative Bob Livingston of Louisiana–who, in the tumultuous days to follow, also resigned the post after Clinton's attack dogs unearthed Livingston's own marital infidelities. They did the same to two other House Republicans, Helen Chenoweth of Idaho and kindly, silver-haired Henry Hyde, whose moral lapse was three decades old.

Though there obviously is an enormous difference between having an affair and lying about one to a grand jury, Clinton and his defenders tried hard to convince the public that his case was "just about sex." They continued to largely prevail in the court of public opinion, where Clinton was overwhelmingly supported by African Americans and, ironically, by most women.

While some predicted the election results meant the House would not press on with impeachment, a constitutional machine with a life of its own had already been set in motion. Nobody could find the switch to turn it off.

Days after the election, Hyde, who would preside over House deliberations as chairman of that body's Judiciary Committee, said of the impeachment, "how I'd like to forget this. I mean, who needs it?" By mid-December, staff lawyers for Hyde's committee had drawn up four articles of impeachment–two on perjury, or lying under oath, and one each on tampering with witnesses and abuse of power.

On the eve of the House taking them up, Clinton suddenly unleashed a major attack on Iraq, ordering hundreds of cruise missiles onto military targets after a year of unfulfilled threats for Baghdad's refusal to permit destruction of its chemical and biological weapons.

Though Congress and most of the nation rallied around the President–typical in time of war–there was nagging suspicion that he had "wagged the dog," following a recent movie title, by fostering war to detract attention from a personal scandal. Senator Hatch, however, was among those applauding Clinton for what the Utahn considered a far too-belated action.

If Clinton thought bombing Iraq would slow his impeachment, he was wrong. On December 19, 1998, a Saturday, the House voted to impeach the President of the United States for the first time in 130 years, charging Clinton with "high crimes and misdemeanors" for lying under oath to a grand jury, tampering with witnesses, and helping to hide evidence.

Article I, perjuring himself before a grand jury, was approved 228-206, with five Republicans voting against it and five Democrats voting for it. Seventeen minutes later, Article III, obstructing justice, was adopted 221-212. The two other articles were defeated 205-229 and 148-285.

Now the Senate would decide the issue.

Immediately after the vote, congressional Democrats drove to the White House, where the President emerged, Hillary on his arm. Still defiant, he vowed to remain in the White House "until the last hour of the last day of my term."

Vice President Al Gore, leading the pep rally, said the House vote for impeachment, without giving members a chance instead to vote for censure, "does a disservice to a man I believe will be regarded in the history books as one of our greatest presidents...." Gore's over-the-top endorsement would become a GOP slogan on roadside billboards and would return to haunt him in the 2000 general election.

Clinton also said "We must stop the politics of personal destruction," but not everyone was listening. That same day out west, Utah Attorney

General Jan Graham, the state's highest-ranking Democrat, added her own ingredients to the coarse cauldron. Charging that the entire federal government was "run by egotistical liars with no morals and no values," Graham in a prepared statement challenged members of Congress, including the five from Utah, to sign affidavits that "they have never engaged in extramarital sexual conduct and...they've never lied about it."

Fellow Utah Democrat David Magleby, a political scientist at Brigham Young University, called Graham's suggestion "inappropriate" and a "smoke screen" that attempted to obscure the difference between extramarital affairs and lying in a legal proceeding. At any rate, Graham was way off the mark. There are many honorable men and women in Washington; scoundrels on the public payroll probably are in about the same proportion as among those who elected them.

Constitutionally, Senator Hatch had no more role in a Senate trial than any other senator. It would be presided over by his good friend Chief Justice William Rehnquist. However, as chairman of the Judiciary Committee Hatch felt a particular responsibility to help guide the Senate through its onerous task. More than that, Hatch had long been considered a bellwether figure in the Clinton saga and was among a handful of outsiders Clinton had turned to for personal advice.

Hatch's views were avidly sought by the media, and he was a constant presence on TV talk shows and in newspaper columns.

Despite yeoman efforts, the Senator had failed to save Clinton from himself and the likely harsh judgment of history. Now Hatch turned his attention to the lessons future generations would take from this pivotal moment in American democracy.

Hatch, one of the keenest nose-counters in Washington, knew it was highly unlikely the Senate–55 Republicans and 45 Democrats–would cobble together the 67 votes needed to sustain Clinton's impeachment. If they failed to do so, he worried that history would record that perjury and obstructing justice were not offenses worthy of impeachment and removal from office.

Facing the near certainty that the Senate would not vote to oust Clinton, Hatch initially supported a proposal–pushed by former Presidents Ford and Carter among others–that the Senate vote to convict Clinton but not remove him. That way, Hatch reasoned, it would be crystal clear that both houses of Congress agreed Clinton had disgraced the presidency.

The beginning point, he said, was to determine if there were 34 or more senators who would not vote to remove Clinton under any circumstances. "If we find that there are, then it's apparent that we shouldn't put the country through a three-, four-, five-, six-month trial," he said. "We should find some way of reconciling and resolving this matter." If at least 34 senators would not vote to remove Clinton, "we're going to have to do what is the next best thing, and that is point out to the American people how really bad his actions were." Conviction without removal would do that, argued Hatch.

Despite the clear partisan split, there was also a sense of comity in the Senate as its members settled in for the historic trial. There was scarcely a good word to be heard about Clinton from any member, Republican or Democrat. Both sides were largely captive to the prevailing sentiment of their parties, with Democrats excoriating their President for the predicament he had put them in.

Venerable Senator Robert Byrd, D-West Virginia, publicly warned the White House against any tampering with the 100-member jury. There was considerable bargaining over procedure, including the number of witnesses to call and whether they would appear in person before the Senate. Then, on January 7, 1999, the first impeachment trial of a U.S. president in 131 years began.

Chief Justice Rehnquist swore in the 100 senators but proceedings soon ground to a halt amid wrangling over how to proceed. Senators were determined to take a more bipartisan approach than the House had done, but they remained divided on key issues, including whether to call witnesses and whether, in the clear absence of the votes to convict Clinton, to censure him and call it a day.

Clinton broke his self-imposed silence on January 13 by arguing that his conduct, while wrong, did not constitute "high crimes and misdemeanors," the level of seriousness specified in the Constitution to remove a federal official from office. The following day, a team of House GOP prosecutors opened their case against Clinton, imploring the Senate to uphold "the rule of law" by showing the world that "the President of the United States has no license to lie under oath."

The President's chief lawyer, Charles Ruff, opened the White House defense on January 19, impressing both sides. Ruff already had established credibility on Capitol Hill in his defense of Clinton before the House. There, he said Clinton had been "morally reprehensible" and had "betrayed the trust" of the American people. Before the Senate, however, Ruff called the

House impeachment case a product of "spider webs" of innuendo and "prosecutorial fudgemaking." Clinton had acted shamefully, said Ruff, but had not committed offenses serious enough to forfeit the Oval Office.

Two weeks into the meandering trial, senators still hadn't broken much new ground. Wrote Doyle McManus of the *Los Angeles Times*: "For several days, the Senate's legislative giants tossed out options from dismissal (West Virginia Democrat Robert C. Byrd) and adjournment (Utah Republican Orrin G. Hatch) to some kind of brokered verdict (Connecticut Democrat Joseph I. Lieberman), but none took hold." McManus said the Senate's strained bipartisanship was fraying fast, and predicted "an ugly battle along party lines...and at least several more weeks of trial for the Senate."

Opinion polls continued to show that most Americans were tired of it all and, while disgusted with Clinton's behavior, did not want him removed from office. Republicans were being blamed for even holding the trial, spurring attempts to bring it to a speedy conclusion. Still unsure how to do so, however, senators took the rare step of holding a closed session on January 25 to kick around ideas without the world listening.

House Republican prosecutors then suggested a greatly scaled-back witness list of just three key figures–Lewinsky, Clinton confidant Vernon Jordan who had found her a job in New York, and Sidney Blumenthal, the Clinton political aide who had worked hard to cover Clinton's trail and confuse the public.

Prosecutors suggested that just one of them appear in person before the Senate: Monica Lewinsky. Senators soundly voted down that proposal, 70-30. Clinton and his surrogates feared that if she were on live television in the Senate chamber, a hundred million voters would tune in, confirming for themselves how young she was.

Many others resisted inviting Lewinsky into that hallowed hall because of her infamously stained character. Hatch, however, was among the 30 voting for Lewinsky's appearance. "Even I was surprised by how many Republicans voted not to allow her to appear," said Hatch. "I felt that she should appear and the American people should be able to judge whether she is telling the truth or not."

In the end, all three testified via videotaped depositions. None shed significant new light on the case. Lewinsky came across as friendly toward Clinton and, to Hatch, seemed "young, vulnerable, and credible."

Hatch meanwhile came up with a creative new approach out of the quagmire: adjourn the trial with "substantial reasons" but without taking the vote that Clinton clearly would win. He ran the idea past a number of House managers, including chairman Henry Hyde who, according to Hatch, was "100 percent for it." The Utahn explained his proposal in a column he wrote for the *New York Times*. The interests of the country will not be well served if the Senate acquits the President, now a foregone conclusion, said Hatch.

> The Senate should seek a conclusion that protects the integrity of the House impeachment articles by avoiding a historic vote on the merits, which could be interpreted as vindicating the President....The message the House sent to our posterity is that Mr. Clinton's behavior is immoral and wrong. In history books, he will go down as only the second president of the United States to be impeached. Any vote that acquits President Clinton, in essence, minimizes the importance of the articles....
>
> The Senate does not have the votes to convict the President, and more than one-third of the Senate (all but one of the 45 Democrats) has said it never will. Since it appears that the President will stay in office, the Senate should seek a conclusion that brings Democrats and Republicans together and also avoids the formal ruling that President Clinton's conduct is not removable. The Senate should vote to adjourn the trial sine die (permanently, without return) on these grounds:
>
> 1. President Clinton gave false and misleading testimony under oath in federal court proceedings and has, in several ways, impeded the justice system's search for truth.
>
> 2. He will be subject to federal criminal jurisdiction for his acts after he leaves office.
>
> 3. The Senate acknowledges, recognizes and accedes to the articles of impeachment passed by the House as Impeachment Without Removal, the highest form of condemnation, other than removal.
>
> Were the Senate to adjourn and make these findings, it would deny the President an acquittal–the result he craves for his own historic legitimacy....By permanently adjourning, the Senate will not have formally acquitted the President....The House's vote to impeach President Clinton will stand as a rebuke forever, and the search for truth will have trumped political expediency.

While some saw Hatch's proposal as ingenious, others considered it legally dubious, including conservative soul mate and fellow constitutional scholar Robert Bork, who believed the Senate had no alternative but to proceed with a full trial and vote. Republican senators, he said, "ought to face up to the fact that they're going to lose."

Too few senators saluted the flag Hatch had run up the pole, and the impeachment ground on toward Clinton's certain acquittal. Senators voted to end the trial by February 12.

On February 9, the Senate once more cleared the galleries and closed its doors to go into private session, though the outcome now was a foregone conclusion. Senator Hatch was proud of the way his colleagues comported themselves in the secret session. "We were talking with each other rather than at each other," he said. "If there is ever a good example as to why we should have closed sessions in impeachment deliberations, this would be it."

During final deliberations, Hatch submitted for the *Congressional Record* a scholarly and comprehensive treatise on impeachment generally and on Clinton's especially. He began it poetically, quoting from Daniel Webster, that a "sense of duty pursues us ever. It is omnipresent like the Diety. If we take to ourselves the wings of morning, and dwell in the uttermost parts of the sea, duty performed or duty violated is still with us...."

"The duty which has faced each United States Senator is the obligation to do impartial justice in a matter of significant historical import with lasting consequences for our constitutional order," said Hatch. He also quoted Theodore Roosevelt: "Honesty is not so much a credit as an absolute prerequisite to efficient service to the public. Unless a man is honest, we have no right to keep him in public life; it matters not how brilliant his capacity...."

During the final vote on the two articles of impeachment, Hatch also noted that "I wanted to be able to support President Clinton. I believe that I have been more than fair. I have tried not to rush to judgment. All of my life, I've been taught to forgive and forget....Indeed, to the dismay of some, I had expressed a hope and a desire early on in this constitutional drama that the President would acknowledge his untruthful statements. He chose to do otherwise and perpetuated his untruthfulness."

> Although some believe this is solely a private matter, I believe this is really about the President's fidelity to the oath of office and the rule of law....After weighing all the evidence, listening to witnesses, and asking questions, I have concluded that President Clinton perjured himself

> and obstructed justice. Committing [such] crimes of moral turpitude...go to the heart of qualification for public office.
>
> This great nation can tolerate a president who makes mistakes. But it cannot tolerate one who makes a mistake and then breaks the law to cover it up. Any other citizen would be prosecuted for these crimes. But President Clinton did more than just break the law. He broke his oath of office and broke faith with the American people....
>
> I will vote for conviction on both articles of impeachment....Upholding our Constitution–a sacred document that Americans have fought and died for–is more important than any one person, including the President of the United States.

On February 12, 1999, thirteen months after the impeachment saga began with Clinton's false testimony about Monica Lewinsky, the Senate acquitted him of perjury and obstruction of justice. Senators voted 55-45 to reject the perjury charge, with 10 Republicans joining all 45 Democrats in acquittal.

"Not guilty as charged," declared Chief Justice Rehnquist.

Senators split evenly–50-50–on the second charge of obstruction of justice.

"Not guilty as charged," Rehnquist intoned again.

Senator Hatch voted "guilty" on both counts.

The Senate reached the conclusion favored by most citizens. A *Washington Post* poll, taken immediately after the trial, showed that 64 percent approved of the "not guilty" verdicts, while 35 percent disapproved. Nearly half–48 percent–said Clinton should "face criminal charges at some point," with most saying he should be charged after leaving office.

Otherwise, public opinion held little comfort for those aching to bring the President to account. Among other responses: More than half–56 percent–said the Senate should "drop the case without censuring Clinton." By 52 percent to 35 percent, Americans said they trusted Clinton more than congressional Republicans to deal with the country's biggest problems. Forty-six percent approved of the job Congress was doing–virtually the same as a year earlier.

Most stunning of all, by virtually every important measure, Clinton's job performance ratings were higher at the end of the impeachment trial than before the scandal broke thirteen months earlier. At the end, 68 percent of Americans approved of the job he was doing–up 8 percentage points from a *Post* poll taken immediately before the scandal began in January 1998.

Titanic had hit an iceberg–and the iceberg sank.

The Senate trial did not end America's trial with its morally bankrupt chief executive. Exactly two hours after winning the Senate votes that assured him 708 more days in office, Clinton strode onto the south lawn of the White House–alone and somber, in sharp contrast to his defiant demeanor that was roundly criticized after the House impeached him.

"Now that the Senate has fulfilled its constitutional responsibility," Clinton said, "bringing this process to a conclusion, I want to say again to the American people how profoundly sorry I am for what I said and did to trigger these events and the great burden they have imposed on the Congress and on the American people." With that, he walked away from shouting reporters and disappeared into the White House.

Off the record, Clinton was far from contrite. "President Clinton shows no remorse for the conduct that got him impeached, according to several people who have spoken with the President recently," reported the *Washington Times*.

New York Daily News columnist Tom DeFrank wrote that Clinton recently reassured an old pal that "this was 'much ado about nothing. I've beaten the odds,' the President happily told well-wishers. According to well-placed sources who have spoken with Clinton, his private demeanor is notably lacking in remorse. Privately, some of these presidential intimates worry that in his understandable relief that the impeachment ordeal is almost over, he still doesn't get it. 'There's no contrition for what he has done,' echoes another dismayed counselor who regularly speaks with the President. 'That's all just an act. He is only sorry he got caught.'"

Clinton's attitude more than a year after his impeachment continued to suggest he was still unrepentant. "In recent days, Clinton has made breezy, even joking comments about the impeachment," noted the *Washington Post* in April 2000. "Last week in Louisiana, for example, he thanked a controversial local political figure 'who proved to me that you could get bad press and the people would stay with you. So I simply decided to test the theory, and it got a little out of hand.'"

Justice did have at least a few final words for Clinton. U.S. District Judge Susan Webber Wright, who oversaw the Jones lawsuit, held the President in contempt of court and fined him for providing misleading testimony about Monica Lewinsky–giving Clinton another dubious presidential first and raising the likelihood he would later be disbarred. Clinton also faced the very real possibility he would be indicted for perjury once he left office.

Within days of the Senate verdict, another Clinton accuser went public after years of refusing to be dragged into the limelight. Juanita Broaddrick, a highly credible and well-to-do businesswoman in Arkansas, was known in government documents as "Jane Doe No. 5." For years her story had circulated in Arkansas, but she had refused to discuss it. When Paula Jones's private investigators showed up on her doorstep in the tiny town of Van Buren, the nursing home owner still wouldn't talk. "I wouldn't relive it for anything," she told them.

Those who knew of her story urged that it be verified and used during the House impeachment and Senate trial. But it was not, and it will never be known if it might have made a difference in the outcome.

At any rate, investigative reporters from NBC, the *Wall Street Journal*, and other major media outlets confirmed the story to their satisfaction–and publicized it shortly after the Senate trial concluded. Although Broaddrick's narrative was more than twenty years old, it was compelling in that it accused Clinton not simply of harassment and infidelity, but of rape.

Finally prodded into talking, Broaddrick said she first ran into Clinton when he was Arkansas' young attorney general, then making his first run for governor. He met her briefly at a political stop in Van Buren, and invited her to visit his campaign headquarters in Little Rock. A week later, on a visit to Little Rock, she called Clinton's campaign office and he suggested they meet at her hotel. Once in the lobby, he suggested they have coffee in her room to avoid reporters.

"Stupid me, I ordered coffee to the room," says Broaddrick. "I thought we were going to talk about the campaign."

Instead, she says, they spent a few minutes chatting by a window. Then Clinton began kissing her. She says she resisted his advances but he pulled her back onto the bed and forcibly had sex with her, leaving her upper lip bruised and swollen where he had bitten it. "The last thing he said to me was 'You better get some ice for that.' And he put on his sunglasses and walked out the door."

Will Clinton ever get it? Will he ever be sincerely sorry for the carnage he has strewn across the national landscape and in so many individual lives? Evidence, sadly, suggests the answer is no.

In April 2000, more than a year after he became the first justifiably impeached president in U.S. history, Clinton spoke to the American Society of Newspaper Editors. Asked if his presidential library would have a "wing" dealing with his impeachment, Clinton again showed the quality of his character, and what he had learned from that dismal chapter.

"I'm not ashamed of the fact that they impeached me," he said as jaws dropped, "that was their decision, not mine, and it was wrong." The real culprits, he indicated, were those who exposed his sordid behavior, and congressional Republicans who had the audacity to call him to account for it.

"On the impeachment, let me tell you, I am proud of what we did there, because I think we saved the Constitution of the United States."

Haul out the jackhammers and start carving Clinton's face on Mount Rushmore, right beside Washington, Lincoln, Jefferson and Roosevelt. Surely someone who has saved the Constitution deserves no less.

20

Utah and the West

There was no consultation with the Governor, no notification to the congressional delegation, no hearings, no town meetings, no media discussion, no nothing . . . .Those of us in public land states cannot afford to have the large majority of the land area of our states subject to the whims of any president.

EVEN LAME DUCKS HAVE WINGS."

That's what Interior Secretary Bruce Babbitt reminded Clinton as the President's legacy turned to toast late in 1998. Babbitt sent Clinton notes suggesting he could still leave his mark for posterity in the wide open spaces of the West, home to over 90 percent of all land owned by the federal government. He urged Clinton to set aside huge tracts as national monuments.

Clinton, with a stroke of a pen and no consultation with local citizens or officials, already had done so in September 1996, creating the 1.8 million-acre Grand Staircase-Escalante National Monument in southern Utah. On that occasion, citing an obscure 1906 law called the Antiquities Act, the Clinton-Gore Administration acted in virtual secrecy, keeping its plans under wraps until the last possible moment.

"This declaration has nothing to do with preserving land in southern Utah–which is a goal we all share–and everything to do with scoring political points with a powerful political-interest group just forty-eight days before the presidential election is to take place," charged Senator Hatch. "In all my years in the U.S. Senate, I have never seen a clearer example of the arrogance of federal power. Indeed this is the mother of all land grabs."

Utah Governor Mike Leavitt made a last-minute appeal to White House Chief of Staff Leon Panetta, telling reporters afterwards that "I made...a strong case that there's a win-win opportunity here. That we share their desire to protect this land, but that we also need to be concerned about preserving the assets of the land and [be] true to the deliberative process of democracy." Panetta insisted Clinton still hadn't decided on the specifics.

Less than twenty-four hours later, Clinton, Vice President Al Gore, and their entourage arrived by helicopter at the South Rim of breathtaking Grand Canyon in Arizona. Gesturing toward the Utah border seventy-five miles away, the President said that by his actions "we are keeping faith with the future....On this remarkable site, God's handiwork is everywhere."

Local reaction was fierce. One political cartoonist summed up the feelings of many Utahns, sketching the President on a canyon bluff, pants and shorts around his ankles, mooning the Beehive State. Politically, Clinton obviously felt he had nothing to lose: In the 1992 presidential election, Utah was the only state where he placed third, trailing Republican Bob Dole as well as Reform Party candidate Ross Perot; in 1996 Clinton-Gore got 33 percent in Utah.

Clinton was following in the steps of the U.S.'s previous southern President, Jimmy Carter, who alienated much of the West upon taking office in 1977 by trying to kill ongoing water reclamation projects–lifeblood in the vast, arid region. The Carter Administration also locked up land from multiple use and overregulated ranchers, miners, and timber interests, sparking the "Sagebrush Rebellion." The rebellion, led in part by Senator Hatch, was a quixotic threat by western states to take ownership of millions of federal acres within their borders. At the time Hatch acknowledged it was primarily symbolic, calling it "sort of a punch in the mouth to let the Carter Administration know we weren't going to take it anymore."

Now, nearly two decades later, on September 18, 1996, the Clinton-Gore Administration was about to seize not the West's water but its land. As Clinton and his entourage, including Vice President Gore, were at the Grand Canyon, angry residents of nearby Kane County gathered at a "Loss of Rights" rally at Kanab High School, wearing black ribbons of mourning. The monument covers 70 percent of the county, with the balance in Garfield County. Many local Kanab businesses closed during the rally and the town sported signs such as "Shame on you, Clinton."

In appeasing hard-core environmentalists, the President opened a Pandora's Box of problems. The Kaiparowits Plateau included in the monument is among the nation's richest coal fields, bearing high-quality, environmentally sound low-sulfur coal that emits far less sulfur dioxide than dirtier coal now in use. Andalex Resources was planning an underground coal mine, leaving minimal scars on the earth's surface, that would have provided nearly 500 jobs in Kane County, whose 9.3 percent unemployment was second highest in Utah. If the low-sulfur coal were blended with the dirty, high-sulfur coal produced in the East, the result would reduce air pollution by millions of tons of particulates.

But Clinton's action killed the proposed mine, making losers of local citizens and, ironically, a cleaner global environment.

Utah schools–where spending per pupil is the lowest in the U.S.–also took a hit. About 200,000 acres of Utah school trust lands were within the monument's borders, and educators counted on royalty revenues from coal production to help bolster public education. Since the White House had acted in secrecy, no one knew what would happen to the trust lands or how to make up the potential loss to schools.

However, through negotiations that should have preceded designation of the monument, Governor Leavitt and Secretary Babbitt in1998 signed an agreement to exchange the school trust lands for cash and federal land assets in other parts of the state. Utah education, handed a lemon by Clinton-Gore-Babbitt, had turned it into lemonade: The Beehive State for decades had sought to exchange the school trust lands captured within federal land holdings, to enable other lands to be profitably developed for the benefit of Utah's school children.

Hatch, joined by his Utah colleague Senator Bob Bennett, in June introduced legislation to codify the Leavitt-Babbitt agreement, which Hatch said would "help restore trust in our government and assist the healing process among our rural citizens in Utah." He added that it would "mitigate one of the severest impacts of that presidential declaration."

Under the agreement, 350,000 acres of school trust lands were transferred to the federal government. In exchange, Utah was to receive $50 million in cash, another $13 million from unleased coal sales for a permanent school fund, and access to 160 million tons of coal, 185 billion cubic feet of coal-bed methane resources, 139,000 acres of land and minerals located in nine Utah counties, and a variety of other minerals.

Hatch said the swap–the largest land exchange in the U.S. since the Louisiana Purchase–was "of approximately equal value." He explained that "while protecting the interests of both the State of Utah and the federal government, the agreement and the bill also protect existing stakeholders, such as the affected local governments, and the valid existing rights of permittees, such as ranchers and those with mining leases.

Negotiations on other monument issues continued as Utah's congressional delegation in 1997 introduced legislation to set limits on a president's use of the Antiquities Act. The 1906 act originally was intended to protect small areas of land and specific places of archeological, geological, scientific, or historic importance, and specifies that monuments "shall be confined to the smallest area compatible with the proper care and management of the objects to be protected." Clinton, in creating a monument half the size of New Jersey that needed no protection, obviously had stretched the law's intent beyond all reason.

Hatch introduced the National Monument Fairness Act in the Senate and Utah Congressman Jim Hansen introduced it in the House. Their legislation would allow a president, on his own initiative, to designate a qualified monument of up to 50,000 acres. Anything larger would require consultation with the affected governor and approval by Congress. Although the House passed the bill twice, at this writing the Senate had yet to act on it.

Hatch, testifying for the bill before a Senate subcommittee in February 1998, noted that in the case of Grand Staircase-Escalante, "There was no consultation with the governor, no notification to the congressional delegation, no hearings, no town meetings, no media discussion, no nothing....Those of us in public land states cannot afford to have the large majority of the land area of our states subject to the whims of any president."

Then, in January 2000, Clinton, Gore, and Babbitt struck again. Standing once more on the South Rim of Grand Canyon, the President announced three new national monuments and expansion of a fourth. Two are in California, including the state's entire Pacific coast out to a distance of 12 miles, and two in Arizona, including Agua Fria, 71,000 acres; and Grand Canyon-Parashant, just over 1 million acres along a strip near the Utah-Arizona border.

Clinton, in his remarks, called Secretary Babbitt "a devoted champion of the Antiquities Act" and explained that when he and Babbitt both were governors–of Arkansas and Arizona respectively–they and their wives had dinner together at least once a year. "And he was giving me the speech that he gave here today fifteen or twenty years ago."

"I know we're doing the right thing, because look at the day we've got," added Clinton. We've got the good Lord's stamp of approval on this great day." Hard-core environmentalists also cheered, as a new group of westerners wondered how they would wrest a living from land that may be denied them.

"If anyone needed more evidence that this Administration has written off rural America, this is it," said Hatch. "Rural Utahns have already shouldered too much of the burden of this Administration's frenzy to build a legacy. It saddens me to see more of our rural areas harmed by this president, and it sickens me to hear him claim he has the 'Lord's stamp of approval' on a process that excludes those who would be most harmed by it."

Babbitt explained the Administration's rationale in these words: "It's about a landscape. The people in Chicago and their children are going to live in a big city but know there is open space forever that belongs to them whether they come and visit or not."

To many others, the notion that puny man could somehow destroy magnificent wonders it took nature millions of years to create is preposterous.

"Ranchers here feel like they've been kicked in the gut by their favorite horse," wrote a reporter in St. George, Washington County, Utah. "They thought they had a deal with Interior Secretary Bruce Babbitt to continue grazing as they have for generations in the rugged canyon country just south of here and Kanab....And they are downright angry at what they call self-righteous rhetoric by environmentalists and others that the land has been overgrazed–something used by President Clinton to justify his designation of 1 million acres here as a national monument."

Rancher Tony Heaton, whose family had run cattle in the monument area since the late 1800s, said the condition of the land was "better today than it was fifty years ago." Under pressure, Clinton subsequently said traditional activities including grazing could continue in the area; Utah officials were cautiously optimistic they could hold him to it.

Clinton, Gore, and Babbitt also were determined to block roads used by generations of westerners to traverse the federal lands surrounding them. Under a revised statute (R.S. 2477) roads already in place were to remain open as rights-of-way. Such roads are critical to local access to unreserved federal lands, and form a basic transportation infrastructure in rural communities. But the Interior Department was trying to close many of the roads, mostly in Utah and Alaska.

"In many cases, these roads are the only routes to farms and ranches," explains Senator Hatch. "They provide access for school buses, emergency vehicles, and mail delivery." The Senator in 1997 asked Attorney General

Janet Reno to personally get involved in determining the validity of Babbitt's proposed management of such roads. Reno, however, was typically unhelpful, and the controversy festered. Meanwhile, to defend itself, Utah has been busy verifying roads on federal land across the state, notably through satellite mapping technology.

The Clinton-Gore Administration also proposed closing about half of the 8 million acres of Forest Service land in Utah and 40 percent of such lands in the rest of the nation. Under the Administration's proposal, citizens are to consider stretches of their forests "closed" unless they are expressly posted as "open."

"This latest move by the President is not simply about managing roads in our national forests," testified Hatch in November 1999 before the Senate subcommittee on forest and public land management. "It is nothing short of an attempt to wrest from Congress and the American people the power to designate wilderness in our national forests. It is, for all intents and purposes, a vast one-size-fits-all 40-million-acre wilderness designation. Only it comes without any public input or congressional sanction."

In the Wilderness Act of 1964, Congress made it clear that some lands should be set aside for wilderness, severely restricting their use. But the act specifies that such areas are to be designated in a public process, with Congress having the final say. Nearly four decades later, there is still arm-wrestling over which areas of the U.S. should fall under that designation.

"Forest Service records show that recreation is the fastest growing use of our forests," testified Hatch. "Yet the Forest Service acknowledges that only 2 percent of recreationists make use of the 35 million acres of existing wilderness. The other 98 percent of the public who use our forests will lose access to an additional 40 million acres, so that the elite 2 percent will have sole access to 40 percent of our national forests. No wonder the President has not sought public input for this proposal."

Hatch said, with the forest roads proposal, "the President is once again attempting to secure political points with extreme environmental groups on the backs of rural communities....I cannot believe that responsible advocates for the environment would support this blatant circumvention of the established processes for designating wilderness."

What perplexes many westerners is the claim by self-proclaimed environmentalists–usually city dwellers far away–that they love nature best and know best how to care for it. Hatch believes that such elitism is at the root of the Clinton-Gore Administration's environmental policies. While earlier generations of environmentalists sought to save the environment for man's use, today their hard-core cousins seek to save it from man's use.

The truth is that farmers, ranchers, and others whose livelihoods depend on renewable natural resources, *must* tread lightly on the land for their very survival. Polluting of streams and watersheds and destruction of vegetation are not compatible with sustaining rural life. Those who have coaxed a living from the barren earth in the West for a century and a half are the region's real protectors and environmentalists.

"Surely those of us who care about the environment can learn from history," says Jim Nicholson, head of the Republican National Committee and a former Coloradan who, as a member of the state's Air Quality Control Commission, helped to substantially cut Colorado's carbon monoxide emissions.

"History shows, over and over, that when resources are owned publicly–streams, rivers, forest, park lands, even animals–there's a great risk that no one will do what it takes to preserve them. In Africa, when they tried to protect elephants by prohibiting their slaughter, the local people killed them for their tusks and meat. But where those same local people have been given ownership of the elephants, [and] a share of the profits to be made from enterprises such as tourism, the poachers became the elephant's zealous guardians."

Hatch is chief cosponsor of a clean-air bill taking such an incentive approach. The bill, introduced in the Senate in May 1999 by Democrat Jay Rockefeller of West Virginia, includes a package of tax incentives for alternative fuel vehicles and their infrastructure. Hatch said it is "the means to help improve the air quality in the Salt Lake Valley."

"As air pollution was introduced at the beginning of [the twentieth] century," said Hatch, "it is fitting that, at century's end, we should find solutions to this vexing problem." He explained that in Utah, automobiles account for 87 percent of carbon monoxide emissions and most of the pollutants that lead to ozone. "Yet it is impractical for Utahns to give up their cars. That's why I believe that a movement toward alternative fuels is the answer."

Their bill would create a fifty-cent-per-gallon tax credit for the purchase of alternative fuels, such as hydrogen, natural gas, propane, methanol and electricity. It provides a tax credit of 10 percent of the purchase price for alternative fuel vehicles, up to $4,000, and an additional $5,000 credit toward any electric vehicle with a range of at least 100 miles. It also offers a $100,000 credit for installing new filling stations for alternative fuel vehicles.

Leading Utah clean-air advocates support the measure, including the Salt Lake Clean Cities Coalition, the Wasatch County Clean Air Coalition, and the American Lung Association. "Our proposal is a fresh approach because it achieves cleaner air through incentives, not through federal mandates," said Hatch. "Consumers will never be interested in alternative fuel vehicles until a strong infrastructure is developed for these cars."

Senator Hatch endorses an approach of federalism, balance, and stewardship, such as that supported by the bipartisan Western Governors Association. It would give state and local officials far more say in matters related to the environment and natural resources. The Senator has a strong record of supporting environmental protections that work hand-in-hand with local need for multiple use of public lands.

The Utahn, along with Senator Max Baucus, D-Montana, sponsored the Community and Open Spaces Bonds Act, to provide special bonds to communities that wish to preserve open space. The bill would help local communities improve the quality of life for citizens without federal mandates.

With the support of local officials, Senator Hatch has also:

- Led the fight for full funding of the Colorado River Recovery Program, which protects and restores endangered and threatened fish species in the Upper Colorado River. He has also helped secure funding to protect endangered fish species in southern Utah's Virgin River.

- Worked to improve water quality of the lower Colorado River, including supporting a salinity control program to reduce agricultural and natural runoff. He has also sought additional funding for the Rural Water and Ground Water Protection programs, which provide technical assistance to Utah's rural water districts, helping them provide clean water to local residents.

- Introduced a bill that was signed into law to build an interpretive center at the Four Corners Monument, the only point in the U.S. common to four states–Utah, Colorado, Arizona, and New Mexico. It will especially help Native Americans in the region, who have some of the nation's highest rates of unemployment.

- Found funding to protect the Deseret Tortoise, an endangered species in Southern Utah. The state ranks fifth in the nation in the number of its native endangered plants; Hatch was one of few senators to fight for funding for the Center for Plant Conservation, which works exclusively to recover endangered plants throughout the country.

• Cosponsored a bill in 1998 with Utah Senator Bob Bennett that expanded the boundaries of Arches National Park to conform to the area's natural basin. The measure was signed by President Clinton in October of that year.

• Cosponsored a bill to reauthorize the North American Wetlands Conservation Act that became law in 1999. In the past, the act has led to the acquisition or improvement of about 3.7 million acres of wetlands, without using burdensome government regulations or taking private property.

Met Johnson, a rancher in southern Utah and for many years the leading public voice of rural Utah, is high in his praise of Hatch. "I'm his number one fan," says Johnson, who headed a coalition of 3,000 elected officials from throughout the West which brought top Washington officials to the region for a first-hand view before it disbanded recently.

"In rural Utah, what we appreciate most about Orrin is that he's willing to take on the Clinton Administration. When the president of the United States doesn't understand the West, and when the Secretary of the Interior tries to lay waste to our water, grazing, and mining issues, it is extremely important to us, and to our way of life, that Orrin Hatch is our chief defender."

Johnson calls Clinton and Babbitt "wackos" in their outlook toward the West. But many observers feared the worst was yet to come if Vice President Gore succeeded his boss in the Oval Office. Unlike Clinton, who is moved primarily by politics, Gore is a dedicated environmental extremist. He is a leading world proponent of an alarmist scenario based on global warming, and a prophet of doom who seeks to radically alter life in the industrialized world.

Gore proposes the opposite approach to change favored by Senator Hatch. While the Senator offers the carrot of tax incentives to encourage the pursuit of cleaner-burning fuels and technologies, Gore threatens the stick of new taxes on current fuels. In the early 1990s, other Administration officials suggested dropping the gasoline tax to encourage production and bring down prices, but insiders say Gore got emotional, dug in his heels, and the tax was retained.

Gore published *Earth in the Balance* in 1992, and in 1999 said "There is not a single passage in that book that I disagree with, or would change."

Among views Gore wouldn't change:

- "It seems an easy choice–sacrifice the tree for a human life–until one learns that three trees must be destroyed for each patient treated....Suddenly we must confront some tough questions. How important are the medical needs of future generations?"

- "Any child born into the hugely consumptionist way of life so common in the industrial world will have an impact on the environment that is, on average, many times more destructive than that of a child born in the developing world."

- "[We ought to] be able to establish a coordinated global program to accomplish the strategic goal of completely eliminating the internal combustible engine over, say, a twenty-five-year period."

- "What if we . . . raised [taxes] on the burning of fossil fuels...."

- "I am convinced that a [carbon dioxide] tax...is rapidly becoming feasible."

By the spring of 2000, the Clinton-Gore Administration's dire view of the world and war on fossil fuels was coming home to roost, as Americans paid higher prices at the pump than ever before. The gang that rejected the harvesting of a trillion dollars worth of relatively clean-burning coal on the Kaiparowits Plateau, and discouraged domestic drilling for new deposits of oil, was the same gang that years earlier had strangled, to no good purpose, America's promising nuclear energy industry.

That leaves hydroelectricity. Or does it? A hair-brained proposal to drain Lake Powell and dismantle Glen Canyon Dam on the Utah-Arizona border was met with laughter a couple of years ago. But at this writing, what was formerly a joke has gathered steam, albeit slowly, and nervous observers aren't laughing. " . . . only a mental suspension of the real world could allow a person to entertain thoughts of [the dam's] destruction," said the *Salt Lake Tribune* in an editorial titled "Dam Foolishness."

The idea is propelled by the Sierra Club, whose president Adam Werbach and a former leader David Brower testified in 1997 before a House subcommittee chaired by Utah Congressman Jim Hansen. Their goal: Restore Glen Canyon to its former pristine state by returning the Colorado River to its natural flow through southern Utah and northern Arizona.

Lake Powell, visited by nearly 3 million recreationists each year, was created in 1964 as the nation's second-largest artificial reservoir. Glen Canyon Dam holding back the water on the river is some 700 feet tall–fourth tallest dam in the U.S.–and contains nearly 5 million cubic yards of concrete. The dam creates no pollutants, uses up no natural resources, and has the capacity to provide energy for some 600,000 households each year. Nearby Page, Arizona was created with the dam, which pours about $500 million annually into local economies, and the city of 10,000 would likely become a ghost town without Lake Powell.

Such details be damned, says Brower, a legendary environmentalist, who blames himself for not taking stronger action against the dam when it was under construction nearly four decades ago. "But as surely as we made a mistake years ago, we can reverse it," he writes. "We can drain Lake Powell and let the Colorado River run through the dam that created it."

In September 1999 the Senate passed legislation authored by Senator Hatch, prohibiting the Interior Department from moving forward on any plan to drain Lake Powell. And on the House side of Capitol Hill, Congressman Hansen has vowed such a plan will never succeed on his watch.

While most observers shake their heads at the thought of draining Lake Powell, in recent years the federal government has come to believe that dams do more harm than good. In 1998 the Interior Department began tearing down six small dams in the West. That summer, Interior Secretary Babbitt, in a speech to the Ecological Society of America, said the removal of those dams "rings in an entirely new era of conservation history, moving beyond preservation or protection, towards a deeper, more complex movement, the affirmative act of restoration."

If there is a single mantra that unites most environmentalists, it is the perceived threat of global warming caused by greenhouse gas emissions. Cars and factories are among culprits blamed for gases that accumulate in the atmosphere, and eventual consequences predicted by Gore and others include rising sea levels that cause flooding, more extreme weather, and disruption to agriculture.

While the earth recently has slowly been getting warmer, scientists disagree on whether the trend will continue and, if it does, what the outcomes will be. "Though some scientists insist there is cause for alarm, evidence indicates otherwise," writes Dennis T. Avery of the Hudson Institute, a think tank based in Indianapolis. "Global warming may be coming, but if it does, it won't necessarily be extreme. And it might actually be a boon for the environment."

Avery says that such warming trends earlier in history led to new food production in formerly frigid places, including Greenland, fewer storms at sea, and less severe weather changes because of reduced differences in temperatures at the poles. "History and the science of climatology indicate that we have nothing to fear but fear mongers themselves."

Enter Al Gore. In 1997 the Vice President journeyed to Kyoto, Japan and, on behalf of the Administration, signed a treaty under which thirty-eight industrialized nations are required by 2012 to reduce greenhouse gas emissions from 1990 levels. Gore pledged that the U.S. would decrease its emissions by 7 percent. The Senate must ratify all treaties, and, while it has not acted on this one, if Gore becomes president there is no doubt he will lean hard on the Senate to do so.

There are many loopholes in the Kyoto accords. Most glaringly, less industrialized countries including China and Mexico are not signatories. Yet it is predicted that, within a few decades, more than one-half the world's carbon emissions will come from currently underdeveloped countries, with China generating more than any other nation. Does anyone really believe China will ever sign on to a treaty slowing its headlong rush to become the world's dominant economic force?

The Argonne National Laboratory, operated for the U.S. Energy Department, predicts the Kyoto accord would lead 20 to 30 percent of the U.S.'s basic chemical industry to move to developing countries within two decades, cut the number of steel producers by 30 percent, the number of steel jobs by 100,000, and reduce U.S. petroleum output by one-fifth. The United Mine Workers' Union predicts Gore's Global Climate Treaty would put 1.7 million American workers into unemployment lines, including 12,700 in Utah.

Senator Hatch, during his 1999 run for the presidency, said that if he were in the Oval Office, one of his first acts would be to revoke the Kyoto accords. "As responsible stewards of the earth, we should strongly encourage the development of alternative energy sources, including new cleaner-burning fuels, solar, biomass and wind," said Hatch. "But for the foreseeable future, we must rely primarily on fossil fuels. We should accept that reality and encourage their production here in the United States, to control our own destiny, instead of driving development to other parts of the world the way this Administration has done."

Rural citizens have ample reason for anxiety over Clinton-Gore-Babbitt policies. But the reality is that the Old West inevitably is changing and what is commonly called the New West is fast emerging. The family farm and ranch are disappearing, giant agri-business concerns are taking their place, and rural residents are as liable to carry a cell phone as a lariat.

Earlier in U.S. history, most Americans worked the land. Thanks to undreamed of advances in productivity, today only about 2 percent of Americans are on the land, producing the world's safest and cheapest supply of food, which costs the average family about 10 percent of its disposable income.

The question is not whether change will continue and even accelerate–it will–but whether change will be directed by the environmental left and a politically motivated administration in Washington, or whether states, counties and communities will be allowed to act reasonably and rationally to help ease their rural populations into the New West.

Senator Hatch has been in the forefront in anticipating change and proposing creative policies to deal with it. As chair of the Senate's taxation and IRS oversight subcommittee, he introduced a bill to repeal the capital gains tax and the "death tax," whose confiscatory approach makes it virtually impossible in many cases for parents to pass on farms or small businesses to their children. Congress passed the Hatch bill but President Clinton vetoed it.

The Senator has helped recruit many new businesses to Utah. He has also introduced and pushed into law numerous bills dealing with intellectual property rights, research, education, anti-trust, trade, and other issues vital to Utah's modern economy.

Among many other actions to attract or protect Utah jobs, Hatch and Congressman Jim Hansen have led the fight in Congress to keep Hill Air Force Base–Utah's largest employer–off the list for future base closings. The Senator helped blow the whistle on the Clinton-Gore Administration's blatantly political attempt to shift Hill's work to two Air Force bases in vote-rich Texas and California, even though the two bases had been ordered closed by a nonpartisan closure commission.

Then, in May 1999, Hatch won a Senate vote rejecting Clinton's request for more rounds of base closures. Hatch and most others in Congress do not trust the current Administration to conduct such hearings fairly. Hill is now scheduled to pick up about 3,000 more jobs from the bases closing in Texas and California, boosting its workforce to 24,000 by the end of 2001.

While agriculture is still extremely important in Utah, the state in fact is one of the most urbanized in the country. More than three-fourths of its population is concentrated along a narrow band of the Wasatch Mountains between Provo in the south and Brigham City in the north. Utah has one of the best-educated and highly motivated workforces in the country, along with a diverse economy and huge high-tech industry.

Thanks in good part to excellent leadership, including the state's congressional delegation and its forward-looking governor, Mike Leavitt, who also chaired the National Governors Association in 2000, this has been a golden era for Utah as a whole. In 1999 alone:

- Utah's economy was one of only two in the nation receiving straight A's from the Corporation for Enterprise Development.

- Utahns enjoyed the nation's second-lowest poverty rate and tenth-highest median household income.

- The Salt Lake-Ogden area was rated the best place to live in North America by the *Places Rated Almanac.*

- Utah had the nation's lowest smoking rate and lowest rate of alcohol-related traffic deaths.

- Utah's college students had the fifth-lowest student loan default rate in the nation.

- Utah's prison system was the least crowded among all fifty states, and in 1999 its crime rate dipped sharply.

While laboring hard for Utah in Washington to help win such results, Senator Hatch and his dedicated staff also work tirelessly for individual constituents, helping about 16,000 Utahns each year solve problems with the IRS, Social Security Administration, and other federal agencies. Hatch returns to Utah on most weekends, and he or his staff are readily available to Beehive State residents through offices he maintains in Salt Lake City, Ogden, Provo, Cedar City, and St. George.

Some reviews of Hatch's efforts by Utahns:

- B. Howard Beckstead, Woodruff: "I'm very grateful to you for the help you gave me in getting my retirement money . . . so now my wife and I can live a better life....You care for the people and the elderly and we appreciate all the hard work you do."

- Dennis W. Peterson, president, Ace Fab and Welding Inc., Ogden: "I am indeed grateful for the assistance offered by you....I had been under the impression that politicians merely pay lip service to the small business community. The speed of your response simply amazed me and my employees. My faith in you now knows no bounds."

- Margaret Watt, Elsinore: "On behalf of the Central Utah Veterans and myself–thank you for your support and help; it is truly appreciated. I now feel our work down here is not being ignored."

- Marie W. Huff, former mayor of Spanish Fork: "On behalf of the citizens of Spanish Fork City, we extend to you our sincere thanks regarding the new post office scheduled for construction. Your rapid response to our concerns is appreciated...."

- Pia Byrd, Salt Lake City, program director of the Children's Dance Theater: "You've made one little girl very happy." The troupe was about to leave for a London tour and the girl, Amy, had no passport. Hatch asked the federal passport office to cut its red tape and issue the passport, which arrived in Utah just in time by special delivery.

Those who have worked closest with Hatch are his biggest fans. "There's never been an issue that I've gone to Orrin with, that he wasn't willing to pick up the battle lines and go to work hard," says former Utah Governor Norm Bangerter. "On the issues that affect Utah the most, Orrin is at the forefront of every battle. He's willing to take on his colleagues, and he's always fought for Utah. With his clout, Orrin will keep Utah at the forefront–and that's essential."

Former Republican Senator Alan Simpson of Wyoming said he liked working with Hatch because "his word is his bond. If he says he's going to do something, put it in the bank." Without Hatch in Washington, Simpson added, the Clinton-Gore Administration would have "picked Utah like a chicken."

Utah's Mike Leavitt says "Most Utahns see Orrin Hatch battling in Washington against the bureaucracy. I've seen him in his kitchen. I've seen him with his family....I've seen him call at times he had so much else to be doing...to check on a person who was sick. This is not just a great senator, he's an extraordinary human being."

21

Orrin at Ease

I don't ever remember [Orrin and Elaine] fighting. When Mom visits alone, Dad calls her three or four times a day.

–Daughter Kimberly Catron

IN A CONVENTIONAL SENSE, Senator Hatch seldom relaxes. He simply changes one type of productive activity for another. Even in sleep, an internal mainspring seems to urge him onward. He developed lower back pain several decades ago, and long, deep slumber has eluded him most of the years since. Rarely does he enjoy more than three or four consecutive hours of sleep. Nonetheless each weekday he arises well before dawn and heads for his Capitol Hill office, usually arriving well ahead of most other members of Congress.

One key to the Senator's stamina and generally excellent physical condition is rigorous, sweat-drenched daily exercise, either at the Senate gym or at home on a stair-step machine on the lower floor of the Hatches' split-level home, while catching a game or evening news on television.

Hatch's work habits were learned at his parents' knees. Other than skipping out on his share of weeding–one chore he couldn't abide then or now–he otherwise was a hard worker from a young age, notably picking up slack around the family home in Pittsburgh after his brother Jess went off to World War II. Among other duties, he helped care for the chickens and sell eggs. Then, starting as a teenager, he worked beside his father in the construction trade.

Family vacations were few when he was a boy, and as a young father they tended to be infrequent and frugal. His children still remember the 1,800-mile drives from Pittsburgh to Utah each summer to visit Elaine's family in Cache Valley. To save money, the Hatches drove straight through, stopping only for gas and food, rather than pay for overnight lodging.

"When Orrin went to law school, someone remarked that 'the law is a jealous mistress.' The Senate is the same," said Elaine. "The first time Orrin ran, he said, 'When I win we'll have every weekend off to go see the historic sites in the East.' Five years later I asked him, 'When are those weekend outings going to start?'" In truth, they never did.

Orrin's father loved to fish, and the two occasionally went on fishing trips before Jesse's death in 1992. The Senator also took up golf, and was a natural, occasionally scoring below eighty. Sometimes he took one or more of the children golfing with him.

As others learned of the Senator's driven nature, demands on his time from outside the family became enormous. He came more and more to appreciate Elaine, a traditional homemaker who cared for their six children, and whom he calls a "pioneer."

Orrin creatively sought to balance family and outside demands, sometimes taking a child when speaking out of town. He also tried hard to make it to the children's special school and other events. Although his family unquestionably was first in his heart, it was not always first on his schedule–a reality that troubled his conscience as he recalled a familiar Mormon aphorism: "No other success can compensate for failure in the home."

While they didn't get a lot of Orrin's time, the now-grown Hatch children are quick to say they never doubted his love. Their father never left home or parted from a family member without saying "I love you," usually accompanied with a hug. By the final measure of parenting success–how children turn out–Orrin and Elaine have passed the test. They have outstanding, well-adjusted children who are rearing beautiful families of their own and contributing to their communities and church. By the start of 2000, their six children had produced nineteen grandchildren.

Brent Hatch is a partner in a Salt Lake City law firm. He and his wife, Mia Ensslin Hatch, have four children, including the oldest Hatch grandchild, a girl, who is a high school senior.

Marcia Hatch and husband, Randy Whetton, have five children and recently moved from California to North Ogden, Utah, where he is a chiropractor.

Scott and Wendy Dalgleish Hatch and their two children live eight miles from Orrin and Elaine in Fairfax, Virginia. Scott is a researcher for a lobby firm.

Kimberly Hatch and husband John Catron have four children and live in Kent, Washington, where he is an attorney with Boeing.

Alysa Hatch and husband Jamie Whitlock and their two children live in Yucca Valley, California, where he is the second son-in-law chiropractor.

Jess and Mary Alice Marriott Hatch have two children. In 2000 they were in Boston where Jess attended Harvard Business School.

Orrin and Elaine have done the single most important thing they could do for their children: They have loved each other faithfully throughout forty-three years of marriage. Their devotion has given the children a model and a sense of security not found in many families. "I don't ever remember them fighting," says Kimberly Catron. "When Mom visits alone, Dad calls her three or four times a day." Kimberly's brother Scott adds that "I look at them as the perfect couple."

Elaine has largely avoided the public spotlight but gives no hint of resentment toward Orrin's life in it. After all these years, she still arises with him early each weekday, and fixes the oatmeal he eats while commuting the forty minutes to his office. She still launders and irons his shirts, and once made her own dress for a White House function. "She's extremely bright, very well-read," said a close friend, Jan Bennett, who has known them most of their married life.

In 1995 the *Salt Lake Tribune* ran a large feature article on Elaine, with subheadings that called her "Orrin's Match" and a "Quintessential Wife, Mother [who] Stays Out of Limelight." It noted that Elaine is one of the most down-to-earth Senate wives, and that her heart is at home or in charitable service, and not on Washington's busy social circuit. Her favorite first lady, with whom she has been compared, is Barbara Bush. The *Tribune* quotes her as saying about Mrs. Bush, "She's a friendly, wonderful, warm woman. She knew your name, knew something about you, asked personal things."

When the *Tribune* article appeared, a district judge in Utah sent a letter to the Hatches commenting on it. The Senator answered him with a note saying "As you no doubt know, having a wonderful woman by one's side makes life so sweet. I have been truly blessed beyond my imagination . . . I owe everything I have achieved to my eternal sweetheart, Elaine."

Once their children had all left home and she had more free time, Elaine and Orrin found ways to spend more time together even when he was on Senate business. She has accompanied him to speaking engagements in the U.S. as well as on a number of extended trips abroad.

There have also been genuine vacations on occasion. During the Senate's summer recess in August 1995, they joined their son Jess and his wife Mary Alice, and her parents Dick and Nancy Marriott, for three days in Lake Winnipesaukee, New Hampshire, where the Marriotts have a compound with a number of homes. Dick is an executive with the Marriott Corporation, founded by his late father, J. Willard Marriott. Staying in one of the family homes which extends over the lake itself, the Hatches walked the shoreline, and Orrin played golf and sped around the lake with Dick in his souped-up racing boat.

"The time in Lake Winnipesaukee was one of the most enjoyable relaxing times I have had in the last 19 years," Orrin wrote to a friend. "Nancy is a terrific cook and she and Dick couldn't have been better hosts. We love them."

Also that summer, the Hatches traveled to Ketchikan, Alaska, an island, where Elaine's sister Doris and her husband David Crockett, a school teacher, lived. A pilot in a float plane picked the Hatches up at the island and took them to Waterfall Resort, for two days of fishing in the inland ocean waterway with some other senatorial couples. Both Orrin and Elaine caught their limits of coho salmon, and he landed an eighty-four-pound halibut on light tackle after a half-hour fight.

They returned from Alaska just in time to go to Park City, Utah, for the Congressional Golf Challenge, the Senator's annual charity golf tournament. The event raises money for needy individuals and families. It especially has helped numerous women in jeopardy, through funding programs and facilities dealing with rape crisis and spousal abuse. The tournament is organized by the Utah Families Foundation, which Hatch created. Its mission is to assist children who are parentless or those who face the problems of homelessness, poverty, unemployment, hunger, illness, abuse, hospitalization, and cultural or educational illiteracy.

In nine years, through 1999, the foundation donated some $2.6 million to such charities as Ronald McDonald House, Shriner's Children's Hospital, Guadalupe School, the Utah Food Bank, Utah Boys Ranch, YWCA and YMCA, National Abilities Center, Centro de la Familia, Caring Program for Children, The Children's Center, The Family Support and Children's Justice Centers, Make a Wish Foundation, New Horizons Women's Center, and many other women's shelters throughout Utah.

Crowning the 1995 charity golf tournament for the Hatches was the surprise arrival of their good friends Muhammad Ali and wife Lonnie. "They came just to be with us," wrote Hatch in a letter. "On Monday, Ali stayed with me at the 11th hole almost all day and had his picture taken with countless groups. Finally, he tired [Ali has Parkinson's syndrome] and we had a young man assigned to him take him back to his room."

Orrin and Elaine collect art. As a poor boy, often he visited Pittsburgh museums and marveled at the grandeur he saw and felt. Years later, in addition to his regular law practice, Orrin opened an evening general law office with an attorney friend named Roy Riehl. It was located on the second floor of a small shopping center where Riehl's wife owned an art gallery. The Hatches bought a number of pieces from the Riehls–including a landscape that is still a favorite–sparking a lifelong interest in collecting.

Included in their collection, which especially showcases western artists, are more than twenty works by Valoy Eaton, a gifted Utah landscape painter and the Senator's cousin. A number of pieces hang in Hatch's Utah and Washington offices, including a favorite of Orrin's depicting Elaine and hollyhocks in a field of corn, which is on a wall in his Salt Lake office.

Hatch has been a strong ally of the nation's artistic community and supporter of the National Endowment for the Arts–despite fierce criticism from other conservatives for aiding a public agency whose funding occasionally has gone to individuals who have betrayed the public trust by creating filth. Hatch has cheered the NEA's restriction of funding to some of those so-called artists, supporting their right to prepare and display their works, but not at taxpayer expense.

Yet he has considered various attempts by Congress to crack down on the NEA overkill. "Some of these fundamentalists wouldn't have allowed the Sistine Chapel to be painted," said Hatch. Crippling the NEA, Hatch believes, would threaten too many legitimate artists and art groups, which typically operate on a shoestring–many of them in his home state of Utah.

"Utah is dotted with art museums from St. George to Logan," wrote Utah art critic Frank McEntire in 1997 after the House voted to abolish the agency. "We can slip into the background as unobtrusive observers and marvel at the enrichment our museums and arts organizations bring into our lives. Art isn't a luxury. It's a veritable necessity."

Hatch continued to hold firm that year when the issue reached the Senate floor, helping to pull the agency from the jaws of death once again. In appreciation, NEA Chairman Jane Alexander wrote him, saying "Your stand has given encouragement to millions of Americans who care about the arts...thank you so much for your strong and consistent support." She added a hand-written postscript: "Many thanks for your unfailing arts support."

Hatch also is an avid sports fan. Once a fine multi-sport athlete himself, he is intensely loyal to a cadre of teams, including colleges in Utah, the NFL's San Francisco 49ers, Washington Redskins, and Pittsburgh Steelers; and baseball's Pittsburgh Pirates. Vernon Law, the Pirate's onetime great pitcher, was a hero to Orrin when he was growing up and remains a close family friend. Other good friends include Jerry Sloan, Phil Johnson, and other coaches of the Utah Jazz; BYU football coach LaVell Edwards, and two head coaches at the University of Utah–Rick Majerus in basketball and Ron McBride in football.

After major league baseball ground to a halt in 1994 with–take your pick–a lockout by owners or strike by players, Hatch jumped into the fray by introducing a bill to strip baseball owners of their antitrust exemption in labor matters. The exemption was first granted by the Supreme Court in 1922, which ruled inexplicably that baseball was not in interstate commerce and therefore immune from federal antitrust laws. No other sport had such an exemption.

He explained in the *Washington Times*:

> When I was a kid growing up in the late '40s, baseball was one of the few entertainments my family could occasionally afford. My dad and I would walk a couple of miles to catch the streetcar; then, two dimes and a transfer later, we would arrive at Pittsburgh's Forbes Field. The admission price to watch the Pirates play was about 50 cents or a dollar.
>
> In a way, baseball was a great equalizer. For a couple of hours, my dad, who was in the construction trades, and I could sit in the sun and become part of a grand tradition. The fact that we wore overalls or didn't have much money was irrelevant. Our support for the home team was important regardless of our social or economic standing. We were part and parcel of the Great American pastime.

Hatch added that "Sadly the ballfields and the bleachers were empty last summer," and given the stalemate between owners and players under current law, "Congress must now step up to right an old wrong. It must pass the limited legislation to repeal the antitrust exemption. Next, it must get out of the way. Then, and only then, will the boys of summer and their bosses get down to serious negotiations so the ball games will begin again."

Hatch clipped a copy of his commentary from the *Times* and sent it to

Vernon Law, by then retired and living in Provo, Utah, along with a note that said "I thought you'd enjoy reading my op-ed piece on baseball and the law. You and Vance [Vernon's son, also a baseball player] have had a good influence on me."

In introducing the bill in Congress in February 1995, Hatch said "The players have already voted to end their strike if this bill becomes law." Without it, he said, "owners can act like a monopoly, with no incentive to bargain in good faith. Meanwhile, the hundreds of minor league players who do not make the million-dollar salaries are stranded out in left field...watching their limited lifetime in the game and their futures tick away."

The measure, coauthored by Democratic Senator Daniel Patrick Moynihan of New York, did not impose specific terms of settlement and did not affect baseball's ability to relocate franchises or run the minor league system. It was limited to labor negotiations. Nonetheless, House Speaker Newt Gingrich at the outset refused to support the bill, charging it was "a club to beat up the owners on behalf of the players."

However, faced with a tidal wave of anger from baseball fans, and fearing retribution at the gates, owners themselves fell into line and supported the concept. Three sessions later, in 1998, the measure passed both houses of Congress and was signed into law by President Clinton.

It was called the Curt Flood Act, after the great center fielder for the St. Louis Cardinals, who in 1970 refused to be traded to the Philadelphia Phillies and battled for the right to free agency all the way to the Supreme Court, which ruled against him. Flood didn't live to see his vindication, dying of throat cancer in 1997.

While Hatch enjoys other sports and teams, his real passion is reserved for the Utah Jazz. He has become for the Jazz what actor Jack Nicholson has been to the Los Angeles Lakers–a celebrity good luck charm and symbol of steady support. Some Jazz players feel they have a better chance of winning when Hatch is there. He catches every game he can, sitting near the Jazz bench, and visits players in the locker room immediately after home games. In June 1998 the Jazz were down 3-1 to the Chicago Bulls in the NBA finals. On Friday, the twelfth, the Senator was scheduled to be in Williamsburg, Virginia, for a charity golf tournament sponsored by two senatorial colleagues. However, four days earlier he had wrenched his back, which had gone into complete spasms, and he was too ill to go to Williamsburg. But he was *not* too ill to board a plane heading the other direction–Chicago for the fifth NBA championship game.

As Hatch wrote to a friend:

> It was a nightmare. We left Washington at 5:30 p.m. and could not get through the weather into Chicago. So we stopped in Nashville, Tennessee, and refueled. By the time we got there it was quite late and we had to go way west to get around this weather front and then came into Chicago at 9:30 p.m. By then, the first half was over and Utah was losing 36 to 30.

At the airport, Hatch ran into a young man also headed for the game who, fortuitously, had ordered a limousine with a color television. He invited the Senator to ride along with him and they caught the third quarter on the way. Once there, security people took Hatch to his seat, next to an owner of the Chicago Bulls. Close by were Jerry Rice, the great all-pro receiver for the San Francisco 49ers, and Kevin Johnson, a guard for the NBA's Phoenix Suns.

Hatch was in heaven–confirmed when the Jazz pulled out the game in the last few minutes. He wrote:

> I was taken down by security to the Jazz locker room where I ran into [Karl] Malone who swept me up in his arms on his way to the media, and I met a number of others inside the locker room, including Coach [Jerry] Sloan. Antoine Carr grabbed me in his arms and nestled his head against my neck, he was so happy to see me. He particularly had played well. Even Jeff Hornacek was bright and friendly. Generally he is so shy he hardly talks to you.

Antoine Carr told a reporter, "Mostly he comes in to tell us how proud he is of us, on the court and for stuff we do in the community. It means something to us, having someone of that clout come in and say something like that. It's cool." The Jazz's Adam Keefe, one of the brightest and best-educated men in the NBA, has talked to Hatch about a possible future career in politics. Hatch has met with and written Keefe a number of times to encourage him to prepare for public service when his playing days are over.

In addition to public appearances at game time in Salt Lake's Delta Center, Hatch sends individual players hand-written notes. In April 1995, for example, he wrote Malone, the Jazz's great power forward, to say "You were sensational as always the other night....We are all fans of your on-court talents. But I am also appreciative of how much you give of your time to the Salt Lake community." A year later he wrote Malone again, saying "I'm so proud of you....You are playing so well. It is a pleasure to watch you and John [Stockton] whenever and wherever I can. I admire your basketball ability but I admire your attitude of goodness even more."

The bread cast by Hatch upon that water was returned many fold in the summer of 1999 after Hatch belatedly threw his hat into the ring for the White House. Malone, the National Basketball Association's 1998-99 Most Valuable Player, joined Hatch in Ames, Iowa to help attract voters in that state's straw poll. Hatch had called Malone three weeks earlier. "He said, 'I need your help on something. I want you to come to Iowa. I think we can make some noise,'" recalled Malone.

The Mailman was in Ames all day beside Hatch, signing autographs and posing for numerous photos. He also addressed the Teamsters Union for the Senator, wearing a Teamsters hat and telling truckers about growing up in Louisiana and dreaming of owning eighteen-wheelers–a dream he has fulfilled.

"The thing with Senator Hatch is he has always supported me in basketball, win or lose," Malone explained. "If he tells you something, he does it."

Days later, back in Utah, Malone and his wife Kay threw a fund-raiser for Hatch at their Capitol Hill bed and breakfast, netting a critical $300,000 for his underdog campaign. "I don't think that fellow down in Texas [George W. Bush] is going to do a hell of a lot for Utah," Malone told guests, who paid $1,000 a plate for dinner. "We should support who supports us."

Hatch has written many other athletes as well, often when he felt they could use a lift. In 1995, stirred by a newspaper article, he penned a note to former middleweight boxing champion Gene Fullmer, then 63, who long ago dropped from public view. "It's important that people know what a great fighter you are," wrote Hatch to the lifelong Utahn. (Note the "are" instead of "were.") "My Dad and I never missed your televised or radioed fights. We always pulled for you. Hang in there. I'm your friend. Orrin." Hatch also has gotten Fullmer together with Ali when Ali has visited Utah.

The Senator has a special fondness for Steve Young of the San Francisco 49ers, a fellow practicing Mormon who played football at his alma mater BYU and arguably is the best quarterback ever to play the game.

Young's value to the 49ers was dramatically demonstrated in 1999 when he missed most of the season with a possible career-ending concussion. With Young out of the lineup the 49ers fell apart, posting a rare and dismal losing season.

In 1994 the 49ers and Young had one of the best seasons in National Football League history, capped by beating the San Diego Chargers 49-26 to win their record fifth Super Bowl championship. In guiding his team to a 16-3 season, Young set a league record with a quarterback rating of 112.8 and became the first player to lead the NFL in passing for four consecutive seasons. In the Super Bowl he passed for a record six touchdowns and was named the game's MVP.

"We are all thrilled by your Super Bowl achievements," Hatch wrote Young. "You were terrific....Keep that great humble, good-guy attitude and you will own the NFL."

During the next season, starting later that year, when Young hurt his shoulder, Hatch wrote to say "Our faith and prayers are with you. I know it must be a little discouraging for you to be sidelined at this time in your career. Just know that when you are back on the field, your offense will do better by you, and you will hit your stride well ....You are a great human being and your faith and that of a great number of others will see you through. Somehow, you'll be better after this is over."

Young missed five games but returned to quarterback the 49ers for the final four regular-season contests, ending with their winning the NFC West Championship. He was selected to the Pro Bowl for the fourth straight year.

Months later, Hatch wrote Young again, saying "Just today, I told Jerry Jones [owner of the Dallas Cowboys], in my office, how I feel you don't get nearly the credit you deserve! Jerry Agreed!....You and I know, however, there are far greater things that are far more meaningful in our lives than being a great football player or a U.S. Senator....Merry Christmas and have a great New Year. Your brother, Orrin."

22
Friends

So I went up to Washington and met him in his office, and he was such a gentleman....I could tell he wasn't patronizing me like some people do. He was sincere....He makes an attractive appearance too. You know, he's pretty. Not as pretty as I am, but he's still pretty.

–Muhammad Ali

IF A MAN IS KNOWN BY THE company he keeps, what is one to make of Orrin Hatch? Few public officials have a more eclectic group of friends–potentates and paupers, billionaires and blue-collar workers, professional athletes, writers, musicians, statesmen, religious leaders, and the list goes on.

For most politicians, "keeping fences mended" with diverse people is simply a way to avoid trouble. Hatch's relationships tend to go deeper. He thrives on emotional connectivity and is fiercely loyal to friends, many of whom appear to need him far more than he needs them. His loyalty sometimes has come at a high political price, since Hatch tends to befriend individuals who are shunned by many others.

Many of Hatch's best friends are basically nonpolitical. Their correspondence suggests his impact on their lives. Monzer Hourani, for example, is a Lebanese American businessman in Houston befriended by Hatch in 1985. They have since worked on a range of mutual interests. "Your kind emotional and spiritual support has been a very important factor in my life," wrote Hourani to Hatch in 1997. "Through your care and concern, you have shown me the noble and beautiful aspects of life . . .I will always be grateful to have you as a brother and part of my family. I love and respect you a great deal, and am blessed to be your brother."

Hatch's most storied friendship–which most people will never understand–is with Ted Kennedy, the Massachusetts Democrat. They are the quintessential odd couple: Kennedy born to wealth and a political dynasty, Hatch to scarcity and obscurity. Kennedy noted for many years of a reckless lifestyle, Hatch consistently a model of rectitude. Kennedy the icon of American liberals, Hatch the Senate's conservative wizard.

Most of the time they oppose each other in the Senate. In 1989, for example, among the ninety-nine other members, Hatch voted most often with conservative Republicans William Armstrong of Colorado and Trent Lott of Mississippi. He voted least often with three liberal Democrats, including Kennedy. In 1996 a leading conservative watchdog group, the American Conservative Union, rated Hatch as voting 100 percent "correct" on the issues they deemed of most importance that year. ACU gave Kennedy 0 percent for his votes on the same set of issues. During that same year, a leading liberal group, Americans for Democratic Action, gave Hatch a scorecard of 5 percent and Kennedy 90 percent.

Despite different philosophies of government–Hatch considers it an essential but last resort to solving most problems, and Kennedy the first resort–they share a hunger to hurdle politics in order to answer human need. When they have reached agreement on particular issues, locked arms, and marched together, political seas have parted and, often, new laws put on the books.

Theirs is a mutual fondness that germinated slowly and has withstood nearly a quarter-century of battering. One notable battering came in June 1997 after Hatch had fought successfully in the Senate Finance Committee for more funding for the Hatch-Kennedy child health insurance bill. Their original bill called for $20 billion. Hatch, against all odds, fought successfully in committee to add another $4 billion to make it a total $24 billion.

Kennedy didn't learn about the deal until after the committee meeting. Already he was on edge because funding for child health care was going to states as straight block grants, the conservative approach Hatch insisted on, rather than through Medicaid which would have included strings Kennedy wanted to attach. Then, because he was not consulted by Hatch before Hatch agreed to the additional amount, Kennedy came unglued. No sooner had Hatch emerged triumphant from the closed-door committee meeting than Kennedy was on the phone.

"This is the greatest betrayal I've had in all my years in the Senate!"

screamed Kennedy as only he can scream.

"What are you talking about?" answered Hatch, dumbfounded. "Don't you understand that our total bill was for $20 billion, and we've got more than that? I've done everything I said we'd do." But Kennedy wouldn't listen. He told Hatch he was going to take the issue to the Senate floor and embarrass him, again emphasizing "This is the greatest betrayal I've ever suffered in the Senate."

Hatch reminded Kennedy that timing was everything. Had he left the tense committee long enough to consult with Kennedy on the final amount, all of it might well have been lost. But Kennedy wouldn't listen. Finally a fed-up Hatch said sharply, "I just think you're wrong," and abruptly hung up.

News of Kennedy's irate phone call soon spread across Capitol Hill and, ironically, helped solidify support for the agreement. Republicans felt that if Kennedy was unhappy with the outcome, maybe it wasn't so bad after all. Even many Democrats, long since tired of Kennedy's bullying and hogging the spotlight, found in his frustration a further reason to support the measure.

The following morning, a Friday, Hatch arrived early at his Russell Building office. One of his first visitors was a sheepish Ted Kennedy. He apologized for the outburst and again explained his concerns–including that states, left unconstrained, would not ensure that special needs children got adequate vision, hearing, or emotional care. Hatch understood.

Business over, Hatch took the initiative to make Kennedy feel even more chagrined. "Ted, I've written a song for you and Vicky," he said.

"You, you have?" stammered Kennedy.

"Yes, do you want to hear it?" said Hatch. He did. Hatch fired up the stereo compact disc system behind the desk in his private office. Out blared "Souls Along the Way," an arresting ballad written by Hatch and Madeline Stone for Ted and Victoria Kennedy, the woman many observers credit with finally reeling in his out-of-control life. Among the lines, written for Vicky to sing to Ted:

All those days of bitter cold
and nights without an end,
You showed me time and time again
the meaning of a friend.
You will always be
The one who reaches me.

[Chorus]
We are souls along the way,
in my heart you stay.

You know my secrets,
I have cried your pain.
When the winding road takes us up and down
We'll keep holding on,
It's love we've found.
Forever and a day
We are souls along the way.

As the last lilting notes of soloist Felicia Sorensen faded away, tears filled Kennedy's eyes. "Orrin, can I have a copy of the tape?" he asked. Hatch, of course, said yes. "Our fifth wedding anniversary is next week, July third," Kennedy explained. "Vicki and I are going to take a sailing trip, just the two of us, down the East Coast. On our anniversary, I'm going to play this for her."

Once more their uncommon friendship had survived a tough test. It was not the first test and it would not be the last. Cynics who say the friendship is based on political convenience and not mutual affection are wrong. The two have been there for each other too often for their friendship to be anything but genuine.

Hatch and Kennedy are now two lions in winter. What each has become is owed in no small part to the other. Insiders credit Hatch with helping to turn Kennedy from his self-destructive ways. That in turn helped pave the way for Kennedy's marriage in 1992 to Victoria Reggie, a beautiful, statuesque, disciplined attorney who was heaven-sent. What Hatch began with Kennedy, Victoria apparently has maintained. In the years from their marriage to this writing, it has been rare to see Kennedy's name or face in the supermarket tabloids–a routine occurrence prior to that time.

Victoria appreciates Hatch's influence on her husband, and occasionally sends him warm personal notes. "Dear Orrin," she penned after the sailing trip, "What a beautiful, beautiful song! The words are so meaningful and touching–they really moved me. Many, many thanks. Ted and I had a wonderful, peaceful sailing trip and anniversary, and 'Souls Along the Way' added to our joy. Thanks for always being such a dear and thoughtful friend. Love, Vicki - 7/97."

In another letter, Victoria thanked Hatch for his generous comments to a writer doing a piece on the Kennedys for the *New Yorker*. "It's easy to see why Ted has so much respect for your friendship and leadership," she wrote. "You certainly helped to capture a more private side of Ted, and I'm grateful for your kind words and sound advice."

When Rose Kennedy, venerable matriarch of the Kennedy clan, died in January 1995 at the age of 105, Hatch attended the funeral at his own expense, walking half a mile down Boston's streets–perhaps the only Republican in the procession–as appreciative residents yelled their thanks to him for coming.

Hatch also sent hand-written notes of condolence to Ted and his three sisters, Jean Kennedy Smith, Patricia Kennedy Lawford, and Eunice Kennedy Shriver. The notes help explain Hatch's attraction to the Kennedys. To Jean he wrote "In a world too often cynical and self-serving, she loved, served, and triumphed." To Pat: "Your mother illustrated, through her profound faith, good works, and devotion to family, Christ's admonition to let her light so shine."

To Eunice: "Her legacy lives on in her children, as each of you embodies her ardent devotion to public service and compassionate outreach."

To Ted, Hatch wrote that he saw in him and other family members Rose's "fierce devotion to justice and equity, to education and responsibility." Of the mother who saw a procession of her promising children, including a U.S. President, go to early graves, Hatch added:

> I appreciate, too, how Rose Fitzgerald Kennedy's individual grief never overshadowed her sense of service and obligation to those less blessed. She truly fulfilled Christ's dictum that "For unto whomsoever much is given, of him shall be much required."
>
> Ted, I admire the tremendous role you have fulfilled as father and surrogate father. Your home, filled with Kennedy photos and memorabilia, always reminds me of the sacred and eternal nature of family bonds. Your friend, Orrin.

Two months later, when Hatch's own mother Helen died, Ted and Victoria were among those attending her funeral in Utah. Afterward, Victoria sent Orrin and Elaine a hand-written note thanking them for making her and Ted "feel so welcome and a part of your lovely family."

> We both commented afterward that we really now had a sense of Helen Kamm Hatch as a mother, a grandmother, a friend and a woman. We

> know in the deepest sense possible what you are going through right now. It is so hard to lose someone you love so much. But you must take comfort in knowing what joy and pride you brought to her during this earthly life. God bless both of you and your wonderful family. Our thoughts and prayers are with you.

Hatch answered with a note to "Dear Vicki," telling her "You are such a blessing to Ted. I've never seen him happier. I've never seen him more in charge of his life than since you have come into it. As you know, he is a great human being, and despite our political differences, I consider him a brother."

While Hatch has changed Kennedy, the reverse is also true. In each case, change has been more personal than political. Hatch is still a mainstream conservative–easily provable by voting records–but lacks the hard edge that is so unseemly in many ideologues of both the right and left. Hatch's relationship with others on the wide band of political thought has helped him appreciate other facets of public policy, and realize that laws have real impact on real people.

Kennedy has also helped Hatch laugh–at life and himself. The Massachusetts liberal has a riotous wit. He is known for throwing an annual Christmas party for his large staff, strictly off the record, in which Kennedy does impersonations and joins skits lampooning the latest national scandal.

One year, with Hatch attending as special guest, Kennedy cavorted on stage as Elvis, complete in black sideburns, wig, dark glasses, and body-hugging white suit open nearly to the navel. Another time he donned a blond wig and dressed as Fawn Hall, a comely secretary who became famous during the Reagan years for spiriting sensitive documents out of a government office in her pantyhose. One year he was Batman–reminding the audience, "That's *Bat*man, not *Fat*man."

Kennedy has a habit of gaining thirty or forty pounds and periodically going on a liquid diet to shed it. In August 1997, after Hatch suggested a new way to lose weight, Kennedy wrote him to say "The ice diet sounds interesting, but I find it works better in combination with cream!" On Hatch's office wall is a lithograph by Kennedy, an amateur painter, of his family's Hyannis Port compound. The inscription warns Hatch to handle carefully because "if the paint comes off the numbers will show."

In 1998 Hatch and Kennedy were invited to conduct the Boston Pops Orchestra. Afterward, Kennedy sent photos of their guest appearances to

Hatch–Kennedy in a white tuxedo and Hatch in black. The accompanying note said: "Dear Orrin, Drop by and see the originals in my office. I think we make pretty good conductors, even though some people are saying, if we want to be conductors, we should stick to railroads. As ever, Ted. P.S. I told Trent you're practicing to conduct the Senate!"

Another noted partner in adventure has been Muhammad Ali. They first met when Ali walked into Hatch's office unannounced in 1988, to thank him for helping a friend land a federal job. Since then the legendary world figure and his wife Lonnie have kept in regular touch with Hatch, campaigning for him in election years and as a guest at Hatch's annual charity golf tournament in Utah. During the tournaments, Ali usually stays with Hatch all day at a designated hole, where they have photos taken with countless groups of players and onlookers. Together they have raised hundreds of thousands of dollars for charity.

Ali suffers from Parkinson's syndrome, possibly brought on by boxing, which slows his speech and gait. But his mind remains quick and his wit enchanting. The once self-proclaimed "Greatest" rarely talks of his glory days in the ring, where he won the title three times before hanging up the gloves in 1980.

Instead, Ali spends most of his time in the service of Islam, praying toward Mecca five times a day and traveling the globe as a volunteer missionary, preaching God's word as he finds it in the Koran. "God gave me this condition to remind me always that I am human and that only He is the greatest," Ali told Hatch. He also told him that "I feel like a very intelligent man who is trying to break out of this body so I can speak."

Their mutual love of religion and children–Ali visits sick youngsters throughout the world–has forged strong bonds. "He is probably the most electrifying, charismatic man I have ever known," says Hatch. "He has the softest, gentlest, kindest eyes of anybody I've ever seen. He also has a magnificent way with children."

Ali's status as one of the world's most revered citizens was confirmed memorably in the summer of 1996. As 3.5 billion people watched on TV, Ali slowly climbed the stadium steps in Atlanta to light the flame starting the Olympic games. Said NBC-TV commentator Bob Costas: "Like everyone else in that stadium, I was deeply moved. Here's a guy who was once the most alive of men–the most dynamic and beautiful athlete we'd ever known–and now, to an extent, he was imprisoned by Parkinson's. His lighting that torch said something about the human spirit."

Ali once told *Insight* magazine that, while he has friends in both political parties, his favorite is Hatch. "I like Orrin. He's a nice fella," said Ali. "He's a capable man and he's an honest man. And he fights for what he believes in." Ali told the magazine he became impressed with Hatch during several televised Senate hearings.

> So I went up to Washington and met him in his office, and he was such a gentleman. He was so polite and courteous. And I could tell he wasn't patronizing me like some people do. He was sincere. You meet as many people as I do and you learn who the phonies are....He's conservative, but that doesn't prevent him from recognizing the rights of the individual. I don't think he's got a prejudiced bone in his body....He makes an attractive appearance too. You know, he's pretty. Not as pretty as I am, but he's still pretty.

One day Ali showed up at Hatch's office carrying a display in a glass box. It was a gift for Hatch: a framed copy of the *Insight* article–alongside one of Ali's world championship belt buckles. Hatch protested the rare gift, but Ali insisted he take it. The display, which hangs on Hatch's office wall, is inscribed, "to my dear friend Orrin Hatch, the man who *should* be President of the United States. With the highest respect and the deepest affection–From one champion to another. Love, Muhammad Ali."

Hatch's friends cover the full range of the political spectrum. On the left, in addition to Kennedy, have been such figures as former South Dakota Senator George McGovern, one of the most liberal men ever to run in a general election for President. McGovern wrote Hatch in 1995, saying "I've always regarded you as a friend. Your compassion for Teddy in the Senate and in his personal problems is admirable."

The late Hubert Humphrey, a former Democratic vice president whose quest for the White House likewise failed, also had a warm relationship with Hatch. Shortly before his death in 1978, Humphrey sent Hatch a note calling him "indeed a dear friend" and thanking him for a Bible he and Elaine had sent as a gift. "It graces our home and is in fact the centerpiece of my library," wrote the Happy Warrior.

Many prominent conservatives who have taken the time to search Hatch's heart likewise have remained steadfast friends. They include Cleon Skousen, a prolific Utah author and constitutional scholar who was one of Hatch's early supporters when he first ran for the Senate, and has remained close through the years. Skousen was among a circle of friends on hand in

June 1999 when Hatch informally announced his attention to run for president, and was there again in January 2000 when Hatch announced his candidacy for a fifth Senate term. They continue to correspond, with Skousen writing in 1995, for example, that "Your whole letter was very interesting as it always is....Our prayers are with you and we join in sending all our love!"

Another highly respected conservative friend was the late Ezra Taft Benson, who had been Secretary of Agriculture in the Eisenhower Administration and was later president of the LDS Church. Upon Benson's death in 1994, Hatch wrote to a relative that "During the campaign of 1976 he supported me. After elected, he would meet with me in his office and showed great kindness....From time to time he would ask me, 'Orrin, why in the world did you vote this way?' I would always answer him and he would say, 'Well, I have to be governed by what you say because you are there and I am here. I believe in you and I know you will do what's right.'"

One of Hatch's most intriguing close friendships was with Rabbi Baruch Korff, a longtime Jewish community activist who died in 1995 at eighty-one. Korff was best known as "Nixon's rabbi" for his steadfast support of the beleaguered former president even after he was forced from the White House in disgrace. Korff developed a personal relationship with Richard Nixon during the 1968 presidential campaign and was credited with influencing Nixon's strong support for Israel.

The crimes of Watergate seemed small to Korff, who had suffered true government-sponsored evil. As a five-year-old boy in Ukraine in 1919, he hugged his mother as she lay dying in the streets, shot by a soldier carrying out an anti-Jewish campaign. Korff, who came from an unbroken chain of family rabbis dating back nearly a thousand years, moved to the U.S. in 1926 and devoted his life to helping his people. He fought for the right of European Jews to emigrate, and during World War II petitioned world leaders to help save Jews in Nazi concentration camps.

Hatch's friendship with Korff began soon after Hatch was first elected to the Senate. They shared a deep love of country and humanitarian values, and Korff became an unofficial foreign affairs advisor to Hatch. They made a number of forays abroad, including to Poland where they joined Polish Solidarity leader Lech Walesa at a Catholic mass conducted by the famous Solidarity priest Father Henryk Jankowski, celebrating the fall of communism. "You're going to get me excommunicated!" Rabbi Korff joked to Hatch during the mass. Hatch explained that "He's a very dear friend who has taught me so much about Israel, about Judaism, about an awful lot of things. He's a great ethical and moral philosopher."

Weeks before Korff's death, as the rabbi lay critically ill with pancreatic cancer, Hatch abruptly canceled a trip to Utah and flew to his friend's bedside in Providence, Rhode Island. During their reunion, reported a local newspaper, Korff sat up in bed and told Hatch that their friendship over the years had been "woven with joy and happiness." He added, "When I found myself in failing health, I couldn't have wished for a closer friend at my side than Orrin Hatch. Thank you for coming."

Hatch turned to a reporter and quipped, "I think he's trying to make up now for all those Nixon years."

The *Washington Post*, in a eulogy to Korff, highlighted traits which happened to be those he had in common with Hatch. "He was rock-hard, yet ineffably sweet," the *Post* said of Korff. "And if his loyalty seemed hidebound, perhaps it's because what usually passes for loyalty is so wobbly. People are loyal to rising stars and winning teams. But when things go bad, loyalty becomes a flexible concept. If you want a friend in official Washington, get a dog. In a world of situational ethics, this man paid no attention to his situation."

Korff's dedication to Israel and to the Jewish people lives on in Hatch. Today, on a thin chain beneath his shirt, the Senator wears a mezuzah–a small Hebrew parchment in a gold container, a constant reminder of Israel's importance.

Hatch often has given succor to those who have fallen from public favor, such as the late Paul H. Dunn, once a popular general authority of the LDS Church whose reputation was scarred when it was revealed he had exaggerated his early history. Dunn wrote Hatch upon his reelection to the Senate in 1994, thanking him for his steadfastness and saying: "You are a rare individual who has the unique qualities of both a good reputation and a sterling character."

In 1987 Hatch and others received a letter from far-right leaders Paul Weyrich and Phyllis Schlafly, warning them to withdraw as sponsors of a Washington dinner that spring honoring U.S. Surgeon General C. Everett Koop. Originally opposed by liberals for his opposition to abortion and homosexuality, the nation's top doctor was in the conservative doghouse for his aggressive campaign against AIDS. But Hatch, noting Koop's trailblazing efforts across a broad range of health issues, including smoking and diet, continued to regard Koop as "a remarkable human being."

The Weyrich-Schlafly letter succeeded in scaring off a number of sponsors, including Senator Bob Dole, Congressman Jack Kemp, and several other presidential aspirants. On the evening of the banquet, only two members of Congress–Representative Henry Waxman, a California Democrat, and Hatch–showed up to honor Koop. Hatch gave a glowing tribute to the seventy-one-year-old Koop, who looked like Captain Ahab with his trademark beard and uniform.

"Dr. Koop exhibits all the qualities that we want in our nation's top doctor," said Hatch as Koop, in a rare moment of vulnerability, dabbed at his eyes with a napkin, "compassion, skill, leadership, and dedication to preserving human life." He added that Koop "has helped focus the debate regarding a new group that needs our compassion–citizens dying from AIDS....Dr. Koop and I have not always seen eye to eye....But by working together, we can develop effective solutions."

Privately, Hatch was angered that some government workers were "very frightened" to be at the dinner. One man told Hatch he might be fired if his photo got into the newspaper. "This type of mind control really bothers me," Hatch wrote that evening. "This is where the conservatives really hurt themselves." Koop wrote a note to Hatch, saying it was "so like" the Utahn "to come and speak to that gathering on my behalf that it didn't surprise me nearly as much as it pleased me."

A decade later, Hatch received this hand-written letter, dated May 21, 1997:

Dear Senator Hatch,

As I walked by your office on my way to work today, I just wanted to drop you a note to let you know what a special meaning your name has to my grandparents, Dr. and Mrs. C. Everett Koop, and to our family. During my grandfather's confirmation as Surgeon General, you were both a strong leader and a steady encouragement, and my grandmother's eyes light up as she recalls your loyal dedication. A true friend you have been.

Best,

Heather Koop

23
Music Man

I think he's talented. Particularly the religious songs have a real authentic voice. I think he feels them very deeply and that comes through in the writing.

–Marilyn Bergman, president of ASCAP and Oscar, Emmy, and Grammy award winner

THE AUTHOR, IN HIS BIOGRAPHY on Senator Hatch (*Leading the Charge: Orrin Hatch and 20 Years of America*) noted that "During his public career, Hatch would be as zealous as a missionary, as tenacious as a trial lawyer, and as aggressive as a prize fighter. He had, in fact, been all three."

Now add another successful calling: songwriter.

"Although it is no mystery to those who know him well, the public image of Hatch betrays the private person his friends describe as a true Renaissance man," said *The Hill*, a Washington newspaper, in a profile.

Senator Ted Kennedy told *The Hill* that Hatch "has got author friends and painter friends. I think in some respects that is what the founders wanted in the Senate, people with different interests. Hatch accepts people who disagree with him, added Kennedy, because he is "a man of a lot of different dimensions and interests."

Hatch loves the cadence of well-turned phrases, believing with playwright Tom Stoppard that "Words are sacred. They deserve respect. If you get the right ones, in the right order, you can nudge the world a little." The Senator has nudged the world in numerous speeches, bills, debates, talk show appearances, opinion pieces, and several non-fiction books. He has even written two lengthy, unpublished adventure novels.

Hatch relishes the life of the mind and, in the reckoning of close observers, is an intellect of the first rank. That helps explain why he is on the short lists of TV networks, who often call on him–sometimes with virtually no advance warning–to explain to viewers the issue of the day.

He devours both fiction and nonfiction, reading whenever he has a spare minute and isn't writing, and often alternating among several books at once. As he finishes a volume, he adds it to a bedside stack that sometimes gets several feet deep before Elaine finds another corner for their unwieldy library. "I now have an excellent light and a comfortable chair for reading," Hatch once mused, "What more could a man ask for?"

During one period a decade ago, he was simultaneously reading *Decision*, a novel by Alan Drury about a Supreme Court case; *The Constitution* by Edward Samuel Corwin; and two books by John Fowles, *The Magus* and *The French Lieutenant's Woman*. He kept a dictionary beside him, noting *The Magus* had 148 words new to him.

Hatch has been one of Congress's leading champions of effective intellectual property laws. Diverse interests ranging from those seeking patents to music writers to software programmers count on him to protect their creations. He also has promoted the careers of favorite musicians and authors, some of whom have become personal friends, including best-selling mystery writers Patricia Cornwell, Robin Cook, and Scott Turow. All three have something in common with Hatch: They have had other, highly successful professional lives–Cornwell as an award-winning crime reporter and analyst in the chief medical examiner's office in Virginia, Cook as a medical doctor, and Turow as a U.S. and private attorney.

Turow, author of such bestsellers as *Presumed Innocent* and *Burden of Proof*, wrote Hatch in January 1995 to thank him for "your tireless efforts in behalf of this [intellectual property rights] bill of yours (and mine) that seems to be a near-miss every session. I heard from your staff that it was derailed last year in conference – makes me ashamed to be a Democrat (I'd change, but there already seems to be so few left)....All of us who know you realize that in this arena the public's business will be done with judiciousness and principle."

In February 1995, the Senator sent copies of Robin Cook's latest book, *Contagion*, all across Washington, including to President Clinton at the White House, with a note calling it "a wonderful read" and saying "I hope one of these days when Robin is in town, I can bring him down to meet you." Then, worried that the President would not share the book with the First

Lady, Hatch that same day sent another copy of *Contagion* and a similar note to Hillary Clinton.

Cook, who has produced a book a year for more than a decade, sent Hatch an autographed copy of *Chromosome 6* in March 1997, with a note "To Orrin–Here's one of the very first copies hot off the press. I think this is far and away my best book....What's your opinion? Your admiring friend, Robin Cook."

Crime novelist Patricia Cornwell told a reporter that she and Hatch get along well despite the fact her political and lifestyle choices are far different than his. "He weighs everything he does and says on the scales of his beliefs and his decency," said Cornwell, a fixture on national bestseller lists. But "he's very well aware that not everybody believes what he does."

Cornwell noted that, while the public sees the "steely" Hatch on television, the Senator is an emotional man. In 1994 she dedicated her fifth book *The Body Farm* to "Senator Orrin Hatch of Utah for his tireless fight against crime." Cornwell recalled that "When I showed him the page he was overwhelmed and his eyes filled with tears. He still hasn't gotten over it."

Hatch not only admires good writers, he has worked hard to become one. He has succeeded in some genres, including as an essayist. His articles–on a wide range of issues–have appeared in the *New York Times*, *Washington Post*, *Chicago Tribune*, and *Barrons,* among other major general-circulation publications. Longer scholarly pieces have been published by the *Harvard Journal of Law and Public Policy* and the *Fordham Law Journal*.

A few years after Hatch entered the Senate, a leading Utah political reporter, Rod Decker, sifted through a thick packet of Hatch's writings and concluded that "Hatch writes well. He is clear and smooth. He marshals arguments well, and makes engaging jokes." However, added Decker, Hatch "too often seems determined to overpower rather than persuade."

Columns on current issues failed to slake Hatch's creative thirst. He began working late into the night at home and during down time on airplanes on his novels. By 1995 he had written three full-length books, including one on religion called *Higher Laws*, published by Deseret Book, and two novels with the working titles of *Crisis* and *Bump.* He circulated the novels among a number of author friends and publishers, and made revisions based on their input.

Since he was an undergraduate in college, Hatch has also written poetry–mostly for his own eyes, but sometimes as gifts. As a senator he bought an anthology of modern poetry and made a half-dozen pages of notes on favorite thoughts, including a quote from Coleridge, "Prose equals words in their best order; poetry equals the best words in the best order." He also liked these from Aristotle: "Poetry is something more philosophical and more worthy of serious attention than history," and "Plato is dear to me, but dearer still is the truth."

Hatch also liked Jean Cocteau's enigmatic epigram: "Victor Hugo–a madman who thought he was Victor Hugo."

He also identified with a famous Robert Frost poem:

The woods are lovely, dark and deep,
But I have promises to keep,
And miles to go before I sleep.

Robert Frost he isn't. But Hatch's poetry consistently conveys a point. Often his verse has dealt with immediate events in the Senate. After the 1984 elections, for example, Republicans met to choose their leadership for the new Congress. As his fellow conservatives lost one Senate leadership post after another in the secret balloting, possibly putting the Reagan Revolution in jeopardy, Hatch penned a poem of telegraphic phrases, ending:

Conservative losses stupendous,
Some thought impossible,
Unity was not tremendous,
Jealousy's cup so full.

This President's next four years,
Endangered by what has been done,
Explicating all our fears,
Neutralizing all that's been won.

Finally, after years of searching, Hatch in 1995 discovered songwriting–the creative style that best fit his talents and temperament. Early that year he was attending a funeral in Utah and ran into Janice Kapp Perry, a popular Mormon songwriter.

"Is it true you write poetry?" asked Perry.

"I confess it is," said Hatch. "But I don't let many others see it."

"Why don't you send me some poems and maybe I could turn them into songs," she suggested. He agreed. Shortly afterward, Perry followed up with a letter to Orrin and Elaine, explaining that she had recently finished reading *Leading the Charge.* She said that "I have always had the greatest respect for your family and now that has just increased greatly....Thank you so much for your integrity and ambition for good causes."

"Also, Senator, I wasn't sure if you were serious about a collaboration...I can hardly imagine you have time for anything else. But sometimes busy people can find time, so I wonder...."

Three months later they bumped into each other at another event, and she again brought up the subject. That weekend he sat down and wrote ten songs for Perry, sending them along with a cover note: "I'm very enthusiastic about giving you some lyrics you can use, therefore, I'll submit these to you....I'll also begin some work on some patriotic themes. Change these anyway you desire. I will be honored with whatever you decide."

"He had a little bit to learn about the difference between lyrics and poetry, as far as putting them into the form of a bridge and chorus," said Perry. "Otherwise he writes beautiful thoughts." Perry, who sings with the Mormon Tabernacle Choir, studied music at Brigham Young University, then reared a large family before embarking on a musical career. By 1997 she had composed more than 600 songs and produced 33 albums and songbooks of sacred music.

The ten songs Hatch sent her became the heart of their first album together, "My God is Love." From the first verse of the title song:

> *My God is love/He lifts me from the depths/He gives me hope/He grants me daily breath/ My God is love/He rules with tenderness/And when I pray/He hears and loves to bless.*
> [chorus] *My very soul requires His daily love/In darkest hours His spirit bears me up/ My love for Him is built upon the rock of perfect trust/For this I know: My God is love.*

A second hymn on the album likewise would help elevate Hatch's new career. It has four verses and is called "My Dearest Savior."

> *My dearest Savior/Who gently guides me/Into that kingdom/Free from all care/ My dearest Savior/Thou art my guide star/Kindly persuading/Leading me there.*
> [last v.] *My dearest Savior/when shall I see Thee?/I want to greet Thee/Free from all sin/ My dearest Savior/Please stay beside me/Lead me through darkness/Bring me back home.*

Hatch has since written hundreds of lyrics for Perry. As word got around that he was writing music, others came calling. Near the end of 1995 Billy Hinsche, instrumentalist with the Beach Boys, asked Hatch to write some songs with him. By then Hinsche apparently had forgiven the Senator for a joint appearance a year and a half earlier in Salt Lake City. The occasion was a fund-raising dinner for the Caring Foundation–just hours after a dentist had completed three root-canals on Hatch, leaving him a bit disoriented.

The Senator had been talked into playing "Georgia on My Mind" on the piano, with Hinsche on guitar. "There were 500 people there, many of whom were probably Democrats and anti-Hatch," he explained later. "We were the first to perform and when I got up to do it, having played 'Georgia' thousands of times in the past, my mind went completely blank and I was unable to play it. I tried and tried and tried. Finally, I was able to pick it up and we did stumble our way through. I about ruined Billy Hinsche's career."

Hinsche obviously sensed talent in Hatch, however, and asked the Senator to collaborate. One result was "I Believed She Loved Me," which Hinsche recorded into a country western ballad.

The following January, Hatch flew to Los Angeles and spoke at a fund-raiser for Senator Fred Thompson of Tennessee, who has acted in a number of motion pictures. Hatch was introduced by Jack Valenti, a longtime personal friend who represents the industry in Washington as head of the Motion Picture Association of America. Hatch just "happened" to have brought along his portable cassette player and played some Hatch/Hinsche songs for Valenti, who promised to shop them to major recording companies.

That same week, Hatch attended a function at the J.W. Marriott Hotel in Washington honoring the centennial of Utah statehood. A chorus of two dozen students from Utah State University, Logan, was on hand to entertain, but without microphones the commotion of a thousand milling people drowned them out. After event chairman Tom Korologos decided to cancel the students' last performance because no one could hear them, Hatch invited the group into a side room and gathered a number of others who stood in a circle while the chorus sang for them. "They were terrific," he said. "I could tell it made their evening."

Hatch's own music soon received similar kindness. Marilyn Bergman, one of the nation's preeminent lyricists, telephoned Hatch, whom she had met while lobbying for arts' causes.

"Orrin, I understand you are writing music?"

"Yes, and enjoying it," he answered.

"How about letting me look at it?"

"I'd be delighted," said Hatch. "It would mean a lot to me."

Bergman's interest would turn any songwriter's head. With her husband, Alan, she won Oscars in 1968, 1973 and 1984 for the songs, "The Windmills of Your Mind," "The Way We Were," and for the score for *Yentl*. They have been nominated for seventeen Oscars and have won three Emmy and two Grammy awards. Collaborators include Marvin Hamlisch, Henry Mancini, John Williams and Johnny Mandel. Marilyn is the first woman elected to the board of directors of the American Society of Composers, Authors and Publishers (ASCAP), which protects the royalty rights of members, and in 2000 was the group's president and board chairman.

Hatch sent her the Billy Hinsche cassettes and three songs with Janice Perry–"My Dearest Savior," "My God is Love," and "Sweet Gentleness."

A short time later Bergman called the Senator. She wasn't wild about the Hatch/Hinsche songs, but said "I love your lyrics with Ms. Perry's music. The music and lyrics match perfectly. Would you mind if I send these to my friend Donna Hilley, who is on the board of directors of ASCAP, and manages Sony/ATV/Tree in Nashville?"

"I'd really be honored," said Hatch.

Soon thereafter Donna Hilley telephoned Hatch.

"Senator, on any given day here in Nashville, we receive 200 good songs written by good writers," she began. "What we're really looking for are *great* songs."

Hatch's heart sank, certain he was being let down gently.

Hilley continued: "We think two of these three are great songs."

"You're kidding!" said Hatch, flabbergasted.

"No, I'm not. In fact, Senator, we believe 'My God is Love' and 'My Dearest Savior' will still be around a hundred years from now."

Hilley continued: "We'd like to demo them for you here in Nashville. Would you be willing to come down and watch how we do it in our forty-eight-track digital studio with good orchestration, top musicians, and top singers?"

"That would be wonderful," said Hatch.

In June 1996 Hatch, despite a bad head cold, flew to Nashville. A driver and limousine met him at the airport and took him directly to the downtown mansion of Donna Hilley and her husband Rayford, where

Hatch was ensconced in a second-floor bedroom. That evening they threw a party for him around their outdoor swimming pool, inviting some of the nation's greatest country songwriters and musicians. Already in place was a white grand piano and an assortment of acoustical and electric guitars, along with a complete sound system.

Guest performers included Kix Brooks and Ronnie Dunn, whose last eleven albums all had been number one on country music charts; Waylen Jennings, who wrote "Could I Have This Dance For the Rest of My Life," and Sy Coleman, the great Broadway songwriter and a longtime friend of Hatch's, who flew in from New York just for the evening.

After a salmon dinner, Randy Cox, who had prepared the orchestration recordings of the two Hatch-Perry songs, had a vocalist perform "My God is Love" and "My Dearest Savior." The crowd applauded enthusiastically. Then a number of other artists performed, including Brooks and Dunn who sang gospel songs of their own. Finally, Sy Coleman performed for the better part of an hour. Hatch, who usually lives far more humbly, was enthralled with it all.

The next day he visited the studio where Randy Cox and an assistant were preparing to record Hatch's two songs. They put sound track over sound track on the forty-eight-track digital studio system. Then a young guitarist–a Robin Williams look-alike, with long hair and wearing a beat-up baseball cap–read the music over carefully and moved into the studio. Immediately the youngster began playing some of the most beautiful guitar music Hatch had ever heard. He did the background music with few retakes. Finally, five singers–three women and two men–performed the two songs.

Hatch, cassette in hand, floated back to Washington.

One of Hatch's favorite Nashville singers is Chris Willis, a dedicated young African American Christian with a beautiful tenor voice, who is also a talented, self-taught pianist. After hearing Willis sing Hatch's songs in Nashville, the Senator brought him together with Santita Jackson, Jesse Jackson's daughter and another Hatch favorite, for duet performances. Santita, also a strong Christian, has performed at a number of patriotic programs Hatch has helped organize.

Hatch also financed a CD featuring the two young singers, called "Put Your Arms Around the World," and including a number of songs written by Hatch and Janice Kapp Perry. It was scheduled for release early in 2000. The duo sang at Hatch's fourteenth annual Utah women's conference in 1998.

The saga continued. A month after Hatch's first trip to Nashville in 1996, Larry Gatlin of the Gatlin Brothers telephoned Hatch at his office. Getting a phone mail message instead, Gatlin proceeded to sing the last few bars of "My God is Love," and then explained that he was writing an autobiography and was going to produce an album to go with it. He wanted permission to include Hatch's two songs in it.

Hatch also took the recordings to Gerald Ottley, director of the Mormon Tabernacle Choir. Ottley told him the songs were too close to "gospel pop" for the choir to perform that way. However, since then the famed choir has performed at least one of Hatch's songs, "Sweet Gentleness."

By May of 1997, the first Hatch-Perry CD was out, titled "My God is Love." Later that month the Senator spoke in Arizona to the Church Music Publishers Association (CMPA). To his surprise and delight, Geoff Lorenz of Lorenz Corporation, the largest Christian music publisher in the country, had done a beautiful arrangement of the CD's title song and passed copies out to the CMPA's executive officers, who sang it to Hatch.

The Senator discussed a music licensing bill, and also took the occasion to confront head-on a disturbing bias against LDS Church-produced music in the industry. Janice Kapp Perry, for one, has had great difficulty breaking into the general Christian community with her music. Some producers even return her packages unopened when they see the return address is Provo, Utah.

"If, in the end, all I accomplish through my music is opening doors for Janice and other talented LDS musicians, it will have been worth it," says Hatch.

To the CMPA's executive officers, Hatch said "I've understood that there is some prejudice against the Mormon Church among some Christian music publishers. That prejudice comes from the fact that some believe that Mormons are not Christians. I want you to know that Mormons definitely are Christians. I testify of Christ, and you cannot listen to one song on this CD without knowing that Mormons are devoted believers in Jesus Christ."

Hatch left believing he had done some good for the industry as well as for his church, but knowing only time would tell.

In September 1997 the second Hatch-Perry CD, "Freedom's Light," was out, featuring ten patriotic songs. The last verse of the title song:

> *So many say our glory days/Will never be again/And angry voices undermine/ The works of honest men/But God above will strengthen us/*

If valiant hearts unite/ We'll raise our voice in freedom's song/We'll walk in freedom's light!
[chorus] *This land, the arc of freedom's light/Is home to you and me/*
And we must keep it burning bright/From sea to shining sea/
We'll feed the fire of freedom's flame/We'll keep our dream alive/
So this blessed land may always feel/The glow of freedom's light.

The CD was well received. General Colin Powell called it "a wonderful and successful effort to illustrate through music the freedoms and blessings we all take for granted as Americans." Air Force Captain Scott O'Grady, the F-16 fighter pilot who was shot down over Bosnia two years earlier and survived six harrowing days on the ground before being rescued, said "I have never listened to an album that has made me feel so proud to be an American."

Also that fall, Hatch and Perry collaborated on a beautiful song called "Many Different Roads," honoring the late Mother Teresa and Diana, Princess of Wales, who died within days of each other in the summer.

Of Princess Diana: *Many different roads can lead to glory/Many different lamps can bring the light/In majesty she walked in humble places/Her common touch a candle in the night.*

Of Mother Teresa: *Many different roads can lead to glory/Many different paths a saint may walk/In poverty she shared a wealthy spirit/And helped the poor to see the face of God.*

Bridge: *A princess and a pauper walked the lonely roads of life/In many ways so different and yet so much alike.*

Last verse: *Many different roads can lead to glory/Many different lamps can bring the light/Both rich and poor may write a golden story/That shines through time like candles in the night.*

Hatch's musical career has continued unabated. By early in 2000 he had produced eight CDs with Perry or other composers, including inspirational and patriotic songs as well as love songs. The latter have included three songs written for Elaine for three wedding anniversaries. Some of the country's leading musicians have collaborated with Hatch, including singer/songwriter Peter McCann, whose soft rock songs have sold over 120 million records while being performed by such stars as Whitney Houston and the late Karen Carpenter.

At least five major music publishers have produced four of the original songs from Hatch's first CD, "My God is Love." Gladys Knight, formerly of the Pips, in 1998 recorded two Hatch-Perry songs–"Jesus' Love is Like a River" and "Many Different Roads"–on a CD taking the latter name as its title. Knight added a verse of her own:

> *There was my mother/A strong, yet humble soul was she/She's resting now in heaven/ But she left a legacy/She represents the mothers of all nations/Her love more precious than the rarest pearl unrecognized/She is an unsung hero/ Who's gentle, loving hands/ Helped shape the world.*

The Hatch-Knight connection was noted in *Parade* magazine in January 2000. Dee Coons of Memphis, Tennessee, wrote *Parade* to say "I just bought a Gladys Knight tape and was surprised to see that the title song was written by Orrin Hatch. Can this be the same straight laced Senator from Utah who is also running for President?" Parade affirmed it was, adding that "Knight is his best-known collaborator. Others are Janice Kapp Perry and Madeline Stone."

Late in 1998 the Senator spoke to a thousand of his fellow ASCAP writers and publishers, meeting in Washington. Hatch–the only member of Congress eligible to belong to the prestigious group–mentioned he had just received his first royalty check. At that, audience members came to their feet spontaneously in applause.

Hatch looked quizzically at ASCAP President Marilyn Bergman, who helped start it all. "You don't know what this means," she explained. "Many of these people have never had a royalty check. It's just so incredibly hard to break into this business."

A reporter for *Capitol Hill Blue*, a Washington publication, asked Bergman about Hatch. "I think he's talented," she said. "Particularly the religious songs have a real authentic voice. I think he feels them very deeply and that comes through in the writing."

"Music industry officials say Hatch's cachet as a senator hasn't and won't help him in the music business," wrote the reporter. "In the end, no one cares who wrote the song if it isn't any good." It quoted Hatch collaborator Peter McCann as saying "They wouldn't care if I co-wrote with John Paul II. If they didn't like the song, it would end up on a shelf."

Despite such clear proof of Hatch's ability, not everyone has applauded. Just as a prophet sometimes is without honor in his own land, so it is for a poet–especially a politician-poet.

"Bad luck seems to come in threes and Salt Lake City has recently suffered from disasters that have left the populace reeling," wrote a Utahn in a letter to the *Salt Lake Tribune* in fall 1999. "First came the Olympic scandals, next came Orrin Hatch's latest CD and so, with the tornado, maybe our misfortunes have ended."

As every artist knows, critical success often does not equate to financial success. While Hatch's songs have sold steadily, they cost a huge amount to produce. At this writing, he has not yet netted enough to cover the expense. The first Hatch-Perry CD, for example, cost a cool $50,000 to produce. To help recoup that and other monies, the Senator occasionally has helped market the music in store malls and other venues. In January 1997 he even went to Tampa, Florida, and appeared on the Home Shopping Network–three times during the day, for nine minutes each.

"I know I am going to be lampooned for this," he wrote. "Nevertheless, I'm willing to do any reasonable thing to try to get these beautiful songs out to change people's lives."

Lampooned he was. Anti-Hatch Utah commentator and columnist Tom Barberi wrote in the *Salt Lake Tribune* that "Our own senator-songwriter was sitting there...recounting with a straight face to Miss Gush how his patriotic and spiritual tunes actually cured some people of depression....I suppose it was a trade-off. Instead of trying to solve the collapsing Social Security system he was penning some smarmy rhymes that would empty hospital beds and fill the nation's houses of worship. What a guy."

In answer to Barberi, another writer sent a letter to the *Tribune*. It read, in part:

> I believe it was Will Rogers who said, "If you done it, it ain't braggin'." Orrin Hatch has done it again by unveiling yet another talent–as a songwriter–and he deserves congratulations for being successful, instead of the sour grapes tossed by Tom Barberi....
>
> The real issue for Utahns is whether their senior senator is taking his eye off the legislative ball...a serious student of Hatch must conclude that his "fringe activities" have not kept him from being uniquely productive in carrying out the people's business. No legislator from Utah in the past half-century has put his imprint on more American laws....
>
> Hatch's outside interests are, in fact, important to his effectiveness.

He seeks and carries such an enormous public load that, without the mental relaxation of his private writings, he would be like a bow whose elasticity and power were sapped by constantly being strung.

The frustration of Hatch's critics is obvious....Despite two decades of trying, they have yet to put a serious dent in his political armor. If the best they can do is criticize his selling of some songs, then Utahns can be pretty confident that Sen. Hatch is representing them faithfully and well.

In summer 1999, soon after Hatch threw his hat into the presidential ring, Jeffrey Goldberg of the *New York Times* spent a couple of days with him. He talked to Hatch about doing a Hanukkah song, and they discussed some themes. Then Goldberg got the inner office treatment Hatch often hands out these days. On a weekday morning for an hour in Hatch's personal office, which is equipped with a stereo set behind his desk, they kicked back and listened to Hatch's CDs when, as Goldberg wrote, "the other dozen or so Republican candidates for president were presumably squeezing donors for money."

In a long *Times* piece afterwards, Goldberg wondered why Hatch was running for president. Hatch said it was because he was the best alternative to George W. Bush and that he was prepared to be a good president.

"But then I put this question to him: If he had a choice between the presidency and superstardom in the world of popular music, which would he choose? 'President,' he said. With all due respect, I didn't really believe him."

Senator Hatch on a visit to Southern Utah.

Against the backdrop of the beautiful Wasatch Mountains, Orrin relaxes in 1986 with (from left) Dale and Clint Ensign, and Paul Dunn.

Running the Nike Capital Challenge.

Preparing to run the slalom in the annual Ski Cup Classic in Park City, Utah.

Senators Hatch and Patrick Leahy, D-Vermont, with Supreme Court Chief Justice William Rehnquist, at the start of the impeachment trial, January 7, 1999.

Planting a Utah tree on the grounds of the U.S. Capitol.

Receiving a poster of the Utah Statehood Centennial Stamp from Gerald McKieman, U.S. Postal Service vice president of legislative affairs, 1996.

Giving
The Greatest
a bit of a sting.

Receiving "Commander
in Chief" boxers from
Senate colleague
Ted Kennedy.

Orrin in one
of his favorite
pastimes–reading.

The Music Man conducts the Boston Pops Orchestra, 1997.
This photo also appears on the sleeve of one of Hatch's eight CDs, "Whispers of My Heart."

Janice Kapp Perry and Orrin Hatch, Utah's "Rogers and Hammerstein."
(Scott Hancock Photo)

The Senator and Lee "God Bless the USA" Greenwood.

In 1995, Lynn Sherr of ABC News writes, "For Senator Orrin Hatch–With thanks for your concern for so many women's rights–and for being such a gentleman always."

KUTV reporter Rod Decker with Hatch. In the background is the famed Salt Lake LDS Temple.

Appearing on ABC's "This Week" with (from left) Sam Donaldson, Cokie Roberts, and George F. Will.

Charles Sherrill of Utah's KSL-TV with the Senator outside Capitol.

Recognizing Ryan Tripp, Utah's "Lawn Ranger," for mowing all 50 state capitol grounds. The youth was urging Americans to become organ donors; registration was made easier by a law Hatch authored in 1984.

Mingling with military personnel during a compaign event in 1999.

Being interviewed by CNN's Wolf Blitzer at the 1996 Republican National Convention.

Senator Hatch is on the short list for TV networks. Here, the Senator appears on CBS's "Face the Nation."

Utah Jazz superstar Karl Malone supports presidential candidate Hatch at a rally prior to the Iowa Straw Poll, August 1999.
(AP Wide World Photos)

The presidential candidate from Utah was No. 1 with four of his grandchildren in New Hampshire, summer 1999. (AP Wide World Photos)

Orrin and Elaine's youngest child, Jess, and Mary Alice Marriott, daughter of Dick and Nancy Marriott, tie the knot at the Washington, D.C. LDS Temple, 1993.

Alex Barney, son of Hatch's Utah press secretary Heather Barney, is one of the Senator's favorite friends. Apparently the feeling is mutual, judging by this photo signed by Alex.

Elaine and Orrin surrounded by their six children and seventeen "hatchlings." Two more grandchildren were added before June 2000.
(Photo by Ron Osborn)

Orrin and Elaine during the annual "Days of '47 Parade," commemorating the arrival of the first pioneers in the Salt Lake Valley in 1847.
(Howlett Photography)

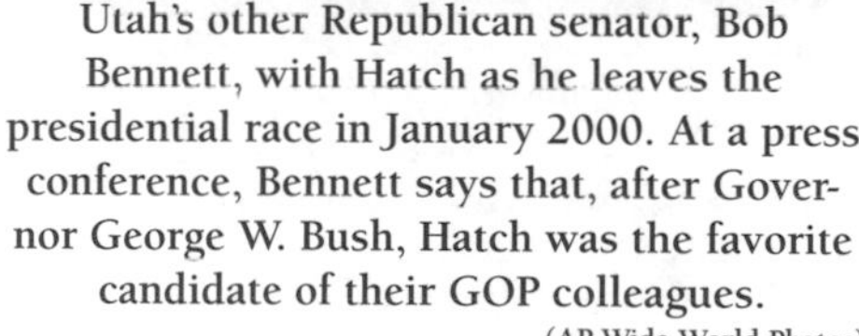

Utah's other Republican senator, Bob Bennett, with Hatch as he leaves the presidential race in January 2000. At a press conference, Bennett says that, after Governor George W. Bush, Hatch was the favorite candidate of their GOP colleagues.
(AP Wide World Photos)

Football legend Steve Young of the San Francisco 49ers backs Hatch in his reelection bid for U.S. Senate, January 2000.
(Photo by Janie Moltrup)

A young supporter is coddled by proud grandparents Elaine and Orrin.

Epilogue

It is not the critic who counts; not the man who points out how the strong man stumbles, or where the doer of deeds could have done them better. The credit belongs to the man who is actually in the arena, whose face is marred by dust and sweat and blood...[who] if he fails, at least fails while daring greatly, so that his place shall never be with those cold and timid souls who know neither victory nor defeat.

–Theodore Roosevelt

On July 1, 1999, Senator Hatch publicly declared his candidacy for president on CNN's Larry King show.

"I'd like to empower families so we have a vision to help mom and dad realize there's a future for their children," he told King. "I want to make sure the streets are safe....I want to get the country rid of drugs. I want to make sure homes are safe...and that the family isn't taxed to death." Above all, he wanted to return honor and integrity to the White House.

Eleven other Republicans already were in the race, including Texas Governor George W. Bush, front-runner by far, who had $36 million in the bank and the support of most of the GOP establishment. Republicans, aching to recapture the White House, had united behind a candidate unusually early. For some voters, Bush presented an irresistible opportunity to atone for kicking his father out of the White House in 1992 and putting Clinton-Gore in.

King called Hatch "a real long shot." On ABC's "Good Morning America" the next day, Hatch was introduced as "the longest of long shots." A media mantra had been pronounced, and it would cling to him throughout the campaign. In almost every interview thereafter the reporter praised Hatch as a giant in the Senate, but ended with the words "You don't have a chance." His Senate colleagues–a full dozen of whom had run for president or seriously tested the waters in the past–also uniformly told him he had no chance.

Despite outward evidence, Hatch felt inner peace. He heeded something said by another sure loser, Abraham Lincoln, who persevered despite being defeated numerous times, including for the Illinois House of Representatives, twice for the U.S. House, twice for the U.S. Senate, and once for vice president. "To sin by silence when they should protest makes cowards of men," said America's sixteenth president.

Hatch's hopes were based on more than blind faith: Polls showed that, while political junkies were tuned in to the presidential election, still seventeen months away, a large majority of other citizens scarcely were aware the contest had begun, and were undecided on whom to support.

The Utahn entered the race to ensure there was a strong backup candidate who could unite Republicans, in case front-runner Bush didn't go the distance. He wanted to make sure that the most important national issues were discussed. He also was tired of prejudice he often had encountered against Utah, a relatively small state with only five electoral votes and domination by one major religion. "I was eager to offer Utah values–including freedom, faith, and family–to the rest of the nation."

Bush had already been fishing in Utah waters, and had landed key GOP leaders while sopping up many of the available campaign dollars. Nonetheless, pollster Dan Jones found that, by 57 to 30 percent–about two to one–most Utahns believed it was a good idea for Hatch to also run.

A national survey by Wirthlin Associates showed that 68 percent of voters recognized Hatch's name, a level considered remarkably high for someone untested on the national scene. In a simulated match-up of Hatch as president and Elizabeth Dole as his vice president vs. a Democratic ticket of Al Gore and California Senator Dianne Feinstein, Hatch-Dole won the contest 53 to 39 percent. When focus groups in California and New Hampshire were asked about possible parings, Hatch did as well as anyone in the race.

"Candidates for president all falter," said Hatch's first national campaign director Sal Russo, "and Bush will too. The question is, when he's knocked down, can he get back up?" Russo, a Californian and veteran of three decades in politics, added that there was a place for Hatch's candidacy because "The feeling of the party hierarchy is if Bush falters and cannot get up, we do not have another candidate with a good chance of unifying the party."

Veteran political columnists Jack Germond and Jules Witcover agreed with Russo. "It's a commentary on how screwy our presidential campaigns have become that when [Hatch] announced his intention to seek the presidency the other day–about 17 months before the next presidential election–the consensus reaction was that he was too late," they wrote.

They noted that decades ago when another senator–John F. Kennedy–also sought the presidency, he didn't declare his candidacy until January of election year 1960. Although many members of Congress have tried since then, Kennedy was the last one to go directly to the White House. This time around, wrote Germond and Witcover, if belief in Bush "is somehow shaken between now and the end of the 2000 primary season, who can blame Hatch, even at this supposedly 'late' date for putting himself in position to ask voters: 'Why not me?'"

"Never count Orrin Hatch out," said Russo, noting the Utahn had pulled off other near-miracles before, including almost single-handedly defeating big labor's attempt at rewriting the rules to force millions of Americans into unions. "This is a historic moment," Russo emphasized, the first presidential candidate from Utah."

Money is the mother's milk of politics, and without a substantial amount a candidate usually cannot get his message out and will not be taken seriously by the media. Hours before formally announcing his candidacy, Hatch told a group of credit union officials who questioned him at a meeting that he knew the odds were long, in part because Governor Bush and others already had rounded up the traditional fat-cat donors.

Michele Hodgkins, president of the small Varian Credit Union in Salt Lake City, and a Democrat, had an idea. She noted to the Senator that if one million people each gave him $36, he would match Bush's campaign war chest. Hodgkins pulled out her checkbook and offered the first donation. An idea was born: Let others have the fat-cats; Hatch would wage a grassroots "Skinnycat" campaign, inviting citizens from every walk of life to donate $36 and join his quest for the presidency.

That evening, with millions of viewers watching, Hatch was about to show that first check on "Larry King Live," when it slipped from his hands. "I about passed out," he said later. When the station went to break, he retrieved the check and brandished in the next segment. As he left the CNN studio, he shook hands with everyone in sight, including the security guards.

Lack of funds continued to plague Hatch, as did the lack of execution by paid campaign leaders. True believers in Hatch found their offers of help going unanswered. The first boilerplate speech prepared by campaign headquarters was wooden and predictable. Many weeks into the effort a simple flier outlining Hatch's background and platform had yet to be prepared. Hatch did not complain to outsiders about such obvious campaign shortcomings, but others close to him did.

Bright lights among the organizational malaise were those not motivated by money but by the chance to do something important by offering their country the leadership of an uncommonly good man. They included Kevin McGuiness, Hatch's former chief of staff who took a long leave from his law practice to volunteer his time; Heather Barney, Hatch's former Utah press secretary who picked up the same duty for the campaign; Tony Dolan, once a top advisor to President Reagan, who helped with overall strategy and speeches; and Marie Woolf, Hatch's talented and hard-working webmaster.

The 2000 presidential race marked a new milestone in campaign communications, with the Internet a major factor for the first time. Woolf, a nationally recognized art director, graphic and Internet designer, and syndicated political cartoonist based in California, produced what the mainstream media called the most creative and comprehensive web page of the presidential contest. It attracted some five million hits–about a million a month while online during Hatch's campaign.

While other candidates, notably Arizona Senator John McCain, preached campaign finance reform, Hatch practiced it–listing every contributor on his web site, in alphabetical order for easy reference. The Utahn genuinely wanted to run his campaign by and for the common man and woman, and was supported largely by small donations.

Senator Hatch's candidacy offered more than twenty years of distinguished Senate service, an unparalleled record of legislative accomplishment, a history of uniting factions to conduct the nation's business, and a solid reputation for integrity in both his public and private life. But communicating those strengths to unknowing voters would prove extremely difficult.

"Unlike the other Republican munchkins," wrote Jeffrey Goldberg of the *New York Times*, "[Hatch] has stature to lose. He has an impressive record and the chairmanship of a powerful committee."

Hatch faced such daunting odds that many people speculated he was really angling for something else, perhaps the vice presidency or a seat on the Supreme Court. The truth was elusively simple: The Senator genuinely was running only for president, propelled by a conviction he was doing the right thing, whatever the odds. He had things to say that other aspirants weren't saying but the country needed to hear; if his candidacy did not endure, perhaps his message would.

He gave a major speech in Alabama saying what he would do as president:

- Give taxpayers back more of what they earn.

- Work for a country in which our children can be "safe, healthy, and well-educated."

- Make a principled defense of the Second Amendment.

- Cut down the size of the "bloated government and its bureaucracy."

- Offer a "just, noble, humane defense" of the right to life.

- Restore a strong military "capable of fighting terrorism, not only abroad, but also here at home."

- Restore to the White House "the time-honored principles of integrity, honesty, and candor."

"Let's face it, after eight years of Clinton-Gore, we need conservative ideas more than ever," said Hatch. "As we head into the next millennium, our country has a glorious future. But we are kidding ourselves if we don't admit our nation has a number of problems we simply have to face."

Among problems, Hatch listed high federal/state marginal tax rates, averaging 40 percent–usually a wartime rate; many who no longer believed in marriage; almost 80 million citizens who had experimented with drugs; teenage gangs that were ravaging cities; children who were killing other children. Also: financial peril to Social Security and Medicare; military personnel on food stamps and dramatically low levels of military readiness; family farms and small businesses being sold to pay "astronomical" estate taxes; and a growing divide between class and race.

The first test came in a non-binding straw poll in Iowa just six weeks after Hatch entered the race. Some advisors urged Hatch to skip the beauty contest, for which other candidates had been preparing for months if not years. But Hatch plowed ahead, eager to prove that personal merit and good ideas could beat big money.

Joining the Senator's entourage in the carnival-like atmosphere in Ames, Iowa, were his wife Elaine, three daughters, and eight grandchildren, wearing white Hatch-for-President T-shirts. Also along was Karl Malone of the Utah Jazz, the NBA's current most valuable player. Hatch had called him three weeks earlier, explained Malone. "He said 'I need your help on something, I want you to come to Iowa. I think we can make some noise.'" Malone added "The thing with Sen. Hatch is he has always supported me in basketball, win or lose. If he tells you something, he does it."

The Utahn's tent also held a couple of other prominent supporters who drew and entertained a standing-room-only crowd: singer Vic Damone and pianist Roger Williams, a native of Des Moines. Among the crowd was Miriam Beck, a registered nurse from Council Bluffs and a strong Hatch supporter. "Why? He's a very religious man and has a lot of the same values as I have. He did get in late, but of all the candidates, he has the most experience. Who can compete with that? He knows his stuff."

Unfortunately there weren't enough Miriam Becks on hand that day, and Hatch finished ninth in the balloting, garnering 558 votes out of some 24,000 cast. "We're not discouraged," Hatch insisted. "We had twelve days in the state. I think we did phenomenal." He added that "Actually, we were told if we could get 250 votes we'd be lucky...we exceeded expectations....We've just got to keep exceeding expectations."

Hatch had to get almost all his votes from people who had never participated before. More than 1,200 showed up indicating support for him, but a two-hour wait on a sweltering ninety-degree day took its toll, and more than half of them left without voting and went to the state fair.

Hatch did better in several lesser-publicized campaign events. He beat Bush in the Alabama Straw Poll in August, and came in a close second to him in October at the Western Republican Regional Conference, held in Jackson Hole, Wyoming, after flying there at the last minute.

Along the campaign trail, Hatch took principled stands that went against the grain of other candidates. What to do about Elian Gonzalez, the

Cuban boy who was in the United States after his mother and nine others drowned trying to reach the U.S.? Ignore politics, said Hatch, and do only what is best for the little boy.

What about the bitterly divisive Confederate flag flying over the capitol of South Carolina? Bush and McCain, fearful of losing support in the hotly contested primary state, refused to take a stand. But Hatch was unequivocal. While the issue was up to the people of South Carolina, he said in a written statement, if given a choice "I would remove the Confederate flag. No one doubts that brave, innocent and honorable men died fighting under both the Confederate and the Union flags during the Civil War. That is not the issue. To many in South Carolina, the Confederate flag is a symbol of slavery, and I believe that should be enough to cause people of good will to want to find a better way to honor their heritage."

By fall a half-dozen GOP candidates had left the race, leaving Hatch and five others to duke it out in six televised debates. Also still running, along with Bush and McCain, were Christian activist Gary Bauer, wealthy publisher Steve Forbes, and former ambassador and talk show host Alan Keyes. The latter, emphasizing basic moral principles, was a surprisingly strong and eloquent candidate whose support belied his scarce financial resources.

After a slow start, the debates proved generally lively. "Never in American political history have so many debated so often in such far-flung places," wrote one weary reporter. When the Republicans aren't debating, the Democrats [Al Gore and Bill Bradley] are."

But the debate formats, often dictated by celebrity moderators, offered little opportunity for significant give-and-take. The limitations frustrated Hatch, whose chance to rise in the polls rested largely on the nationally televised debates, since he could not afford to purchase the TV time or the newspaper ads bought by better-heeled candidates, and the news media itself continued to largely ignore him and the other candidates far behind Bush.

Much of the media treat national political contests more like horse races than critical exercises in democracy. Since money and opinion polls are far easier to track and describe than are policy nuances, those are the things the media focus on.

In Hatch's case, it was telling that the biggest coverage he got throughout the campaign was for a humorous quip to Bush in a debate in Phoenix, Arizona. Under that debate format, candidates asked each other questions. Bush, who drew Hatch's name, commented on his own efforts to reach out to minority voters, and asked Hatch about his attempts to do so.

The Utahn complimented Bush, then said "My only problem with you governor is you've only had four, and you're going into your fifth year of governorship in a constitutionally weak governorship. And, frankly I really believe that you need more experience before you become president of the United States. That's why I'm thinking of you as a vice presidential candidate."

As the audience of 1,300 broke up in laughter, Hatch continued: "Just think, Ronald Reagan picked your father because he had foreign policy experience. Somebody suggested the other day that you should pick me because I have foreign policy experience. They got it all wrong. I should be president; you should have eight years with me and boy, you'd make a heck of a president after eight years." The audience again erupted in laughter, this time joined by Bush.

In another debate, when publisher Steve Forbes said "I'd better hold onto my wallet," Hatch answered "Steve, I couldn't even *lift* your wallet." The audience exploded with laughter as Governor Bush leaned over to Hatch and said sincerely that "I'd give you some of my money if I could." Of McCain, Hatch said "John has such a love affair with the media. He's going to find out that his love affair with the media is about as stable as a love affair with Bill Clinton."

Despite debate limitations, those traveling with Hatch said no matter how weary he was beforehand, the contests always seemed to energize him. By most reckoning, Hatch held his own in the debates, especially hitting his stride in the latter ones. A page-one story in the *Washington Post* on January 7, 2000 reported that "A group of Republican and Republican-leaning independents who watched [last evening's] debate with Washington Post reporters gave their highest marks to Hatch, finding him more impressive than either McCain or Bush."

On the Fox Television Network after the same debate, former New York Republican Senator Alphonse D'Amato asked moderator Paula Zahn "Do you know who has been doing absolutely fabulously?....Orrin Hatch." D'Amato, who had served in the Senate with both Hatch and McCain, called Hatch "sensible" and said "he's accrediting himself well...he's done a heck of a job."

During his first response in that debate, Hatch noted that a new poll by the Kennedy School of Government at Harvard showed 74 percent of Americans had yet to pick a favorite candidate in either party–up from 64 percent a month earlier. "This poll shows the race is still wide open," said Hatch.

While gratified by critical acclaim for his debate performance, Hatch repeated a call he made throughout the campaign season for more substantive exchanges. "What is missing from these debates is any discussion of the vision of America that the candidates will bring to the White House," he said. "We need to get beyond the repetitive debate over a limited handful of issues and begin talking about other problems that are troubling Americans, such as the security of our families, our homes, our schools, and our nation. You cannot be free if you are afraid."

While confident in his own prescriptions for the U.S., Hatch was complimentary to other GOP candidates. A day after entering the race, he told ABC's "Good Morning America" that "I have to say [Bush] is a fine man And they tell me he's a quick learner. But you've got to be really quick to be able to meet that steep [presidential] learning curve."

John McCain became the media darling of the campaign, traveling through primary states in a well-appointed bus dubbed the "Straight Talk Express." His candidacy was based largely on removing wealthy special interests from national campaigns–even as he himself exploited his chairmanship of the Senate Commerce Committee and continued to accept corporate donations by hitting up the same people who had to come before his committee.

Most Republicans, including Hatch, believed if McCain's reforms were passed into law, a lot of get-out-the-vote funding now going to the GOP would dry up, while soft money benefitting Democrats, notably from labor unions, would continue unimpeded, putting Republicans at great disadvantage. Each election cycle, unions spend millions in independent expenditure campaigns for Democrats.

Hatch also believes the McCain-[Russell] Feingold campaign reform bill is patently unconstitutional because it narrows first amendment rights of free expression by restricting citizen groups from spending what they feel is needed to disseminate their messages.

Hatch and the hot-tempered McCain had clashed often in the Senate, over this and other issues, and relations between the two men were cool. When it was reported during the campaign that McCain had intervened at the Federal Communications Commission on behalf of a contributor, the Arizonan was widely accused of hypocrisy. Hatch had a golden opportunity to even several scores at once by piling on McCain. Instead, Hatch issued a press release in which he said "Senator McCain and I disagree on a number of issues...but I know John and he is the same man of integrity today that he was a week ago. Let's not rush to judgment."

A reporter for the Sioux City, Iowa *Journal* wrote that the Utahn met with her paper's editorial board and "I thought Hatch was exceptionally impressive for several reasons–and a significant part of why I found him impressive was what he didn't say. First of all, during the interview, he said nothing bad about the other candidates for the Republican nomination....When he disagreed with them on issues, he said so, without announcing that the other candidate had a screw loose.

"It was refreshing, to say the least. But there was more. He also didn't trash Democratic candidates Vice President Al Gore or former New Jersey Sen. Bill Bradley...instead of commenting on why the country will go to blazes with a Democrat or any of the other candidates in the White House, Hatch focused on what he had to offer....The civility was refreshing in a presidential candidate."

While Hatch was civil, he was also concerned by his GOP colleagues' sharp criticism of each other and their lack of focus on the key imperative for Republicans: ridding the White House of Clinton and Gore and returning respectability to the presidency.

He struck a major blow for substance, issuing a detailed plan of what he would do for America on his very first day as president. He would begin by revoking five executive orders issued by President Clinton. Included was an edict allowing clinics that receive federal aid to offer abortion counseling, one that freed federal contractors from posting notices informing employees of their right to object to the use of union dues for political purposes, one prohibiting the hiring of permanent strike replacements, and one that attempted to abolish the presumption of state sovereignty when federal bureaucratic policy conflicted with state law.

Also on his first day in the Oval Office, said Hatch, he would withdraw from the Clinton Administration's planned lawsuits against firearm manufacturers, and order the reassignment of 100 Justice Department attorneys to prosecute criminals who use guns. He would have a plan drawn up to consolidate the FBI and the Bureau of Alcohol, Tobacco and Firearms; create a multi-agency task force to investigate terrorist threats and organized criminal activity directed at the U.S. from abroad; and withdraw from the Kyoto Accords treaty on global warming.

Hatch would create a "code of conduct" for his administration, prohibiting fund-raising on White House property, illegal drug use by his staff, and the abuse of executive privilege when administration officials were asked by Congress for information–all characteristics of the Clinton-Gore Administration. "I believe no day in the tenure of the next president will be as important as the first, when it can finally be made clear that the Clinton Administration is over and that the presidency once again embodies traditional values," said Hatch.

In the closing weeks of Hatch's campaign, while wealthy candidates were flooding the airwaves with slick sound bites in Iowa and New Hampshire–the first primary states–Hatch gambled one last time that voters could be influenced by an important, concrete message. He sat before a camera and, for the first time by a public figure of his caliber, tied the most important misdeeds of the Clinton-Gore Administration into one powerful package for mass consumption.

In the twenty-eight-minute fireside chat, Hatch didn't even mention Clinton's personal scandals. Instead he focused on national security interests compromised by Clinton-Gore, including political misuse of such sensitive agencies as the FBI, Secret Service, and IRS, and the raising of millions of dollars in illicit campaign funds tied to foreign interests, notably China.

Clinton-Gore has been an administration "whose abuses of power have done grievous damage to the democratic process and to the bonds of trust and respect for the truth that unite us as a people," said Hatch. "Defenders of the Administration say 'This isn't Watergate.' You know, they're right. It's worse than Watergate."

Hatch's campaign scraped the bottom of its coffers, buying two half-hours of time on television in Iowa and another two in New Hampshire to air the fireside chat. Thousands of videotaped copies were also sent to individuals in Iowa, encouraging them to invite friends to also view it before voting in the state's caucuses on January 24.

Conservative columnist Tony Blankley wrote that it was "gratifying to see, in one speech, a seamless description of Mr. Clinton's policy deceits and constitutional breaches. Mr. Clinton's criminalities are not a theoretical matter to me. His political operatives pawed through my FBI file. I was told in 1995 that my tax returns were seen on the desk of a Clinton political appointee." Blankley said "Mr. Hatch possesses the moral acuity to recognize that Bill Clinton's corrupting example must be explicitly extirpated from the body politic."

A *New York Post* editorial called the fireside chat "a devastating indictment of what can reasonably be termed the crimes of the Clinton-Gore administration....Good for Orrin Hatch for raising these issues. Let's hope the American people are paying close attention."

Alabama's *Mobile Register* said Hatch was "correct to criticize the front-runners" for not addressing what the paper called "one of the great unmentioned issues of the presidential campaign: the dangerous precedent set in the past eight years by a corrupt, imperial presidency...a consistent pattern of misuse of White House power to thwart justice and run roughshod over the rights of political opponents." The *Register* added that "Insofar as Sen. Hatch is successful in making the rule of law a pre-eminent issue in this campaign, he will have performed a hugely praiseworthy service for this country."

By November Hatch's campaign had raised and spent about $2 million and was $200 thousand in debt. Campaign director Sal Russo urged the Senator to apply for federal matching funds, which he had qualified for by raising contributions across a broad swath of the country. Hatch had nearly $1 million coming in matching funds, which could have paid off the debt, leaving approximately $800 thousand to spend on media in Iowa. Russo believed the media buy might push Hatch into at least third-place in the Iowa caucuses, giving him momentum heading into the New Hampshire primary.

However, asked Hatch, "Why would I turn to taxpayers to finance my election when I know I cannot win in New Hampshire?" The Senator easily could have acted in his own self-interest and taken the federal funds, thereby paying off the campaign debt and assuring himself of a stronger, face-saving showing in Iowa. But he did the principled thing and turned it down.

As the money ran out and the Senator refused to accept federal matching funds, Sal Russo and gang jumped ship, leaving a tiny band of mostly unpaid volunteers to see the campaign through.

Efforts of some volunteers echoed Hatch's heroics. David Breck, a software entrepreneur in Epping, New Hampshire, for example, contributed his car and personal time to drive Hatch throughout New Hampshire looking for anyone who would listen to his message. "I'd take a bullet for him," said Breck. "I don't say that about many people." After first meeting the Senator and carefully researching his career, said Breck, he considered him a "living mentor" who would make a great president.

Hatch and the volunteers tramped frozen cornfields to meet with hundreds of small groups, stayed in cheap motels, and ate fast food–including canned Slimfast while on the run–all out of sight of the rest of the nation, whose mainstream media early on had pronounced Hatch's candidacy futile, and were not about to do anything to threaten their predictions. Most of the national press covering candidates daily on the campaign trail blatantly ignored Hatch throughout the campaign. Occasionally a reporter apologized for the snub, explaining his or her editor had specified no coverage of those running far behind the leaders.

A major CNN story on January 22–two days before the crucial Iowa caucuses–mentioned the activities of every candidate in the race, Republican and Democrat alike, except Hatch. That same day, Yahoo, one of the most popular Internet sites, featured "Iowa campaign photos" on its presidential web page. They included 112 shots, even family photos, again featuring every candidate but Hatch.

"It's really outrageous that the liberal media are determining who the people should consider," Hatch told Utah's *Deseret News*. "And they do it on one single issue: money....I filed late, I have the least amount of money, and they just automatically discount my [candidacy]."

Only near the end, after their refusal to acknowledge his efforts had long since helped kill any hope of rising in the polls, did some national media take notice of Hatch. With little money and little media attention, noted a *Washington Post* reporter, "the mighty senator, lion of the Judiciary and Finance committees, is forced to live as an also-ran in Iowa, accepting even the lowliest appearances." When a button fell off Hatch's coat before a New Hampshire event, marveled the reporter, "Hatch, to the amazement of onlookers, pulled a sewing kit from his pocket and stitched it back on."

The *Post* reporter blamed the Utahn himself for "being out here in a snowstorm, campaigning for president and sleeping at the Mason City Holiday Inn. He could be tucking into a nice steak at the Palm. Hatch disagrees. 'I feel I do have to be out here,' he says."

Tom Barberi, a liberal Utah commentator who often uses Hatch for a punching bag, wrote that the Senator's real reason for running was to land a job in a Bush administration, adding absurdly that Hatch "even fantasizes about a VP spot or Cabinet post." Such nonsense was another burden for Hatch to carry as his campaign headed into its last lap.

As such critics mocked Hatch for staying in the race, a friend sent him a note of encouragement, including something said by Theodore Roosevelt:

> It is not the critic who counts; not the man who points out how the strong man stumbles, or where the doer of deeds could have done them better. The credit belongs to the man who is actually in the arena, whose face is marred by dust and sweat and blood; who strives valiantly; who errs, and comes short again and again, because there is no effort without error and shortcomings; but who does actually strive to do the deeds...who at the best knows in the end the triumph of high achievement, and who at the worst, if he fails, at least fails while daring greatly, so that his place shall never be with those cold and timid souls who know neither victory nor defeat.

Timely encouragement came from other quarters as well. Frank Layden, popular former president of the Utah Jazz, sent a long open letter to the *Salt Lake Tribune*, urging Hatch to hang tough: "Orrin Hatch has been one of the most effective senators in the history of Utah. Orrin Hatch has always been the 'go-to' man. People often remark that if you want something done, Orrin Hatch will work until the very end to accomplish what he believes is right."

Layden noted Hatch's working-class background, saying that for the Senator, "obligations to family, church and community are not campaign slogans but the normal responsibilities of daily life....For the press, however, none of this matters. While decrying the role of money in politics and the lack of substance in most campaigns, many in the news media are fixated only on campaign contributions and have all but declared a winner before a single vote has been cast....

"I am glad that Sen. Orrin Hatch is running for president. It is refreshing to be able to finally support a proven, principled leader whose record is more impressive than his promises and who has the ability, temperament, and moral compass to restore much needed dignity and honor to the White House."

Hatch was also buoyed by thousands of Skinnycats throughout the U.S., who sent him small donations and caring messages, usually after watching the televised debates. Some of the messages:

- Derek, a U.S. Air Force officer on the East Coast: "I have been very impressed with your policy stances over the past several years and with your attempt to get the media to hold Clinton accountable for his perjury and misuse of office."

• Tamara, a company manager in Winter Springs, Florida: "I have been a Democrat since the day I was born. I could be shot for investing in you....I'm tired of the welfare state. I'm tired of the taxes. I am encouraged by your tolerance."

• Jeff, in Smyrna, Georgia: "I'm 12 yrs old and I think you're great. About a month ago I had a tumor removed from my brain, now I'm going through radiation treatments. I said if Orrin wouldn't give up, I won't give up either."

• Greg, in Pottsville, Pennsylvania: "I'm a 39-year-old Pennsylvania man who for the last 3.5 years has been living each day with Lou Gehrig's disease. I can no longer walk, dress or feed myself....I'm down to using one finger on each hand to type this e-mail message to you....Don't give up and keep plugging away!"

"I have been asked many times why I ran and why I stayed in the race despite the odds," said Hatch. "One answer is that I ran for Derek, Tamara, Jeff, Greg, and all other Americans who believe as I do that something is seriously wrong with the current administration in Washington, and want a better approach to leading our country. I will continue to work and fight to focus attention on critical issues facing us, and to restore integrity to the White House."

Another favorite letter, which Hatch carried in his breast pocket, came from Pierre Salinger, colorful press secretary to President John Kennedy. "I feel very strongly that you are the best Republican candidate for president," wrote Salinger, who enclosed a $144 contribution for himself and three other Skinnycats. "You have done incredible work in the Senate for years, something that makes me feel that you would be an important president."

In addition to media apathy, Hatch faced a disturbing amount of prejudice against his religion, notably from some fellow Christians. In one of his first campaign interviews, a reporter said "The polls show that 17 percent of the American people will not vote for a Mormon for president. What do you say about that?" The question repeatedly came up during the year, leading Hatch to say "I intend to get my 51 percent vote out of the other 83 percent."

Appearing at a national conference of the Christian Coalition, Hatch, in unscripted remarks, said "I can't do anything about bigots or bigotry, but I can do a lot to help those who are misinformed about my faith. I take my Christian faith very seriously and I try to live it. Besides, I thought that kind of bigotry and intolerance went out when John F. Kennedy was elected our first Catholic president."

As Hatch noted, religion supposedly had been laid to rest as a political liability with the election of Kennedy in 1960. In a key speech during that campaign, Kennedy said "I believe in an America...where no man is denied public office merely because his religion differs from the president who might appoint him or the people who might elect him...where religious intolerance will someday end...and [all religionists] will refrain from those attitudes of disdain and division which have so often marred their works in the past, and promote instead the American ideal of brotherhood."

There was one final factor that cost Hatch dearly: his determined dedication to the duty Utahns had entrusted to him. Fellow senator and presidential aspirant John McCain simply deserted the Senate in 1999, spending more time on the campaign trail than in Washington. But Hatch is made of different stuff, and could not bring himself to do the same, no matter the cost to his presidential quest. The Utahn was on the Senate floor 98 percent of the time for its votes in 1999, passing a dizzying array of legislation.

By the time his presidential bid drew to a close, Hatch had succeeded in advancing important issues that became part of the continuing national political dialogue.

They included holding Clinton-Gore responsible for administration misdeeds; the critical importance of the election on the federal judiciary, especially the Supreme Court; the growing threat of terrorism and the consequences of losing U.S. counterintelligence capabilities; and promulgating a code of conduct for the White House. He also practiced real campaign reform, listing every contributor on his web site as donations were received–an example that Bush, who would carry Republican hopes in the fall election, picked up and followed.

Among those who know Washington best, the Utahn's reputation was enhanced in the presidential race. "Hatch, many in Washington agree, is a decent, smart and powerful man," wrote a *Washington Post* reporter near the end of the campaign. "In a few days, mercifully, his obligation to posterity will be fulfilled–and Hatch can go back to being a giant again."

Senator Hatch scored just 1 percent in the Iowa caucuses on January 24. That evening he flew home to the biggest snowstorm to hit Washington in a decade, slowly making his way to Vienna on slippery roads and dropping exhausted into bed at 1:30 a.m. No sooner was Hatch in bed than a constituent who had an international problem called, waking him up. The Senator stayed up until 2:30 a.m. solving the problem.

He arose the next morning prepared to announce at a press conference that he was leaving the race that day, but learned that the freak snowstorm had paralyzed the city, closing almost everything in Washington.

"Elaine, maybe this is God's will that I shouldn't withdraw," he said with a wistful smile.

"No, Orrin," she smiled back, "The Iowa caucuses were God's will."

The following day, at a large press conference on Capitol Hill, he withdrew from the race and endorsed Governor Bush, saying the Texan had grown on the campaign trail and would make a good president.

"Some say that in politics, if you want a friend, get a dog," said Hatch in exiting without a trace of rancor. "Well, they are wrong. I can never thank the thousands and thousands of friends and supporters I have in Utah and around this nation who had the courage to stand with me, who have helped me in so many countless ways. They come from every conceivable background, from every political perspective. Yet we have one thing in common: We share a belief in the promise of this nation."

He also said "I leave the race with no regrets for having tried. The goal of public life is service. In a democracy, each of us has an obligation to step forward if we believe we can make a difference for the better."

Fellow Utah senator Bob Bennett appeared with Orrin and Elaine, their children, and grandchildren at the event. Had Bush's campaign faltered, said Bennett, most Republicans in Congress would have thrown their support to Hatch as the best alternative.

Accolades poured in. "Hatch lost everything in this race except his sense of humor," wrote the *Washington Post's* David Broder, dean of political reporters. "But the Utah senator was as gracious and uncomplaining in his farewell remarks as he had been droll and direct during the earlier Republican debates." Broder added that Hatch "found, at a moment of maximum pressure, a way to express something that was so genuine it made you want to cheer."

The *Deseret News*, in an editorial headlined "A brave attempt, senator," said "Hatch represented his state well. His experience and solid values were evident in the televised debates, as was his warm sense of humor....Hatch pursued his dream for the right reasons. He ran a good, clean race. Well done, Senator."

Weeks earlier, while still in the race, Hatch had turned reflective after giving a humorous speech at the annual Gridiron Dinner in downtown Washington. He ended by saying, in part:

> Trust me, there is no more humbling experience than running for president. A couple of weeks ago, I found myself in New Hampshire, sitting at the very desk where so many presidential candidates have sat to fill out the forms to declare their candidacy. It hit me again–we are a fortunate people to live in this country. Imagine a country where someone like me can run for the highest office in the land. When I was growing up we were dirt poor, but I didn't know it....When Elaine and I were first married forty-two years ago, we converted my parents' chicken coop into an apartment so we could have a place to live. I can still see those mildew spots on the wall. By today's way of measuring things, we didn't have much, but it never mattered. We had our family. Today that family is six children and nineteen grandchildren strong. There are many reasons we have survived and succeeded, but one of the most important was that Elaine and I never forgot how to laugh and, more importantly, how to laugh at ourselves. If we can take the time to laugh...then we will not only make the most of our brief run in the arena of life, but we will find the race much less tiring and the company far more enjoyable. Thank you and God bless.

Tears have leavened the laughter through the years, but there has been far more sunshine than shadow. Orrin Grant Hatch indeed has come a long way since those days of want in Pittsburgh. And he has lifted millions of others with him–citizens whose lives are better in measurable ways because he is in the Senate. He has achieved because he stands for something, and believes passionately that every citizen, however humble his beginning, also has the right to pursue the American Dream.

Hatch has made the most of his God-given gifts, adding to them a remarkable resilience of spirit. "There is a need of a sound body, and even more need of a sound mind," noted Theodore Roosevelt, who cherished men like Hatch. "But above mind and body stands character–the sum of those qualities which we mean when we speak of a man's force and courage, of his good faith and sense of honor."

On January 28, Hatch faced three hundred Utahns gathered on the University of Utah campus. "I have tried hard to live up to the trust you have placed in me, and hope you feel that I have served our state with vigor, honor, and integrity," said Hatch. "Today, in the sincere belief that I have done so–and will continue to do so–I come before you to announce that I will again be a candidate for the United States Senate this fall."

"I truly believe America's and Utah's best days lie ahead of us. I will continue to do all within my power to see that they are realized–for us and for our posterity."

With that, Orrin Hatch was off to move another mountain.

Sources

WHILE WRITING MY FIRST BOOK on Senator Hatch in 1993, *Leading the Charge: Orrin Hatch and 20 Years of America*, the Senator and I routinely began to correspond about public events in which he has been a participant. Lengthy, highly detailed letters from him continued to arrive into 1999, and are a key resource for the present volume.

I interviewed Senator Hatch a half-dozen times specifically for this book. I also interviewed key individuals who know him best, including his wife Elaine and other family members, political supporters as well as critics, current and former staff members, and others able to shed significant light on his public career and private interests.

In addition, I was given virtually unrestricted access to the Senator's private papers, including correspondence to and from him involving both his professional and personal lives. Primary and secondary research was conducted in Washington, D. C., and in Utah.

When the Senator is quoted directly in this book, without other attribution, the quote usually originated either in an interview or in a letter from him to me.

Introduction

xi *"Bill Clinton may not be the worst president America has had,..."*; George F. Will, "Will Clintonism ever end?" *Washington Post*, March 30, 2000.

Fifty-eight American historians agree.; New York Times, February 21, 2000.

xii *"I knew that by getting in late, by raising money from small donors...",* Hatch, *Salt Lake Tribune*, January 27, 2000.

xiii ...the structure of America "has been erected by architects...", Joseph Story, *Commentaries on the Constitution of the United States* (2nd edition, Vol. 2, 1851), 617.

"...Here you are with a 100% conservative voting record having to put up with..."; President Bush, letter to Hatch, March 15, 1997.

xiv ...*"The very first mention of a compassionate conservative that I found..."*; Glenn Kessler, "New! Improved! Recycled Rhetoric!" *Washington Post*, April 1, 2000.

Part I

Chapter 1 A Gentleman Up Close

1 *"Senator Hatch is a fine Christian gentleman..."*; Garrison Keillor, "The Republicans Were Right, But–," *Time*, February 22, 1999.

2 *"Compassion is what most defines* Orrin..."; Ruth Montoya, interview, 1999. Other quotes from Montoya in this chapter are from that or subsequent interviews.

What is remarkable about this incident..."; Kris Iverson, letter to author, December 17, 1998. Other quotes from Iverson in this chapter are from the same letter.

Another staffer, Becky Shipp, had a different problem....; Shipp, memo to author, December 16, 1998.

3 *"I was very nervous about the operation and how it would affect my job"*...; Larry Block, memo to author, December 17, 1998.

"I didn't want to bother Orrin, but when he found out..."; Heather Barney, letter to author, March 19, 1999. Other quotes from Barney in this chapter are from the same letter or subsequent interviews with Barney.

4 *George Thomas Scott just wanted to be an American...*; JoAnn Jacobsen-Wells, *Deseret News*, July 4, 1990.

5 *Thank him for "the spirit of compromise and fairness which marked..."*; Bayh, letter to Hatch, December 1, 1978.

Pulitzer prize-winning columnist Jack Anderson...; Anderson interview, 1999.

8 *"No thanks," answered Matulic, "I'm not big on foreign royalty..."*; Memo, Matulic to author, December 17, 1998.

9 *...the Manchester Union Leader, charged that Hatch was driven by ego...*; *Union Leader*, June 25, 1999.

As for those "Italian Shoes," Orrin's unusually narrow feet...; Author thumbed through Lands End and Paul Fredrick catalogues in Hatch's office in 1999.

10 *"Hatch's Senate career has been shaped by two impulses..."*; Michael Barone and Grant Ujifusa, *The Almanac of American Politics 1998* (Washington, D.C.: National Journal, 1998), 1414.

11 *In 1997, George magazine named him one of a half-dozen living "Legends..."*; *George*, December 1997, cover story.

12 *"an independent-minded and enigmatic politician..."*; Julie Kosterlitz, "Tough to Typecast" (profile of Orrin Hatch), *National Journal*, August 19, 1989.

"I just read the wonderful biography 'Truman,' by David McCullough..."; Walter Scott, *Parade*, June 26, 1994.

Chapter 2 The Early Years

13 *His great-grandfather...was...one of the first settlers in Utah's Ashley Valley...*; For the Hatch family's role in settling Ashley Valley, see the Hatch File, Historical Collection, Uintah County Library, Vernal, Utah.

Six years later, at the age of seventeen, Jesse,...; Information about Jesse's youth, his courtship with Helen Kamm, and their early family life, including Orrin's childhood, comes from Helen Kamm Hatch, interviews, 1993, and from interviews the same year with Orrin's sisters Nancy Hatch Scott and Frances Hatch Merrell.

16 *A "B" in arithmetic during the last six weeks was all that marred an all-"A"...*; Orrin's sixth grade report card was kept by his mother and shown to author in 1993.

18 *"He was a great basketball player," she remembers...*; Joyce Strong, interview with Dawn Souza, the Lawrence, Massachusetts *Eagle-Tribune*, January 19, 2000.

19 *"Basketball whiz...hardworking union man..."*; *The Balthi*, 1952; photocopy in author's possession.

"Senator Hatch won the election. Congratulations."; The Purbalite, May 21, 1952, photocopy in author's possession.

Chapter 3 Molding the Man

22 *Centuries later, a local farm boy named Joseph Smith said God...*; Joseph Smith–History 1: 17-19; 59. This account was canonized in 1880 as part of LDS Scripture, *The Pearl of Great Price: A Selection from the Revelations, Translations, and Narrations of Joseph Smith*...(Salt Lake City, Utah: The Church of Jesus Christ of Latter-day Saints, 1981 edition).

His mission president was a Utah dentist named Lorin L. Richards...; Florence Richards, interview, 1993. She is also the source of other statements, either as attributed to her, or quoted from her late husband, in this chapter. Florence Richards died in August 1996.

"I'm going to blow your head off..."; Orrin Hatch, missionary diary, read by author. Other mission-field incidents cited in this chapter likewise are from Hatch's missionary diary.

24 *"Now, Sister Hatch, I am going to let you in on a little bit of special news..."*; Florence Richards, undated letter to Helen Hatch on letterhead of Great Lakes Mission. Her husband, mission president Lorin Richards, sent a letter to Orrin, aka "Elder Hatch," September 28, 1955, closing with this unusual plea: "We hope you won't work too hard so that it will interfere with your health, but keep up the good work."

25 *"To the most wonderful fellow I know. I love you."*; Both photos are in a family album at the home of Orrin and Elaine Hatch.

Chapter 4 Into the Arena

30 *Early in his Utah legal career, Hatch tried a case before Willis Ritter..."*; In addition to Hatch's memories of Ritter, and accounts in newspapers, Utah attorney Scott Savage told

several Ritter stories and appraised Hatch's courtroom competence, as attributed in this chapter.

32 *"Why don't you run against Moss? He asked."*; Jackie Nokes (widow of Grey Nokes), interview, 1993.

34 *"I cried for three days," she recalled. "I didn't like politicians..."*; Interviews with Elaine Hatch, 1993 and 1999.

37 *Skousen...sent a fund-raising letter on Hatch's behalf...*; Cleon Skousen, letter to Freemen Institute members, mailed ca. August 25, 1976; photocopy in my possession.

"I feel so badly that I am the culprit..."; Helen K. Hatch, letter to the editor, *Deseret News*, September 10, 1976.

38 *"THE TIME HAS COME FOR ME TO DO EVERYTHING I CAN..."*; Reagan, advertisement, *Salt Lake Tribune*, September 12, 1976.

39 *"Hatch was completely a blank page to me..."*; Frank E. ("Ted") Moss, interview, 1993. Relevant campaign papers are in the Frank E. Moss Papers, Special Collections, Marriott Library, University of Utah, Salt Lake City.

"Senator Moss just didn't take Hatch seriously."; Dale Zabriskie, interview, 1993.

"...[Hatch] certainly gets around everywhere..."; Ernest Wilkinson, diary, September 17, 1976. Copy in Special Collections, Marriott Library, University of Utah.

40 *In a traditional luncheon before Utah clergy..."*; *Salt Lake Tribune*, October 14, 1976.

Chapter 5 Labor Law 'Reform'

42 *Hatch "was expected to be one of the most intriguing new figures..."*; "Largest Turnover in Senate since 1958," *1976 CQ (Congressional Quarterly) Almanac*, 830.

43 *"Back then, Orrin was a lot like Ronald Reagan..."*; Paul Laxalt, interview, 1993.

44 *"...bright, articulate, unafraid to beard liberal lions..."*; Bruce H. Jensen, "Thunder on the Right," *Utah Holiday*, February 1978, 121.

46 *"Mail being received in the Senate is beyond counting..."*; "Why the Bitter Fight over a New Labor Law," *U.S. News & World Report*, April 10, 1978.

50 *Lugar writes in the New York Times: "The Majority Leader's duty..."*; *New York Times*, June 20, 1978.

51 *This week's Kiplinger Washington Letter arrives.*; Kiplinger Washington Letter, June 16, 1978.

54 *[Hatch is one of five new senators] "most often named as leaders of the future."*; Richard E. Cohen, "Freshmen in the Senate Being Seen–and Heard," *National Journal*, March 17, 1979.

Chapter 6 Growing Into a Giant

56 *"My candidacy brings an opportunity for our state to elect a senator..."*; Photocopy of Wilson speech, Special Collections, Marriott Library

"Nobody's outworked me in six years, not one senator...", *Salt Lake Tribune*, October 12, 1982.

57 *"You'd think the honor of challenging Hatch would be fought over..."*; *Deseret News*, March 17, 1994.

"Imagine Mark McGuire slamming twice as many hits as the rest..."; *Deseret News*, December 5, 1999.

59 *Microsoft put an "oppressive thumb on the scale of competitive fortune..."*; *Washington Post*, April 4, 2000.

61 *In Spring 2000 GOA distributed a flier calling Hatch...*; Undated flier from Gun Owners of America to "Dear Gun Rights supporter."

Since even the National Rifle Association says Hatch in fact...; Charlton Heston, president of the NRA, wrote to Utah members in April 2000: "For 24 years, Senator Hatch has been one of the most committed, principled, and consistently effective advocates of your Second Amendment rights on Capitol Hill."

"Gentlemen, suppose all the property you were worth was in gold..."; Lincoln, cited by Francis B. Carpenter, "Anecdotes and Reminiscences of President Lincoln," in Henry Jarvis Raymond, *The Life and Public Services of Abraham Lincoln...*, (1865) 752.

"The true rule in determining whether to embrace or reject anything..."; Congressman Abraham Lincoln in the U.S. House of Representatives, June 20, 1848. *The Collected Works of Abraham Lincoln* (edited by Roy P. Basler, Vol. 1, 1953), 481.

Chapter 7 The Club

63 *"Just think, Ronald Reagan picked your father [for vice president]..."*; *New York Times*, December 7, 1999.

"Utah Sen. Orrin Hatch, the high-collared Mormon elder..."; Mary McGrory, *Washington Post*, December 12, 1999. Months earlier, in a personal letter to the author, dated July 12, 1999, McGrory wrote that "...your subject is not my kind of politician. I am used to wicked Irishmen who are put up with only because they make us laugh a lot. Humor is not [Hatch's] strong point."

64 *The Senator occasionally cites these reported quotes...*; From Hatch's personal file of favorite jokes and anecdotes.

"Comedian Scotty Kowall called that line 'funny...'"; *Salt Lake Tribune*, January 3, 2000.

66 *On December 4, 1999, Hatch regaled the national press corps.*; From a photocopy of the Senator's speech.

68 *"Politics is one of the great sources of tensions..."*; Brooks Hays, *A Hotbed of Tranquility* (New York: The Macmillan Company, 1968), 3.

69 *"I thought he had a save-the-world complex..."*; Paul Laxalt, interview, 1993.

Laxalt...called Hatch "a true leader in the United States Senate...; Letter dated January 15, 1982.

"You may come to my office at S-243 at which location upon..."; Simpson, letter to Hatch, June 17, 1987.

72 *Hatch: "I just wish my colleague from West Virginia were on our side..."* The two-day exchange in the Senate is in the *Congressional Record* of February 23, 1997, S-1291-1293, and February 24, 1997, S-1448-1452.

73 *"He has a very strong sense of justice..."* Edward M. Kennedy, interview, 1993. Additional quotations from Kennedy in this chapter are from this interview.

Part II

Chapter 8 Suffer the Children

78 *"Orrin's reaction was priceless."*; Heather Barney, interview, 1999.

80 *"We are cannibalizing our children," said Dr. Edward Zigler...*; *New York Times*, June 19, 1989; reprinted in *Congressional Record*, June 22, 1989, S-7225.

"Since the 1950s, when the conservative movement coalesced out..."; George F. Will, *Washington Post*, January 10, 1988.

81 *...Majority Leader George Mitchell...[praised Hatch] for "the remarkable..."*; *Congressional Record*, June 23, 1989, S-7477.

...Elizabeth and two friends...met around a kitchen table in 1988...; A brief history of the Elizabeth Glaser Pediatric AIDS Foundation is on the web at www.pedaids.org/history.

82 *"My son and I may not survive four more years of leaders..."*; Recounted by combined wire services, *Salt Lake Tribune*, upon Glaser's death, December 4, 1994.

83 *"It's one thing for an older fellow like myself..."*; Hubert Humphrey, undated memo to Hatch.

85 *...who told pollsters that health insurance was their fifth-highest concern.*; Poll by the Kaiser Foundation, *Salt Lake Tribune*, March 18, 1997.

86 *"There may not be two more relentless legislative advocates..."*; Al Hunt, *Wall Street Journal*, April 17, 1997.

87 *"The issue involves a substantial increase in federal cigarette taxes."*; Don Gale, KSL editorial, May 20, 1997.

89 *...the New York Times reported: "At the insistence of Mr. Hatch..."*; *New York Times*, June 2, 1997.

90 *..."Yet again you have proven that deep commitment and hard work..."*; Marian Wright Edelman, letter to Hatch, July 13, 1997.

Chapter 9 Women and Families

92 *... to "Senator Hatch, for his tireless fight against crime"*; Patricia Cornwell, *The Body Farm* (New York: Charles Scribner's Sons, 1994), dedication page.

She tells interviewers "he's a truly good man."; *USA Today*, September 25, 1994.

"The main ingredients of Hatch's senatorial style..."; Nadine Cohodas, "Orrin Hatch: The Mace and the Olive Branch," *Congressional Quarterly*, October 10, 1981, 1955.

93 *"I've called her morning and night to make sure she's all right..."*; Hatch, letter to his mother, Helen Hatch, August 11, 1994.

"It was great to be reunited with Elaine..."; Hatch, letter to the author, June 10, 1997.

94 *"That you would take the time to be so thoughtful speaks to..."*; Shtasel, letter to Hatch, November 28, 1984.

95 *"On average, Hatch Pays Women More Than Men..."*; *Salt Lake Tribune*, December 19, 1993.

96 *"I wish you well," he told Hill, who had hoped to kill...*; These were virtually Hatch's only comments to Hill. Second set of Judiciary Committee Hearings on the Nomination of Clarence Thomas to Associate Justice of the U.S. Supreme Court, October 11, 12, and 13, 1991, 111.

97 *"Dear Orrin," it began, "To echo the famous cry of one who was betrayed..."*; Schlafly, letter to Hatch, January 30, 1989.

"Asked about his priorities," wrote Al Hunt...; *Wall Street Journal*, February 24, 1981.

99 *"Thank you for your courtesy and decorum at this morning's hearing..."*; Feldt, letter to Hatch, March 11, 1981.

101 *"I remember when legislation was pending..."*; Jan Bennett, Interview, 1993.
103 *In 1996 Ginsburg sent Hatch a note on Supreme Court letterhead...*; Letter is dated April 25, 1996.

Chapter 10 Health and Longevity

104 *"We talk about new visions on aging..."*; Hatch, remarks opening his twelfth annual seniors conference, May 10, 1999.
A Harvard study in 1997 found that men in Utah's Cache and Rich...; *New York Times*, December 4, 1997. Dr. Christopher Murray, study director, said in 1990 men lived longest, to 77, in these two northern Utah counties, and women lived longest, to 83, in Stearns County, Minnesota.
105 *Life expectancy for older Americans has continued to increase.*; "Health, United States, 1999," Department of Health and Human Services.
"Many older people are in good health and leading active lives..."; Jeffrey Koplan, "Annual Report on Nation's Health Spotlights Elderly Americans," HHS News, October 13, 1999.
106 *"Retirement security is a topic on everyone's mind these days..."*; Hatch, statement before the Senate Finance Committee hearing on pension legislation, June 30, 1999.
109 *"Today the Medicare program is on more solid financial ground..."*; Hatch, remarks at the "Save our Seniors" rally, September 22, 1999.
111 *...older Americans spent another $2,400 out of pocket for health care...*; *USA Today*, December 8, 1999.
112 *...it "balances the interests of dietary supplement users..."*; *Salt Lake Tribune* editorial, October 12, 1994.

Chapter 11 The AIDS Crisis

114 *Through December 1998, at least 410,800 citizens had died...*; Report, Centers for Disease Control and Prevention (CDC), May 13, 1999.
...HIV mortality has dropped out of the fifteen leading causes of death...; HHS (Department of Health and Human Services) News, October 5, 1999.
115 *"In those early years, the federal government viewed AIDS..."*; Randy Shilts, *And the Band Played On: Politics, People, and the AIDS Epidemic* (New York: St. Martin's Press, 1987), xxiii.
...Reagan administration officials who "ignored pleas from government scientists..."; Ibid, xxii.
"Although he was a conservative Mormon from Utah..."; Ibid, 296.
116 *Later that year Hatch was instrumental in having Dr. James Mason...*; Ibid, 399.
117 *"I find it strange that we can pass veterans' legislation so speedily..."*; *1988 CQ (Congressional Quarterly) Almanac*, 302.
"Let us quit judging and let us start doing what is right..."; *Washington Post*, May 2, 1988.
Hatch: "I do not agree with [gays'] sexual preferences."; *1988 CQ Almanac*, 302.
118 *In thirty-nine days of hearings, Watkins said later, nearly 800 witnesses...*; Ibid, 301.
121 *"I am honored to say a few words about the legacy [Terry Beirn] left..."*; From text of Senator Hatch's remarks at memorial service, July 31, 1991.

122 *Consider these sobering numbers at the end of 1998...*; See CDC reports: "Basic Statistics - Cumulative Cases," "HIV/AIDS Among African Americans," and "HIV/AIDS Among Hispanics in the United States," on the web at www.cdc.gov/nchstp/hiv_aids.

An estimated 95 percent of AIDS sufferers live abroad.; CDC Division of HIV/AIDS Prevention, citing the Joint United Nations Programme on HIV/AIDS, above web site.

In 1998, wars in Africa killed 200 thousand people. AIDS...killed 2 million...; Associated Press, datelined United Nations, January 10, 2000.

123 *"AIDS has never posed a bigger threat to development than it does now,..."*; AP, Kuala Lumpur, Malaysia, October 23, 1999.

"the AIDS epidemic is in the midst of ...the crisis of complacency."; AP, Indianapolis, former home of the Ryan White Foundation. Jeanne White-Ginder said she would join forces with the AIDS Action Council, to continue focusing on AIDS education for young people.

Chapter 12 Education

125 *"Many Americans may be unaware that many teachers subsidize their schools..."*; Hatch news release, March 1, 2000.

126 *"She gave me a love for English literature which has been with me all my life..."*; Hatch, National Parent-Teacher Association, Questionnaire on "The Public School Teacher Who Most Influenced My Life," completed June 12, 1986.

"Of all the occupations in America, teachers may deserve their own..."; *Congressional Record*, May 5, 1999, S-4732.

127 *"It will help de-bureaucratize our schools," said Hatch.*; Hatch news release, March 12, 1999.

128 *"Anything we can do through tax incentives to help families and the state..."*; Statement before the Senate Finance Committee, March 3, 1999.

"I do have to brag a little about my home state..."; Ibid.

130 *"We saw more in-depth, complex demonstrations than we've currently seen..."*; Hatch Senate website, www.Senate.gov/~hatch/distance., as of September 25, 1999.

131 *"We are providing seed money for the construction and expansion of clubs..."*; Hatch, Senate speech, March 19, 1997.

In Salt Lake City...the number of gang members increased 146 percent...; Hatch statement, hearing before the Senate Judiciary Committee, April 23, 1997.

133 *In a keynote speech when receiving an honorary degree at Dixie College...*; Hatch speech "What Will You Build?" was delivered June 5, 1998.

Chapter 13 Toward a Colorblind Society

134 *"William T. Coleman Jr., the black man appointed by President Gerald Ford..."*; *Washington Post*, November 13, 1997.

135 *"Taking into account women, the disabled, nonwhite immigrants..."*; Victor A. Walsh and Thomas E. Wood, "Bakke and Beyond," a study issued by the California Association of Scholars, November 4, 1996.

Jennifer Riel, the daughter of hard-working Filipino immigrants...; Her case and that of Janine Jacinto, Ibid.

136 *Patrick Loen was denied admission to an elite public magnet school...*; His mother, Charlene Loen, testified before a hearing chaired by Hatch, reported in a letter from the Senator to the author, July 11, 1997.

137 *"I believe Mr. Lee is a very fine man, a man of conviction..."*; *Salt Lake Tribune*, March 6, 1999.

President Clinton said the rejection "provides strong evidence for those..."; *Washington Post*, October 6, 1999.

138 "Using race as a political tactic to advance controversial nominees..."; Hatch, *Congressional Record*, October 7, 1999, S-12186.

Helms...said "I'm going to sing 'Dixie' until she cries."; *Chicago Tribune*, August 6, 1993.

139 *As of the 1990 census, his home state of Utah was about 96 percent white...*; Official 1990 census figures for Utah: population 1,722,850; white 95.9%; black .7%; American Indian 1.5%; Asian and Pacific 2%; possible Hispanic origin 4.9%. (Breakdown equals more than 100% because of overlap.)

140 *"This is really, really wonderful. I had been praying for a long time..."*; Hatch's private notes, written at the time; read in 1993 by the author.

"Your endorsement was perfectly timed and politically potent." Brooke, letter to Hatch, September 29, 1978.

141 *"Karl Malone is a bigger fool than I thought if he lends his support..."*; Thomas Ladanye, letter to the *Salt Lake Tribune*, August 22, 1999.

142 *...Hatch was in Utah when Jesse Jackson called, asking for help.*; The events involving the Jackson family in Utah were reported in both the *Deseret News* and *Salt Lake Tribune*, August 24, 1998.

Chapter 14 And Justice for All

143 *"The due administration of justice is the firmest pillar of good government..."*; George Washington, response when Congress passed the Judiciary Act, 1789.

145 *...the two liberal senators "are not exactly [the] Lewis and Clark team..."*; George F. Will, *Washington Post*, August 3, 1986.

"a tall, superbly dressed senator...the real leader of the pro-Rehnquist forces...", *Baltimore Sun*, September 22, 1986.

146 *Reagan...said in a note: "Your comments during the committee hearings..."*; Letter to Hatch, August 15, 1986.

Rehnquist wrote Hatch: "You have been a tower of strength..."; Letter to Hatch, August 1, 1986.

"We will fight Bork all the way until hell freezes over..."; *U.S. News & World Report*, September 14, 1987.

Molly Yard, ...president-elect of...NOW, called Bork "a Neanderthal."; *Washington Post*, July 20, 1987.

"By any standard of fairness, the judgment must be rendered in your favor."; Typescript of speech, September 19, 1987, in Hatch's files.

147 *"We're going to Bork him," vowed Patricial Ireland, president of NOW.*; *Miami Herald*, July 8, 1991.

148 *"How important was Senator Hatch to my confirmation?"*; Clarence Thomas, interview with the author, 1993. This was the first media interview given by Justice Thomas after his confirmation to the Supreme Court.

"I hope that President Clinton...will choose someone who appreciates..."; Hatch written statement, March 19, 1993.

149 *"You might be able to get him confirmed...but there would be blood everywhere..."*; Hatch, interview with the author, 2000.

150 *Senate Democrats...favor judicial activists "who are willing to change..."*; Free Congress Foundation news release, "Democrats Work Harder Than Republicans to Promote Their View of Judiciary, Report Says," August 16, 1999.

...Hatch has "worked hard to keep politics out" of the confirmation process...; *Deseret News*, August 28, 1999.

151 *In a series of speeches, and in a chapter written for a recent book...*; See Orrin Hatch, "Judicial Activism and Politics: Twin Dangers to the Constitution," in *Charting a New Millennium: The Latter-day Saints in the Coming Century*, edited by Maurine and Scot Proctor (Salt Lake City, Utah: Aspen Book, 1999).

153 *...the Constitution "will...demonstrate as visibly the finger of providence..."*; Washington, letter to Lafayette, May 28, 1788.

Chapter 15 Patriotism and Foreign Policy

154 *"[True patriotism] is a sense of national responsibility..."*; Adlai E. Stevenson, speech to the American Legion convention, New York City, August 27, 1952. Speeches of Adlai Stevenson (1952), 81.

155 *"While a man can have no greater love than to be willing..."* Hatch, manuscript of speech, October 19, 1984.

157 *"I urge the Senate not to tinker with the First Amendment..."*; Senator Robert Bennett, *Congressional Record*, March 27, 2000, S-1711.

"A nation is defined by its symbols, its citizens, and its values."; Major General Patrick Brady, "H.J. Res. 33 Passes in U.S. House of Representatives," June 24, 1999, Citizens Flag Alliance (CFA), on the web at www.cfa-inc.org/index.

158 *General Norman Schwarzkopf...said "I regard legal protections for our flag..."* CFA news release, May 10, 1999

Washington attorney Adrian Cronauer...told Freedom Forum's...; Freedom Forum news release, February 5, 1998.

"We need not alter the Bill of Rights. Instead we should restore its meaning..."; Hatch, statement before the Senate Judiciary Committee on the Flag Protection Amendment (S.J. Res. 14), April 20, 1999.

"Love of liberty does not reside merely on a battlefield, in a parade,..."; Ibid.

159 *Legionnaires..."reserved their most enthusiastic applause for Sen. Orrin Hatch..."*; *Orange County Register*, September 9, 1999.

The American Security Council...routinely rates the Senator 100 percent correct...; The ASC's rating for each Congress is called the National Security Index, and is available, among other places, in *The Almanac of American Politics*, published every two years by National Journal.

162 *"The battle for Angola is...a battle over ideologies..."*; Hatch, "Savimbi Deserves Support," typescript of article, January 27, 1986.

163 *"Throughout our trip...Jonny and I kept coming back to your courage..."*; McFarlane, letter on personal stationery to Hatch, June 9, 1987.

164 *"Your songs are simply beautiful. Sara and I have enjoyed them immensely..."*; Israeli Prime Minister Benjamin Netanyahu, letter to Hatch, April 14, 1998.

165 *A member of Hatch's delegation...Bill Bradley, graphically described their visit...*; See Bradley, *Time Present, Time Past* (New York: Alfred A. Knopf, 1996), especially 131-132.

166 *Hatch's pivotal role in the drama remained concealed until...*; *Washington Post*, July 20, 1992.

168 *"Clinton missed the moment because he came into office believing..."*; Hatch, "American Strategic Renewal: Foreign and Defense Policies for a New Century," speech delivered during the presidential campaign, January 22, 2000.

169 *...Hatch peppered Milosevic with tough questions...*; Paul Matulic, a participant in the meeting, memo to the author, December 17, 1998.

Chapter 16 Religious Freedom

170 *"Do not neglect your spiritual growth,"*; www.familyforever.com/art/OHatch.

171 *"How important would you say religion is in your own life...?"*; Gallup News Service, July 14, 1999.

"Most adults say they pray to a supreme being, such as God, the Lord..."; The Gallup Organization, Princeton, New Jersey, May 6, 1999.

"The potential impact of the Smith case is frightening..."; Myrick, *Congressional Record*, July 15, 1999, H-55801.

173 *Among those encountering problems during the following year:...*; *Deseret News*, June 9, 1998.

174 *Brigham Young University law professor W. Cole Durham found...*; *Deseret News*, July 1, 1998

"These protections are necessary, not because there are systematic pogroms..."; Hatch, statement before the Senate Judiciary Committee, June 23, 1998.

175 *...Alexander Lebed...pointedly calling Mormons..."mold and filth..."*; *New York Times*, June 29, 1996

Faced by a storm of protest, Lebed backtracked somewhat a week later.; Combined Wire Services, *Salt Lake Tribune*, July 3, 1996.

176 *LDS Church spokesman Don LeFevre said "We have noted and appreciate..."*; *Salt Lake Tribune*, July 3, 1996.

The gruff Lebed, regarded by some Russians as their best bet...; Two Internet sources with significant biographical information on Lebed are www.russiatoday.com/bio/lebed and especially www.cs.indiana.edu/hyplan/dmiguse/Russian/albio.

"[Democracy] doesn't completely suit our historical experience, our traditions..."; *Deseret News*, March 9, 1997 .

177 *Once more Hatch helped lead the fight against the latest threat...*; Speech on religious liberty in Russia, U.S. Senate, *Congressional Record*, July 16, 1997, S-7521.

One letter...said Congress's intent...[means] "Accept our religion, or be burned..."; Bill Revene, letter to the *Salt Lake Tribune*, July 14, 1997.

178 *"I can't adequately express my appreciation to you..."*; Jeffrey R. Holland, letter to Hatch, July 31, 1997.

180 *In May 1998, a month after Hatch and Smith returned home, Russia officially...*; *Salt Lake Tribune*, May 16, 1998.

"There is a conceptual problem whenever we seek to apply...sanctions..."; Hatch speech in Senate, *Congressional Record*, October 9, 1998, S-12095.

Part III

Chapter 17 Clinton and Gore

183 *"We made a serious mistake...by not listening more to the reporters in Little Rock..."*; David Broder, discussion with author and other journalists, 1999.

184 *...early Clinton traits included a tendency "to block things out..."*; David Maraniss, *The Clinton Enigma* (New York: Simon & Schuster, 1998), 43. The early life sketch of Clinton came from this book and Maraniss's *First in His Class: The Biography of Bill Clinton*, Touchstone Books, 1996.

Other traits came later, including "a sex drive so powerful..."; *Enigma*, 43.

"He was so young, barely four, when he was scarred by abuse...;" Hillary Clinton, interview, *Talk* magazine, September 1999, 174.

185 *Helen called Jesse "the kindest man I ever knew."*; Interview with author, 1993.

"Senator," said Clinton, "I just want you to know..."; Conversation recapped in letter from Hatch to author, 1993.

186 *They included a notorious luncheon attended by Gore...It netted $109,000...*; Robert Novak, *Washington Post*, March 13, 2000.

187 *Clinton and Gore also have had money ties to two other Asian women...*; Edward Timperlake and William C. Triplett II, *The Year of the Rat: How Bill Clinton Compromised U.S. Security for Chinese Cash* (Washington: Regnery Publishing, 1998).

"The fund-raising disclosures have blown up into the biggest political scandal..."; *New York Times*, April 16, 1997.

188 *"The Clinton-Gore Administration has used every conceivable means to dissemble..."*; Hatch, fireside speech televised in Iowa and New Hampshire, January 2000; author has transcript.

189 Huang later testified before a House committee that the money was raised... ; Associated Press, December 16, 1999.

In 1994 Huang also arranged a $100,000 payment to Clinton's close friend...; Ibid.

...[Reno] has a "legal and ethical obligation" to request a special counsel...; *Salt Lake Tribune*, November 25, 1998.

190 *...more than forty White House employees...had used illegal drugs...*; Hatch, letter to the author, August 6, 1996.

"The statistics confirm an upward spiral of drug abuse across the nation...;" Hatch, letter to the author, November 15, 1996.

"Law-abiding citizens are being killed and wounded by criminals using firearms..."; Hatch, speech to National Rifle Association, February 2, 2000.

193 *"The great mystery when we look at the actions of the Clinton-Gore..."* *The Cox Report: U.S. National Security and Military/Commercial Concerns With the People's Republic of China,* edited by Kenneth deGraffenreid (Select Committee, U.S. House of Representatives, declassified in part on May 25, 1999 and printed by Regnery Publishing, Washington, D.C.), Foreward.

194 *...just one in four Americans believed he had high personal...standards.*; *Washington Post-*ABC News poll, December 21, 1998.

"I think most of us learned...if you don't like the President's position..."; Congressman David Obey, *Washington Post*, June 14, 1995.

...Clinton was "an unusually good liar. Unusually good. Do you realize that?" Senator Bob

Kerrey, *Esquire* magazine, January 1996.

"*Clinton's as popular as AIDS in South Carolina.*" Senator Ernest Hollings, *Atlanta Journal and Constitution*, February 7, 1996.

196 ...*Gore has claimed to be father of the Internet, said he and wife Tipper*...; *Washington Post*, December 1, 1999.

"...*at times...Gore...can't find the level beneath which he will not sink*..."; Margaret Carlson, "Stretching the Fabric," *Time*, February 14, 2000.

197 "If he does really think that there is no distinction between virtue and vice..."; Charles Krauthammer, *Time*, July 9, 1984.

...*Richard Cohen described a "full Clinton" as*...; *Washington Post*, October 24, 1995.

"*Plainly put, almost no one thinks [Clinton] believes a word he says*..."; George F. Will, *Newsweek*, November 13, 1995.

"[Clinton] gives the appearance of taking stands..."; Joe Klein, *Newsweek*, October 23, 1995.

198 "*Lots of power. Big. Sexy. Thinks he's invulnerable, like the builders of the ship*..."; Psychiatrist E. James Lieberman, quoted in Maraniss, *The Clinton Enigma*, 43.

Chapter 18 Bill and Monica

199 ...*Danny Ferguson, apparently leaked a distorted account of what happened*...; See "Criminal Laws Implicated by the Clinton Scandals: A Partial List," *American Spectator*, February 1994.

"*My guess is she's lying*..."; Stuart Taylor Jr., cited in the *Washington Post*, November 19, 1996.

200 *After entering his hotel room, said Jones, Clinton began*...; Jones affidavit in civil suit filed against President Clinton in U.S. District Court in Little Rock, Arkansas, May 6, 1994.

201 *Paula Jones's evidence of "predatory, if not depraved, behavior by Bill Clinton*..."; Stuart Taylor, *The American Lawyer*, November 1996. Stuart is a Harvard-educated lawyer as well as a journalist.

203 *Here is a comparison of points, quoting directly from Clinton's deposition*..., Clinton deposition by Jones's attorneys was taken on January 17, 1998.

204 "*I did not have sexual relations with that woman, Miss Lewinsky.*"; *Washington Post*, January 27, 1998.

...*the controversy had been fabricated by a "vast right-wing conspiracy."*; Hillary Clinton, NBC's "Today" show, January 27, 1998.

...*Gore told them "It's important that Democrats support the president*..."; *Salt Lake Tribune*, January 27, 1998.

..."*Mr. Blumenthal stated that Monica Lewinsky had been a 'stalker' and*..."; Christopher Hitchens, affidavit filed in the District of Columbia, February 5, 1999.

205 "If these allegations are true, then there's been a tremendous abuse of power."; *Deseret News*, February 12, 1998.

"*This president would go down as the greatest canoodler in history.*"; *Deseret News*, February 12, 1998.

...*[White House attorneys] had grown from four to eighty-four*...; Hatch letter to author, April 1, 1998

206 "*The fact that he would ignore and violate a subpoena*..."; Reuters News Service, July 27,

1998.

207 *...reporter Helen Dewar called Hatch and ... John Kerry..."Honest brokers"*; *Washington Post*, September 28, 1998.

"I've spent a lifetime helping people who have difficulties..."; *Washington Post*, September 28, 1998.

"I kept glancing at Orrin to gauge what he was thinking..."; Heather Barney, interview, 1999. Other details of Hatch's reaction to Clinton's speech also are from Barney.

209 *"Last time I saw [Clinton]," said maverick Democrat James Traficant, Jr...."*; *Washington Post,* September 11, 1998.

The Senator reached the White House on his car phone.; Hatch letter to author, November 2, 1998. Many news accounts reported the conversation took place; this is the first time the details have been revealed.

211 *"I'm a Secret Service agent," the agent said in a hushed voice...*; Hatch letter to the author; personal details on the two agents purposely have been left vague to protect them.

Chapter 19 The Impeachment

213 *...a law professor...said "I think it's plain that the President should resign..."*; Professor Bill Clinton, quoted in *Arkansas Gazette*, August 6, 1974.

214 *A visit to the White House by Mexican president Ernesto Zedillo...*; Starr report to Congress.

"Clinton is, in a sense, being protected by his scandals, which distract attention..."; George F. Will, *Washington Post*, September 10, 1998.

In March 1998 the annual white-tie Gridiron Dinner was held...; Satire quoted below is from a transcript of the event, held on March 21, 1998.

216 *"...it was clear that the most important thing to Bill Clinton is...Bill Clinton..."*; Peggy Noonan, *Wall Street Journal*, September 14, 1998.

"The transgressions the President has admitted to are too consequential..."; Senator Joseph Lieberman, *Congressional Record*, September 3, 1998, S-9925.

217 *"All of us are pulled in many directions...but mostly...by our consciences." Hyde, Salt Lake Tribune*, October 9, 1998.

218 *Throughout 1998 Clinton defied the laws of political gravity.*; Gallup poll numbers reported by the American Policy Center, July 31, 1998.

...[Clinton's poll numbers] went up to 67 percent–something no one could...explain.; *Salt Lake Tribune*, October 13, 1998.

...a majority could not name a single accomplishment of the just-ending [Congress]...; The *Detroit News*, October 16, 1998.

219 *"The Republicans...assembled a firing squad in the shape of a circle..."*; *Salt Lake Tribune*, November 5, 1998.

"...issues do matter...some agenda will beat no agenda every time."; Ibid.

220 *[Hyde] said of the impeachment, "How I'd like to forget this...who needs it?"*; *Salt Lake Tribune*, November 16, 1998.

[Gore says Clinton] "...will be regarded...as one of our greatest presidents...", *Washington Post*, December 20, 1998.

221 *...Utah Attorney General Jan Graham...[asks members of Congress] to sign affidavits that "they have never engaged in extramarital sexual conduct..."*; *Salt Lake Tribune*, December 20, 1998.

222 *If at least 34 senators would not vote to remove Clinton "we're going to have to..."*; *New York Times*, December 28, 1998.

223 *Clinton had acted shamefully, said [White House lawyer] Ruff, but had not committed....*; *Washington Post*, January 20, 1999

"*...the Senate's legislative giants [including Hatch] tossed out options...*"; *Los Angeles Times*, January 24, 1999

"*I felt that [Lewinsky] should appear and the American people should be able to judge...*"; Hatch, letter to author, February 25, 1999.

224 "*The Senate should seek a conclusion that protects the integrity...*"; *New York Times*, February 2, 1999.

225 *Republican senators [said Bork] "ought to face up to the fact...*"; *New York Times*, February 4, 1999.

...Hatch submitted for the Congressional Record a scholarly and comprehensive...; The Senator read from his treatise during final deliberations on the Senate floor, February 10, 1999. The full text appears in the *Congressional Record* on February 23, 1999, S-1781 to S-1790.

227 "*President Clinton shows no remorse for the conduct that got him impeached...*"; *Washington Times*, February 8, 1999.

...Clinton recently reassured an old pal that "This was 'much ado about nothing...'"; *New York Daily News*, February 9, 1999.

"*...Clinton has made breezy, even joking comments about the impeachment...*" *Washington Post*, April 14, 2000.

228 "*I wouldn't relive it for anything," [Broaddrick] told them.*; *Washington Post*, February 20, 1999.

"*Stupid me, I ordered coffee to the room," says Broaddrick.*; Ibid.

229 "*On the impeachment, let me tell you, I am proud of what we did there...we saved the Constitution...*"; *Baltimore Sun*, April 17, 2000.

Chapter 20 Utah and the West

230 *Babbitt [told Clinton] he could still leave his mark for posterity in the [West]...*; *New York Times*, January 16, 2000.

"*This declaration has nothing to do with preserving land in southern Utah...*"; *Salt Lake Tribune*, September 19, 1996.

...Leavitt made a last-minute appeal to White House Chief of Staff...; *Salt Lake Tribune*, September 18, 1996.

231 *Less than twenty-four hours later, Clinton...Gore, and their entourage...*; *Salt Lake Tribune*, September 19, 1996

233 "*There was no consultation with the governor, no notification to..." Hatch* testimony before the Senate subcommittee on national parks, historic preservation, and recreation.

"*I know we're doing the right thing...We've got the good Lord's stamp of approval...*"; transcript, *Deseret News*, January 12, 2000.

234 "*Ranchers here feel like they've been kicked in the gut...*"; *Deseret News*, January 11, 2000.

235 "*This latest move by the President is not simply about managing roads...*"; Hatch, public statement, November 2, 1999.

236 "*Surely those of us who care about the environment can learn from history...*"; Nicholson speech to Environmental Defense Fund, Denver, October 7, 1999.

238 "*I'm his number one fan," says Johnson [of Hatch]...*"; Interview with author, 2000.

Johnson calls Clinton and Babbitt "wackos" in their outlook toward the West.; Ibid.

239 *Gore published Earth in the Balance in 1992...*; Al Gore, *Earth in the Balance: Ecology and the Human Spirit* (New York: Houghton Mifflin, 1993).

...*"There is not a single passage in that book that I...would change."*; Gannett News Service, March 23, 1999. Page references for quoted sections: "It seems an easy choice..." 119; "Any child born into..." 308; "[We ought to] be able..." 325-326; "What if we..." 349; "I am convinced..." 349.

"...*only a mental suspension of the real world could allow a person...*"; *Salt Lake Tribune* editorial, March 23, 2000.

240 *"We can drain Lake Powell and let the Colorado River run through the dam..."*; Cited in a public notice by Congressman Jim Hansen, R-Utah, announcing hearings, September 18, 1997.

241 *"Global warming may be coming, but...it might actually be a boon..."*; Dennis T. Avery, *American Outlook*, March 1998, published by the Hudson Institute, Indianapolis.

In 1997 [Gore] journeyed to Kyoto, Japan and...signed a treaty...; The Kyoto Protocol to the 1992 Climate Change Treaty was signed December 10, 1997. It is binding on individual countries only after their governments complete ratification.

The Argonne National Laboratory...predicts the Kyoto accord...; The study, issued in February 1997, is cited in the *Journal of Commerce*, December 18, 1997, 6A.

244 *Some reviews of Hatch's efforts by Utahns:...*; Correspondence to Hatch was furnished by his Salt Lake City office, after writers agreed to be publicly quoted.

"There's never been an issue that I've gone to Orrin with..."; Bangerter co-chaired Hatch's Senate campaign in 2000, along with former Utah Senator Jake Garn.

Chapter 21 Orrin at Ease

247 *"When Orrin went to law school, someone remarked..."*; Elaine Hatch, interview, 1993. She also was interviewed by the author in 1999.

While they didn't get a lot of Orrin's time, the now-grown Hatch children...; Among other correspondence in Hatch's private files is a letter from oldest daughter Marcia Hatch Whetton, dated November 8, 1992, that says, in part: "I was sitting here thinking how much I love you. You are such a great dad...You are always such a strength and support...I owe so much to you and I pray I will make you proud of me."

248 *"She's extremely bright, very well-read," said a close friend, Jan Bennett...*; *Salt Lake Tribune*, February 5, 1995.

In 1995 the Salt Lake Tribune ran a large feature article on Elaine...; Ibid.

"...*I owe everything I have achieved to my eternal sweetheart, Elaine.*" Hatch letter to Judge Michael Murphy, February 21, 1995.

250 *"Utah is dotted with art museums from St. George to Logan,"...*; *Salt Lake Tribune*, July 20, 1997.

...*NEA Chairman Jane Alexander wrote him, saying "Your stand..."*; Alexander letter is dated September 22, 1997.

251 *"When I was a kid growing up in the late '40s, baseball was..."*; *Washington Times*, February 23, 1995.

252 ...*Newt Gingrich [initially charged]...it was "a club to beat up the owners..."*; Associated Press, February 14, 1995.

253 *In April 1995...he wrote Malone, the Jazz's great power forward...*; Hatch letter, April 21,

1995.

254 ..."*I'm so proud of you...You are playing so well.*" Letter to Malone is dated February 2, 1996.

"*The thing with Senator Hatch is he has always supported me...*"; *Washington Post*, August 16, 1999.

"We should support who supports us,"; Malone, *Salt Lake Tribune*, August 20, 1999.

"*It's important that people know what a great fighter you are,*"...; Hatch's hand-written letter to Fullmer is dated February 27, 1995.

255 "We are all thrilled by your Super Bowl achievements,"...; Hatch, letter to Young, January 30, 1995.

... "Our faith and prayers are with you. I know it must be a little discouraging..."; Letter to Young, October 8, 1995.

..."*Just today, I told Jerry Jones [owner of the Dallas Cowboys]...*"; Letter to Young, December 20, 1995.

Chapter 22 Friends

256 "*Your kind emotional and spiritual support has been...*"; Monzer Hourani, letter to Hatch, April 24, 1997.

257 "*This is the greatest betrayal I've had in all my years...*"; The Kennedy-Hatch exchange is reported in a letter from Hatch to the author, July 11, 1997.

260 "*It's easy to see why Ted has so much respect for your friendship...*"; Victoria Kennedy, letter to Hatch, March 24, 1997.

"We both commented afterward that we really now had a sense..."; Victoria Kennedy, letter to Orrin and Elaine, undated.

261 ..."*The ice diet sounds interesting, but I find it works better...*"; Ted Kennedy, letter to Hatch, August 8, 1997.

262 "*Dear Orrin, Drop by and see the originals...*"; Ted Kennedy, letter to Hatch, February 9, 1998.

"*Like everyone else in that stadium, I was deeply moved.*"; Bob Costas, *People*, January 13, 1997.

263 "So I went up to Washington and met him in his office..."; Ali, *Insight*, August 8, 1988.

Humphrey sent Hatch a note calling him "indeed a dear friend..."; Note dated September 26, 1977.

264 ..."*Your whole letter was very interesting as it always is...*"; Cleon Skousen, letter to Hatch, October 14, 1995.

..."*From time to time he would ask me, 'Orrin, why in the world did you...*"; Recounted in letter from Senator Hatch to his mother, Helen, June 30, 1994.

[Rabbi Korff] is a very dear friend who had taught me so much about Israel..."; Providence [Rhode Island] *Journal-Bulletin*, June 25, 1995.

265 "*[Korff] was rock-hard, yet ineffably sweet...*"; *Washington Post*, July 27, 1995.

"*You are a rare individual who has the unique qualities...*"; Paul H. Dunn, letter to Hatch, November 21, 1994.

266 "*Dr. Koop exhibits all the qualities that we want in our nation's top doctor...*"; Typescript of speech, May 20, 1987.

Koop wrote a note to Hatch, saying it was "so like" the Utahn...; Koop, letter to Hatch, July 23, 1987.

Chapter 23 Music Man

267 *"Although it is no mystery to those who know him well..."*; *The Hill*, July 24, 1996.

268 *Turow...wrote Hatch...to thank him for "your tireless efforts in behalf of this..."*; Turow, letter to Hatch, January 9, 1995.

...including to President Clinton...calling it "a wonderful read"...; Hatch, letter to Clinton, February 3, 1995.

269 *"To Orrin–Here's one of the very first copies hot off the press."*; Cook, letter to Hatch, March 10, 1997.

"He weighs everything he does and says on the scales of his beliefs..."; *Cornwell, The Hill*, July 24, 1996.

"Hatch writes well. He is clear and smooth. He marshals arguments..."; *Deseret News*, November 30, 1979.

271 *"Also, Senator, I wasn't sure if you were serious about a collaboration..."*; Perry, letter to Hatch, March 28, 1995.

"He had a little bit to learn about the difference between lyrics..."; *Salt Lake Tribune*, May 13, 1997.

273 *Bergman's interest would turn any songwriter's head.*; Her arts resume is on the web at www.ascap.com/about/bergman-bio.

277 *The Hatch-Knight connection was noted in Parade magazine...*; Walter Scott, *Parade*, January 23, 2000.

Hatch–the only member of Congress eligible to belong to [ASCAP]...; The American Society of Composers, Authors and Publishers has some 80,000 members. Its function is to protect the rights of members by licensing and paying royalties for the public performances of their copyrighted works.

"I think he's talented," she said. "Particularly the religious songs..."; Bergman, *Capitol Hill Blue*, October 13, 1998.

278 *"Bad luck seems to come in threes and Salt Lake City has recently..."*; *Salt Lake Tribune*, September 28, 1999.

"Our own senator-songwriter was sitting there...;" *Salt Lake Tribune*, December 28, 1997.

"I believe it was Will Rogers who said, 'If you done it, it ain't braggin'." Lee Roderick, *Salt Lake Tribune*, January 17, 1998.

279 *"But then I put this question to him: If he had a choice..."*; *New York Times*, August 4, 1999.

Epilogue

281 *"I'd like to empower families so we can have a vision..."*; *Deseret News*, July 2, 1999.

282 *"Candidates for president all falter,"* said... *[campaign director]* Sal Russo,... "; Russo was at Ronald Reagan's side in five campaigns–one for governor of California and four for president. In an interview with the AP, Russo said he joined Hatch's uphill effort because "I think he is as close as there is to the Reagan-Kemp heir among the candidates." *Washington Post*, November 9, 1999.

283 *"It's a commentary on how screwy our presidential campaigns have become..."*; Germond and Witcover, *Denver Post*, June 30, 1999.

284 "Unlike the other Republican munchkins,"... *New York Times*, August 4, 1999.

285 *He gave a major speech in Alabama...*; "Vision for America," Birmingham, Alabama, August 28, 1999.

286 *"The thing with Sen. Hatch is he has always supported me in basketball..."*; Malone, *Washington Post,* August 16, 1999.

"Why? He's a very religious man and has a lot of the same values..."; Beck, Ibid.

287 *"I would remove the Confederate flag. No one doubts..."*; Hatch, written statement, issued January 20, 2000.

"Never in American political history have so many debated..."; *Washington Post,* January 10, 2000.

288 *"My only problem with you governor is you've had four,..."*Associated Press, December 7, 1999.

"Do you know who has been doing absolutely fabulously?....Orrin Hatch."; Former Senator Alphonse D'Amato, transcript from "The Edge," Fox News, January 6, 2000.

289 *"I have to say [Bush] is a fine man."*; Hatch, *Houston Chronicle,* July 3, 1999.

290 *"Senator McCain and I disagree on a number of issues...but I know..."*; Hatch, press release, January 6, 2000.

"I thought Hatch was exceptionally impressive for several reasons..."; Kate Thompson, "Hatch Campaigns Without Using Negative Tactics," *Sioux City Journal,* December 27, 1999.

He struck a major blow for substance, issuing a detailed plan...; ABC News, December 13, 1999; also *Salt Lake Tribune* of same date.

291 Conservative columnist Tony Blankley wrote that it was "gratifying..."; *Washington Times,* January 19, 2000.

292 ...*"a devastating indictment of ...the crimes of the Clinton-Gore administration." New York Post* editorial, January 18, 2000.

...Hatch was "correct to criticize the front-runners" for not addressing...; *Mobile Register,* January 15, 2000.

"I'd take a bullet for him," said Breck. I don't say that about many people."; Massachusetts/New Hampshire *Eagle-Tribune,* January 19, 2000.

293 *"It's really outrageous that the liberal media are determining who the people..."*; *Deseret News,* January 17, 2000.

... *"the mighty senator, lion of the Judiciary and Finance committees..."*; *Washington Post,* January 21, 2000.

...Hatch "even fantasizes about a VP spot or Cabinet post." Such nonsense...; *Salt Lake Tribune,* January 30, 2000.

294 *"It is not the critic who counts;..."*; Theodore Roosevelt, address at the Sorbonne, Paris, France, April 23, 1910. "Citizenship in a Republic," *The Strenuous Life* (Vol. 13 of The Works of Theodore Roosevelt, national edition, 1926), 510.

"Orrin Hatch has been one of the most effective senators in the history..."; Layden, *Salt Lake Tribune,* December 1, 1999.

Hatch was also buoyed by thousands of Skinnycats...; The messages cited below all were sent to Hatch by e-mail.

295 *"I feel very strongly that you are the best Republican candidate..." Washington Post,* January 21, 2000.

296 *"I believe in an America...where no man is denied public office merely..."*; Senator John F. Kennedy, address to the Greater Houston Ministerial Association, Houston, Texas, September 12, 1960.

Fellow senator...John McCain simply deserted the Senate in 1999...; By the end of that year, McCain had missed more than 160 Senate votes. From the sidelines, he criticized fellow senators, angering many of them, for example, in calling a difficult year-end budget deal "obscene." Cox News Service, November 28, 1999.

"Hatch, many in Washington agree, is a decent, smart, and powerful man"... Washington Post, January 21, 2000.

297 *Fellow Utah senator Bob Bennett appeared with Orrin and Elaine...*; Bennett issued a press release, dated January 26, 2000, in which he said "Orrin understood that he was facing very long odds. We believed that if the front runner stumbled, Sen. Hatch was clearly the best choice for the Republican nomination...."

"Hatch lost everything in this race except his sense of humor."; Broder, *Washington Post*, January 28, 2000.

"Hatch represented his state well. His experience and solid values were evident..."; *Deseret News* editorial, January 27, 2000.

298 *"Trust me, there is no more humbling experience than running for president."* Hatch, speech at Gridiron Dinner, December 4, 1999.

"There is a need of a sound body, and even more need of a sound mind,"... Roosevelt, address at the Sorbonne, April 23, 1910.

Index

A
AARP 111
ABC's Good Morning America 51, 272, 281, 289
Abortion 98-9
Act for better Child Care (ABC) 81
ACLU 157, 172
Adoption 99-100
Afghanistan 165-66
AFL-CIO 18, 44-47, 56, 96-7
AIDS 81, 82, 102, 114-23, 194-95, 265-66
Albright, Madeleine 192
Alcohol, Tobacco, and Firearms (ATF), Bureau of 190
Alexander, Jane 250
Alexander, Lamar 67, 175
Alexi II 179-80
Alger, Horatio 147
Ali, Lonnie 249, 262
Ali, Muhammad 70, 141, 249, 256, 262, 263
Allen, James 31-3, 36, 43, 46-8, 51
Allen, Maryon 50
Almanac of American Politics 9
American Bar Association 137, 157
American Cancer Society 102
American Conservative Union (ACU) 257
American Lawyer 201
American Security Council 159
American Society of Newspaper Editors 229
American Spectator 199
Americans with Disabilities Act (ADA) 138
Andalex Resources 231-32
And the Band Played On 115
Anderson, Jack 5
Angola 161-62
Anti-Terrorism and Effective Death Penalty Act 159, 191
Antiquities Act 233
Arizona Republic 6
Armstrong, Senator William 257
Aum Shinri Kyo 175
Avery, Dennis T. 241
B
Babbitt, Bruce 149, 230, 232-34, 238, 242
Baer, Judge Harold, Jr. 151
Baker, Senator Howard 51-2
Baird, Zoe 185
Baker, Senator Howard 46
Bakke, Allan 135
Balanced Budget Act 109-10
Baldwin High 17-19
Balkans 168
Ballard, M. Russell 172

Bangerter, Governor Norm 244
Bank of Credit and Commerce International (BCCI) 183
Barberi, Tom 278, 293
Barney, Alex 78
Barney, Heather 3, 4, 8, 77, 207, 208
Barry, Dave 205
Base Realignment and Closure Act (BRAC) 129
Baucus, Senator Max 237
Bauer, Gary 287
Bayh, Senator Birch 5, 139
Beaty, Judge James 151
Beck, Miriam 286
Beckstead, B. Howard 244
Beirn, Terry 120-21
Bennett, Jan 101, 102, 248
Bennett, Senator Robert (Bob) 61, 86, 157, 297
Bennett, William 118
Benson, Ezra Taft 264
Benson, Steve 6
Bergen, Candice 74
Bergman, Alan 273
Bergman, Marilyn 267, 272, 277
Bible Way Church 141
Blackmun, Justice Harry 149
Blankley, Tony 291
Block, Larry 3, 4
Blumenthal, Sidney 204, 223
Blythe, William Jefferson III 184
Body Farm, The 92, 201
Book of Mormon 22
Borger, Gloria 209
Bork, Robert 146, 152, 225
Boston Pops Orchestra 261
Bowen, Melanie 92
Boxer, Senator Barbara 7, 82
Boys and Girls Clubs 131
Bradley, Bill 12, 165, 190, 195, 287, 290
Brady, Patrick 157
breast cancer 101-02
Breck, David 292
Brennan, Justice William J. 147
Breyer, Justice Stephen 148-49
Brezhnev, Leonid 1
Brigham Young University (BYU) 20, 21, 25, 27, 28, 39, 66, 174, 221, 254, 271
Broaddrick, Juanita 228
Broder, David 183, 297
Brooke, Edward 140
Brooks, Kix 274
Brower, David 240
Bryant, William Cullen 48
Buchanan, Pat 67
Buchwald, Art 11
Buckley, William F. xi
Buffalo News 215
Bumpers, Senator Dale 2, 47
Bureau of Alcohol, Tobacco and Firearms (ATF) 190-91
Burger, Justice Warren 145
Burrell, Keile 79
Burrell, Rochelle 79
Burrell, Wayne 79
Burton, Dan 12
Bush, Barbara 81
Bush, President George xiii, 81, 147, 152
Bush, Governor George W. xiv, 281, 288
Business Software Alliance (BSA) 60
Byrd, Pia 244
Byrd, Senator Robert 43, 45, 49, 50, 53, 71-3, 117, 222-3

C

Cabral, Anna 139
Cabranes, Jose 140, 148
California State University 135
Campbell, Senator Ben Nighthorse 12
capital gains tax 107
Capitol Hill Blue 277
Caring Program for Children 249
Carlson, Jack 33, 35, 39
Carlson, Margaret 196
Carlson, Thure 31
Carpenter, Karen 276
Carr, Antoine 253
Carter, President Jimmy 32, 41, 42, 44, 45, 53, 55, 56, 64, 160, 221, 231
Cassidy, Virginia 184
Catron, Kimberly Hatch & John 246, 248
Catholic Church 172, 179-80
CBS's *Face The Nation* 206
CBS News 10

Centers for Disease Control (CDC) 105
Centro de la Familia 249
Chenoweth, Helen 219
Chicago Bulls 252
child support 100
Children's Center 249
Children's Health Insurance and Deficit Reduction Bill (CHILD) 84
Chiles, Senator Lawton, 47
China 166, 187
Christensen, Mac 9
Christian Coalition 296
Christopher, Warren 192
Chuck-A-Rama 9
Chung, Johnny 187
Church of Jesus Christ of Latter-day Saints (LDS) (Mormon) 16, 21, 22, 23, 25, 29, 30, 67, 254
Church Music Publishers Association (CMPA) 275
CIA 166
Cleland, Senator Max 157
Clinton, President Bill 12, 60, 64-5, 67, 91, 98, 103, 108, 128-29, 136-37, 140, 143, 148-52, 159, 164, 167-69, 172-76, 183-235, 238-45, 252, 268-69, 290
Clinton, Chelsea, 208, 211
Clinton-Gore Administration 60, 96, 128, 85, 152, 188, 190
Clinton, Hillary Rodham 91, 184, 189
Clinton, Roger, Jr. 185
CNBC 10
CNN 10, 281, 283, 293
Cocteau, Jean 270
Coffer, Charles 141
Cohen, Richard 197
Coleman, Sy 274
Coleman, William T., Jr 134
Collins, Senator Susan 125
Confederate flag 287
Congressional Record 54, 225
Congressional Quarterly 42, 92
Contagion 268, 269
Cook, Robin 268
Coons, Dee 277
Cornwell, Patricia 91-2, 268
Corwin, Edward Samuel 268
Costas, Bob 262
Couric, Katie 68
Cox, Randy 274
Cox Report, The 193
Crim, Diane 127
Crockett, David and Doris 249
Cronauer, Adrian 158
Crosby, Kathryn 99
Curie, Betty 203
Curt Flood Act 252

D

Dallas Cowboys 255
D'Amato, Senator Alfonse 89, 288
Damone, Vic 286
Darrow, Clarence 19
Daschle, Senator Tom 157
Davidson, Lee 10, 55, 58
Deaver, Michael 38
Decker, Rod 269
DeConcini, Senator Dennis 6, 160
DeFrank, Tom 227
De Gaulle, Charles 64
DeLaurentis, Susan 81
Democratic National Committee 56, 82
Denniston, Lyle 145
Denver & Rio Grande Railroad 31
Deseret News 10, 37, 56, 57, 293, 297
Diamond, Neil 68
Dietary Supplement Health and Education Act 112
Dixie College 133
Dolan, Tony 284
Dole, Senator Bob 6, 59, 198
Dole, Elizabeth 67, 282
Drury, Alan 268
Dubinin, Yuri Vladimirovich 161
Dunn, Paul H. 265
Dunn, Ronnie 274
Durham, W. Cole 174

E

Earth in the Balance 239
Edelman, Marian Wright 90
Ed-Flex 127
Education 124-133
Edwards, LaVell 251
Eisenhower, President Dwight 20, 147, 152

Elementary and Secondary Education Act 128
Employment Division v. Smith 171
Equal Rights Amendment (ERA) 95, 96
Esquire 194
F
Family Support and Children's Justice Centers 249
Fawson, Kristine 77
Fawson, Shane 77
FBI 96, 139, 189, 190, 192, 290
Feinstein, Senator Dianne 7, 282
Feldt, Gloria 99
Ferguson, Danny 199
Ficken, Bill 83
Fifteenth Air Force 16
Finance Committee 59, 98, 129
First in His Class 184
Flores, John 139
Flowers, Gennifer 198
Food and Drug Administration 31, 81, 102, 111,
Forbes, Steve 287
Ford, President Gerald 32, 41, 43, 64, 221
Forest Service 235
Fowles, John 268
Fox Television 10, 288
Fredrick, Paul 9
Free Congress Foundation 150
Freeh, Louis 189, 192
Friedan, Betty 218
Frost, Robert 270
Fullmer, Gene 254
G
Gale, Don 87
Gallo, Robert C. 116
Garfield County 231
Garn, Jake 70
Gash, Adele 184
Gatlin, Larry (Gatlin Brothers) 275
generic drugs 111
George 11
Gephardt, Richard 217
Germond, Jack 283
Gingrich, Newt 219
Ginsburg, Douglas 146, 147
Ginsburg, Justice Ruth Bader 103, 148-49
Giuliani, Rudolph 190
Glaser, Elizabeth & Ariel 81, 82
Glaser, Paul Michael 81
Glen Canyon Dam 239
global warming 240-42
Goldberg, Jeffrey 279, 284
Gompers, Samuel 19
Gonzalez, Elian 286
Good Morning America 281, 289
Good Morning Vietnam 158
GOP 2, 33, 35, 41, 46, 56, 61, 64, 69, 87, 145, 160, 198, 213, 219-20, 281-82
Gorbachev, Mikhail 1, 166
Gordon, Dick 29
Gore, Vice President Al 64, 67, 144, 159, 167, 185, 220, 231-35, 238-39, 241, 242, 245, 282, 287, 290
Graham, Jan 221
Gramm, Senator Phil 89
Grassley, Charles 89
Gravelet, Jean Francois 61
Greenspan, Alan 193
Gridiron Club 66, 214-15, 298
Gun Owners of America 61
H
Haile-Mariam, Mengistu 162
Hale, Edward 68
Hamlisch, Marvin 273
Hand, Judge Learned 158
Hansen, Elaine 21
Hansen, George 6, 7
Hansen, Congressman Jim 233, 240, 242
Harrington, Dave 200
Hatch, Abram 40
Hatch, Alysa 27, 248
Hatch, Brent 25, 29, 247
Hatch, Chloe 14
Hatch, Elaine 1, 26, 28-9, 32, 35, 41, 93 247-50, 268, 286, 297
Hatch, Frances 14
Hatch, Helen Kamm xv, 26, 37, 93, 260
Hatch, Jeremiah 13, 40
Hatch, Jesse (Father) 13, 16, 35, 93, 185
Hatch, Jess Ramon 16, 29, 246, 248
Hatch, Jesse (Jess) Morlan (brother) 14, 155
Hatch, Jessica 14

Hatch, Josephus 13
Hatch, Kimberly 27
Hatch, Lorenzo 40
Hatch, Marcia 26
Hatch, Marilyn 14, 15
Hatch, Mary Alice Marriott 7, 248-449
Hatch, Martha Luella Thomas 13
Hatch, Mia Ensslin 247
Hatch, Nancy 14, 15
Hatch, Scott 26, 247, 248
Hatch-Waxman Drug Competition Act 111
Hatch Wendy Dalgleish 247
Hayakawa, Senator Sam 44, 70
Hays, Brooks 68
Head Start 78
Heaton, Tony 234
Helms, Senator Jesse 47, 10, 117, 138
Hess, Stephen 213
Higher Laws 269
Hill Air Force Base 79, 242-43
Hill, Anita 75, 91, 95-6, 147, 218
Hill, The 267
Hilley, Donna 273
Hilley, Rayford 273
Hinsche, Billy 272, 273
Hitchens, Christopher 204
Hodgkins, Michele 283
Holland, Jeffrey R. 178
Hollings, Senator Ernest F. (Fritz) 46, 52, 53, 194
Hornacek, Jeff 253
Hourani, Monzer 256
Hsai, Maria 187
Hsi Lai Temple 187
Huang, John 187, 188
Hubbell, Webster 189
Hudson, Rock 115
Huff, Marie W. 244
Humphrey, Vice President Hubert 43, 83, 263
Hunt, Al 97
Hyde, Congressman Henry 12, 217, 220, 224
I
Impact Aid 128
Indian Affairs Committee 59, 140
Insight 263
Intelligence Committee 59, 108, 159, 161
Internal Revenue Service 4, 6, 31, 106, 243
Iran-contra affair 162-64
IRAs 129
Iraq 220
Ireland, Patricia 147
Israel 164-65
Iverson, Kris 2, 8
J
Jacinto, Janine 135
Jackson, Jesse Jr. 142
Jackson, Jesse Sr. 82, 141, 142, 216
Jackson, Santita 82, 142
Jackson, Judge Thomas Penfield 59-60
Jankowski, Father Henryk 264
Jefferson, Thomas 60, 229
Jehovah's Witnesses 173
Jipping, Thomas 150
John Birch Society 27
Johnson, Andrew 217
Johnson, Gregory 156
Johnson, Kevin 253
Johnson, Met 238
Johnson, Phil 251
Johnson, Samuel 154, 197
Jones, Brian 139
Jones, Dan 7, 39, 282
Jones, Jerry 255
Jones, Paula Corbin 198, 199, 202, 206, 216,
Jordan, Michael 131
Jordan, Vernon 67, 223
Judiciary Committee 3, 59-60, 95, 103, 112, 131, 139, 143-144, 150, 158, 174, 185, 206
K
Kaiparowits Plateau 231
Kamm, Helen 13
Kamm, John Bernard 13
Kampelman, Max 161
Kanab High School 231
Kanchanalak, Pauline 187
Kane County 231
Kassebaum, Senator Nancy 12
Kassin, Gennady 1
Kassin, Natasha 1

Kearney, Charmaine 139
Keefe, Adam 253
Keillor, Garrison 1, 12
Kennedy, Senator Edward M. (Ted) 66, 73, 84, 116, 138, 172, 257-62, 267
Kennedy, President John F. 283, 295-96
Kennedy, Rose Fitzgerald 260
Kennedy School of Government at Harvard 288
Kennedy, Victoria Reggie 258-61
Kerrey, Senator Bob 158, 194, 216
Kesler, V. L. 29
Keyes, Alan 287
KGB 1
Kiplinger Washington Letter 51
Kirkpatrick, Ambassador Jeane 103
Klein, Joe 197
Klinghoffer, Leon 164
Knight, Gladys (Pips) 277
Knight, Patricia 92
Kohl, Herb 12
Koop, Surgeon General C. Everett 81, 118, 265, 266
Koop, Heather 266
Koplan, Jeffrey 105
Korff, Rabbi Baruch 264-5
Korologos, Tom 272
Kosovo 169
Kowall, Scotty 64
Krauthammer, Charles 197
KSL Television 3, 4, 87
Kudrayvtsev, Aleksandr 179
Kyoto Accords 241
L
LaBella, Charles 189
Labor and Human Resources Committee 59, 78, 110, 124
Ladanye, Thomas W. 141
Lafayette, Marquis de 153
Lake Powell 239-40
Lake Winnipesaukee 249
Landerman, Dick 29
Larry King Live 10, 208, 211, 281, 283
Law Review 26
Law, Vance 252
Law, Vernon 252
Lawford, Patricia Kennedy 260
Laxalt, Senator Paul 55, 69, 160
Layden, Frank 294
(LDS) (see Church of Jesus Christ-)
Leahy, Senator Patrick 137, 157
Leavitt, Governor Mike xii, 56, 87, 124, 230, 232, 243, 245
Lebed, Alexander 175-76
Lee, Bill Lann 136-37
LeFevre, Don 176
Leno, Jay 214
Letterman, David 214
Lewinsky, Monica 97, 148, 184, 198, 199-212-16, 223,
Lewis and Clark College 202
Lieberman, Senator Joseph 107, 216
Lincoln, Abraham 61, 229, 282
Lippo Group 188-89
Livingston, Congressman Bob 219
Loen, Charlene 136
Loen, Patrick 136
Loginov, Andrey 179
Long, Senator Russell 47, 49, 53
Loos, Bill 57
Lopatto, Jeanne 150
Lorenz, Geoff 275
Los Angeles Times, 11, 223
Lott, Senator Trent 86, 88, 205
Lugar, Senator Richard 46, 50
M
Macdonald, Dr. Donald Ian 119
Maddox, Mark 123
Madison, James 143
Madsen, Ron 142
Magleby, David 221
Majerus, Rick 251
Make a Wish Foundation 249
Malone, Karl 55, 58, 67, 141, 253, 254, 286
Malone, Kay 254
Manchester *Union Leader* 9
Mann, Reverend Gerald 68
Maraniss, David 184
Marriott, Dick 249
Marriott, Nancy 249
Marshall, Ray 50
Martin, C. J. 7, 8, 141
Martindale-Hubbell 27

Marx, Karl 86
Mason, Dr. James 116
Matheson, Governor Scott 56, 155
Matulic, Paul 8
Maxwell, Neal A. 140
McBride, Ron 251
McCain-[Russell] Feingold Bill 289
McCain, Senator John 284, 289, 290, 296
McCann, Peter 93, 276
McCullough, David 12
McElroy Mr. 126, 127
McEntire, Frank 250
McFarlane, Robert 163
McGibney Elementary School 15, 125
McGovern, Senator George 263
McGrory, Mary 63, 134
McGuiness, Kevin 284
McGuire, Mark 55, 57
McManus, Doyle 223
McNeil-Lehrer News Hour 10
Meany, George 44, 47, 50, 96
Medicaid 83, 100, 195, 257
Medicare 108, 285
Metzenbaum, Senator Howard 81
Microsoft 59-60
Milosevic, Slobodan 168-69
Missing Children's Act 78
Mitchell, Senator George 81
Mobile Register 292
Mohamad, Prime Minister Mahathir 123
Montoya, Luben 139
Montoya, Ruth 1-4, 11, 139
Moran, Minnie 14
Mormon (See Church of Jesus Christ -)
Mormon Tabernacle Choir 271, 275
Morris, Philip 87
Moseley-Braun, Senator Carol 138
Moss, Frank E. (Ted) 32-6, 39-41, 56, 57
Mother Teresa 276
Moynihan, Senator Daniel Patrick 89, 216, 252
Mr. Mac's 9
Murkowski, Senator Frank 89
Murphy, Betty Southard 94
Myrick, Representative Sue 171
N
NAACP 137, 146
National Abilities Center 249
National Endowment for the Arts (NEA) 250
National Journal 54
National Monument Fairness Act 233
National Rifle Association 61
NATO 167, 178
Netanyahu, Prime Minister Benjamin 164
New Horizons Women's Center 249
Newsweek 11
New York Daily News 227
New York Post, 218, 226, 292
New York Times 11, 50, 71, 187, 199, 200, 206, 218, 224, 251, 284
Nicholson, Jack 252
Nicholson, Jim 236
Nickles, Senator Don 89
Nixon, President Richard 32, 64, 213, 264
Noonan, Peggy 215
North, Lt. Col. Oliver 162, 164
O
O'Connor, Justice Sandra Day 146
O'Grady, Jane 96
Olson, Elder 23
orphan drugs 112
Orthodox Jews 173
Orton, Bill 57
Ottley, Gerald 275
Oxford University 57
P
Packwood, Senator Bob 7, 94
Parade 12, 277
Pataki, Governor George 90
Patient's Bill of Rights 101, 110
People 95
Percy, Senator Charles 48
Perry, Janice Kapp 155, 270, 274-5, 277
Peters, MaryBeth 130
Peterson, Dennis W. 244
Phoenix Suns 253
Pitney, Jack 219
Pittsburgh Pirates 251
Pittsburgh Steelers 251
Places Rated Alamanac 243
Planned Parenthood 99
Plumb, Walter 29
Poindexter, John 162

Pope John Paul II 277
Powell, General Colin 276
Powell, Justice Lewis F. 146
Pratt, Larry 61
Primary Children's Hospital 79
Princess Diana 276
Princess Margaret 8
Purbalite, The 19
Q
Quayle, Dan 67, 74
R
Radiation Exposure Compensation Act 112
Rampton, Governor Calvin 56
Rappaport, Jack 26
Reagan, President Ronald 29, 41, 55, 56, 64, 69, 79, 81, 101, 119, 145, 160, 215, 288, 382, 384
Redford, Robert 56
Rehnquist, Chief Justice William 145-46, 221-22
Reid, Senator Harry 12
Religious Freedom Restoration Act 172
Reno, Janet 75, 173, 186, 189, 192, 202, 235
Republican Hispanic Task Force 139
Republican National Committee 65
Republican National Convention 134
Riady, James 188
Rice, Jerry 253
Richards, Florence 22, 24-5
Richards, Lorin L. 22, 25
Riehl, Roy 250
Riel, Jennifer 135
Ritter, Judge Willis 30, 33, 34
Rockefeller, Senator Jay 236
Rockefeller, Vice President Nelson 42
Roe v Wade 98-9
Rogers, Will 278
Ronald McDonald House 249
Roosevelt, Theodore 19, 225, 229, 281, 294, 298
Roth, Senator Bill 89
Roukema, Representative Marge 90
Rowan, Carl 214
Rubin, Robert 193
Ruff, Charles 222-23
Rusher, William 62
Russia 175-79
Russian Orthodox Church 177, 179-80
Russo, Sal 282, 292
S
Salinger, Pierre 295
Salt Lake Tribune, 64, 95, 112, 141, 177, 239, 278, 294
Sanders, Dave 127
San Diego Chargers 255
Sandinistas 162
San Francisco 49ers 251, 253, 255
Sarokin, Judge J. Lee 151
Savage, Scott 30, 32
Savimbi, Jonas 161
Sawyer, Diane 195
Scalia, Justice Antonin 145
Scarpetta, Kay 92
Schieffer, Bob 209
Schlafly, Phyllis 97, 265
Schlessinger, Dr. Laura 103
Schwarzkopf, General Norman 158
Scott, George Thomas 4
Scott, Jessie 4
Secret Service 211-12
Senate Commerce Committee 289
Sharansky, Anatoly 1, 164
Shea, Pat 57
Sherrill, Charles 3, 4
Shilts, Randy 115-16
Shipp, Becky 2
Shriner's Children's Hospital 249
Shriver, Eunice Kennedy 260
Shtasel, Sana 94
Sierra Club 240
Silver, James 141
Simon, Senator Paul 139
Simon, William 42
Simpson, Senator Alan xii, 63, 69, 244
Skousen, Cleon 37, 263-64
Sloan, Jerry 251, 253
Small Business Administration 98
Smeal, Eleanor 96
Smith, Eleanor 126
Smith, Senator Gordon 177-80
Smith, Jean Kennedy 260
Smith, Joseph 22
Smith, Paul 209
Social Security 106, 108, 243, 278, 285

Souter, David 147
Soviet Union 1, 42, 45, 54, 161-62, 164, 175-77, 179, 193
Sparkman, Senator John 47, 49, 50, 52
Specter, Senator Arlen 71
Starr, Kenneth 202, 203, 205, 208, 211, 216, 217, 218
Starsky, David 81
Steel, LaVar 20, 21
Stephanopoulos, George 215
Stevens, Justice John Paul 145
Stevens, Senator Ted 53, 70, 145
Stevenson, Adlai 20, 154
Stockton, John 254
Stone, Madeline 82, 93, 277
Stoppard, Tom 267
Story, Justice Joseph xiii
Strong, Joyce 18
Summerhays, Lowell 29
Sununu, John 138-39
Syria Mosque 18
T
Taft-Hartley Act 44
Talbott, Strobe, 164
Tate, Randy 219
Taylor, Elizabeth 119-20
Taylor, Nancy 121
Taylor, Stuart Jr. 199-201
Texas v Johnson 156
Thomas, Justice Clarence 91, 95, 141, 147, 201, 218
Thompson, Senator Fred 272
Thompson, Robert 52
Thurmond, Senator Strom 70, 71
Time 11, 38, 71, 164, 165, 196, 251, 269, 279, 267,
Time Present, Time Past 165
Titanic 198, 227
Title IX 100-01
Todd, Ruth 208
Torrijos, Omar 160
Traficant, Congressman James, Jr. 209
Travolta, John 215
Trie, Charlie 187
Tripp, Linda 202, 204
Truman, President Harry 12
Tunney, John 70
Turner, Douglas 215
Turow, Scott 268
U
UC Davis Medical School 135
University of Nebraska 79
University of Pittsburgh 26
University of Utah 57, 142, 251
U.S. Chamber of Commerce 47, 52
U.S. News & World Report 45, 46
Utah Boys Ranch 249
Utah Food Bank 249
Utah Holiday 44
Utah Jazz 77, 141, 251, 252, 286, 294
Utah State University 124, 130, 272
USA Today 209
V
Valenti, Jack 272
VanCott Bagley Cornwall & McCarthy 30-32
vitamins and minerals 102, 112
W
Walesa, Lech 264
Wall Street Journal 11, 86, 97, 209, 228
Wang, Nina 187
Warren, Chief Justice Earl 147
Washington, George 143, 153, 229
Washington Post 11, 63, 166, 183, 207, 209, 218, 226, 227, 265, 269, 288, 293, 296-7
Washington Times 11, 227, 251
Watkins, Admiral James D. 118
Watt, Margaret 244
Waxman, Congressman Henry 115, 266
Webster, Daniel 225
Weekly Standard 11
Weicker, Senator Lowell 117
Weinberger, Caspar 193
Werbach, Adam 240
Weyand, Mildred 16
Weyrich, Paul 36, 118, 140, 265
Whetton, Marcia Hatch 247
Whetton, Randy 247
White, Justice Byron 148
White-Ginder, Jeanne 125
White, Jeanne 120
White, Judge Ronnie 137
White, Ryan 119, 120, 123
Whitlock, Alysa Hatch 248

Whitlock, Jamie 248
Wilcox, Paul 17
Wilkinson, Ernest 36, 37, 39
Will, George F. 80, 145, 197, 214
Willey, Kathleen 202
Williams, Brian 139
Williams, Senator Harrison (Pete) 5, 47
Williams, Roger 286
Williams, Bishop Smallwood 141
Willis, Chris 82, 274
Wilson, Ted 56, 57
Wirthlin, Richard 38
Witcover, Jules 283
Women, Infants and Children (WIC) 79
Woolf, Marie 74-5, 284
Wordsworth, William 48
World War II 16, 246
Wright, Judge Susan Webber 200, 227

Y

Yard, Molly 146
Yeltsin, President Boris 175-79
YMCA 249
Young, Bruce and Nancy 172
Young, Steve 254, 255
YWCA 249

Z

Zabriskie, Dale 39
Zahn, Paula 288
Zedillo Ernesto 214
Zeegen, Susie 82
Zeibel, Rabbi David 174
Zia ul-Haq, Mohammed 165
Zigler, Edward 80
Zimmer, Norma 104
Zorinsky, Senator Edward 47, 50, 52, 53, 174